ALSO BY CHANDRA MANNING

What This Cruel War Was Over:
Soldiers, Slavery, and the Civil War

Troubled Refuge

Troubled Refuge

STRUGGLING FOR FREEDOM
IN THE CIVIL WAR

Chandra Manning

ALFRED A. KNOPF   New York
2016

THIS IS A BORZOI BOOK
PUBLISHED BY ALFRED A. KNOPF

Copyright © 2016 by Chandra Manning

All rights reserved. Published in the United States by Alfred A. Knopf,
a division of Penguin Random House LLC, New York,
and distributed in Canada by Random House of Canada,
a division of Penguin Random House Canada Limited, Toronto.

www.aaknopf.com

Knopf, Borzoi Books, and the colophon are registered trademarks
of Penguin Random House LLC.

Library of Congress Cataloging-in-Publication Data
Names: Manning, Chandra, author.
Title: Troubled refuge : struggling for freedom in the
Civil War / Chandra Manning.
Description: First edition. | New York : Alfred A. Knopf, 2016. |
Includes bibliographical references.
Identifiers: LCCN 2015039724 | ISBN 9780307271204 (hardcover)—
ISBN 9781101947791 (ebook)
Subjects: LCSH: United States—History—Civil War, 1861–1865—
African Americans. | Slaves—Emancipation—United States. |
United States—History—Civil War, 1861–1865—Social aspects.
Classification: LCC E453 .M24 2016 | DDC 973.7/11—dc23
LC record available at http://lccn.loc.gov/2015039724

Map concepts and research by Tom Foley
Additional cartography by Robert Bull

Jacket image: Slaves sitting near their cabins on a Port Royal
South Carolina plantation by Timothy O'Sullivan, 1862.
Everett Historical/Shutterstock
Jacket design by Perry De La Vega

Manufactured in the United States of America
First Edition

Dedicated to Georgetown

Contents

Troubled Refuge

Introduction

I
t was August 1862 and mercilessly hot near Fredericksburg, Virginia. Union soldiers in their shirtsleeves were supposed to be on picket duty, but they could barely stand up, even in the shade. As they wilted, they looked on in wonder as more than eighty women and children, barefooted, bareheaded, with nothing to eat, little water, and no protection from the sun, walked with grim determination across a shadeless plain and into Union lines. All were "faint and hungry." One woman's blouse had been reduced to ribbons by the same whip that had cut her back "to pieces." Another woman's hair was entirely gray, and her back was so stooped that she walked practically at right angles to the ground, but there was nothing frail about the way she grasped the hand of a little girl about three years old. The old woman's daughter had been sold "to the far Southern market," and she had been taking care of her granddaughter ever since. Then she overheard her owner's plans to ship her to Richmond, leaving her granddaughter with no family to shield her from the violence of slavery. So the woman ran, and she took the little girl with her. The Union soldiers she found were mainly farmers who thought they knew what physical demands on the body were, but in the presence of this woman the men were awestruck. At least one was moved to tears. Wordlessly, they placed their day's rations into the hands of the women filing by, knowing that the procession might try to make its way west to the Orange and Alexandria Railroad, or maybe ride the rails from Fredericksburg to the Potomac River and from there

get to Washington, D.C. Within Union lines, the women and children could see tracks leading out of slavery. Where those tracks led to was far less clear.[1]

. . .

Winter winds along the Ohio and Mississippi Rivers were cold, but the aging man barely noticed. Francis Lieber, Prussian immigrant, veteran of the Napoleonic Wars, famous jurist, and soon to be the author of the Lieber Code, the world's first written guidelines for military conduct in "civilized" warfare, was looking for his son. A Union soldier, Hamilton Lieber had gone missing after the February 1862 battle at Fort Donelson in Tennessee. The grim trip was not Lieber's first wartime journey. The previous summer, he had visited General Benjamin Butler at Fort Monroe, Virginia, and pondered what the United States ought to do about "run-away slaves" there. This time, he checked Cincinnati, St. Louis, and Paducah, Kentucky, where a captain in Hamilton's regiment confirmed that the young man was alive last the captain knew. Paducah was full of hospitals and soldiers, as well as of black men and women who had run from their masters, some dashing furtively out of sight in case the unfamiliar white man might be in camp to try to drag slaves back into bondage. Lieber found "whole cargoes of wounded, dying and dead" loaded onto steamboats and sent downriver, but he did not find his son. He followed the steamboats to Cairo and then on to Mound City, Illinois. Once again, Lieber made his way among refugees from slavery, ducked his head frantically into tents, and strode determinedly up and down rows of hospital beds until finally he "found the dear boy," minus one arm, but still alive. Lieber had already known "war as [a] soldier, as a wounded man in the hospital, as an observing citizen," but now he knew war as "a father searching for his wounded son." Moreover, he was a father who just weeks later would lose another son, his beloved Oscar, who had already broken his heart by joining the Confederate army in this awful war that Lieber hoped would uproot slavery. In that poignant winter, Lieber confronted a central paradox of war: its chaos brought suffering and new possibilities not merely at the same time, but intimately connected to each other.[2]

. . .

The Hungarian-born major general Alexander Asboth needed forti-fications faster than soldiers could build them. Serving in 1863 as post commander at Columbus, Kentucky, a state that officially stayed in the Union but was filled with civilians who supported the Confederacy, Asboth bore responsibility for defense against guerrillas as well as regu-lar Confederate forces. At first, he hired white civilian laborers, but he found many of them to be the "least efficient" workers he had ever come across. Meanwhile, black men, women, and children fleeing their Kentucky masters were streaming into his lines, and they proved to be much better workers. Before long, a local civilian, Mrs. V. C. Taylor, insisted that Asboth return slaves who had taken shelter in his camp. The major general refused, on the grounds that "she and her husband not only have many relatives in the Rebel Army, but they warmly sym-pathize with the traitors." No matter how fair Mrs. Taylor's complexion was, and no matter how rich she was, she had forfeited any right to "protection" or "indulgence" from the U.S. government when she chose to betray it. She went away empty-handed, which to Asboth seemed like a straightforward matter of "wisdom and justice," but local civil authorities fought his decision bitterly, and it took constant vigilance to prevent them from kidnapping African Americans and hauling them back into slavery. Moreover, Asboth's surprises regarding the black workers were not over yet: it turned out that the laborers were being paid less than the white workers fired for inefficiency had been. Surely, all who would "work faithfully or volunteer to fight for our common cause" should count the same in the eyes of the government they served, Asboth insisted. He and the black fortification builders had learned that former slaves seeking freedom were likely to get more from mili-tary authorities than from civil ones, but that alliance with the Union army came with its own limits and drawbacks.[3]

The wartime experiences of the grandmother and granddaugh-ter, Francis Lieber, and the fortification builders working for Gen-eral Asboth highlight the phenomenon of enslaved men, women, and children—close to half a million of them—running to the Union army. That mass flight raises key questions about the process, aftermath, and long-term results of emancipation in the U.S. Civil War. What did flee-ing slaves hope to achieve, and why did they go to the army to achieve it? What was it like when they got to Union encampments? How did they first build and then use an alliance with the Union army to attain their visions? What did they gain and what did they lose by doing so? What happened to the alliance after the war? What if any difference did any of it make in the long run?

Looking to the experiences of fleeing slaves in Union army encampments to understand emancipation is a bit like visiting a cyclorama. Very popular in Europe and the United States in the late nineteenth century, cycloramas were giant, panoramic paintings that enveloped viewers, wrapping around the walls of circular buildings constructed specifically to house them. An exquisitely rendered vignette on one side of the painting might not bear much obvious relation to another scene painted on the other side of the room, but they are all part of the same encircling whole. One of the most famous in the United States was the 377-foot-long, 42-foot-high cyclorama of the Battle of Gettysburg painted by Paul Philippoteaux in 1883. A cyclorama is at once overpoweringly vast and painstakingly minute, and the Gettysburg Cyclorama is no exception. It features such lavish detail that viewers can count leaves on trees, nails in horseshoes, spokes on wagon wheels. Hundreds of human figures run and shoot, fall back and charge forward, crouch down and stand up in the painting, and yet individual facial features are still intricately portrayed. When the first viewers walked in, they were overpowered by the painting. "Whoever expects to see a picture merely—even a great battlepiece—must be taken by surprise," reported one newspaper. The Gettysburg Cyclorama opened first in Chicago, moved to Boston in 1884, and finally landed at Gettysburg in time for the fiftieth anniversary of the battle in 1913.[4]

Now the cyclorama is in the Visitor Center at Gettysburg National Military Park, and if you want to see it but are short on time, you can view it in a couple of different ways. You can choose one or two square feet of the painting, peer in closely, allow yourself to be captivated by the realism, and soak in everything about that one particular scene, while forgoing any sense of the greater whole. Alternatively, you can stand back, take in the encompassing panorama, allow yourself to be swept up by the vast, swirling movement, but not notice much about any of the people or places in the painting. In either case, you would have *looked at* the cyclorama, and you would know something real and important about some part of it, but you would not really have seen or understood its totality. The reasons for preferring a limited visit are not hard to understand. Beyond the pressures of time, fully experiencing the cyclorama is disorienting, even vertigo inducing. Especially if there is music playing, to visit is to be bombarded by intense stimuli, literally from all sides. You have to spend some time disconcerted and utterly unsure of where you are. But spend enough time, be willing to live with some disorientation, and there is a whole that exceeds the sum of its parts.

This book functions like a cyclorama. Part 1 peers in closely at Civil War contraband camps, which were refugee camps for slaves who ran to the Union army. Contraband camps brought more African American men, women, and children into contact with the U.S. government than had ever happened before. The prelude provides an overview, covering what and where camps were, how they got started, and general factors that affected camps wherever they were located. Chapters 1 and 2 focus on the lives, objectives, aspirations, and challenges of people in the camps, first in the eastern theater and then in the western, because experiences in the two theaters differed. Not every camp will appear in these pages, not because I am unaware of black people or the Union army at Natchez, Huntsville, or Harpers Ferry, but because it is simply impracticable to discuss each of the hundreds of places in which formerly enslaved men, women, and children encountered Union forces. It is one thing to be willing to invest time in the cyclorama room; it is another to get trapped inside and never leave.

Still, many camps do appear in chapter 1 about the eastern theater of the war, where refugees from slavery most often made their way to a camp and stayed put, as well as in chapter 2 about the western theater, where both Union forces and former slaves running to them remained in motion throughout the course of the war. Think of reading these chapters as walking up as close to the cyclorama wall as the railing of elapsed time and source survival allow. Squint, and take in all the tiny detail. Try to feel and hear and smell what it was like to exit slavery in each particular place. Remember that people who ran to freedom during the Civil War could not see the outcome of their actions. No analytical thread, no clear narrative arc, gave order to their days. Instead, they had to try to make their hopes for freedom real in the gritty detail of what each day in a difficult place brought them. Part 1 invites readers to immerse themselves in the camps and the stories of people who sought freedom there without reassuring signposts to indicate where it would all end up, because part I aims to convey a sense of what it was like to exit slavery, and one aspect of exiting slavery was to be disoriented and left with no alternative but to proceed anyway.

Parts II and III, in contrast, are like standing in the middle of the cyclorama room, taking the whole thing in for the meaning collectively created by and transcending the individual people and places. The impulse for freedom and the first steps toward it unquestionably came from enslaved people, but enslaved people had yearned for freedom for centuries, and yet slavery continued. Slavery was, among other things, a state of perpetual war between slaves who desired autonomy for themselves, their loved ones, and their communities, on the one hand, and slave owners determined to deny those things to bond people, on the other.[5] Before the Civil War, slave owners had the support of the U.S. government, and they won the ongoing daily war. Neither slave owners nor slaves changed their minds, but beginning with the election of 1860, and then increasingly throughout the war, the U.S. government switched sides. With an army pointing guns at slave owners near Fredericksburg, the elderly grandmother who had always wanted to care for her granddaughter now had access to a source of power mighty enough to help her defy the slaveholders who would stop her from doing so. Meanwhile, that source of power—the Union army—had aims of its own. It needed to take and hold territory and transit routes, and it needed to reestablish the economy, both to pay for the war and to prove that slavery was not necessary for the economies of the region or the nation to flourish.

The army and refugees from slavery, then, did not need exactly the same things, but they knew that they needed each other, and so they built a tenuous alliance. The relationship was not one between equals. Sometimes it hit the sensitive nerve of proper relations between civil and military authority, a nerve that had caused collective wincing among Americans since before the Revolution. The alliance remained in flux throughout the war, and it definitely did not achieve everything people fleeing bondage hoped it would. Nonetheless, it helped reinvent the relationship between the U.S. government and the individual person. Chapter 3 analyzes the first part of that process, military emancipation, which began in 1861 and continued in 1862. Chapter 4 examines the alliance building, which participants called citizenship, from 1863 to the spring of 1865.

Part III stays right in the cyclorama room to consider the months of May through December 1865, because those months following the surrender of armies were connected to the years of hostilities preceding them, even as they also constituted their own distinct moment equally crucial to making sense of war and emancipation. In books and classrooms, the Civil War story often takes a flying leap from the Army of Northern Virginia's surrender at Appomattox to *Plessy v. Ferguson* and the long reign of Jim Crow, and then to the civil rights movement of the 1960s. Yet for people who lived through the conflict, the latter half of 1865 stood as a distinct and definite moment, when everybody involved knew that much had changed, and nobody knew for sure what would come next. The moment was full of violence and foreboding. It brought the troublesome relationship between civil and military authority urgently to the fore. Yet it was also a moment of possibility, when later events were anything but inevitable. Part III stays in rather than bypasses that distinctive postwar moment.

The interludes are like the pauses you might take to close your eyes and regain your bearings when visiting a cyclorama. They are hiatuses for taking stock, reflecting on implications, and preparing to shift perspective. The conclusion is like taking one last look around the full 360 degrees of the cyclorama and taking its measure before stepping out into the lobby.

· · ·

The Gettysburg cyclorama portrays the third day of a three-day battle that took place in the middle of the war, which means that visitors can better appreciate what they are looking at if they have some idea of what had happened up to that point. Similarly, this book is joining a number of existing conversations about emancipation and the evolving relationship between the U.S. government and individual people—generally known as citizenship—and it helps to know a little bit about the state of those conversations.

Collectively, a rich body of work on the unraveling of slavery has uncovered the political strategies of the enslaved while cautioning against exaggerating the agency that black people could exercise, given the realities of massive power arrayed against them.[6] Among other things, this book is an extended meditation on the tension between structure and agency in the wartime destruction of slavery in the United States. There is no question that the originating impulse toward emancipation came from the courage, determination, and resilience of slaves who wanted freedom, but no amount of human courage, determination, or resilience is invincible. Sometimes immense structural forces—like firepower and state power—overcome people, no matter how resolute their will. Sometimes tiny forces—like germs—defeat even the most brave and persistent individuals. It is also indisputable that leadership mattered. Union officers' responses to arriving refugees, War Department dictates, presidential orders, and laws passed by Congress all helped demarcate the limits of the possible and the impossible, but military and political leaders were not omnipotent, either. They, too, were often overcome by forces unleashed by war and full of more fury than any human could harness.

At the same time, an exclusively structural account cannot tell us how emancipation happened, for slavery did not just end by chance or on its own. People had something to do with it, and historians have long debated which people, decisions, and actions really destroyed slavery. For a long time, historians tussled over whether Lincoln or slaves themselves "freed the slaves," but lately attention has been moving away from *who* ended slavery to concentrate on *how*.[7] Shifting the question has fostered widespread recognition of emancipation as a complex and multifaceted process in which individuals and institutions in Washington and on the ground all played key roles.[8]

While veritable consensus surrounds the idea that emancipation was the work of many hands carried out in multiple places, no such agreement has been reached on the *timing* of emancipation. Historians continue to dispute whether emancipation happened quickly once the war began or only belatedly and with reluctance on the part of U.S. authorities.[9] Part of the impasse comes from understanding enslavement in slightly different ways, which in turn leads scholars to use the word "emancipation" to mean different things that happened at different times. In Orlando Patterson's classic formulation, enslavement was "social death," meaning a state so consuming and overpowering that enslaved people's basic markers of human identity like kin and community were wiped out and they were left with no meaningful checkpoints of social identity. Emancipation, then, would consist of a return to social life by reconstituting ties of family and community. From that perspective, emancipation came reasonably quickly for freedpeople who exited slavery accompanied by families and loved ones, but was very slow in coming for others, and sometimes never came at all in cases where death, time, and distance made it impossible for former slaves to put their families back together again.[10] Recently some scholars point to networks of kin and community that enslaved people managed to maintain in bondage—albeit amid great struggle—to question the notion of enslavement as "social death" and in so doing disaggregate family reconstitution from emancipation. These historians do not argue that reassembling kin networks was unimportant to former slaves, but rather they see that process as a separate one that could happen before, during, or long after emancipation.[11]

If by enslavement we mean the state in which one human being is the legal property of another human being, then emancipation consisted of one person's ceasing to be the legal property of another person. This definition makes a distinction between the core of enslavement—being property—and its horrific effects, which included abuse, exploitation, assault, family separation, and more. Emancipation undid the core of enslavement but could not by itself cure the effects or heal the damage caused by them. In this understanding, emancipation is not a perfect synonym for freedom. Emancipation itself was not enslaved people's longed-for destination but rather one important—indeed crucial—step in the journey from slavery to freedom. Without it, none of the rest of the journey could take place. In this limited but important sense of what emancipation was, emancipation began almost as soon as the war did, but that answer leads immediately to a trickier question: What did former slaves become once emancipated?[12]

That second question is easy to miss if we assume that the only two conditions a person could occupy were either enslavement or full inclusion within the American polity complete with enjoyment of equal rights, or, in other words, citizenship as we currently conceptualize it. If we assume only two states, and we reason from that assumption that emancipation happened when a former slave became a full and equal citizen of the United States with the same rights as all other citizens, then emancipation took a very long time. After all, it is easy to point out the myriad ways in which African Americans were denied equal rights with white Americans for the entirety of the Civil War (and long after), which is precisely what many works arguing for slow, reluctant emancipation generally do. But the assumption that a person had to be either a slave or a citizen because those were the only two possible conditions is faulty. A quick glance at slavery's end elsewhere in the world demonstrates that when bond people ceased to be slaves, they almost never became immediate citizens. In most places in the Caribbean, emancipated slaves entered a nebulous "apprenticeship" stage. Brazilian-born slaves went through a prolonged transition from "first freedom" to "full freedom," which took years if it ever happened at all. The list could easily continue through several other types of indefinite, in-between status that formerly enslaved people have occupied. Sometimes, liberated slaves even returned to slavery.

Enslaved men, women, and children did not exit slavery and step directly into American citizenship, any more than enslaved people anywhere else in the world immediately joined the body politic the moment they ceased to be owned by someone else. Instead, emancipated slaves in the U.S. Civil War entered a liminal state, just as liberated slaves the world over and throughout time did.

The key institution that ushered former slaves through that liminal state during the Civil War was the Union army. It was no smooth passage. Lately, scholars have become more attuned to the Union military as a key instrument in slavery's destruction while bearing in mind that armies trying to win wars generally prove to be "unreliable vehicles for emancipation, bringing heartbreak as well as liberation."[13] Just as the institution of slavery was shot through with violence and tragedy, so too was its destruction, in the United States no less than in the rest of the world. Several historians have been working with great seriousness of purpose to temper an excessively celebratory view of wartime emancipation with unflinching depictions of the heartbreak.[14] Their attention to the jaggedness of the wartime destruction of slavery makes it even more surprising that U.S. emancipation in the midst of the Civil War actually happened, and therefore all the more important to understand with some precision the Union army's role in that transformation.

It is also important to understand exactly how wartime emancipation operated in the Civil War, because Civil War emancipation, for all its shortcomings, turned out to be permanent, whereas in most other times and places wartime emancipation proved to be reversible.[15] In the American Revolution, some former slaves gained freedom while others were resold into slavery by their purported liberators. The War of 1812 manumitted some slaves but ultimately led to the strengthening of the institution of slavery. In the Caribbean in the late eighteenth and early nineteenth centuries, and in several South American countries throughout the nineteenth century, slaves who gained freedom during war, rebellion, or uprising were re-enslaved afterward, sometimes immediately and sometimes years later. After the 1835 Ragamuffin Revolt in Brazil, for example, slave soldiers enjoyed a decade of freedom, only to be forcibly transported ten years later from their homes to the capital and compelled to labor for the imperial government. Only in Haiti had war led to abolition over the long haul, and even there re-enslavement followed liberation for a brief period before the world's only successful slave rebellion finally destroyed Haitian slavery for good. Moreover, most antebellum white Americans regarded Haiti as nightmare and anathema, certainly not as an example to follow.[16] There was no a priori reason why Civil War emancipation would defy the norm, even as late as 1865. Indeed, a central theme of this book is the real and persistent threat of re-enslavement.

So how was that threat averted? Why did permanent wartime abolition happen in the U.S. Civil War despite so much precedent to the contrary and in the face of slaveholders' determined efforts to resist it during the war and reverse it afterward? Many factors contributed, but two essential reasons are the Thirteenth and Fourteenth Amendments to the U.S. Constitution, which abolished slavery and secured African Americans' U.S. citizenship. In some ways, the two amendments are integrally connected: it is much more difficult to re-enslave a citizen than a noncitizen, and so the Fourteenth Amendment helped secure the Thirteenth Amendment. Yet the two amendments are also distinct and different, because emancipation and citizenship are not the same things, and the former does not and did not lead automatically to the latter.

How the Civil War led to black citizenship, then, represents another robust conversation among U.S. historians into which this book enters, but only after a fashion. "How the Civil War led to black citizenship" is less a single conversation and more an entire cocktail party of numerous conversations all going on at the same time. When attending a party, some people are very skillful at circulating throughout a room and socializing with everyone there, but I generally find myself drawn into good, long chats with a smaller number of people. This book takes after me in that regard. In broaching the topic of black citizenship, this book is not joining in conversations about the origins of the Fourteenth Amendment or the antebellum evolution of state and federal citizenship from the perspective of legal history, and it makes no pretense of intervening in debates over whether jus soli, jus sanguinis, or any other theoretical foundations undergird citizenship in the United States. Neither is it designed to help readers think differently about the ideological origins of black citizenship among free African Americans or the history of voting rights. Rather, this book means citizenship in the way that refugees from slavery meant it as they sought freedom during the Civil War: as a mutually beneficial alliance with the national government that could help both the Union and the freedpeople achieve specific ends.

To black men, women, and children who ran to the Union army, "citizenship" was less the ultimate objective than it was a means to the particular goal of autonomy for themselves, their loved ones, and their communities.[17] The word "citizen" does not contain some magical power that could ward off bullwhips, shelter children, keep families together, or nurse babies back to health, and *those* aims were the ones that African Americans desperately sought in the maelstrom of war. Not even voting—the pinnacle of political rights and badge of equal citizenship to decades of free black Northerners and to formerly enslaved community leaders after the Civil War—offered much direct promise of what fleeing slaves most urgently sought during the war. Direct access to the power of the national government *could* help freedpeople do or achieve the things that mattered most to them at the moment they exited slavery, and so they sought a direct relationship—an alliance—with the national government to help them attain their visions of what freedom should be and mean. They called the alliance citizenship, and while it had manifest shortcomings, it also had much to recommend it. We miss their achievement in obtaining as much of it as they did if we conflate citizenship with voting and conclude that their efforts completely failed.

When this book talks about black citizenship, it is talking about that alliance. In these pages, I explore why freedpeople thought such an alliance would aid them in pursuit of their aspirations, how they helped craft it with the army and the national government in wartime, and the extent to which it succeeded in realizing their goals. The origins of black citizenship go back much earlier than the Civil War to black abolitionists (and their white allies) who imagined a fully realized national union of hearts and minds, but no matter how fully and creatively black Americans conceptualized their own citizenship, and no matter how strongly they desired to bring it to fruition, the power to deny or recognize black citizenship remained firmly in white lawmakers' hands. That power showed no signs of bending to black people's purposes before the Civil War.[18] Historians have generally explained why the Civil War led to the Fourteenth Amendment's enshrining black citizenship by agreeing with Frederick Douglass, who famously noted, "Once let the black man get upon his person the brass letter, U.S., let him get an eagle on his button, and a musket on his shoulder and bullets in his pocket . . . and . . . there is no power on earth . . . which can deny that he has earned the right to citizenship in the United States."[19] Black Union soldiers, in this interpretation, fought for and obtained their own citizenship.

Crucial as the black soldier-to-citizen narrative is, it remains by itself incomplete for a number of reasons. Long ago, W. E. B. DuBois pointed out bitter flaws in anything, including citizenship, that some men could obtain only by killing other men, and recent historians have echoed his critique of citizenship procured via violent military service.[20] Black enlistment also cannot by itself account for the attainment of citizenship because, Frederick Douglass aside, plenty of powers on earth continued to withhold equal citizenship despite black soldiers' service in the American Revolution and the War of 1812, as well as any number of conflicts outside the United States. Clearly, fighting alone was not enough.

Moreover, the emphasis on soldiering omits black women, who could not fight but who became citizens. Some historians have argued that black women traveled a "marital" path to citizenship by marrying black soldiers and then "pin[ning] their own hopes on the soldiers," and without question black enlistment was linked to emancipation for a recruit's family members, both in official policy and in the eyes of many men who enlisted. Yet a citizenship-through-marriage paradigm cannot account for what happened during the Civil War, partly because emancipation and citizenship were not the same thing, but even more because the decided majority of contraband camp inhabitants were *un*married women and their children. One historian critical of the "marital route" interpretation has emphasized black women's own labor in working for their own emancipation but holds that women's labor and loyalty "simply never assumed the strategic significance of men's loyalty" and therefore played no role in procuring black citizenship.[21] Yet while white Union soldiers might not have begun the war with much interest in black women's loyalty, finding themselves in harm's way amid a hostile white population made them consider black women who provided intelligence and labor differently. It was not as soldiers or as spouses to somebody else but as *themselves* that most black women came into contact with the U.S. government, aided the breakdown of slavery, and built alliances with soldiers, the Union army, and the national government in the era of the Civil War.

The version of citizenship as an alliance between former slaves and the national government, which freedpeople could call on to protect their rights to things that mattered to them, was fundamentally different from what citizenship generally meant in the antebellum era. Before the Civil War, citizenship's meaning was contested but had primarily to do with membership within a political community (what one historian calls "belonging to a common association"), inclusion, and obligation. Moreover, state governments, not the national government, were in charge of it.[22] The American Revolution had created the category and idea of the "American citizen" predicated on consent, as distinct from the "natural, personal, and perpetual" British subject predicated on birth, but neither the Revolution nor the Constitution as drafted in 1787 provided much additional guidance.[23]

One thing that was clear was that state governments, not the national government, determined citizenship. The antebellum constitution inserted the federal government into citizenship only by giving

Congress the right to determine naturalization requirements and in the comity clause in Article IV, which entitled citizens of the individual states "to all privileges and immunities of free citizens in the several States," thereby establishing that one's home state determined if a person met basic eligibility requirements for membership within the national citizenry.

States used the "ascriptive characteristics" of race and gender to limit eligibility for citizenship and voting, but alongside the obvious motives of racism and sexism they did so for complex ideological reasons as well. The result was that in every state, native-born white men were citizens and could vote, native-born white women were citizens and could not vote, and with rare exceptions black men and women were not citizens and could not vote, but if you had asked an antebellum state legislator why that was, his answer would have been more involved than "I do not like black people, and I think women are inferior." He could very well have said both of those things (and it is even more likely that he would think them), but he would also talk to you about the notion of usefulness. A comparison between the Constitution's comity clause and the clause in the Articles of Confederation that it replaced, along with close examination of antebellum state constitutions and the conventions that hammered them out, can help explain what he would have meant.[24] Article IV of the U.S. Constitution substitutes the single word "Citizens" for the Articles of Confederation's more cumbersome phrase "free inhabitants of each of these States, paupers, vagabonds, and fugitives from justice excepted," but it incorporates the prohibition against non-contributing community members within the sleeker prose.[25] Similarly, antebellum state constitutional conventions demonstrated that a citizen was someone seen by others in the community as independent, self-reliant, and capable of contributing to "the harmony, well-being, and prosperity of the community" either because of property ownership, the capability to grow or build or make things, or the ability to direct others to do so.[26] An antebellum citizen, in short, was a full member of the community not necessarily by virtue of earning power (free blacks earned a living) but because the members of the political community of the state in which the individual resided affirmed that individual as useful to that community.[27]

White men were citizens (or, if foreign-born, could become citizens with relative ease) because white men were most readily associated with responsible property ownership and productive or directive capacity, while black people were excluded from citizenship in almost every state in large part because the white members of the political community of that state, "the people," could not conceive of African Americans as useful contributors. Those presumptions are evident in the pervasive antebellum rhetoric (especially in the North) about black "dependence" and "indolence." They are evident in Henry Clay's widely shared (especially by white Americans wielding the power of the federal government) assumption that "African descendants . . . possess no part . . . in our political system." And it was on those presumptions that Roger Taney's repeated insistence in the *Dred Scott* decision that black people formed no part of the "community" and could not be citizens was in substantial measure based.[28]

Recognizing that states rather than the federal government adjudicated citizenship, and that white Americans believed that they merited citizenship because of their usefulness to the community, helps clarify who could be a citizen and why, but it does not tell us very much about individual rights, because citizenship before the Civil War was about membership and obligation more than about rights. A vigorous literature on women, gender, and citizenship confirms that antebellum notions of citizenship centered on usefulness and obligation, which white women were expected to exhibit, more than rights, of which they enjoyed fewer than white men.[29] It was not that antebellum Americans (especially white men) did not have rights, but the "actual bundle of rights" they enjoyed came from complex webs of voluntary institutions, hierarchical relationships, and associative communities, not from either citizenship itself or the state government that granted citizenship. A white husband and father who hired laborers to help him work his farm during the day, attended Odd Fellows meetings on Tuesday evenings, and worshipped at the Baptist church on Sunday enjoyed a wider range of individual rights and privileges than his wife, children, or hired hands did because his standing as husband, father, employer, Odd Fellow, and church member permitted him to do so, not because a state government, or still less the federal government, said so.[30]

To say that the federal government had little to do with citizenship before the Civil War is not the same as saying that the federal government did nothing before the Civil War; it just did different things. Tired, unexamined assumptions about a small, weak antebellum federal government have been authoritatively replaced by compelling portrayals of an antebellum U.S. government whose power was large, widespread, and palpable in people's everyday lives, even if it operated differently from contemporary European states.[31] Yet vigorous though the antebellum federal government was, it was not chief protector of individual rights. It did protect property rights, but other than that its role where individuals were concerned was chiefly negative: it did not "infringe," to use the language of the Bill of Rights. Where the rights of certain groups were concerned, in contrast, the national government assumed an active role. Most notably, the federal government did a lot before the Civil War for white slaveholders who disproportionately benefited from the government's positive actions in claiming land, removing Indians, and recapturing runaway slaves.[32]

Antebellum citizenship, individual rights, and the federal government, then, were separate things before the Civil War, but during the war they merged. We understand part of how and why, thanks to the collective work of several scholars. We already know, for example, that the war's massive death toll forced newer, more direct relationships between individuals and the national government (in the Confederacy as well as the Union) and compelled the governments of both the United States and the Confederacy to deal directly with previously marginalized individuals like women and slaves.[33] Existing scholarship also illuminates how African Americans capitalized on wartime circumstances to put themselves into direct contact with the national government through the army and establishes that their interactions with the army placed their status up for debate within the Northern public.[34] This book picks up with that understanding and aims to take it further by exploring what the interactions themselves (distinct from what white people in the North thought and said about them) looked like, achieved, and did not achieve in the immediate context of Civil War contraband camps, in freedpeople's lives, and in implications for the meaning of citizenship to all residents of the United States.

One of the chief duties of the historian is to explain how we know what we know, and that duty of transparency is especially acute in this case, because retracing the circuitous path out of slavery and into citizenship means piecing together many different types of evidence from lots of different sources. The first places in which many enslaved men, women, and children encountered the U.S. government were Union army camps. Some of those encounters appear in the multivolume *War of the Rebellion: A Compilation of the Official Records of the Union and Confederate Armies* (commonly known as the *Official Records*), and many others appear in the Freedom series of document collections edited by the Freedmen and Southern Society Project. Both of these published resources offer invaluable starting points for investigating freedpeople's wartime flight out of bondage. They draw on military and governmental records measured in whole floors of archive shelf space, thanks to the Union army's and the U.S. government's predilection for writing things down.

Because no published project could possibly fit more than a tiny fraction of those records between the covers of its books, I turned to the archival record collections sampled in the *Official Records* and the Freedom volumes to sift among tens of thousands of additional army records housed in some key collections at the National Archives. One such collection was the post command records of each Union army installation (National Archives Record Group 393), which include day-to-day happenings in army encampments, orders given and received, correspondence between officers about everything to do with the war (including what to do about fugitive slaves), rosters of names—of laborers, rations recipients, jail inmates, and more—ledgers detailing port activity (including the arrivals and departures of former slaves), maps and camp diagrams, requisitions, telegrams, passes, and literally countless scraps of paper churned up by the day-to-day functioning of places that operated as military posts and refugee camps at the same time. Other military collections, such as the Quartermaster General's Records, the Adjutant General's Records, and the Provost Marshal General's Records, provide additional perspectives on freedpeople in Union army camps. To understand what was going on in wartime camps, this book has also drawn on the major legal histories and volumes of military law available to and used by officers during the Civil War.

Branches of the U.S. government besides the army generated voluminous records about freedpeople during the war. The Department of the Treasury vied with the army for control over parts of the occupied South, and its records include material on the land and labor experiments inaugurated on Treasury-controlled lands, especially along the South Carolina and Georgia coasts. Congress discussed emancipation endlessly, and its deliberations are readily available in the *Congressional Globe*, but members also recognized that they needed more information about conditions on the ground in contraband camps and authorized numerous investigations and reports from 1863 to 1865. Members of Congress, cabinet members, President Lincoln, prominent Union generals, state governors, and legal thinkers like Francis Lieber all corresponded during the war, and their exchanges shed valuable light on the changes in the relationship between the U.S. government and formerly enslaved individuals that unfolded throughout the war.

While lawmakers and statesmen surveyed the shifting landscape of U.S. citizenship from the altitude of their offices, Union soldiers walked in its midst on the ground. The letters and diaries of soldiers often described former slaves in camps and discussed soldiers' interactions with freedpeople. Sometimes soldiers just reported matter-of-factly, and other times they recorded their own thoughts or ideas, favorable or unfavorable, about changes they could clearly see afoot. Sometimes they even reflected upon the meaning and significance not just of what they saw but of what they felt transforming within themselves. Regimental histories penned by soldiers during or shortly after the war also narrate things that happened to soldiers and freedpeople, and while I have not used them to gain insight into wartime attitudes or opinions, they offer useful factual data on events that took place.

Not all Union soldiers were white, and especially in the second half of the war, when black Union troops sometimes guarded contraband camps, black soldiers' sources also provide valuable insight. Fewer letter collections survive from black Union troops than white (partly due to lower literacy rates among soldiers who had recently been slaves), but some do exist. Black soldiers also wrote to prominent black newspapers like *The Anglo-African* and *The Christian Recorder*. Enlistment and enrollment records and the pension applications filed by black veterans after the war augment letters and diaries.

To hear the voices of former slaves in contraband camps who did not become Union soldiers requires more and different types of evidence.

Pension records filed by the widows and orphans of black Union veterans often narrate wartime experiences in contraband camps, sometimes in astonishing detail. Occasionally, antebellum plantation records from areas near large contraband camps (eastern North Carolina, for example) provide bits of information that can be carefully assembled with wartime data to piece together family relationships among freedpeople in camps. Despite antebellum laws prohibiting black literacy, some freedpeople who spent time in contraband camps did write about their experiences; Susie King Taylor's *Reminiscences of My Life in Camp* offers one book-length example, and other shorter memoirs appeared in religious magazines in the decades following the war. Some African American families accumulated their own family paper collections, consisting of newspaper clippings, oral histories, birth and marriage certificates, pension claims, and other family memorabilia dating back to Civil War days, and donated them to archives; I have used those collections whenever I have found them.

A whole category of invaluable evidence from the perspective of black men, women, and children in contraband camps consists of transcribed spoken testimony they offered about their experiences. One of the richest caches of such testimony comes from the files of the American Freedmen's Inquiry Commission, the AFIC. Headed by Samuel Gridley Howe, James McKaye, and Robert Dale Owen, the AFIC was authorized by Congress and instructed by Secretary of War Edwin Stanton to send agents throughout the occupied South in 1863 and 1864, investigate camp conditions, and offer recommendations for how the U.S. government should expedite slaves' transition from bondage to freedom. On its own initiative, the commission extended its inquiries to Canada and Haiti. The AFIC is best known for its published *Preliminary Report* and *Final Report,* which are often credited with inspiring the creation of the Freedmen's Bureau, but even more valuable are the raw data the AFIC collected in the form of eyewitness testimony. Agents conducted interviews and transcribed thousands of pages of testimony from U.S. Army personnel, Northern aid workers, local whites, slaves, freedpeople, and free blacks. The files do not use dialect to capture African Americans' testimony, but rather render it in standard prose, just as with testimony from white speakers. They provide an enormous archive of black voices describing their wartime transition out of slavery.[35] Former slaves also testified on their own behalf in court, to the provost marshal, and before congressional committees during and after the war, and such testimony also offers telling evidence of the transition out of slavery as experienced by those who went through it.

Another group of people present in contraband camps were missionaries and philanthropists connected with private aid societies and religious institutions, and they too left detailed records of life in contraband camps. Some, like the abolitionist Edward Pierce, published articles and reports. Others, like Clara Barton, left behind collections of personal papers. Many wrote letters to loved ones that have survived in manuscript published form. Others wrote to the churches or societies—the American Missionary Association (AMA) or the New England Freedmen's Aid Society, for example—that sent them, and still others wrote for newspapers or religious periodicals. Meanwhile, the meeting minutes, records, and annual reports of churches and philanthropic organizations like the Northwestern Freedmen's Aid Commission, the Boston Educational Commission, and the Western Freedmen's Aid Commission offer abundant detail on relief sent to camps and instructions issued to aid workers ministering there.

Members of the Northern public, black and white, knew something extraordinary was going on in contraband camps, even if they were not there to witness it firsthand, and newspapers, periodicals, sermons, speeches, and circulars all offer insight into how Northerners made sense of and reacted to emancipation and the transformation it set in motion. Moreover, free black Northerners held conventions and public meetings, published proceedings, and issued pamphlets.

New agencies created during and just after the Civil War also generated records of the interactions between freedpeople and the U.S. government. The records of the Freedman's Bank, the Bureau of Refugees, Freedmen, and Abandoned Lands (better known as the Freedmen's Bureau), the Southern Claims Commission (SCC), and the Department of Veterans' Affairs all offer glimpses of newly freed men, women, and children working with the U.S. government to secure what it meant to be a U.S. citizen. These records also provide valuable quotidian detail, especially the papers of the Southern Claims Commission and the pension records, for in those places former slaves often narrated what they did during the war. Personal papers of some Freedmen's Bureau agents augment the sometimes antiseptic bureau records with personal detail.

Finally, exiting slavery was a major turning point in many black men's, women's, and children's lives, and they continued to remember and relate it for many years afterward. Employees of the Works Progress Administration in the Great Depression interviewed former slaves and gathered their recollections together into the WPA Narratives housed at the Library of Congress, an oral history resource with its own pitfalls and challenges to be sure, but recently historians have reawakened to the vividness of its offerings when used carefully and in full knowledge of the challenges. In addition, both Iowa and Illinois possess vast collections of raw data collected by WPA workers but not included in the Narratives collection and now housed in boxes at the State Historical Society of Iowa in Des Moines and the Woodson Regional branch of the Chicago Public Library, respectively. The longtime Wisconsin archivist John O. Holzhueter maintained his own Black Settlers in Early Wisconsin Collection, an omnium-gatherum of oral history, scrapbooks, and other ephemera saved by and related to former slaves who settled in Wisconsin, and then donated this treasure trove of otherwise-impossible-to-find gold to the Wisconsin Historical Society.

A brief word about vocabulary or, more specifically, what to call the African American men, women, and children who fled slavery and made their way to the Union army. Many of the contemporary sources on which this book relies referred to such people as "contrabands," for reasons that will become clear in the prelude, but for a number of reasons I have avoided using that term except when quoting. One is that in a strictly legal sense it only applied to a limited number of individuals who fled from certain masters at certain times, before other, more extensive actions took effect. Another reason is that while some descendants of the people known as "contrabands" during the Civil War embrace the term, many others reject it because they believe that it likens human beings to property and in so doing insidiously legitimizes slavery.[36] Finally, to twenty-first-century readers, using the term "contrabands" to talk about people is just plain confusing; most people who hear the word think it must have something to do with the wartime blockade and smuggled cigars. Because other, clearer language to talk about formerly enslaved people who ran to Union lines exists—"freedpeople," for example—it seems more sensible to use it. I also use the phrase "refugees from slavery," because we all need a little variety and because I think it accurately captures the sense of human beings doing their best to flee from something they hated. Some scholars have argued that "refugees" only meant white Southerners displaced by war, but army records, newspapers, and black people themselves all used "refugees" interchangeably with other terms, including "contrabands," to refer to black men, women, and children who fled slavery during the Civil War, and so I follow their lead and use it, too.[37] I do retain the use of the term "contraband camps" to refer to refugee camps for former slaves under direction of the Union army in the occupied South, because that was the term by which they were universally known during the war itself.

· · ·

Whatever words they use, the types of sources on which this book draws seem as unrelated to one another as a tiny leaf on one tree in one section of a cyclorama seems distant from the buttons on a soldier's uniform in another section of the cyclorama. In isolation, many of these sources *are* completely different from each other. The owner or overseer who listed the ages of slave women and their children in the 1850s certainly did not see himself as connected to the recording secretary of the Northwestern Freedmen's Aid Commission, and a Union general might not have perceived much kinship between himself and a young black woman testifying in a provost marshal's courtroom. Yet every little brushstroke of evidence that each of these sources left behind, even the tiny stipple dots, like a name in a list or the docking schedule of a boat, helps paint a vast, imperfect cyclorama. Like a painting with some faded sections or portions compromised by water damage, the cyclorama created by all these sources cannot show us everything with the clarity we would like, yet it still portrays a story that takes a whole room and 360 degrees to tell.

That story is about slaves who wanted freedom, aided the Union army in the hopes that the U.S. government would help them procure it, and ended up with a distinctive version of citizenship, which neither fulfilled all their hopes nor matched exactly what citizenship had meant before the Civil War. Enslaved people desired freedom and autonomy for themselves, their loved ones, and their communities, but they were up against powerful slaveholders determined to deny them those things, just as they had always done. War created new possibilities for black men, women, and children to attain their visions because it brought upheaval and chaos. Chaos itself was a double-edged sword: it brought enormous suffering, but it also weakened slaveholders and introduced an alternative source of power into a South previously dominated by masters. That source was the Union army, and fleeing slaves allied with it, using their demonstrated usefulness to the Union cause to bargain for protection of the rights former slaves needed to pursue their own ends. Again and again, Union pickets and provost marshals were faced with the question of who was most likely to aid the war effort: a black woman who owned nothing and was working for the Union or a white property-owning man who sought the overthrow of it. The alliance that resulted between the army and fleeing slaves was never an easy collaboration. Former slaves' and soldiers' ultimate goals often coincided but were never completely congruent. When goals overlapped, freedpeople enjoyed the most success in achieving their ends. When goals diverged, their gains narrowed. The protection the army provided was never wholly impervious against the threat of re-enslavement. The alliance remained unstable and full of drawbacks, even tragedies. It was always a work of improvisation, and it stayed in flux for the entire war.

Yet for all the shortcomings to the alliance with Union military power, freedpeople enjoyed more success in obtaining their objectives under military authority than they did under civil authority. When formal hostilities ended in 1865 and civil authority once more began to overtake military authority, wartime gains started to shrink. Initial losses under civil authority did not lead the federal government to immediately and inevitably abandon former slaves to oppression. On the contrary, postwar violence and white Southern intransigence alerted freedpeople and their allies, especially in the Republican Party, to the importance of translating the wartime alliance between fleeing slaves and Union soldiers into an ongoing relationship between freedpeople and the national government. That relationship never worked exactly as African Americans envisioned it would, any more than the wartime alliance had, but in 1865 it remained viable, if unpredictable.

The version of citizenship that evolved in contraband camps during the war continued changing afterward, but the wartime version brought about two distinct changes that outlasted the war. One was the national government as arbiter of citizenship rather than the state governments, and the other was the relationship between citizenship and individual rights. Neither of these changes was foreseen or intended. Enslaved men, women, and children running to the Union army did not set out to inspire jurists' legal treatises or to alter the theoretical foundations of citizenship in ways over which legal scholars might puzzle. What they intended to do was build alliances with the Union army and the U.S. government to help them obtain autonomy for themselves, their families, and their communities, but the process of building that alliance called the precedent of state governments controlling citizenship into question and nudged the issue of rights to the fore. Before the war, states adjudicated citizenship by making their own determinations about who could and could not be useful to the community, but with some states out of the Union and the federal government fighting for its existence, the national government suddenly needed to determine usefulness to the national community. It was to federal arbiters that black men, women, and children appealed by proving how very useful they were to the Union army and the national community. In return, they parlayed their usefulness to the Union war effort into protection of basic individual rights. If it was being a Methodist or a Mason that safeguarded an individual's "actual bundle of rights" before the war, it was being a citizen of the United States that did so after the war, at least for the specific rights of basic personal protection, sanction for family bonds, personal mobility, access to schools and the legal system, and equality before the law.

There was no way that a resolute grandmother intent upon protecting her granddaughter could see what was coming when she took her first steps out of slavery and into the unknown under a hot August sun near Fredericksburg, Virginia. All she could know for sure was what unfolded before her as she took each determined step. For her, and for the hundreds of thousands of men, women, and children who fled from slavery and to the Union army, emancipation began not with a clear map to what was coming next but rather in confusion. What it felt like to go through that experience varied from place to place. Wringing out wet cloths to place on the heads of children delirious with fever as a contract employee of a U.S. smallpox hospital was not the same as pounding spikes to maintain a rail line through cotton country. The experience of emancipation began in the intimate details of the everyday, in the specific settings to which black men, women, and children ran. That is where this book will begin, too.

PART I

Out of Egypt

Prelude

A s the story goes, Old Point Comfort at the tip of the peninsula formed by the James and York Rivers, about midway down the Atlantic coast of North America, got its name from weary, grateful travelers who had spent months at sea in a seventeenth-century ship guaranteed to make any landfall look like a refuge. To judge by first appearances, the spot is in fact beautiful, girded by the Atlantic Ocean and the Chesapeake Bay, with sandy beaches and rocky outcroppings, and the breeze that blows on a summer day brings cool relief. The oysters that once littered its shores even added a touch of luxury. Certainly compared with a reeking, disease-ridden seventeenth-century ship, Old Point Comfort must have seemed a haven or even a paradise . . . until sojourners noticed that it had, in the pithy quip of Benjamin Butler, "plenty of oysters, but no water," no matter how deep they dug. In the 1860s, U.S. soldiers set out to drill a well; they dug nine hundred feet into the ground without finding a drop, realized the futility, and gave up.[1] Without massive human intervention, the refuge Fort Monroe could provide was neither healthful nor permanent, for in the absence of freshwater no place can sustain human life for long.

So, too, was the case with Civil War contraband camps, the first one of which took root at a U.S. Army installation at Old Point Comfort called Fort Monroe. Fort Monroe was the first of many contraband camps, for camps spread wherever the Union army went throughout the occupied South. They were the specific places in which emancipation began for nearly half a million former slaves. In contraband camps, black men, women, and children sought refuge from slavery. They found it in the basic sense of escaping their owners' grasps, but the environments, both natural and man-made, they encountered in the camps made for troubled refuge.

When the Commonwealth of Virginia left the Union on April 17, 1861, Fort Monroe remained in the hands of the U.S. Army, and it was to that army that three enslaved men ran on May 23, 1861, thereby making themselves the business of General Benjamin Butler, the officer in command at Fort Monroe. There was more to the story of Butler and his "contraband decision," and to the lives of the three men, than meets the eye, and we will look at both more closely later, but the brief outline goes like this: Shepard Mallory, Frank Baker, and James Townsend had been put to work building Confederate fortifications when they learned that their owner, the Confederate colonel Charles Mallory, planned to remove them farther south to labor for the Confederate army, separating them from their families. They decided to try their luck at Fort Monroe. The colonel sent an agent to demand their return, in compliance with the federal Fugitive Slave Law. Butler refused on the grounds that Colonel Mallory had used the men to build fortifications that would aid a force in armed rebellion against the United States, and so the rules of war conferred authority to confiscate the three slaves as contraband property.[2] In a stroke, Butler used slaveholders' own insistence that slaves were legal property to release slaves from owners' grasps and illustrated how war could create possibilities unavailable in peacetime. The phenomenon of the Civil War contraband camp was born.

Contraband camps followed and affected the course of the war, beginning in the eastern theater. The first camps formed in locations that never left Union hands, such as the northern tier and eastern coast of Virginia, followed soon by northwestern Virginia when Union forces took control in June 1861, and Washington, D.C., itself, especially once Congress abolished slavery in the District of Columbia in April 1862. Coastal regions farther south became the sites of camps almost as soon as Union forces captured them, from North Carolina's shoreline in the summer of 1861, to the South Carolina Sea Islands in November 1861, to coastal Georgia and Florida shortly thereafter. Once a camp formed in the eastern theater, it generally remained for the duration of the war, and many fleeing slaves seeking refuge there tended to stay for the duration, too. To go to a contraband camp required a huge leap of faith, but once a man, woman, or child had taken that step in the East, he or she was likely to stay put for the rest of the war; that relative stability made life in eastern camps different from life in western camps.

Camps in the West followed rivers and railroads and then fanned out from there, just as Union forces did. Control of the transportation, communication, and commercial artery of the West, the Mississippi River and its fertile valley, was a Union war aim from the start, and the army worked from all directions to obtain it. First successes came along the Mississippi's tributaries and their feeders. As Nashville fell to the Union in the winter of 1862, a camp took shape there, and others soon tracked Union progress along the Ohio and Cumberland Rivers at places like Clarksville and Gallatin, Tennessee; Smithland, Paducah, and Louisville, Kentucky; and Huntsville, Alabama. More camps came later in northern Alabama as the Union presence thickened there. Meanwhile, following the capture of the Mississippi's southern outlet at New Orleans in the spring and Memphis in the early summer of 1862, camps first blossomed in and around New Orleans and Memphis and then sprouted at Natchez, Davis Bend, and Helena on the river and from there deeper into Arkansas. Camps also tracked the railroad, following the army to Grand Junction, Bolivar, La Grange, and Jackson, Tennessee, and Corinth, Mississippi, as the Union carried out a long campaign to take and hold Vicksburg, the city holding the key to the whole river valley. The Union approached Vicksburg from the other end of the river simultaneously, consolidating forces at the key river and rail junction at Cairo in the southern tip of Illinois in June 1861 and proceeding doggedly down from there. Fugitive slaves followed. Thousands remained in and around Cairo for the duration of the war, while others were resettled in Northern communities by the U.S. government. Tens of thousands more were relocated to other camps along the Mississippi such as Mound City, Columbus, New Madrid, and Island Number Ten. Once Vicksburg came into Union hands, camps burgeoned there and at nearby Lake Providence, Paw Paw Island, Young's Point, and Milliken's Bend. Camps even sprang up in the interior portions of the border states of Missouri and Kentucky, although fugitives who ran to them faced danger of recapture by loyal Unionist slaveholders as well as by Confederate guerrillas, making life in those states extraordinarily precarious. In the West, both camps themselves and the people in them were constantly on the move.

Everywhere the Union army went, refugees from slavery retraced and broadened the path first cut by Shepard Mallory, Frank Baker, and James Townsend at Fort Monroe. One was Solomon Bradley, whose wife and two children had been sold away years before the war came, but that loss did not inoculate him from continuing to witness intolerable cruelty. As an enslaved railroad worker, he worked on tracks from Charleston to Savannah. One morning, the track passed by a plantation where a woman lay with her face flat against the ground, hands and feet tied to stakes, as her owner dripped melting wax into the gashes opened by the beating he had just given her. He then used a riding whip to flick off the hardened wax once it cooled and gave the woman a solid kick in the mouth whenever she cried out too loudly. "The sight of this thing made me wild almost that day," Bradley reported, and as soon as he caught sight of Union gunboats in Port Royal Sound, he made his way to Union forces in South Carolina's Lowcountry. He worked as a cook on the steamer *Cosmopolitan*, which ferried army personnel and Northern missionaries among the Sea Islands, until he joined the Third South Carolina Volunteers later in the war.[3]

Whether propelled by hope of freedom or hatred of slavery, whether motivated by belief in a better future or loathing of the people who had sold, beaten, and used their loved ones for profit, refugees from slavery made their way to the Union military. One woman decided to run off with the army because she "knew they could not take me anywhere where the Lord was not."[4] Perhaps most, like her, simply pressed forward on sheer faith that defies human power to explain. Once news of the Emancipation Proclamation got out in September 1862, even greater numbers of slaves anticipated the proclamation's implementation in January 1863 by running to the Union army wherever they could find it. By war's end, well over 400,000—somewhere between 12 and 15 percent of the entire U.S. slave population according to the 1860 census—had taken refuge behind Union lines, most of them in contraband camps.[5] With the smallest housing hundreds of refugees from slavery and the largest sheltering upwards of ten thousand, contraband camps brought greater numbers of slaves into contact with each other in a single place than had ever happened anywhere in the United States before.

Women and children made up a disproportionate share of contraband camp populations. As soon as slave owners suspected that Union troops might infiltrate, many who possessed the financial means sent their most valuable slaves, especially men of prime laboring age, deeper into Confederate territory. For families in the Mississippi valley, that usually meant heading west of the Mississippi River. Virginians and North Carolinians typically headed for the Appalachian Mountains, where the density of the slave population grew appreciably during the war. Wherever slave owners tried to evacuate themselves and their slaves, the goal was to keep the workers who carried the most capital value and the Yankees away from each other.[6] Not every slave owner could afford the expense or manage the logistics of transporting slaves, and others simply chose not to, so at first men of all ages were present in contraband camps. Sometimes, in the very early days of the war, they even outnumbered women and children.[7] Sex ratios skewed dramatically and irrevocably once the Union army began to enlist black men of military age into its ranks. Contraband camps functioned as instant recruiting stations, and it was not long before the bulk of eligible men had traded (sometimes voluntarily, sometimes not) life in the camps for a suit of Union blue, leaving camps full of women, children, the old, and the sick.

Danger was present in every camp. Deadly disease flourished in crowded conditions. Hostile whites threatened camps, especially in areas where the Union's hold on the territory remained vulnerable to Confederate attack or even recapture. Danger could also emanate from the segment of the Union army that saw slaves as the scapegoats to be blamed for the cursed war.

Certain ideas influenced life in contraband camps everywhere. Chief among them were ideas about dependence and independence, which had been tangled and fraught among first colonists and then Americans since the American Revolution. Before the eighteenth century in Europe or its colonies, "dependency" described an economic relationship that included almost everyone because it meant "to gain one's livelihood by working for someone else." It connoted a particular rung on a social ladder, below aristocratic landowners who were free from the need to labor and who owned sufficient property to qualify for political rights, but it did not carry moral stigma. "Independence" among anyone else indicated a lack of regard for proper social relations, and it fomented social disorder. A confluence of intellectual and economic forces, especially the rise of particular forms of Protestantism like Puritanism and Quakerism, the spread of Enlightenment ideas, and the ongoing development of capitalism, converged in the eighteenth century to redefine the individual, recharacterize independence as the ability to support a household economically, valorize it among (white) men as well as the political entities that comprised them, and stigmatize the once-ordinary condition of dependence as a state fit only for those rendered inferior by race, age, gender, or personal moral failing and as a disqualifier for political rights enjoyed by the growing ranks of the independent. As Nancy Fraser and Linda Gordon put it in their intellectual history of the concept, "Dependency was deemed antithetical to citizenship."[8] These ideas had particular resonance for Civil War–era white Americans, because their nation had gained its political independence amid the froth churned up by them, and so they seemed to be at the foundation of the United States, whose existence was now on the line.

Ideas about dependence and independence could prove confounding in contraband camps, where the enormous fact of immediate material need among sick, starving, and vulnerable refugees from slavery demanded redress. Ungenerous or racist members of the Union army obviously begrudged any aid, but even well-meaning soldiers or aid workers worried that providing direct relief would undermine principled attempts to convince members of the Northern public that former slaves were worthy, upstanding, and deserving of rights, rather than indolent paupers who would drain precious resources. "Proving" that black people were perfectly capable of fending for themselves cut at cross-purposes with supplying rations to the starving or distributing coats to shivering refugees waiting on a dock in a fierce winter wind.

Consequently, benevolent workers wrestled with dilemmas of conscience, official policy reflected confusion at best and heartlessness at worst, and black men, women, and children suffered from unmet needs.

Importantly, all contraband camps brought formerly enslaved human beings and the U.S. government into direct contact with each other. Whereas before the war, the federal government bore an obligation to protect the property of a slave's owner, the idea that the U.S. government would treat with an enslaved person directly as a person and not indirectly as the possession of a white property owner simply made no sense. Yet here were hundreds, and then thousands, and then tens of thousands, and finally hundreds of thousands of exactly such people, right in the lap of the Union army, the most obvious embodiment of the U.S. government outside the White House and the Capitol. Lawyers could argue over whether black people ought to be able to sue in federal courts or carry U.S. passports, but in the urgency of war the army and refugees from slavery had to deal directly with each other right then and there.[9] Manifestations of that new, direct contact between the U.S. government and formerly enslaved people abounded, including the creation of whole new entities, like the AFIC and the Freedmen's Bureau.

All camps were a mix of improvisation, sanctuary, and humanitarian crisis, but the exact ratio of refuge to misery varied mightily from place to place, depending on the interplay of a number of concrete factors. One was camp location. Wherever freedpeople were, the availability of local resources for building shelter, and of land and tools for cultivating gardens to supplement or replace dreary army food rations, quite literally affected the environment in which they began the passage from slavery to freedom. Most camps appeared where soldiers encamped, which was often in large, open areas, but not always. For the many formerly enslaved men, women, and children who encountered the Union army in cities like Alexandria, Washington, D.C., New Orleans, and St. Louis, the urban environment shaped and characterized the particular transition out of slavery in ways quite different from how former slaves outside urban locations experienced that transition.

Proximity to a clean river, creek, or stream was always important, for nothing mattered more than access to freshwater. Drainage also mattered, because it directly influenced the disease environment. Poor drainage led to dismal sanitary conditions, which fostered cholera, dysentery, and intestinal diseases. Faulty drainage also resulted in standing water, which provides an ideal environment for reproduction among certain species of disease-bearing mosquitoes.

People carry diseases, too, especially when they come together in crowded conditions and are sick and starving upon arrival, as undernourished slaves who undertook long and risky journeys to flee bondage generally were. From an epidemiological perspective, camps functioned much like instant and overcrowded cities, in which people exposed to or infected with measles, typhus, smallpox, or other diseases found themselves cheek by jowl with those who lacked immunity and whose weakened conditions left them with little resistance. Almost every camp, as a result, functioned like an epidemiological incubator to a greater or lesser degree, but the exact diseases that ravaged camps varied from place to place, and a camp with cholera differed from one with smallpox.

Political and strategic considerations differed from camp to camp. Whether a camp was located in a Union-occupied part of the Confederacy, where wartime federal policy on slavery prevailed, or in a border slave state, where slavery remained under the jurisdiction of state law, mattered. So did the military progress of the war because, to state the obvious, if the Union army left or lost control of an area, there went the contraband camp. Even in camps that never left Union control, the quality of life often depended on what happened on nearby battlefields, because the army's chief business was to win the war, and if military necessity came into conflict with the needs and interests of freedpeople, military necessity invariably got priority. If the army determined it needed all hands—black and white—on deck, then black men and women could find themselves digging trenches or throwing up earthworks, regardless of whether their gardens needed sowing or harvesting at the same time.

Camps were also populated by different people, black and white, each of whom brought unique experiences, ideas, priorities, and prejudices that influenced the atmosphere in camp, just as the physical environment and the iron demands of the war did. Blacks often brought well-founded mistrust of whites, but they also calculated that anyone fighting against slaveholders had at least one common interest with them. Whites typically brought preconceived notions about black people, ranging from blind and bitter hatred to the so-called environmental view that former slaves lagged behind whites in ability and attainment not because of innate difference but because of the poisonous effects of slavery, for which white benevolence and careful instruction were the only proper antidotes.

Because the army disproportionately wielded hard power, the attitudes of Union army personnel in each location exerted unmistakable influence. Some officers assigned to serve as superintendents of contrabands viewed the camps as nothing more than distasteful and inconvenient encumbrances that only the orders of their superiors could have induced them to accept. Others welcomed the assignments. Still others approved of the idea in theory but quailed at the overwhelming scale of need in the camps. As for the rank and file of the Union army, it consisted of roughly two million men and therefore roughly two million individual opinions about black people. While the war convinced most enlisted soldiers of the necessity of emancipation in fairly short order, and while many did find themselves forced to look hard at hitherto-unexamined racial prejudice, wide variety still prevailed among soldiers' attitudes toward individual black people, and treatment accordingly ran the gamut from vicious and cruel to principled justice to simple human kindness.[10]

Aid workers and missionaries, black and white, who came from the North also brought a range of attitudes with them. Beyond simply opposing slavery, they felt a calling to care for those who had been enslaved: some with insufferable condescension, many with naïveté, and nearly all with earnestness. Sometimes, the experience of war changed benevolent workers, just as it did soldiers. Joanna Moore, for example, attended an Emancipation Eve celebration in Illinois on December 31, 1862, and felt a calling so strong that she abandoned her final year of study at Rockford Female Seminary and with it the opportunity to graduate. Instead of studying poetry, she set sail down the Mississippi River to work with refugees from slavery, confident that "woman's hand and heart must supply their needs." There was no doubting her sincerity when she disembarked on Island Number Ten, nor was there any doubting her initial shock when she was immediately sent to break up a fight between two freedwomen who "laughed at my earnestness" until the humiliated Moore ran to her bunk and "cried myself to sleep." Yet from that experience and "many another," Moore realized that at first she "only pitied those women," which was why she "did them but little good," for "I have learned since that you never can help any one till you love them a little after the way that Jesus loved."[11] The ability to move from pity to love was unevenly distributed among all aid workers and made for another variable affecting life in the camps.

Wherever the Union army went, tens of thousands of enslaved men, women, and children made their way to its blue lines, braving almost unimaginable risks to get there. They gambled against dogs, heavily armed search parties, jittery Confederate or Union pickets who might shoot at the very sound of an unexpected footstep. They defied the dire threats of their masters, such as the Virginia master who swore that if his slaves ran to the Yankees, he would hunt them down, stone them, and sell their children.[12] Still they came. Still they found work where they could. Still they aided the Union army when and where they were able. And they began the long journey from slavery to freedom.

The particulars of the journey varied widely from place to place, and the particulars mattered to the sojourners, for they undertook the journey with no way of knowing its ultimate destination, no sense of unifying themes, no foreknowledge of the coming twists and turns in the road. Refugees fleeing slavery had no real way of knowing anything for certain except for the particulars as they heard and saw and smelled and felt and tasted them, day after day, on the road out of bondage. Exiting slavery to the crash of the surf at Fort Monroe sounded different from exiting slavery to the whine and roar of trains rushing along tracks to Corinth. Exiting slavery looked different to a worker who raised his eyes from a burlap sack to see rows and rows of white cotton bolls than it did to a worker peering down at the burlap sacks she methodically stitched for the Quartermaster Department of the Union army. Exiting slavery smelled different to a man digging graves behind a smallpox hospital than it did to a man piloting a boat through tricky Atlantic inlets. Exiting slavery felt different to a child who crawled into the lap of a welcoming aid worker than it did to a child who had to be pried from the stiffening arms of a dead parent, tattered clothing plastered to cold limbs by mud and frost and blood. Exiting slavery tasted different to a woman gnawing on an unyielding square of Union army hardtack than it did to a woman sipping ginger tea. Contraband camps everywhere provided troubled refuge to the enslaved people who gathered in them, but the version of freedom each refugee from slavery found depended in some ways on exactly where he or she found it.

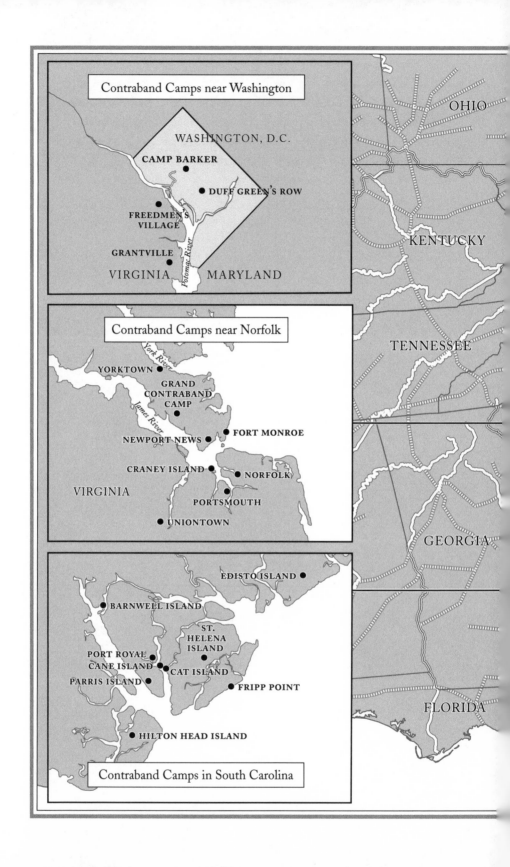

Contraband Camps near Washington

WASHINGTON, D.C.

CAMP BARKER

DUFF GREEN'S ROW

FREEDMEN'S
VILLAGE

GRANTVILLE

VIRGINIA   *Potomac River*   MARYLAND

Contraband Camps near Norfolk

York River

YORKTOWN

GRAND
CONTRABAND
CAMP

James River

FORT MONROE

NEWPORT NEWS

CRANEY ISLAND   NORFOLK

VIRGINIA

PORTSMOUTH

UNIONTOWN

EDISTO ISLAND

BARNWELL ISLAND

ST.
HELENA
ISLAND

PORT ROYAL
CANE ISLAND   CAT ISLAND
PARRIS ISLAND   FRIPP POINT

HILTON HEAD ISLAND

Contraband Camps in South Carolina

OHIO

KENTUCKY

TENNESSEE

GEORGIA

FLORIDA

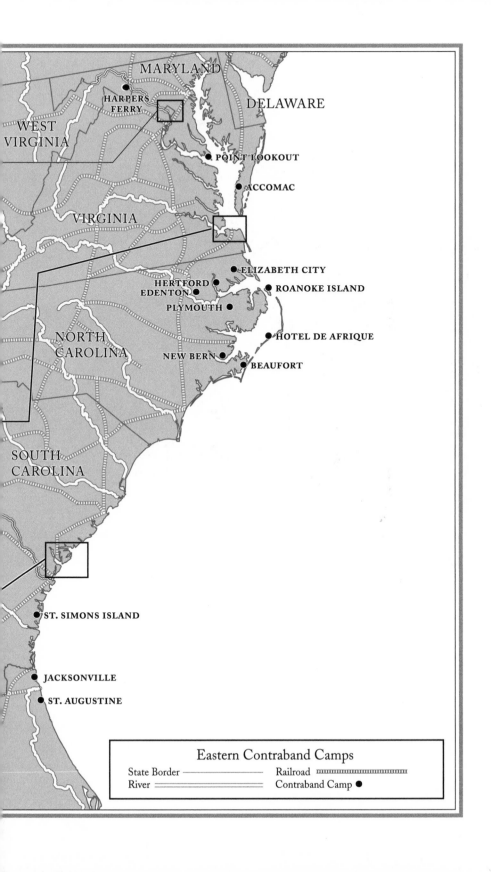

Eastern Contraband Camps

State Border ——————— Railroad ▪▪▪▪▪▪▪▪▪▪▪▪▪▪▪▪▪▪▪
River ════════════ Contraband Camp ●

Edisto Island, South Carolina, 1862

ONE

Grit and Limits

Experiencing Emancipation in Eastern Contraband Camps

The 1862 photograph shows a white clapboard-covered cabin framed by trees and Spanish moss, a cart pulled by a mule or possibly a small horse.[1] It must have been a sunny day, because the branches cast shadows on the cabin. Ten people look straight at the camera: five men, one boy, three women, and one girl who appears to be in her teens. They were all on Edisto, an island in the Carolina Lowcountry under Union control. They stand on sandy soil, the kind that turns into airborne grit when any wind above a slight breeze comes along, not all that different in texture from the desert soil in the story of the exodus, the most potent contemporary metaphor for emancipation. In the exodus, the Israelites fled bondage in Egypt and then woke up homeless every morning to walk through the desert, again and again, for forty years, displaying a kind of determination that we sometimes call grit. Grit is also a harsh, abrasive irritant. It was the sand and dust swirling about the desert for all forty years of the trek, clogging noses, irritating throats, interfering with breathing, getting in eyes so travelers could not see what was up ahead. Grit was everywhere in the story of the exodus, and it was everywhere that fleeing slaves encountered the Union army along the Eastern Seaboard from Maryland to Florida. To glimpse what it was like to exit slavery in the Civil War's eastern theater means getting right down into the grit of daily life in contraband camps in the East.

THE CAPITAL REGION

From the outset, the story of slavery's disruption unfolded not in one linear narrative in a single place among a handful of actors but rather on multiple stages simultaneously among a cast of thousands who were often at cross-purposes with one another. On the very day that Butler refused to return Baker, Mallory, and Townsend to their owner, members of the First Michigan Volunteer Infantry marched down Duke Street, a main thoroughfare in Alexandria, Virginia, and into the so-called slave pen of Price, Birch & Company, a capital-intensive and highly lucrative slave-trading firm.[2] The people held inside stepped out of the pen and into a street coated with some combination of gravel, bird droppings, dried horse dung, and dirt from soldiers' boots, or, in other words, urban grit. Over the next eighteen months, thousands of men, women, and children would join them as the Army of the Potomac crashed forward and curled back like a tide over the Virginia countryside in multiple (unsuccessful) attempts to capture the Confederate capital at Richmond. Each time the army swept through Fairfax County, to Manassas, Gordonsville, Fredericksburg, or anywhere in between, freedom-seeking slaves hurled themselves into it and were rolled about like pebbles in the undertow as the wave receded. They generally found their feet again somewhere on the Orange and Alexandria rail line, which they rode by the hundreds into Alexandria.

Alexandria's urban setting shaped the experience of exiting slavery there. One of its most notable features was a housing shortage, which in turn led to overcrowding, rampant disease, and high mortality rates. Refugees already in the city took in whom they could, but it did not take long for their tight quarters in alleyways and outbuildings to exceed capacity. Newcomers crowded into abandoned railcars and packing crates, and when they filled those up, there was one place left to turn: the old "slave pen" on Duke Street, the very one liberated on the first day freedom-seeking slaves found refuge with the Union army. When Julia Wilbur, a Quaker from Rochester, New York, visited the pen in November 1862, she found about twenty women and children camped out in each of the small, dirty rooms. Many of the children were wrapped in insubstantial rags and huddled around a fire while their mothers searched for work. They had been pushed past the limits of endurance just to escape their masters and make it to Alexandria, and the maladies that Wilbur collectively labeled "fatigue and exposure" mercilessly claimed lives.[3] Albert Gladwin, appointed superintendent of contrabands by the Union army, sought to redress the housing crisis by building group barracks, despite the clear preferences of freedpeople and aid workers for family apartments or cottages to respect privacy and slow down the transmission of disease.[4] Predictably, disease raged. Harriet Jacobs, a former slave famous for the memoir she published about her antebellum escape from North Carolina, left her new home in Boston to help combat measles, diphtheria, scarlet fever, typhoid fever, and, in the winter of 1863, a smallpox epidemic that claimed at least seven hundred lives before spring came and the worst abated.[5]

Alexandria also incubated moral pathogens, like callousness, greed, and corruption. The smallpox epidemic left so many children orphaned that one doctor threatened to send them all to a quarantine "pest house" outside town, before his superiors censured him and overruled his pitiless plan.[6] Meanwhile, two men, Bundy and Pierce, took between eight hundred and a thousand dollars' worth of coffee and meat provided by the Union army for slave refugees, sold it to white Alexandrians illicitly, and pocketed the proceeds before the army found out about it and launched an investigation.[7]

At the same time, Alexandria's urban environment did offer some distinct advantages, which refugees from slavery were quick to recognize. The presence of Union troops made for more of certain kinds of security than an exposed camp on ground tenuously occupied by Union forces deep in Confederate territory could. A busy port city and railroad hub also provided work for men and women who loaded and unloaded at docks, kept rail lines running, nursed in government hospitals, and found a ready supply of city residents looking for domestic help.[8] Schools multiplied quickly, and hundreds of former slaves, both children and adults, flocked to them. When students outnumbered teachers by too unwieldy a ratio, convalescent Union soldiers filled in the gaps to teach the basics of reading and writing.[9] The housing shortage was never fully alleviated, but freedpeople's sheer force of numbers made their preferences felt eventually, and by March 1864 more than seven hundred new cabins had been built for and by families of former slaves.[10] By that November, a freedman named Peter Grant—renowned for his skill as a shoemaker and for his one leg—had built a two-room frame house with a small yard, and hundreds more freedpeople followed his example, creating a tidy little neighborhood called Grantville.[11]

Alexandria's high population density also hastened the forging of direct relationships between freedpeople and the army (and U.S. government) by sheer necessity. Smallpox would have claimed even more lives if not for the Union military governor John Slough's implementation of systematic, cost-free vaccination.[12] Many of those who died were spared the anonymity and indignity that death often brought to refugees from slavery, because the army established the Contrabands and Freedmen Cemetery on the outskirts of the city, buried former slaves there in the same kinds of coffins used for Union soldiers, and kept records of the names of the dead. These actions were grim, to be sure, but they were also measures that the U.S. government had not taken even for soldiers who died fighting for it when the war first began. They certainly did not amount to the attainment of former slaves' visions of freedom, but they did signify the forging of a new and previously impossible relationship between former slaves and the national government.[13]

Maryland is not far from Alexandria geographically, but in many ways it was worlds apart for enslaved people seeking freedom there. Unlike Virginia, Maryland remained in the Union, so there were fewer troops there. In the parts of the state with no federal soldiers, there was also no refuge from slavery. The city jail of Frederick, in the western part of the state, continued to house captives who had run from their masters, only to be snatched by slave catchers and held for safekeeping until their owners came to claim them.[14] Moreover, the logic of rebellion as revocation of the rights of property holders to call on the U.S. government to safeguard personal property—and more specifically, of slaveholders to call on the federal government to enforce the Fugitive Slave Law—did not pertain. In plain terms, the "contraband decision" taken at Fort Monroe did not apply in Maryland, and slaveholders there expected the Union army, acting on behalf of the U.S. government, to protect all their property rights, including their rights to slaves. On General Benjamin Butler's journey through Maryland before arrival at Fort Monroe, he had agreed with that interpretation and vowed to enforce it while he and his troops were in Maryland.

The relative paucity of troops and the uncertainty surrounding the response that refugees from slavery might meet from those troops notwithstanding, many enslaved men and women still identified a Union army fighting against slaveholders anywhere as a potential escape route out of slavery. When the army established a hospital at Point Lookout in the coastal part of the state in 1862, fugitive slaves began to flock to it, and formed a contraband camp there.[15] After the Battle of Gettysburg, Point Lookout also housed a Confederate prisoner-of-war camp, so it meant captivity for thousands of rebel soldiers, even as it meant just the opposite for former slaves like ten-year-old Austin Smith, who had been separated from his family and removed from Maryland by slavery. When the war began, Smith lived and labored for a master in Northumberland County, Virginia, just across a narrow section of the Potomac River from Point Lookout. Somehow, Smith made his way across the river, where he found refuge until a free black family member came for him in April 1863 and took him home.[16] No significant contraband camps developed in the western part of the state, but in the wake of the March 1862 law preventing Union soldiers from serving as slave catchers, the army established a contraband camp on the grounds of the U.S. Armory at Harpers Ferry in Virginia, to which slaves in the western part of Maryland could run. Besides the armory, Harpers Ferry featured rail lines, which offered work to some refugees from slavery and transportation to many others who rode rail lines east to Washington, D.C., especially after Congress abolished slavery there in April 1862.[17]

One year after the outbreak of war, the District of Columbia Emancipation Act freed thirty-one hundred individuals in the district immediately, and it also turned the nation's capital into somewhere enslaved people in Maryland and even Delaware could flee. Emancipation in the District of Columbia was hardly a new idea in April 1862. Enslaved men and women had long fought their own enslavement in small daily ways and in some big, dramatic ways, such as the failed efforts of dozens of slaves in 1848 to escape on a schooner called the *Pearl*, but with the weight of the federal government on the side of slave owners, such efforts made little headway.[18] In 1849, Abraham Lincoln, as a freshman congressman from Illinois, had tried and failed to get the House of Representatives to pass a bill banning slavery in the district, and the matter had continued to come up for debate intermittently but never with much hope of success. The absence of senators and members of the House of Representatives from the seceded states shifted the balance in Congress enough to permit the passage of the District of Columbia Emancipation Act on April 16, 1862. Even then, arrival in Washington did not ensure former slaves' liberation, because masters in loyal Union states could still try to invoke the Fugitive Slave Law to reclaim runaways until the repeal of that law in June 1864. In 1863, before the Fugitive Slave Law's repeal, Washington, D.C.'s superintendent of contrabands, D. B. Nichols, observed that freedpeople "are much afraid of Maryland" and particularly the penchant of Maryland slaveholders for entering the district and kidnapping freed children to force back into slavery.[19]

Despite the chronic threat of kidnapping, refugees from Maryland could at least hope to blend in among the capital city's free black community. Within six months, forty-two hundred refugees from slavery congregated in two major camps in the district. One camp was at Duff Green's Row on Capitol Hill, not far from where a notorious slave market had once carried out its business and literally right in the path of members of Congress as they came and went from the Senate and the House of Representatives. The other was called Camp Barker, and it was located near what is now Logan Circle. In the summer months, President Lincoln passed by it most mornings and evenings as he commuted back and forth between the White House and his family's summer lodgings on the grounds of the Soldiers' Home just a few miles from the city center. The combined number of refugees from slavery within the two camps had approached five thousand by 1863 and continued to climb throughout the war.[20]

In Washington, former slaves found opportunities scattered throughout a cityscape of wartime hardship, but the hardship would have been more immediately visible. One of the most persistent and devastating problems was water, or rather the fact that the camps lacked a clean freshwater supply. One army surgeon described "an accumulation of filth, foul mud, and stagnant water in a deep hollow adjoining the Contraband Camp, which renders the row of buildings next to it unhealthy." Debate raged over whether the best recourse was to pipe in freshwater from the Potomac or to simply cover the foul pits with dirt and transport freedpeople to a larger haven across the Potomac as quickly as possible. Some did move to a camp hastily assembled on the grounds of Arlington House, the estate inherited by Mary Custis Lee (Robert E. Lee's wife) from her father and abandoned by the family when Union forces moved across the Potomac into northern Virginia. There, former slaves built a self-sustaining community called Freedmen's Village, and they buried Union army dead in what would become Arlington National Cemetery. But back in Washington, army doctors and the quartermaster general's office continued to argue, and former slaves continued to suffer.[21] A black physician from Ohio, Dr. R. B. Leach, traveled to Washington to investigate conditions and found plenty to sicken him. Unscrupulous sutlers were shorting former slaves on wood rations and were hoarding clothing that was meant for distribution. Insufficient fuel and clothing led to increased exposure and vulnerability to illness, but woe betide the poor man, woman, or child who took sick because hospital conditions were even worse, according to Dr. Leach. Not even death saved former slaves from indignity, for in contrast to Alexandria the dead were treated with nearly inconceivable disrespect: the average corpse-to-coffin ratio was seventeen to ten.[22]

The persistence of hardship could not erase the symbolic significance of abolition in the nation's capital, for it signaled a shift away from the national government's historic alliance with slaveholders in the ongoing battle between owners and slaves. When rumors of an impending attack roiled Washington in the fall of 1862, black workers were redeployed to guard vulnerable spots along the city's defenses, and news of former slaves defending the national capital crackled "through the rebel states like electricity."[23] Even when the capital was not under direct attack, increasing numbers of former slaves found work. Some new arrivals to Washington found work through the New England Freedmen's Aid Society, and others by word of mouth throughout the African American community, but many sought out the army and the federal government as employers. Drawing wages from the federal government in the nation's capital carried enormous symbolic significance for African American men and women, because before the war laws prohibiting black federal employment were so unbending that an African American was not even supposed to handle the U.S. mail.[24] Meanwhile, leaders of Washington's substantial antebellum free black community, members of Washington's black churches, and black Union soldiers stationed in Washington in the later years of the war all fully appreciated and acted upon the symbolic value of advocating for equal access to public facilities (for example, streetcars) in the nation's capital.[25]

FORT MONROE AND COASTAL VIRGINIA

Farther down the Atlantic coast, enslaved men, women, and children continued to call on their courage, their determination, and their feet to turn Fort Monroe, site of Butler's "contraband decision," into "Freedom's Fortress," but the complicated interplay between the war and the people in camps shaped life there right from the start. By July 1861, "nine hundred negroes," roughly two-thirds of them women, children, or sick and elderly men, had found their way to Fort Monroe and the adjoining city of Hampton, which had been abandoned by Confederates earlier in the spring. Black Hampton residents who stayed put when the whites fled, along with former slaves from surrounding areas who fled to Fort Monroe, worked under the direction of the Massachusetts infantryman Edward Pierce to build a battery. The city soon became "a thriving, free settlement" of former slaves, "supported by fishing, oystering, huckstering, artisanship, gardening, and farming."[26] By that time, more Union troops had arrived, taking Newport News, reinforcing Fort Monroe, and creating a buffer between Hampton's nascent free community and "marauding parties of rebels."[27] Then things went awry for Union troops on the battlefield (not for the last time). A Union loss at Big Bethel, followed immediately by the humiliating disaster at Manassas on the banks of the Bull Run in July, meant that General Butler needed to put his troops into action and could not spare enough of them to guard Hampton. He directed residents to evacuate the city, and on August 7, 1861, black men, women, and children crowded across the moat into Fort Monroe before Confederate forces under General John B. Magruder burned the city from its western edges all the way to the wharves.[28]

Inside the moat, refugees from slavery were safe from Confederate raiders but not from more insidious dangers like germs and shortages. Two days after they all crowded into the fort, General Butler answered a concerned query sent by the American Missionary Association, promising that he would "continue to receive and protect all the negroes especially the women and children." They were "earning the subsistence furnished them by the United States," so going hungry was not the major concern. Clothing was. "Many of them are now dressed in the cast-off clothing and uniforms of the soldiers," Butler wrote of the men, but the garments could be expected to be pretty ragged by wintertime, and unsurprisingly the army had nothing on hand for women and children.[29] Inadequate clothing, drafty tents for housing, crowded conditions, and Fort Monroe's perennial shortage of freshwater all led to predictable results: disease flourished, just as it did anywhere large numbers of soldiers encamped, and mortality climbed.[30] Small wonder that freedom seekers leaped at the chance to recross the moat and look for a little breathing room in and around Hampton as soon as the immediate Confederate threat had passed.

When black men, women, and children made their way back into Hampton, they found a ghostly landscape of charred buildings. They rebuilt with a combination of government lumber, the sides of packing crates, and the kind of ingenuity that could build a church and a school out of the surviving walls of a singed courthouse that had once housed the law offices of Colonel Charles Mallory. Other refugees from slavery took shelter in tents at nearby Camp Hamilton and in the adjacent area, christened the Grand Contraband Camp.[31]

They also turned to Mary Peake, a free black woman who, even before the war, had clandestinely taught slaves to read (in violation of Virginia state law), and asked her to begin a school. She converted the front room of her home into a classroom, and by the end of the week "between fifty and sixty" children clustered together each day. First, they learned the alphabet, then one-syllable words, then multi-syllable words and the fundamentals of arithmetic, all while memorizing Peake's favorite hymns, such as "I Want to Be an Angel" and "There Is a Happy Land." At Christmas, the students staged a festive recital, complete with dramatic readings of Scripture, a potluck supper, and the hymns they had worked diligently to memorize. Cheerful strains of "Merry Christmas to all! Merry Christmas to all! Merry Christmas to all!" rang out crisp and bright on the cold December evening, but no tune could drown out Mary Peake's cough. In two months, children would sing many of the same hymns again, this time at Peake's funeral following her death from tuberculosis.[32]

It was a resilient spirit that inspired the consumptive Peake to teach, children to sing, and former slaves to rebuild charred ruins into a landscape of hope. That same resilient spirit animated freedpeople in all camps, but sometimes willpower is no match for tuberculosis or conflagration. Sometimes, germs and ashes won out in Hampton and wherever freedpeople and the Union army came into contact with each other.

Meanwhile, freedpeople and the Union army continued to influence the progress of the war in the Hampton Roads region and up into Virginia's peninsula. One reason Fort Monroe never left Union hands despite its location deep within the Confederacy was that army personnel there benefited from local knowledge and intelligence gathered by black spies. Benjamin Butler struck up a particularly fruitful working relationship with the militant and ever-inventive Abraham Galloway. Galloway had been born a slave in North Carolina, escaped to the North, traveled to Canada and Haiti in pursuit of society less defined by the color line, and was attracted back to the United States by the opportunity to participate in slavery's overthrow. Galloway's ingenuity, aptitude for navigating by land or water, and charisma in inspiring other black men and women to gather intelligence on the rebels all served Butler so well that he invited Galloway to go with him when he was reassigned to New Orleans later in 1861.[33] African Americans did not stop serving as spies when Galloway departed. After the famous naval battle between the ironclad ships the *Monitor* and the *Merrimack* (renamed the C.S.S. *Virginia*) at Hampton Roads in March 1862, one Union official reported, "The most valuable information we received in regard to the Merrimack and the operations of the rebels came from the colored people."[34]

Fort Monroe's reliance on black labor extended far beyond spying. All black men and women capable of labor were "set to work upon system and under supervision." They dug and built defenses, cooked for soldiers, nursed and scrubbed in hospitals, repaired rail lines, and kept railroad cars full of supplies humming.[35] Once the Army of the Potomac arrived and initiated the massive Peninsula Campaign (an ambitious plan launched from Fort Monroe to capture Richmond), former slaves defied their masters' orders "not to cook anything for the Yankies" and brought "corn cake, eggs, fresh herring & salmon" to Union soldiers on picket and did the thousand and one other things needed to get the vast, lumbering army on its way to Richmond.[36]

Black men and women worked for the army as paid laborers, not slaves, at least in theory, but not only were they paid less than white workers; prompt payment of wages proved more exception than rule. Even today, errors in soldiers' pay are fairly common and can take months or even years to resolve. During the Civil War, both soldiers and black workers went months on end without any sign of the paymaster, but the consequences of unpaid wages were more dire for former slaves locked in a hardscrabble struggle for survival than they were for Union soldiers. Workers in the Engineer, Subsistence, and Ordinance Departments could count on "wages of from 80 cents to one dollar per day, which is regularly and promptly paid," but workers in the Quartermaster Department and in hospitals were not so fortunate.[37] Suthey Parker worked first for the Quartermaster Department and then as a cook for the better part of a year, but he only saw cash wages for about a month of that time.[38] To make up for the shortfall, black men and women did what they could to earn money in other ways, like taking in washing, selling pies and corn bread to soldiers, and even starting "little restaurants where they sell ice cream, lemonade, meals &c" to enlisted Union troops. Their efforts knew no limits, but the results sometimes did, for with neither black workers nor soldiers paid regularly, the available pool of paying customers was too small to keep even the most entrepreneurial endeavor afloat, and soldiers were notorious for simply not paying their bills.[39] The resulting hardship was so appalling that Lewis Lockwood, a Northern missionary investigating conditions at Fort Monroe, accused the army of "government slavery."[40]

General John Ellis Wool, Benjamin Butler's immediate successor as commander of Fort Monroe, took the wages problem seriously, and his actions demonstrate both the impact of conscientious leadership and its limits in the face of structural problems too large for a single individual to overcome. Wool lived by "the principle that Black People should have the same rights as white people," and he brooked no nonsense from anyone.[41] To be sure, as the oldest (born 1784) officer in the army by 1862, Wool was a soldier who followed orders, as he had when accompanying the Cherokee on the infamous Trail of Tears in the 1830s. Yet he also held his fellow army personnel to rigid standards, just as he had done when he court-martialed volunteers for mistreatment of Mexicans in the Mexican-American War and when he clashed with white settlers over their abuses of and encroachments upon the Yakima, Cayuse, and Nez Percé in Washington Territory in the 1850s.[42] Wool launched an investigation, answered inquiries from Congress, and appointed the Bostonian Charles B. Wilder to serve as superintendent of contrabands in exchange for "quarters, fuel and forage" but no wages. Wool also replaced a two-tier wage system with a policy of equal pay for equal work regardless of the race of the laborer and put Wilder in charge of administering it. Under Wool's new policy, Suthey Parker finally got paid in May 1862.[43]

Just as the lot of Suthey Parker and all the men, women, children, and families like him appeared to be improving, more changes in leadership and the progress of the war took over yet again. Once General John A. Dix took command in the summer of 1862, wages became an even bigger problem, and for longer. The two-tier wage scale returned in theory, but in practice it looked more like a no-wage scale to workers who once again went unpaid. In November 1862, Secretary of War Stanton appointed the Boston philanthropist LeBaron Russell to investigate. Russell was a keen and passionate observer with the acuity to realize that camps were not monolithic. As he reported to the secretary of war in December, "The condition of the colored Refugees varies very considerably in the different localities in which they are collected." His careful calculations painted with a fine and detailed rather than overly broad brush; they revealed that some departments were more egregious than others and that Wool's policy made a temporary difference, but overall the picture was stark. The government was in arrears to unpaid black workers in and around Fort Monroe for a total of $33,495.41. Russell sent both a long and a short version of his report, along with hospital payrolls, to the secretary of war, and for good measure also sent a copy of the short report to assistants to the secretary of war. Although Assistant Secretary of War John Tucker acknowledged that the War Department received both reports, the payrolls for hospital workers mysteriously went missing, once again delaying payday, especially for freedpeople who had worked in Union hospitals. AFIC commissioners interrogated Dix, who reported that as far as he knew, wages had been paid up at Fort Monroe and most surrounding areas.[44]

Dix was wrong, but it is just possible that he thought he was telling the truth, for the differences between Generals Wool and Dix went beyond wage policies and underscore both the impact and the limits of individual leadership. Superintendent of Contrabands Charles Wilder testified that General Wool had acted on his egalitarian principles; Dix, on the other hand, "endorses that principle, professedly, but he fails in carrying it out."[45] Dix *intended* "kindness and courtesy," but the challenges he faced were greater than his energy for meeting all of them. In any event, even the best of unfulfilled intentions were of little comfort to the black men, women, and children who knew all too well where the road built by good intentions led.

In November 1862, General Dix ordered that a hospital at Newport News become a shelter for refugees from slavery, but just as he did so, Michael Corcoran's Irish Legion arrived from New York after a stormy journey down the Atlantic coast that destroyed all the tents intended to provide their shelter. Finding nowhere else to house the troops, Dix sent them to the hospital and ordered the removal of the freedpeople there to a contraband camp on nearby Craney Island. It was the sort of decision that might look perfectly sensible on paper, but paper did not take into account the weather, the logistics of getting to Craney Island, or the temperament of some of Colonel Corcoran's men. The soldiers forcibly removed the black men, women, and children from the hospital to the wharf, where they waited their turn for the vessels that could only transport so many at once. As night fell, many had to wait overnight for transportation the following morning, without shelter or food and subject to being robbed by soldiers. One former slave died.[46]

Upon learning of what had happened, Dix exploded at Corcoran. "These people are in our care," he thundered, "and we are bound by every principle of humanity to treat them with kindness and protect them from exposure and injury." Corcoran responded that "the removal was conducted mildly." Coming from a man whose perspective on removals had been shaped by watching families thrown out onto the road and their cottages put to the torch during the famine in Ireland when Corcoran was in his teens, his statement might have been intended truthfully; it is certainly hard to imagine any other perspective that could characterize the removal as "mild." His callous attitude became even more apparent when he brushed aside the death with the statement "One per day is a small proportion of mortality among these people, much smaller than any previous day since our arrival here."[47] The failure of Dix's reprimand to make much impression on Corcoran or some of his men remained obvious. Their continued "intrusions upon the God given rights of man" appalled independent aid workers and so frustrated LeBaron Russell that he fumed, "General Dix speaks of this with regret, as if it were beyond his power to prevent it. I should like to see the experiment tried of the enforcement of the laws, military or civil, against offenders."[48]

Undeterred, refugees from slavery continued to pour into Union lines at Hampton, Newport News, and Yorktown. One woman traveled over two hundred miles disguised as a man to evade her owners' attempt to recapture her.[49] Missionaries and aid workers from the North continued to arrive as well. Lucy and Sarah Chase, Quaker sisters from Worcester, Massachusetts, traveled by train to Baltimore and then sailed to Fort Monroe, amid wild ducks whipping the water into such a fury that it felt as though the sisters sailed through a snowstorm.[50]

Sent to Craney Island in January 1863, the Chase sisters found scarcity, deprivation, and resourcefulness among the roughly eighteen hundred refugees from slavery living there. Most were women, a great many of whom had lost children, some of them three or more. Many had been on the road for a long time and many miles, mainly within a two-hundred-mile radius stretching from Richmond into North Carolina, but some had journeyed from as far away as Tennessee, Kentucky, or South Carolina.[51] The first and most obvious shortage in January was warm shelter. There were a few houses and tents, but none of them provided sufficient protection from the winter wind that "drove over the island all day and was very sharp." The Chase sisters and the freedpeople resorted to burning beams of the ruined C.S.S. *Virginia*, which Lucy insisted upon calling by its Union name, the *Merrimack*, because the island's scant supply of trees had already been exhausted. On the mainland, Superintendent Wilder started a steam-powered sawmill, which was soon "turning out some five thousand feet of boards per day" for "freedmen for their cabins." The boards marked an improvement, but they had to be imported to Craney from the mainland, slowly and tediously, sometimes by boat and sometimes by mule across a ford.

Anything forded by mules had to be used sparingly, and for housing first and burning only a distant second, so to be on Craney in the winter was to be cold.[52]

Bedding and clothing shortages rivaled the dearth of housing and fuel, but they also crystallized white Northerners' dilemma over how to meet need and undercut notions about African American dependence at the same time. Once again, the sunken *Merrimack* came in handy when Lucy and Sarah Chase fashioned work boxes from its salvaged planks and got down to business organizing and overseeing an elaborate sewing operation among the black women and girls. They gathered corn husks and "a quantity of sacking" to fashion into makeshift bedding. Once donations of cloth from Northern benevolent organizations arrived, freedpeople began to sew clothing.[53] "Our women are ready with their needles," Lucy reported, and "eighty or ninety" were already busy "in the manufacture of beds" while she and Sarah prepared to distribute what limited "dress materials" they had to get the women started on sewing clothes. Painfully aware that their meager supply of fabric would not outfit the "nine-hundred unclothed fugitives" already on Craney, let alone the hundreds more they were "daily expecting," Lucy implored Northern "sewing societies" to send shoes, stockings, blankets, and cloth as soon as possible.[54]

Women's and children's skill with the needle benefited the army in a very direct way that went well beyond the "make-work" characterization with which it might, at first glance, seem easy to dismiss sewing operations in contraband camps. Functional grain sacks are not very glamorous, but they were necessary if a nineteenth-century army was to go anywhere, because the horses and mules that pulled artillery and baggage trains needed to be fed, and feed bags were the only way to store and carry grain needed by pack animals on the march. Fort Monroe's quartermaster and wagon master were in for an unpleasant surprise when they discovered that five thousand grain sacks were defective, but the women on Craney "seized upon these bags" with "great readiness" and repaired them back into sturdy utility.[55]

Former slaves' yearning for education was as evident on Craney Island as it was in every other camp, and the combined ingenuity of freedpeople and the Chase sisters found resourceful ways to meet it. Considering it "feasible to unite study and sewing," Lucy hung a large

"A.B.C. card upon the walls" of the sewing room, and the industrious women and girls kept "heads and fingers busy" learning to read and spell while they produced clothing for refugees and repaired army property. Learning to write required a little more in the way of supplies. Specifically, learners needed slates to practice forming letters. Some came from Northern benevolent societies, but it was not long before the supply was "giving out," so Sarah Chase journeyed to an abandoned Confederate battery on nearby Pig Point, climbed onto the roof of "rebel buildings," and "tore off some of the slates to be used in our schools."[56]

Not even the determination to learn to read while sewing feed bags, or the pluck to climb a roof in pursuit of slates, could overcome the limited food capability, overcrowding, and continual Confederate threat that characterized life on Craney. By the summer of 1863, the Union army had moved all but about three hundred women, children, and disabled men to other locations, either to nearby contraband settlements or to the so-called government farms in the region.[57] Government farms constituted a somewhat different approach to the question of what should become of slaves who escaped from their owners during the war than contraband camps did, and while they were more widely used in Louisiana and in cotton-growing regions of the Mississippi valley, some sprang up in Virginia, too. Designed to relieve overcrowding, dilute disease environments, demonstrate black people's capacity for independence, and benefit the army, government farms put black men, women, and children to work on farms abandoned by rebel owners and leased from the U.S. government, usually by Southern Unionists or Northern leasing agents.

Most Craney Island refugees on government farms worked not for wages but for "shares" or "halves," which meant that the Union army and Northern donations provided seeds and farm implements, and black women, children, and elderly men planted, tended, and harvested the fields. The proceeds of crop sales were divided between the Union and the black farmers. Others farmed completely independently. Gibberty Davis, a black man who reckoned his age somewhere between seventy and eighty years old, worked with his wife and the help of two young boys to grow 250 bushels of corn and 150 pounds of cotton on thirty acres in 1862 and 1863, despite an early frost that reduced the yield of both crops. He assured himself a comfortable year when he sold the corn for ninety cents a bushel and the cotton for sixty cents a pound. Nearby, ten former slaves and their young children worked a four-hundred-acre government farm confiscated from an absent Confederate officer named William James, earning enough "on halves" from the 1,000 bushels of corn and 145 bushels of sweet potatoes to live "better than they ever did under their master." Life on the farms certainly beat life in the camps, at least for these "fair specimens of the whole," as one inspector termed Gibberty Davis and the workers on the James farm, but opportunities for cheating former slaves were rife, superintendents of farms varied widely in their treatment of workers, and security from Confederate raids remained a concern. Living conditions also suffered when the transition from contraband camp to government farm went less than smoothly. When several hundred Craney Island refugees were removed from the island at one time, there was no shelter ready for them on government farms. They huddled together in a firetrap of a tobacco drying house until huts could be assembled, a slow process thanks to the many demands on the government lumber supply and the fact that the black men who might have been able to build the fastest were already working for the army elsewhere.[58]

Other Craney Island evacuees traded Craney not for farm life but for another contraband camp at Portsmouth, Norfolk, or Uniontown, a settlement near Suffolk that concentrated both the tenuous promise and the perils of Civil War contraband camps within the right-angled streets radiating out from Washington Square at Uniontown's center. Slaves had begun "leaving their masters by droves" and making for the clusters of Union troops between the Virginia coast and the Great Dismal Swamp as early as the spring of 1862, when a cavalry company of Dubuque, Iowa, men escorting a wagon train from Fort Monroe allied with escaping slaves along the way to Suffolk. Midwesterners shared hardtack with runaway slaves, who in turn alerted soldiers to the spots along the borders of the swamp where they were most likely to find hogs so "impudent" that hungry troops "have to shoot them in order to protect themselves" and could then share fresh pork along with the hard crackers.[59] By the spring of 1863, Uniontown housed 1,320 freed-people within its seventy-eight structures arrayed along orderly, tree-lined streets. Thousands more crowded into Norfolk and Portsmouth.[60]

Former slaves, such as "a 16 year old female former slave who recently learned to read at Craney Island," lost little time continuing the work of education. The sixteen-year-old began "teaching the alphabet and 1–2 syllable words" to younger children nearly as soon as she arrived at the Uniontown settlement, and by the spring of 1863 "130 or 140 children in the colony" gathered in a split-pine building to attend school under the tutelage of "a colored man & woman" who had themselves once been slaves.[61] As elsewhere, black men and women worked for the army maintaining rail lines, laboring for the quartermaster, or nursing in Union hospitals at Norfolk, Portsmouth, and Newport News.[62]

Life was fraught with the usual perils of contraband camp life—delayed or unpaid wages, scarcity, and the like—at Norfolk, Portsmouth, and Uniontown, but it was also even more dangerous in terms of former slaves' personal safety than Fort Monroe or Hampton were.[63] One reason was that the Ninety-Ninth New York was stationed there, a regiment that contained a number of men who directly defied army orders and the Second Confiscation Act by returning former slaves to claimants and pocketing reward money with so little shame that they did not even care that their fellow Union soldiers viewed them with more contempt than they viewed Confederates.[64]

Moreover, the constant threat of Confederate attack, guerrilla activity, and re-enslavement remained deadly throughout southeastern Virginia and adjoining counties of northeastern North Carolina. By late 1863, Major General Benjamin Butler was back from New Orleans and installed at Norfolk. From there, he hatched a plan to strike back at guerrillas and other Confederate irregulars. His partners in that plan would be General Edward Augustus Wild and the soldiers of the "African Brigade," black men recruited from Ohio, Massachusetts, and eastern North Carolina, who launched a two-column raid from Norfolk and Portsmouth in Virginia into North Carolina in December 1863. For nearly a month, Wild's brigade foraged, took hostages, and liberated thousands of black North Carolinians, most of whom clambered aboard anything that would float and ended up behind Union lines in eastern North Carolina or southeastern Virginia.[65] Confederate reprisals were lethal.[66] When Army of Northern Virginia pickets inched their way from Richmond to within sight of Union sentries at Suffolk, Corporal John Williams of the Tenth Virginia Heavy Artillery could hardly wait for the chance to "drive the yankees away and take every negro there." Confederate forces under General James Longstreet laid siege to Suffolk and conducted massive foraging campaigns around it, but despite the fond hopes of Williams and his fellow soldiers neither the Union garrison at Suffolk nor the camp at Uniontown succumbed. Dr. Orlando Brown wrote to the AFIC the following month to confirm that "the contraband village is still there and Corporal Sykes is still in charge."[67] In charge he might have been, but that did not render the settlement immune to the guerrilla activity that continued to pilfer supplies, terrorize Union pickets, and kidnap black people back into slavery.[68]

The chronic danger once again grew acute in 1864, by which time the Second U.S. Colored Cavalry was stationed at Suffolk. That March, North Carolina soldiers in Clingman's Brigade swooped through the region, vowing to "catch the G——d d——d niggers yet!" Blacks fought back, shooting and killing at least one member of the Twenty-Ninth North Carolina State Troops and several members of Ransom's Brigade, but in the end they were overrun, and those who did not escape were killed. One group huddled in a small house until Confederates set the house on fire, giving inhabitants a choice between getting bayoneted to death as they fled the building, burning to death, or dying of smoke inhalation.[69]

From Suffolk, the jagged gash of violence continued to tear south and east to Plymouth, North Carolina. A federal supply depot situated where the Roanoke River met Albemarle Sound, Plymouth had offered haven to hundreds of refugees from slavery since its occupation by Union forces in 1862, and another wave arrived after liberation by Wild's Raid in December 1863. By April 1864, the black soldiers of Wild's African Brigade numbered among the troops guarding the nascent community built by 850 refugees from slavery at Plymouth.[70] On April 17, the Confederate ironclad *Albemarle* attacked Plymouth while infantry converged from three directions, forcing the Union general Henry W. Wessells to surrender the town on April 20.

Surrender, for black soldiers and freedpeople in Plymouth, brought the very opposite of peace. Black men wearing Union blue were stripped and then hanged, lined up along a riverbank to be shot, or "killed by having their brains beaten out by the butt end of the muskets in the hands of the Rebels," as one black witness reported. Any who survived the night were dragged through town by a rope around the neck the following day and then murdered.[71] Meanwhile, black men, women, and children outside the enlisted ranks were less likely to be killed, at least immediately. Instead, Confederate forces either "lodged [them] in some jail" until their masters called for them, put them to work for the Confederate army, or sold them to pay jail fees.[72]

Until Union reoccupation in the fall, Confederate officers at Plymouth fielded requests (sometimes accompanied by deal sweeteners like "good old apple brandy") from masters throughout the eastern counties to return slaves.[73] N. S. Perkins of Edenton, for example, was still smarting over the escape of about two dozen of his slaves, leaving him "not one even to bring up a bucket of water." Then he learned that one of them, Atlas, was among the captured. Worried that Atlas "might make his escape to the Yankees again," Perkins asked Colonel George Wortham of the Fiftieth North Carolina to "deliver one boy Atlas . . . if you are through with him."[74]

As the clause "through with him" suggests, Confederate authorities found plenty of use for the black men, women, and children they captured. The Confederate private James Bracy and his fellow troops holding Fort Holmes at the southeasternmost tip of the North Carolina shoreline were delighted to hear that "four hundred Yankees negroes . . . taken at Plimouth" were being shipped down to do the "heap of work" necessary to keep the fort in rebel hands.[75] The owner of a teenager named Preston, for example, had some trouble getting his slave back because Preston, along with all others found "competent to work on fortifications," had been put to hard labor digging, hauling, and building and Confederate authorities were not keen to give up the unpaid labor they could extract from former slaves or from free blacks, such as John and James Tyner. The Tyner brothers were captured, put to work on fortifications, protested their freedom, tried to run to the Union army, were caught, and forced back to work.[76]

To some of the re-enslaved or potentially re-enslaved, the prospect of returning to slavery seemed even worse than death. A young woman named Louisa, "about twenty years of age," who had somehow managed to elude authorities in the immediate wake of Plymouth's recapture, gave birth in secret without any help, so determined was she to "keep herself concealed" and prevent her child from being born into slavery.[77] A forty-year-old man named Harry, who had followed Wild's Raid to Plymouth from his master's home in Tarboro the previous December, was forced into serving the Seventeenth North Carolina's commissary "under guard" to prevent him from trying "to make his escape again," which he was sure to do, "even at the risk of his life." Harry had good reason to fear, his owner grimly hinted once he learned of Harry's whereabouts, for "he is certain he will have a hard road to travel if we should meet again."[78]

EASTERN NORTH CAROLINA

Northeastern North Carolina's hesitantly emerging terrain of freedom had been connected to coastal Virginia's since August 1861. In that month, fourteen Virginia slaves who had taken refuge at Fort Monroe manned artillery on the U.S.S. *Minnesota* as part of the joint army and navy attack on Confederate forts at Hatteras Inlet. Capturing Hatteras established the beachhead for federal occupation of coastal North Carolina, a mission planned in part on the basis of intelligence gathered by the spying of Abraham Galloway, which was probably how Benjamin Butler became aware of the intrepid Galloway.[79] Fugitive slaves began to arrive at Hatteras immediately, prompting General Wool (the same John E. Wool who would later replace Butler at Fort Monroe) to write to Secretary of War Simon Cameron for guidance on what to do about them.[80] He soon learned that the policy inaugurated by General Butler at Fort Monroe applied, and so the name "contrabands" affixed to refugees from slavery in North Carolina, just as it had done in Virginia. A fort that had been constructed by Confederates in June 1861 was immediately rechristened Hotel De Afrique, and that name stuck even when the first building was replaced by twelve barracks built on the opposite side of the island to accommodate steadily growing numbers and avoid dangerous and unpredictable tides.[81]

As Roanoke Island, Elizabeth City, New Bern, Beaufort, Edenton, and Hertford all fell to the Union and came under the command of General Ambrose Burnside, black men, women, and children kept running to Union lines.[82] When the Forty-Fourth Massachusetts marched eight miles to New Bern, slaves young and old tied belongings into bed quilts, and everyone from great-grandparents to toddlers "trotted along" beside Union troops making their way to camp.[83] One slave woman carefully wrapped up a basket of eggs and put it into a canoe alongside her children. With her hopes of freedom—as simultaneously rich with potential and as fragile as those eggs—she walked the canoe soundlessly through twelve miles of waves, steadying it against sudden swells, quieting it against the wake of other watercraft, keeping it in the shadows. She delivered the eggs to General Burnside and herself and her children to freedom.[84]

The proximity of the Union army gave slaves the opportunity to act on the pent-up desire for freedom. Teenage Gaston Becton decided he had had enough one day and refused his mistress's order to help her son plant peas. Rather than withstand the threatened whipping, Becton bolted for the Yankees. Soldiers "took me to their camp nearby and then on to Newberne," where he "got a job cooking for . . . privates . . . four or five of them, all in one tent."[85] A man named Nero showed that he meant it when he said he was "willing to run all risks for the bare chance of obtaining his liberty." He led half a dozen fellow slaves nearly ninety miles over land from Duplin County, near the Virginia border, eluding Confederate patrols and pickets and surviving on "an occasional ear of corn, for which he ventured into the fields only at night," until arriving "almost exhausted and worn out" inside Union lines at New Bern.[86]

By midsummer 1862, ten thousand people just as determined as Nero, Gaston Becton, and the woman with the basket of eggs had made their way to the Union-occupied areas of eastern North Carolina, and throughout the war more came. More went to New Bern than any other single location in North Carolina. By January 1865, numbers stabilized around eighteen thousand, concentrated chiefly at Beaufort, New Bern, and Roanoke Island.[87] In March 1862, General Burnside appointed Vincent Colyer as superintendent of the poor, a post he held until his resignation in 1863. Horace James, a Congregational minister from Worcester, Massachusetts, carried on Colyer's work under the modified title of superintendent of Negro affairs.

Contraband camps in North Carolina shared a number of characteristics with their Virginia counterparts. Freedpeople endured crowding, shortages of every conceivable kind, and vulnerability to environmental conditions. Themes of dependence and independence colored life there as they did in Virginia, and conditions there as elsewhere were affected by the particular attitudes, inclinations, and personalities of the individuals, black and white, who populated and oversaw them. As in Virginia, men, women, and children who fled to camps in North Carolina craved education. Gaston Becton, for example, learned to "read a little print and . . . sort of write my name at times, if my hand don't tremble too much."[88] Former slaves sought and found work in North Carolina camps as well. Three men, Amos Yorke, Samuel Perry, and Jacob Perry, worked as clerks for Vincent Colyer. Hundreds more built earthen forts for eight dollars a month plus one clothing ration. They loaded and unloaded ships. They served as the crew on roughly forty Union ships, and they labored for the quartermaster, commissary, and ordinance offices of the Department of North Carolina as coopers, carpenters, blacksmiths, bridge builders, ship joiners, and guards. They cooked and laundered in army encampments. They sold "lucturies" like applesauce, milk, potatoes, and pies to hungry Union soldiers tired of dried beef and hardtack. They nursed in hospitals. They piloted the small boats that ferried Union soldiers in and through the inlets and coves that made the coastline so treacherous. They made themselves, in the words of Colyer, "invaluable and almost indispensable," just as they had in Virginia.[89]

In some ways, North Carolina's camps differed notably from Virginia's, and one of the big ones was more overt clashes between military and civil authority. Many such clashes crystallized around Edward Stanly, Unionist governor of North Carolina from May 1862 to March 1863. Benjamin Butler's initial refusal to return slaves to their owners had been predicated upon Virginia's professed departure from the Union, which, as Butler saw things, invalidated state and local laws and made the Union army the only relevant legal authority. The state of North Carolina also seceded, but it did so last and with larger populations of reluctant secessionists and outright Unionists than elsewhere. President Lincoln interpreted such populations as validation of his view of the war as a rebellion by a fractious minority, best solved by allowing the loyal majority to bring their state back into the Union as quickly as possible. To that end, he invited Stanly, onetime Whig from North Carolina, back from his law practice in San Francisco to serve as military governor of North Carolina in May 1862. Stanly's time in California had not shaken his belief that abolitionism was the chief deterrent to a peaceful Union. Upon arrival, he assumed that nothing had altered state laws regarding slavery and was incensed to learn that the army was paying black workers laboring on New Bern fortifications. He wanted Union troops to enforce the Fugitive Slave Law, so when the local farmer Nicholas Bray complained about Massachusetts soldiers inducing his slaves to leave, Stanly launched into testy exchanges with regiments on the ground and with Secretary of War Stanton in Washington. He also closed schools established for freedpeople, citing antebellum state laws that forbade teaching blacks to read. Already fed up with Stanly, Vincent Colyer stormed off to Washington to complain to Lincoln directly. The president overruled Stanly on the Fugitive Slave Law and the schools and turned down Stanly's request to exempt North Carolina from the Emancipation Proclamation point-blank. Stanly resigned in protest and schools reopened, but in the meantime sights like an angry Bray stomping about camp and sounds like the silence of temporarily empty schoolhouses warned of freedom's fragility in the hands of intransigent white civil authority.[90]

The rhythms and tides of a distinctive maritime environment influenced the experience of emancipation in eastern North Carolina. If anyone understood the tides, it was the black watermen, free and formerly enslaved, whose expertise in piloting coastal North Carolina's tricky waters had created an entire maritime world before the war.[91] A Washington County fish merchant named John Chesson operated a thriving fishery before the war, but his business foundered once Union forces showed up, because the slaves who actually conducted the fishery's day-to-day business (both slaves he owned and those he hired from other owners) immediately bolted for Union ships and lines. Cooper, Levi, Bob, John, two men named Tom, and another "hired" slave stuffed bags with clothes and then met up with three more men (Kiah, Jo, and Bill) to steal a boat and "make their exit." Then the wind changed direction unexpectedly, and they were recaptured and beaten until they revealed their plot. White businessmen organized a stringent guard and even burned boats to prevent the escape of such valuable maritime workers, but well over a thousand succeeded in escaping within weeks of the Union military's arrival.[92] So skilled were they at escaping on canoes, oyster boats, or anything that floated that the Confederate army even tried banning the use of *any* boats in the sounds until white oystermen and salt makers complained that the rules were harming their livelihoods while barely slowing down the flight of determined fugitive slaves.[93]

Those black pilots, fishermen, stevedores, shipbuilders, bateau men, female fishmongers, and net repairwomen lent labor and navigational expertise to Burnside's expedition to control the Atlantic coast from Fort Monroe to Wilmington, North Carolina. They also helped maintain the North Atlantic Blockading Squadron's cordon around the Confederacy. All the while, they aided the escape of fellow former slaves. William B. Gould was an enslaved carpenter living in Wilmington rather than an expert waterman, but he knew his way around a boat and around the Cape Fear River. On the rainy night of September 20, 1862, he and six other men crept to the end of Orange Street, where it met the river, helped themselves to a boat fastened there, and sailed down Cape Fear toward a line of U.S. steamers enforcing the blockade. They were picked up by the U.S.S. *Cambridge* and enlisted in the navy. Gould served on the *Cambridge* for a year, enforcing the blockade and shuttling black men and women to Union-held territory, before transferring to the frigate *Niagara*.[94]

Men and women who knew the maritime world made good spies, and the Union occupation of eastern North Carolina relied even more heavily on the intelligence they could provide than the castellated Union garrison at Fort Monroe did. Fort Monroe, after all, had the benefit of being surrounded by a moat, but eastern North Carolina was much more exposed. Both guerrillas and conventional forces constantly threatened to pry off fingers of Union control. Plymouth was recaptured more than once, New Bern and Beaufort came under multiple attacks, and rumors of Confederate reoccupation ran rampant just about everywhere.[95] Black spies proved crucial. One committee of black women, for example, helped keep tabs on Emeline Pigott, a Confederate spy who ran information from Union-held stretches of coastline to the officers of the Twenty-Sixth North Carolina. The women's attentiveness eventually landed Pigott in prison.[96] One Jones County man had been sold and separated from his family after his master died. He spent two months in a Richmond slave pen, stripped naked for easier inspection by prospective purchasers who came to look over what they called the "droves of stock." A trader bought him and put him on a train for Wilmington, where a boat waited to sail slaves to the voracious market in Alabama. As the Wilmington and Weldon Railroad steamed south and east, the man recognized his old neighborhood, "made an excuse to look out the door, and watching my chance while the train was in full motion, passing through a wood, jumped off." Starving, injured in the fall, and confined to swamps to avoid detection, the man made his way to his wife. After "a word of good cheer from her and kisses from my three children," he hid out in the woods, eluded capture by dogs, and made canny bargains with poor blacks and whites to exchange food he caught for goods he needed. As soon as U.S. forces took New Bern, he made his way there and began building fortifications for eight dollars a month, but what he really wanted was to bring his family into Union lines. He struck a deal with Union authorities to head to Kinston to "take a good look at the rebel encampments, make a careful note in his memory of their number and situation, [and] inquire of their negroes in their cabins all about the enemy." Superintendent Vincent Colyer "gave him rations for three days, some small change in silver, and a pass," and off he went. After two weeks of matching wits with pickets, dogs, and armed hunting parties, he returned with his wife, children, and "valuable information" on Confederate tactical movements and use of rail lines.[97]

Benjamin Butler's favorite spy, Abraham Galloway, returned to New Bern in 1862, where he proved indispensable to black enlistment in the Union army. The recruitment process proceeded somewhat uniquely in North Carolina and also entailed unintended consequences. North Carolina's first black soldiers would be organized into Wild's African Brigade, which began recruiting in New Bern in May 1863. The governor of Massachusetts, John Andrew, long interested in black enlistment, sent Edward Kinsley as an agent to accompany Wild, but despite Wild's determination and Kinsley's earnest enthusiasm recruitment's pace was sluggish at best, stock-still at worst. One day, Kinsley received a message to report at midnight to the house of Mary Ann Starkey, a free black woman who kept a boardinghouse in New Bern. Upon arrival, Kinsley was blindfolded and led upstairs. Once the blindfold was removed, he found himself in a candlelit attic facing a roomful of black men and women and flanked by two armed men, one of them

Abraham Galloway. Galloway put a gun to Kinsley's head and made him swear "a solemn oath, that any colored man enlisted in North Carolina should have the same pay as their colored brethren enlisted in Massachusetts; their families should be provided for; their children should be taught to read; and if they should be taken prisoners, the government should see to it that they were treated as prisoners of war." Under the circumstances, Kinsley agreed. "The next day the word went forth, and the blacks came to the recruiting station by hundreds and a brigade was soon formed."

One early recruit was Gaston Becton, who found himself out of a job when the soldiers who employed him as cook were assigned to barracks and compelled to use the company's cook. As he decided what to do next, Becton encountered a recruiting agent who "asked me if I wanted to join the army; and I told him I did." When asked his age, Becton confessed that he had no idea, and the recruiting officer concluded that the young man looked "about 18" and signed him up.

Signifying the black community's considered, but not unconditional, support for the endeavor, the "colored ladies of New Berne" made and presented a "banner of the Republic" to the fully recruited regiment. The brigade was Wild's Brigade, which would serve for the rest of the war and even beyond.[98]

Galloway's insistence on care for soldiers' families made particular sense in eastern North Carolina, where the proportion of refugees from slavery who arrived in family units was higher than most other places. A unique experiment on Roanoke Island developed in response to that higher proportion of families. A genuine island in the Croatan Sound between North Carolina's Outer Banks and the mainland, Roanoke Island was captured by Union forces in February 1862. White residents either took the oath of allegiance to the Union and clustered on the southern end of the island or fled.[99] The upper end of the island became a contraband camp, never attracting as many people as New Bern but complete with the crowding, poor sanitation, and hasty and imperfect response to overwhelming material need that characterizes any ad hoc refugee camp. For more than a year, rows of tents christened Camp Foster flapped in the wind and rain.[100] In the spring of 1863, when Horace James replaced Vincent Colyer as superintendent for the District of North Carolina, he "establish[ed] a colony of negroes upon Roanoke Island" as a permanent settlement rather than a temporary camp. The timing of the colony's establishment just as recruitment of Wild's African Brigade began was no accident; the predominant residents of the colony would be the families of black Union soldiers.[101] The aim of the colony, as Horace James explained in a public letter that summer, was "to colonize these freed people, not by deportation out of the country, but by giving them facilities for living in it; not by removing them north, where they are not wanted, and could not be happy; nor even by transporting them beyond the limits of their own State; but by giving them land, and implements wherewith to subdue and till it, thus stimulating their exertions by making them proprietors of the soil, and by directing their labor into such channels as promise to be remunerative and self supporting."[102]

Ambitions for Roanoke Island as a model "independent, self-governing community" ran high. Fitted with a steam engine, sawmill and gristmill, planned neighborhoods, schools, and churches, the colony would equip freedpeople for, in James's emphatic vision, *"the exercise of civil functions, the care of the poor, and the intelligent discharge of the duties of free citizens, under municipal law enacted and executed by themselves."*[103] The colony at Roanoke was no simplistic imposition of a liberal individualist framework. Its goal was communal autonomy and self-sufficiency, not a collection of acquisitive rugged individualists.[104] Union authorities supported—not dismissed—freedpeople's focus on family needs and control of land. Yet, like so much of Union policy surrounding emancipation, Roanoke Island was an experiment, an act of faith that unfolded a day at a time with no script, no assurance as to the final outcome, and plenty of unforeseen variables. As Horace James himself put it in a masterpiece of understatement, "We had no precedents."[105]

In many ways and at various times, the colony on Roanoke Island seemed to offer great promise. Surveyors and choppers took charts, chains, compasses, and axes into pine groves on the northern end of the island and laid out broad avenues twelve hundred feet apart, running parallel to the shores of the island, transected by streets four hundred feet apart. Next came builders, and soon houses with street frontage and gardens filled the lots.[106] In contrast to drafty tents or pine lean-tos, cabins on Roanoke Island sometimes featured carpets, stoves, and comfortable furniture. In their gardens, former slaves cultivated "vegetables, grapes, and other fruit."[107] By and large, Roanoke Island residents lived in stable family units, albeit often ones with men away fighting in the Union army, and they owned their lots and houses, according to General Orders No. 12, which gave them "full possession of the same, until annulled by the Government or by due process of United States law."[108] Roanoke Island freedpeople also went to school, either at the main schoolhouse situated on "a broad magnificent avenue" and "decorated with holly" or at one of the smaller schoolrooms located about the island. They learned from white Northern women like Elizabeth James and Sarah Freeman but also from Robert Morrow, onetime slave of the Confederate James J. Pettigrew who took himself to Union lines at New Bern and then taught on Roanoke Island while serving as a sergeant in Wild's African Brigade.[109] Freedpeople worked at "oystering, farming, turpentine and tar making, boating, barbering, teaming, baking, and store-keeping . . . washing, ironing, cleaning, nursing, pie-making, house work . . . garden work and . . . needle-work," and great plans for a shad fishery hummed in the air. The shad plan fizzled, but other ventures, including an industrial school and a fledgling sewing business, took their places on an island that for a long time seemed so full of possibility.[110] Garden produce plus vaccination by army surgeons contributed to better overall health on Roanoke Island than at New Bern (or contraband camps in general, for that matter), at least for a while.[111] Roanoke was not immune to danger—the Confederate ram *Albemarle* threatened it on at least one occasion—but it was safer than the mainland, because it was harder for guerrillas or small Confederate forces to slip into camp to terrorize or kidnap freedpeople.

Yet the promise of Roanoke Island was undercut by many factors, beginning with sheer material need. For all the sound planning and steady work that went into Roanoke Island by Union authorities, white missionaries, and black residents alike, relentless material shortage dogged the island, just as it did every wartime settlement of former slaves. When forty-three refugees from slavery, eight of them orphaned children, made it to Roanoke Island after a fraught Christmas Eve escape, there were no vacant cabins, tents, or barracks on that bitter cold night, so they had to huddle in a freezing-cold schoolhouse just hoping to make it through to morning.[112] The long-awaited sawmill eventually helped mitigate the housing crisis, but the cold was so cruel that Union soldiers and freedpeople vied with each other over the insufficient supply of stovepipes, and the clothing shortage never abated.[113] "My heart sometimes sickens at the thought of the suffering that must ensue," Sarah Freeman confided as she surveyed "3,000 bodies, nearly naked" and nothing more than "about 800 vests, 100 old coats of the poorest quality, and in all not over twenty pairs of pants" to distribute. Meanwhile, millworkers labored barefoot in water, women cut and hauled wood in their bare feet, and boys and girls stayed away from school for "want [of] shoes and stockings."[114]

Even the basic need for food went unmet, partly because of war-related shortfall and distribution problems but also because of ideas about dependence and independence.[115] Much of Horace James's enthusiasm for the Roanoke Island project emanated from his sincere conviction that the colony could best bring long-term benefits to freedpeople's aspirations by giving the lie to white assumptions about black inferiority, indolence, and limited potential. When asked by AFIC commissioners for his assessment of former slaves' capacity as fully independent and contributing citizens of the Republic, James confidently expressed "no doubt" that they could become "self-supporting and independent, like free communities at the North." As he saw it, one big obstacle was white skepticism, which was where an experiment like Roanoke came in, for if freedpeople could demonstrate "personal responsibility for their own support," white Northerners would recognize the experiment as "an exodus out of Egypt, and a full answer to the question, 'What shall be done with the negro?'"[116] The key idea was "self-supporting and independent . . . communities," leading James to go to great lengths to demonstrate that on his watch former slaves were not *given* necessities like bacon, flour, soap, and tea; rather they paid for them (albeit at low prices) and then shared the goods among themselves. The difficulty with such reasoning was that no matter how low prices might be, they were out of reach for workers who had not been paid, a description that applied to almost everyone in the District of North Carolina at one time or another and to residents of Roanoke Island most of the time. James was certainly aware that "the wages of the freedmen in this District have not been regularly paid" and indeed railed against the problem to military authorities, as well as underscoring it with extra-dark ink and underlining when he wrote to tell the AFIC, *"Next to none have been fully paid."*[117]

That realization did not stop James or his subordinate, Holland Streeter, from instituting measures that are hard to see as anything other than draconian. By the spring of 1865, most of the Roanoke colony's full-grown men were in the Union army serving in Virginia. When Confederates once again menaced the district, James and Streeter pulled boys as young as twelve out of the freedmen's school on the island and put them to work on Union fortifications at New Bern. Meanwhile, they sharply reduced or even cut off rations to all island inhabitants who could not pay for them or were not directly laboring for the government, including the wives and young children of soldiers in the army and the families of the boys who had been shipped to New Bern. Alarmed Northern schoolteachers reported that "the sweeping reduction of the rations brings hundreds suddenly face to face with starvation."[118] Yet Captain James defended his actions by saying that they were for the freedpeople's own good. Generous rations and lenient work requirements, in his view, had eroded the freedpeople's self-sufficiency, the very quality the Roanoke Island colony most needed to demonstrate. "The truth is *they have had too much* given them," James claimed, and if former slaves were ever to demonstrate their capacity to a doubting public, then the government ought to give them the opportunity to show that they could fend for themselves.[119]

Nobody had much chance of fending for themselves where disease was concerned. A smallpox outbreak tore first through New Bern, leading to the establishment of the Contraband Smallpox Hospital there just in time for Christmas 1863. On top of all else, smallpox intensified the clothing shortage as cold weather set in, because the clothes of anyone infected with or exposed to smallpox had to be burned.[120] As the winter wore on, the "pestilence that walketh in darkness . . . among us, in the form of smallpox," had made it to Beaufort.[121] Improving weather helped abate that threat, but the swampy summer brought mosquito-borne diseases, and yellow fever hung over the region through October and November.[122]

The worst ravages from disease were still to come. After months of reasonably stable demographic and disease environments, a new wave of refugees followed the blue columns of General William T. Sherman's army out of Georgia and South Carolina, arriving in Beaufort, New Bern, and Roanoke Island in the spring of 1865. By the time they got to North Carolina, freedpeople had walked hundreds of miles, "mostly without covering for either their feet or heads, some of them emaciated" from keeping up with a fast-marching army without the benefit of hearty rations. Many were "afflicted with hoarse hollow coughs, with measles, [and] with malarial chills." The rapid influx left little choice but to crowd into close quarters, thus ensuring that disease would spread rapidly, defeating hundreds of former slaves just as the Union finally claimed victory over the Confederacy.[123] On the very day that news of the Army of Northern Virginia's surrender arrived in Beaufort, a former slave woman who had walked out of bondage in South Carolina collapsed on the beach, dying "with sand on her face and in her mouth."[124]

Marching Through Georgia

The woman who succumbed on the Beaufort beach might have died alone, but she certainly had not marched alone. As Sherman's columns had left Atlanta in November 1864, heading first for Savannah and then through South Carolina, they cut through interior and upland regions formerly untouched by a federal presence. Like slaves in coastal Virginia and North Carolina who had identified Union lines as their best shot at freedom, thousands of black men, women, and children in the interior regions of Georgia and South Carolina saw the moving lines of Union soldiers as the most promising route out of slavery and dashed for them. Samuel Arms was only twelve or thirteen when whispers about oncoming Yankees reached his ears, but twelve or thirteen years of slavery in Georgia was more than enough to ready him to leave the first chance he got. Determined to beat any thought of flight out of young Samuel, his mistress snuck up to him one fall day as he washed dishes and began to whip him with a riding crop. Emboldened by the proximity of troops, Samuel snatched the whip, whirled the woman around, and whipped her across the back until her fine silk dress hung in shreds. As she fell to the ground, he fled, running smack into a Wisconsin regiment. As that regiment's drummer, he marched out of bondage, sounding a beat that called more field hands and house servants, blacksmiths and railway laborers, washerwomen and draymen, out of the possession of whites who claimed to own them and into long columns that snaked behind the army.[125]

All of them took enormous risks. As the Twenty-First and Twenty-Second Wisconsin Infantry Regiments crossed in and through Jefferson County in the Georgia interior, legions of women and children made their way through thick groves of fan palms to cross the Ogeechee River and the Rocky Comfort Creek on army pontoons, constantly struggling to stay ahead of Confederate stragglers and deserters who chased behind setting fires to the bridges.[126] Word of their coming preceded them across the Savannah River, which divided Georgia from South Carolina, and nearly five hundred slaves in then Hampton County, including young Will Sherman, "abandoned their masters' plantations 'to meet the Yankees,'" cutting down fences, dodging pickets, and reassuring the skittish Union soldier standing guard duty of their friendly intent. Once in the Union encampment, most of the "volunteer slaves," as Sherman proudly called himself and his fellow freedom seekers, elected to continue marching with federal troops, and they counted among the many who arrived in North Carolina in the spring of 1865.

Others were not so lucky. Former slaves who could not keep up with the fast pace of Sherman's hardened veterans were seized by Confederate "bush whackers . . . decapitated and their heads placed upon posts that lined the fields" as warnings "of what would befall [other slaves] if they attempted to escape."[127] They might also be betrayed by the Union army, the most infamous incident of which took place at Ebenezer Creek in December, shortly before the Union's march from Atlanta reached Savannah. Calling the body of water a "creek" misses how deep, wide, and swift Ebenezer Creek actually was, and it stood between the Union general Jefferson C. Davis's Fourteenth Corps and the city of Savannah. With Confederate cavalrymen close behind, Union troops threw pontoon bridges across the water and marched over as the long columns of black men, women, and children who had been following them waited to go next. As soon as the last soldier touched land, Davis ordered destruction of the bridges. Appalled but unwilling to defy orders, the men of the 126th Illinois watched as "men, women, and children rushed by the hundreds into the turbid stream, and many were drowned before our eyes." Others were killed or re-enslaved when

captured by Confederates. The cries of "anguish and despair" continued to haunt both survivors and Union soldiers long after.[128]

South Carolina's Sea Islands and the Department of the South

Will Sherman made it safely to Savannah and then continued following
the army to Beaufort, South Carolina, where large numbers of former
slaves had begun the transition out of slavery as far back as November 7,
1861. On that day, the Union navy entered Port Royal Sound and together
with the army took the Sea Islands of Hilton Head, Port Royal, and St.
Helena in the Carolina Lowcountry, a fabulously wealthy region of rice
and high-end long-staple cotton plantations. Confederates fled, leaving
great stacks of luxurious and lucrative Sea Island cotton—harvested,
ginned, and baled—in storehouses and wagons lining the roads. They
also left behind nearly ten thousand slaves. On November 9, just two
days after gunboats nosed into the harbor, Brigadier General Thomas
W. Sherman appointed B. K. Lee superintendent of contrabands. Lee
supervised gangs of Union soldiers and former slaves as they hoisted
great ropes, tromped up and down ships' gangplanks, and hauled to
shore barrels of flour, crates of ammunition, stacks of blank forms and
ledger books, chests of officers' personal effects, and everything else it
took to effect the Union occupation of the district. They worked until
about four o'clock, when an old, formerly enslaved man reminded Lee
that it was Sunday and called a prayer meeting right at the docks.[129]

Work among ships and boats came naturally to many of the Sea
Island African Americans, just as it had to the men and women of
North Carolina's waterways. Creeks, swamps, and marshes interwove
with dry land to make up the distinctive landscape, connecting rather
than dividing plantations to those who knew how to steer and sail.
With Charleston nearby, the bustling harbor guaranteed that unloading and loading, sailing, steering, guiding, and otherwise working on
larger commercial ships had also figured prominently in many slaves'
work lives.

The most famous was certainly Robert Smalls, a slave with extensive
maritime experience as a stevedore and rigger. Smalls knew Charleston
harbor as well as or better than any pilot, even though, as he told U.S.

officials, "a colored man was not allowed to be a pilot." Official titles aside, in the spring of 1862 the enslaved Smalls was for all intents and purposes piloting the *Planter*, a swift, 147-foot, high-pressure steamer. In peacetime, the *Planter* carried passengers and cotton between Charleston and Georgetown, South Carolina. By 1862, its owner had rented it to the Confederate government, which fitted it with howitzers and thirty-two-pound rifle guns and used it as an army transport between fortifications in Charleston harbor. On the night of May 12, 1862, Smalls, his family, and eight additional enslaved crewmen sailed the *Planter* right past those fortifications, ran up a white flag, steamed for the U.S. blockading squadron out in open water, and delivered the boat to the service of the U.S. Navy. *Harper's Weekly* and various Northern daily newspapers reported the dramatic story and hailed Smalls as its hero. Smalls himself continued to pilot the *Planter* as a dispatch and supply vessel for several months. He remained on as pilot when it was transferred to the U.S. Army Quartermaster Corps later in 1862 and then to the Freedmen's Bureau in 1865 for ferrying freedpeople from Port Royal to nearby islands.[130] Other black South Carolinians might not have made the pages of *Harper's Weekly*, but they still knew their way around the water and lent that expertise to the Union by navigating, steering, crewing, and unloading all manner of steamers, gunboats, supply ships, and flatboats that supported the Union war effort and daily living in a landscape of indistinct boundaries between land and sea.

Just as North Carolina and South Carolina were very different states, in some ways contraband camps in the Department of the South (into which coastal South Carolina, Georgia, and Florida were consolidated in March 1862) were distinctive. For one thing, almost everything about the Department of the South was large, starting with the numbers of former slaves there. Upwards of ten thousand remained in place when the Union came and whites fled, and more came in from surrounding areas every month, sometimes singly or in small groups but more often in "parties of 10, 20, 50 and 100." The longer the occupation lasted, the more they came, especially once the Union began recruiting black soldiers, who in turn conducted raids to liberate the enslaved who were otherwise beyond the reach of the Union. In June 1863, three hundred black Union troops and their colonel were led by Harriet Tubman, the famed abolitionist who had been born in bondage in Maryland before escaping in 1849 and then earning the nickname the General by aiding in the escape of nearly seventy slaves for the next eleven years. When the Civil War came, she channeled her expertise and courage into making sure that the Union's war was also an escape route for the enslaved. She spied for the army and led raids like a June 1863 venture up the Combahee River, which "brought off nearly 800 slaves and thousands of dollars' worth of property."[131] By that time, between seventeen thousand and eighteen thousand freedpeople came under the supervision of the Department of the South. Numbers zoomed higher after the influx of refugees from Sherman's March in 1864 and 1865.[132]

At first, because Lowcountry black men, women, and children remained on their home turf rather than fleeing for unfamiliar Union lines, life featured fewer disruptions than in some other regions.[133] Initially, neither food nor housing ran as short there as elsewhere, because former slaves remained in their dwellings and continued to grow corn, peas, and potatoes and to keep chickens, as they had under slavery. In fact, in 1862 food was even more plentiful because former slaves planted not only the vegetables they usually did but also corn on some lands previously used for cotton, for the very sensible reason that growing cotton "had enriched the masters, but had not fed them." The monotony of corn, peas, potatoes, eggs, and poultry grew tiresome because the war disrupted the food trade patterns that usually brought molasses, sugar, and salt to plantations, but for the most part outright starvation did not present an imminent threat until more refugees from slavery began making their way to the coastal region from the interior.[134]

As elsewhere, the most pressing immediate need was for clothing. In ordinary times, slaves received their annual clothing allotment of one or two suits of clothes at the end of each year. By the time clothing distribution rolled around, a year of snags, torn knees and elbows, and the general disintegration of cloth occasioned by hard labor day in and day out meant that most slaves wore fabric shreds held together chiefly by dirt and habit. But in 1861, planters had fled before the annual clothing allotment time. Some black men, women, and children appropriated the fabulous silks and ornate gowns that their years of uncompensated labor had purchased for their owners, and a few of the most resourceful "had taken up their master's old carpet from the floor" and fashioned makeshift garments from the heavy brocade, but even those creative efforts could only go so far. Thousands had "scarcely clothing enough to cover them," and so they stood in the middle of one of the world's richest fiber-producing regions, in the midst of wealth that their labor had created, with wind blowing through inadequate rags.[135]

That same wind swept over hundreds of thousands of acres, demonstrating another way in which the Department of the South was different: in it, the Union controlled far more land than in most places it occupied, and outlandishly valuable land at that, given the profitability of the luxury cotton grown there. As the Union general Thomas W. Sherman scurried to secure Union control of the occupied islands, he hastily appointed Colonel William H. Nobles of the Seventy-Ninth New York Infantry as an agent of the United States authorized to collect and sell abandoned cotton, 94 percent of the proceeds to go to the U.S. government and 6 percent for himself.[136] Nobles lost no time and by Christmas had already sold $30,000 worth, but he had also alienated freedpeople, other soldiers, and Treasury agents alike. Moving quickly to contain discontent, Secretary of the Treasury Salmon P. Chase appointed Colonel William H. Reynolds of the First Rhode Island Artillery to collect and guard the rest of the cotton harvest abandoned by owners in 1861.[137] All told, the U.S. government sold the crop of "some two million five hundred thousand pounds of ginned cotton" for roughly $600,000, which it used to establish a cotton fund overseen by the Department of the Treasury. That fund paid wages of thirty cents per day to the freedmen and freedwomen who worked on the abandoned plantations overseen by the government, and it also paid the salaries of subordinate superintendents of contrabands (who operated under the supervision of B. K. Lee), installed at the rate of about one per every three abandoned plantations.[138]

But that solution was really only a stopgap method for dealing with the 1861 crop, which was no sooner sold off than competing visions for how to plant, cultivate, and harvest the next crop began to clash. The Lowcountry seemed to promise opportunity to many, but different constituencies glimpsed different possibilities. For African Americans whose owners had fled, Confederate departure held out the hope for the independence and autonomy to live their own lives. The strategic value of proximity to Charleston harbor preoccupied army and naval officers, while the prospect of exorbitant cotton profits beckoned to Northern speculators and Treasury officials (who had a war to pay for) alike.

Meanwhile, members of benevolent societies and some Northern industrialists saw the chance to prove axioms in which they had no doubt but of which portions of the Northern public remained unconvinced. For committed reformers and abolitionists (black and white), particularly religiously motivated ones, here was a time and place to disabuse whites of racist notions about black people's unwillingness to work or fitness for self-sufficiency. As Edward Pierce (fresh from his earlier assignment at Fort Monroe) put it, "Particularly did it seem desirable that the enemies of free labor in either hemisphere should not be permitted to say exultingly . . . that a product . . . could not be cultivated without the forced, unintelligent, and unpaid labor of slaves."[139] They even received official encouragement when General Thomas W. Sherman issued General Orders No. 9, requesting that Northern churches and the American Missionary Association send teachers for ex-slaves.[140] For others, like the businessman and railroad investor John Murray Forbes, the Sea Islands seemed the perfect chance to prove the truth of his own zealous faith that free labor was more profitable and efficient than slave labor. The availability of land, a crop, and a workforce expert in the cultivation and harvesting of it seemed to make the Lowcountry an ideal laboratory, a sense neatly captured in the widespread use of the term "Port Royal Experiment."[141]

Proponents of each of these visions raced by steamer to South Carolina, and there they met thousands of former slaves as well as Union military personnel and agents of the U.S. Treasury. The mingling of all of these groups, thrown together into necessary but distrustful relationship by their mutual opposition to the Confederate forces and civilians who were never far away, conveyed a distinctive regional cast onto tensions between civil and military authority. Some volunteers came singly, and others came authorized by Secretary of the Treasury Chase, but many came as part of "Gideon's Band," a group of missionaries and philanthropists, backed by aid societies in New England, New York, and Philadelphia, who took oaths of allegiance to "the Constitution and Government of the United States against all enemies, whether domestic or foreign," and then set off for Port Royal and environs.[142] The first wave of Gideonites sailed from New York in March 1862 aboard the steamer *Atlantic* and then boarded a lither craft, the *Cosmopolitan,* on which the escaped slave Solomon Bradley worked as a cook, to navigate tricky Lowcountry rivers.[143]

If there was one constant in the Department of the South, it was disagreement. Missionaries from different denominations disagreed with each other over points of doctrine. Investors who saw maximum profitability as both goal and the best way to discredit the slave regime clashed with reformers, who viewed freedpeople's independence and moral uplift as their chief objectives. Army personnel and Treasury agents prioritized national interest but differed on how to pursue it, and neither constituency was completely devoid of individuals out chiefly for personal profit. Freedpeople disagreed among themselves over whether to grow cotton for their own benefit or eschew the crop that had enriched their masters while starving them, and they disagreed over if, how much, and which white newcomers could be trusted.

All of these disagreements came to a head over cotton and land, and particularly over what the precise relationship between freedpeople and the U.S. government should be in determining land distribution, use, and yield. In May 1862, the same month in which Robert Smalls delivered both the *Planter* and his valuable services to the Union cause, Brigadier General Rufus Saxton was appointed military governor of the Department of the South, and he assumed authority over land and cotton from the Treasury Department. What followed was a patchwork of experimental arrangements. Some plantations remained in government hands, to be administered for one year by appointed agents who would hire former slaves to grow the largest possible crop and then sell the crop to pay wages and help finance the war effort. After the first year, land would be sold. Saxton wanted the cost of government-controlled land (all of it abandoned by Confederates) kept deliberately low so that black families could buy their own land, settle on it in family units, and farm it for themselves. Land commissioners sent by the Treasury Department viewed Saxton's vision as naive. Low-cost land was more apt, as Commissioner A. D. Smith explained, to be snapped up by capitalist investors with the intention of instituting their own cotton-growing regimes that would not improve things much for the former slaves forced to labor there. Better to give "land Commissioners power in their discretion, to bid up on any land," and then purchase it on behalf of the government, which would run plantations differently than profit-minded owners would, to ensure that former slaves not simply undergo "a change of masters from slave owners to capitalists."[144]

Compensation for workers was irregular to say the least. In theory, privately purchased plantations generally paid workers in daily wages, while government-run ones paid by work done. For example, in picking time, workers were paid by the pound, and at planting and hoeing times they were paid by the "task." A task, according to the Quartermaster Department, was work done on a quarter acre, so workers were paid for four tasks for each acre they plowed, planted, or hoed. Workers could earn additional cash for other jobs performed, such as ditch digging, outbuilding maintenance, wood chopping, or any other necessary agricultural labor. Of course, reality did not always match policy where wages were concerned. One aid worker fumed with frustration at the "Red Tape," like problems with payroll printing, which delayed the payment of wages, as well as at the leisurely attitude that army officers and Treasury agents seemed to take toward paying black workers overdue wages in the summer of 1862.[145] Yet overall, nonpayment of wages was not *quite* as pervasive a problem in the Lowcountry as in Virginia and North Carolina, probably because of the existence of the Cotton Fund and because of the availability of alternative methods of compensation, such as growing on shares or renting land for freedpeople to farm themselves.[146]

To former slaves and to Northern abolitionists who came to work among them, the question was less who had a right to the land and more how black men, women, and children should live on the land that was rightfully theirs. Harry McMillan had been born in Georgia, but he had spent most of his four decades of life working as a field hand growing long-staple cotton in South Carolina. He advised distributing land in small to moderate parcels because "people here would rather have the land than work for wages." Individual parcels of "4 to 5 acres to a family" would be best for most, he reckoned, although he believed he "could take care of 15 acres."[147] Clara Barton agreed. Barton had come to the Department of the South chiefly to minister to invalid Union soldiers, but while there she befriended Frances Gage, an abolitionist woman from Ohio whose efficiency and dedication to the well-being of former slaves induced Union authorities to appoint her superintendent of contrabands on Parris Island. Encouraged by Gage, Barton took a much longer, more serious look at the men, women, and children emerging from slavery than her earlier, vague antislavery principles might have elicited. A long carriage ride to and around a plantation called Mitchelville, on which black men, women, and children farmed for themselves, convinced Barton that distributing land to families represented "the commencement of the solving of the problem of negro capacity to self-support." Workers' neat slate houses even had floors, something she had not seen in cabins on any other plantations and that quite convinced her of the superiority of the Mitchelville arrangement.[148] Other freedpeople had still different ideas. In some places, former slaves pooled funds to purchase plots of land, which they farmed not in family units but in common among themselves.[149]

Missionaries to the Department of the South pledged themselves not only "to relieve bodily suffering" and "to inform the public of the needs, rights, capacities and disposition of the freedmen" but also to impart "the rudiments of knowledge, morals, religion and civilized life."[150] Patronizing though they undoubtedly were, benevolent workers attributed perceived deficiencies to the regrettable but reversible effects of slavery and championed what they thought of as black independence and uplift. Those ideas made missionaries and freedpeople allies in one priority they shared: education.

Schools opened with the New Year and especially proliferated once the Gideonites began to arrive in March. As spring advanced, teachers went where pupils were, fanning out to the several plantations. Pine Grove on St. Helena, for example, had five schools and about 140 students by the end of May.[151] Harriet Ware taught in one of them, instructing the youngest children in the morning, older children at 3:30 in the afternoon once they got off work in the fields, and sometimes adults in the evening.[152] In Beaufort, Old Fort Plantation's claim to fame was that it housed a building constructed expressly as a school for former slaves, as opposed to a shed, outbuilding, or tent hastily appropriated to the task. The schoolhouse featured board floors, wooden benches, a tall pine desk and stool, a blackboard, a box stove, and six shuttered and fully glazed windows. Into this comparatively luxurious structure walked Elizabeth Botume, sent from Boston to Beaufort by the New England Freedmen's Aid Society in late October 1864.

Botume's incomprehension of local customs, like naming traditions, Friday wash day, and mutual suspicion between Beaufort children and refugees from surrounding islands, led her to make a number of early missteps, but she came with illustrated primers, Bibles, and a genuine desire to nurture her students' "individuality and personal dignity," for which her pupils were willing to forgive her quite a lot.[153]

Much as Mary Peake was perfectly capable of teaching former slaves at Fort Monroe, some local African American men and women proved ready to take on the role of educator once the limitations of state laws prohibiting black literacy were lifted. Susie Baker was a teenager enslaved in Savannah when the Union navy took Fort Pulaski in April 1862. She and some relatives got themselves aboard a Union gunboat and eventually reached St. Simons in the Georgia Sea Islands. Baker stunned the captain of the gunboat when she told him she could read and then wrote her name and place of birth inside a book to prove that she could also write. He in turn told Commodore John R. Goldsborough, who was in charge of freedpeople at St. Simons, and within three days of Baker's arrival Goldsborough asked her to "take charge of a school for the children on the island." She agreed, on the condition that Goldsborough procure some books for her. When "two large boxes of books and testaments from the North" arrived a week or two later, she began instructing forty children during the day and even more adults at night. Over the course of the war, Baker would marry Edward King (who later joined the Thirty-Third U.S. Colored Troops), work as a nurse and laundress, and continue to teach both children and adults.[154] An old man named Bachus, who suffered a disability that robbed him of the use of his hands, had been a slave on St. Helena before the war, but he could read. From time to time, he took charge of Harriet Ware's school. He taught mathematics by lining children up in rows and having them march around, and he taught reading by setting the alphabet and basic phonetics to song. When Bachus's brother, Lester, died in June 1862, Bachus's students carried schoolbooks like hymnals to Lester's graveside service, "singing their A,B,C, through and through again, as they stood waiting round the grave."[155]

As Harry McMillan's focus on families taking care of themselves emphasized, many former slaves prioritized the ability to order their own lives, removed from white direction. While former slaves everywhere harbored such ambitions at least to some extent, those ambitions were particularly apparent in the Lowcountry. Slaves constituted fully 82.8 percent of the total population of Beaufort County, South Carolina, in 1860, by which time they had been the demographic majority for over a century. As a result, it was possible for African Americans in the South Carolina and Georgia Lowcountry to never or rarely see a white person, a situation that did not spare them from slavery's cruelty but did provide a measure of daily independence different from what slaves constantly under watchful white eyes experienced. With that independence, black men, women, and children might tend a garden patch or keep chickens, weave baskets or craft tools, sell the fruits of their labor, and purchase from each other. This informal economy led to more African American property ownership than was common in many regions and also to the forging of a culture more distinctly separate than in much of the slaveholding South, featuring its own customs, conventions, and even language, known as Gullah or Geechee.[156]

Taken as a whole, the response of Union incoming to the distinctive culture and aspirations of Lowcountry freedpeople varied, which was to be expected given how varied a lot the legions who came to serve the Union in the Department of the South really were. Tunis Campbell, for one, was commissioned by Secretary of War Stanton to leave behind a partnership in a New York bakery and go to Port Royal. Campbell had been born free in New Jersey, worked as a waiter, hotel steward, and business owner in New York, and become active in the antebellum black convention movement. At Port Royal, he put his ideas about the dignity of labor and his evangelical abolitionism to work supporting former slaves' transitions out of bondage.[157]

Some of the missionaries were convinced that African Americans needed careful white tutelage, but other newcomers supported freedpeople's—especially women's—aspirations for autonomy. Harriet Tubman traveled on her own steam, not as one of the Gideonites, but like the Gideonites she sailed on the *Atlantic* to South Carolina in 1862. Along with spying and leading raids, she nursed in Beaufort hospitals and worked among refugees from slavery who had fled surrounding plantations and come into Beaufort. She also built a washhouse in Beaufort and helped women who had fled slavery to set up a laundry business in it. The proceeds from the business purchased not simply food and clothing but also black women's ability to order their families' lives as they saw fit, until the washhouse was commandeered by a sudden influx of soldiers in 1864. The wear and tear of men bunking in the structure that had not been built to withstand such constant or intensive use badly damaged the building, making the financial autonomy of the women who worked there short-lived, to the dismay of Tubman and, no doubt, the women earning their livings there.[158]

Some white Northern women missionaries shared that dismay. Part of their consternation arose from the same irritation anyone over the age of thirty occasionally experiences with men in their late teens and early twenties, a developmental phase not noted for restraint, good judgment, or delicacy.[159] More than just impatience with overgrown boys, though, some white women missionaries sincerely supported freedwomen's ambitions, at least to a degree. For all the preconceived notions she likely brought to South Carolina with her, Harriet Ware was quite adept at recognizing leadership among the black women of St. Helena. She realized, for example, that the only way the freedpeople of the Fripp Point neighborhood would trust her school enough to attend was if "Old Peggy," a woman who decided who "came into the Church," signaled approval. Ware had the good sense to work through rather than ignore or steamroll the network of women and enlisted the aid of Peggy's friend Flora to escort Peggy on a special visit to the school.[160] Ware and other missionaries admired black women's evident agricultural expertise and the self-possession to which that expertise entitled "free, strong, and graceful" women organizing their own work methods in the fields.[161]

They also recognized that such self-possession ought to extend to everyday matters like clothing. When Union forces and early missionaries first arrived, all agreed that the clothing shortage amounted to the most pressing humanitarian need, and Northern benevolent associations responded by sending boxes of dresses, shirts, trousers, and other serviceable garments. But Harriet Ware, Laura Towne, and their counterparts throughout the Lowcountry soon discovered that African American women had their own ideas about personal style, which diverged considerably from staid New England ready-made, and they quickly adapted, requesting that aid societies send cloth, needles, and thread instead, because the women "prefer to make their own clothes and all know how to sew." So, down the coast sailed bolts of denim, calico, worsted, gingham, and flannel, and on designated afternoons schoolrooms doubled as general stores, with teachers selling fabric by the yard out the classroom window until the last scrap was gone and disappointed customers had to be sent away to come back after the arrival of the next shipment.[162]

But willing as the most enlightened of the missionaries might have been to advocate black women's self-direction in some matters, they drew the line at what they considered matters of moral uplift, and here their most off-putting moral chauvinism is acutely on display. Slavery had so distorted ordinary morality among the enslaved, thought Laura Towne, that "I do not think they could work out their own civilization unless led up by white people."[163] Northerners were especially likely to disdain freedpeople's morals in matters of family life. Superintendent of Contrabands B. K. Lee reported in perfect horror that when Union officials asked parents who married them, the "answer we get seven times out of ten" is "Parson Blanket married us." Lee rushed to assure AFIC commissioners, "We commenced trying to instill into their minds the necessity of their being married."[164] In fact, the degree to which everyone from Union army generals to Gideonites fixated on the childbearing patterns of Sea Island women was downright unseemly. Every Union officer who testified to the American Freedmen's Inquiry Commission noted what he called the "looseness" of female morals in the Sea Islands and invariably pointed to the young age at which women began bearing children as evidence.[165] Henry Judd, a civilian superintendent of plantations in Port Royal and Cat, Cane, and Barnwell Islands, similarly bemoaned what he described as a lack of female chastity.[166] Even Robert Smalls, the hero of the *Planter,* spent much of his testimony getting pummeled with questions like the following: "Are [women] not carried away by their passion to have intercourse with men?" "Do they do this for money?" "At what age do the colored girls begin to have intercourse with white men?"[167]

The disproportionate attention paid to women's reproductive patterns sprang partly from prurience but also partly from genuine puzzlement at what white Northerners deemed a mysterious contradiction between such habits and freedpeople's religiosity. "The religious element in their character is very strong," Saxton emphasized, even as he lamented what seemed to him a certain laxity where chastity was concerned.[168] Union officials in other departments sometimes commented on what they saw as a similar dynamic, but nowhere else were such comments so plentiful as in the Department of the South, nor was the particular emphasis on *women's* religious customs and devotion quite the same elsewhere. Perhaps the women of other regions fostered distinctive religious cultures, but if they did so, they kept things quieter than in the Lowcountry, where black women openly cultivated religious devotion within their own religious societies, outside the purview of all whites and also of black men. Laura Towne observed secret religious initiation rituals and societies unique to Gullah women, and Robert Smalls verified that most black girls underwent a women-only initiation ceremony around the age of fifteen, after which the faith lives and leadership roles of women faithful changed.[169] None of the white Northerners who commented on black women's devotional habits doubted the strength of their faith; rather, to someone raised on the clear mandates of white Northern Protestantism, freedpeople's religiosity proved that they knew the Ten Commandments and were willfully choosing to break one of them, which imperiled their souls far more than ignorance of church teachings would have done.

If white Northerners feared that the souls of Lowcountry freedpeople faced eternal danger, they *knew* that their bodies confronted immediate threats. Danger came in many guises in the Sea Islands. Malaria and yellow fever were specters that always haunted the humid, low-lying land, and the close quarters at which refugees lived as more and more bond people fled from surrounding plantations into Union lines created perfect conditions for disease to spread. The most deadly was smallpox. Susie Baker took advantage of her own immunity to the dreaded disease and provided great quantities of sassafras tea and even deeper reserves of energy to afflicted soldiers of the Thirty-Third U.S. Colored Troops early in 1863, going every day to quarantine tents to nurse sick men.[170] The following year, the disease came back, and this time Clara Barton nursed sick soldiers and sent supplies to suffering freedpeople in the environs.[171]

Neither Barton nor the people she served in the Sea Islands were strangers to peril. Barton had literally arrived with a bang in April 1863, docking at Hilton Head at the exact moment that Union forces began bombarding Charleston, reminding her then and readers now that to be in the Department of the South was to be in an active war zone.[172] Freedpeople never had the luxury of forgetting it. To live in the Sea Islands meant to live with raiding parties, jittery pickets, and cannon fire. In the farther reaches of the Department of the South, things were even more precarious. Jacksonville and St. Augustine, Florida, went back and forth between Union and Confederate control a dizzying number of times, which placed former slaves at risk in countless ways, some obvious, such as the danger of getting caught in cross fire or of being subjected to violent re-enslavement if Confederates recaptured territory. The constant military activity made freedpeople vulnerable in more subtle ways as well. Black women in St. Augustine, for example, set out to support themselves by starting a laundry business specializing in washing for Union soldiers, each of whom ran an account at the laundry, to be settled once the paymaster appeared. The trouble was that "the frequent and sudden change of regiments, often between the visits of the paymaster, prevents the soldiers from paying their washbills, and thus the earnings of weeks, as well as the little stock of starch and soap, are swept away." An African American cobbler ran into the same problem when a regiment was redeployed before its members paid him for repairing their boots, and he, too, faced the coming winter with no way to buy necessities like food, clothing, and medicine.[173]

The risk of kidnapping was also ever present. The six hundred men, women, and children on St. Simons Island, Georgia, could not "go very far from our own quarters in the daytime" and after dark did not dare "even to go out of the house" because Confederate troops stationed just across the creek on the mainland "would capture any persons venturing out alone and carry them" off. Lowcountry geography meant that freedpeople throughout the Department of the South generally enjoyed no more peace of mind than the St. Simons refugees from slavery did, for the same surreptitious paths and waterways they had traveled to get to Union troops could also be followed, and nearly as stealthily, by Confederates intent upon nabbing them. Once back in the hands of slave owners, former slaves who had come so tantalizingly close to freedom often found themselves forcibly moved to upland regions too far away from Union lines to make re-liberation feasible.[174]

Besides the threat of kidnapping by Confederates, the Union army sometimes resorted to enlistment practices so coercive that it might as well have called them kidnapping. The distinction between enlistment and abduction remained well-nigh invisible to a middle-aged woman named Susan, who began the war with five sons and the following year found herself with none. Two had been captured "by Secesh," one had voluntarily gone off as a servant to a Union officer and never been heard from again, and two more were rounded up against their will by the Union general David Hunter's dragnet on a single day in May. To Susan, Union or Confederate captors made little difference in light of the basic fact that a mother of five sons had "not so much as that (pointing off the end of her finger) left of one of them."[175] Laura Towne, who up to that point had generally approved of the antislavery general David Hunter, saw so many women made "anxious and depressed" by the disappearance of their husbands and sons as a result of Hunter's coercive recruitment that she called May 12, the day he issued his enlistment proclamation, "the black day."[176]

Hunter's impetuous action met resistance from black men and their families as well as white missionaries but also from Congress, which had not yet authorized the enlistment of black soldiers, and from the Lincoln administration, which consistently reprimanded officers who tried to elevate military over civil authority, especially where slavery was concerned and especially when it still took a delicate balancing act to ensure that the slaveholding border states of Kentucky, Missouri, and Maryland remained in the Union, as was the case in the spring of 1862. That fall, Hunter's May 12 recruits were disbanded, never having been paid a cent for their months of service and with a sour taste in their mouths, which undoubtedly helped explain why legitimate recruiting in South Carolina went slowly and "by means of a great deal of coaxing" when black enlistment officially resumed. "Oh, if the formation of the regiment last spring had only been differently managed!" lamented Harriet Ware in early 1863, "we should have had a brigade by this time." As it was, one man had been "so badly treated" when rounded up by Hunter that he hid in a chimney to avoid getting pressed into service again.[177] The bitter irony was that from the moment war had first broken out, African American men had rushed to join Union forces, only to have their offers rebuked. Still, many placed great hope in the prospect of black military service as a way to destroy slavery and also to contribute to the creation of a new Union in which African Americans counted as full and equal members. Yet the actual way that the hope of black Civil War enlistment played out on the ground along the coasts of South Carolina, Georgia, and Florida frustrated, subverted, and dashed some hopes, even as it fulfilled others.

A similar story of hopes raised and trampled, often at the same time and almost never in the manner anyone predicted, would play out again and again for the freedpeople of the Lowcountry, including where their hopes for land and independence were concerned. Within the first year of war, numerous settlements of former slaves took shape on various islands off the South Carolina and Georgia coasts, and in them freedpeople began cultivating their own crops as well as their own semiautonomous civil societies. Potatoes, corn, and even a mill sprouted up on St. Simons Island, tended by former slaves who took refuge there. Hundreds of acres of cotton and corn thrived on Edisto Island, grown by the black men, women, and children who also built serviceable houses, crowded eagerly onto schoolroom benches, and began to institute their own self-government. Determined and resolute, the refugees from slavery cooperated with Union authorities, for the most part allied with missionaries, and remained vigilant against the threat of Confederate troops just a few miles inland, whose presence nobody could ever dismiss.

Yet the frustrations and failures of unseen armies far away turned out to be more devastating to Lowcountry hopes than predictable nearby perils. The failure of the Army of the Potomac's Peninsula Campaign in the summer of 1862 precipitated a panicked concentration of Union forces in Virginia, which the War Department achieved by hastily dragging regiments from all over the Eastern Seaboard back to the Old Dominion. In the Department of the South, Hunter and Saxton had little choice but to concentrate remaining forces by pulling them closer in to Beaufort and Port Royal, which for all the good sense it made on paper left places like Edisto and St. Simons unprotected. Freedpeople could either remain vulnerable to Confederate recapture or abandon the new communities they were wresting out of the islands' sandy soil. By and large, the Union army and navy made the decision for them, uprooting settlements and relocating former slaves elsewhere within the department, where they were less vulnerable to kidnapping but also distant from the crops they had planted and the relative independence those crops had underwritten.[178]

In 1865, history would come eerily close to repeating itself throughout the Department of the South. As winter settled on the city of Savannah and General William T. Sherman and his men recuperated there from their famed March to the Sea before heading up through Carolina, a group of twenty black ministers and other community leaders met with the general and with Secretary of War Stanton. At the meeting, the black men persuasively made the case for black landownership as necessity, as material grounds for independence, and as basic justice in return for black contributions to the war effort, as well as centuries of unrequited toil. In response (and also as a tactical measure with the twin objectives of keeping strategically valuable land in loyal Union hands and shedding the long lines of freedpeople who had followed Sherman's army from Atlanta), Sherman issued Special Field Orders No. 15 on January 6, 1865. Special Orders No. 15 stipulated that the coastal islands and a thirty-mile-wide strip of land from the St. Johns River in Florida up through South Carolina be "reserved and set apart for the settlement of the Negroes now made free."[179] The establishment of the "Sherman Reserve" inspired optimism and confidence in the black press. The *New Orleans Tribune*, for example, predicted that "the country will be electrified in a few days by an order from [Sherman] partitioning among them the abandoned Sea Island property of fugitive rebel planters, and establishing them in their new free hold, and laying the foundation of a new social condition in the South."[180]

On Edisto, freedpeople once again sank their hopes into the soil, pacing out plots of ground, tilling, planting, cultivating livestock, and looking forward to security for their "articles of furniture" and homes in which to enjoy them.[181] Meanwhile, the *Planter* began ferrying freedpeople to "lands they have selected," carrying axes and adzes for clearing land, a foot lathe, drills, and screw plates to repair mills, muskets for black men to use against "poisonous serpents, ferocious beasts, and rebels," and books to establish a library on at least one of the Sea Islands.[182]

There was discontent, too, to be sure. Sometimes Union officials resented directives from Washington that made little local sense. Sometimes they clashed with each other, such as when Union soldier turned Freedmen's Bureau agent William Eaton saw Tunis Campbell's political organizing among freedmen as overstepping authority, but Campbell saw it as his way of encouraging peace and good order.[183] Sometimes officials and black farmers had incompatible ideas about crops as well as about behavioral norms, and sometimes military personnel had never had freedpeople's best interests at heart to begin with. Sometimes neighboring black families disputed boundaries on plots of land or simply did not get along. And life's material considerations never came easy; necessities remained in short supply, and everybody had the massive upheaval of war to contend with day in and day out.

Nobody, in short, would mistake the Department of the South—or anywhere former slaves met the Union army—for utopia, but at the time of the war's conclusion life looked much different for the tens of thousands of black men, women, and children who had exited slavery there than it had when the war began, or even than it had in 1862, when the photograph of Edisto with which this chapter began was taken. Another look back at that photograph reveals ten people looking straight at the camera. The direct gaze must have cost them, because it would have required them to look into the sun. Yet not one winces or glances away. The determined gazes at first make the scene seem completely motionless, as though the camera caught a moment of still and quiet. A closer look shows a blur where the teenage girl's hand clutches a hoe, as though there were no stillness for her, ever. The edges of one of the women's skirts blur as well, as though she were swaying back and forth, which she might well have been doing, for she was holding a baby, the one figure not looking at the camera but instead twisting and squirming. The baby's protests make clear what everyone in that photograph, and anyone exiting slavery anywhere in the eastern theater of the Civil War, surely knew: even in relatively settled eastern camps, nothing was certain, and any impression of respite was an illusion.

Former slaves of Jefferson Davis at Baton Rouge, ca. 1863

Constant Turbulence

Experiencing Emancipation in
Western Contraband Camps

Women and children and a handful of men gather in a large yard.[1] One woman holds a baby on her lap, the fingers of her left hand splayed around the child's back in a grip both indestructibly solid and infinitely tender. Another woman gazes down at a toddler at her feet as he plays with a stick, in the way very small children do. A group of older children kneels in a circle, entranced by a game, possibly marbles, more deserving of their attention than the photographer. A cluster of women sits together in a semicircle, ages and expressions limning a wide arc of human life span and experience. One of the older women bores right into the camera with eyes that say they have seen it all, while one of the younger women looks just as directly with eyes that announce a readiness to face whatever sights might present themselves. Other women look away or down, the shoulders of one in particular expressing sorrow that goes beyond mere sight. To their left stand more women, one holding her chin contemplatively in her hand. Around the edges of the photograph stand dozens more people, often with arms crossed, too far from the camera for nineteenth-century photography to capture much detail about their faces, but of all ages. The group's size and variety and range of activities insist that life persists, in all its richness and tedium and suffering, in its minutiae and in its vastness. Yet the photograph offers no way to locate where the people are. There are structures that

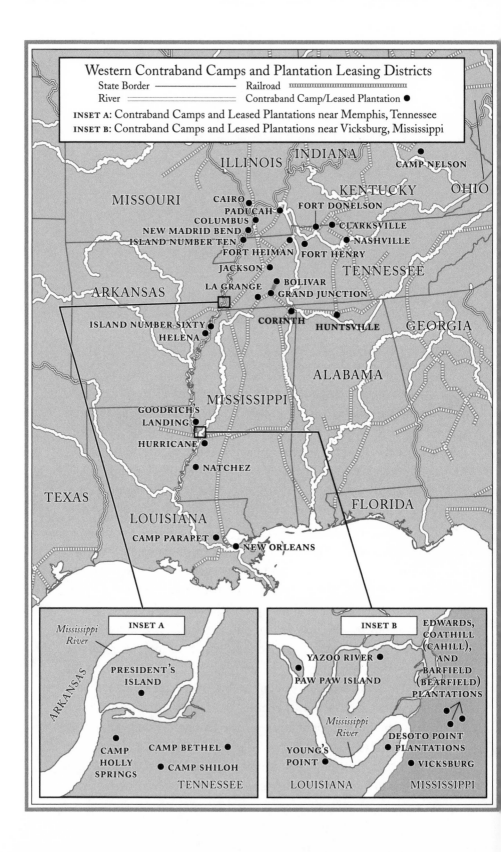

Western Contraband Camps and Plantation Leasing Districts

State Border ———————— Railroad ▪▪▪▪▪▪▪▪▪▪▪▪▪▪▪▪▪▪▪▪▪▪▪▪▪
River ══════════════ Contraband Camp/Leased Plantation ●

INSET A: Contraband Camps and Leased Plantations near Memphis, Tennessee
INSET B: Contraband Camps and Leased Plantations near Vicksburg, Mississippi

INDIANA
ILLINOIS
● CAMP NELSON
KENTUCKY   OHIO
MISSOURI   CAIRO ●
PADUCAH ●   FORT DONELSON ●
COLUMBUS ●   ● CLARKSVILLE
NEW MADRID BEND ●   ● NASHVILLE
ISLAND NUMBER TEN ●
FORT HEIMAN ●   FORT HENRY
JACKSON ●   TENNESSEE
LA GRANGE ●   BOLIVAR ●
ARKANSAS   ● GRAND JUNCTION
ISLAND NUMBER SIXTY ●   CORINTH ●   GEORGIA
HELENA ●   HUNTSVILLE ●

ALABAMA

MISSISSIPPI
GOODRICH'S LANDING ●
HURRICANE ●
● NATCHEZ

TEXAS   FLORIDA
LOUISIANA
CAMP PARAPET ●
● NEW ORLEANS

INSET A

Mississippi River

ARKANSAS

PRESIDENT'S ISLAND ●

CAMP HOLLY SPRINGS ●   CAMP BETHEL ●
● CAMP SHILOH

TENNESSEE

INSET B

EDWARDS, COATHILL (CAHILL), AND BARFIELD (BEARFIELD) PLANTATIONS

YAZOO RIVER ●
PAW PAW ISLAND ●

Mississippi River

YOUNG'S POINT ●   DESOTO POINT ● PLANTATIONS
● VICKSBURG

LOUISIANA   MISSISSIPPI

could be any house and outbuildings, and there are some trees with and without leaves, none of them providing much to navigate by. The caption provided by the Louisiana State Museum, which owns the photograph, tells us that the setting is Baton Rouge, but we must take that location on trust, for to go by the navigable details in the photograph, the people could be nearly anywhere or nowhere in particular.

For most of the black men, women, and children who fled slavery and ran for Union lines in the West, emancipation's landscape was even more disorienting, mobile, and impermanent than it was for those who fled in the eastern theater of the war. With a few notable exceptions, Union grasp on territory in the West was more tenuous and forces changed base, often repeatedly and sometimes rapidly, in constant attempts to control transportation arteries as well as territory. As a result, routes out of slavery tended to follow rivers and railroad tracks, and journeys along those routes tended to consist of one temporary hiatus after another, rather than a single arrival at a permanent location. In contrast with freedpeople who ran to Fort Monroe or to Roanoke Island or to one of the Sea Islands and then stayed put, refugees from slavery in the western theater often floated in and out of multiple camps, but never out of danger. Almost nobody, and nothing, not even freedom itself, stayed in one place for long. If the river Jordan was not rolling through this shifting landscape of slavery and emancipation, the river Mississippi certainly was. The Mississippi was both water of life and force of destruction, much like the army itself. Shaped by the twin forces of the army and the Mississippi, the experience of emancipation in the western theater was relentlessly disruptive, transient, and clouded less by grit blown inland from the sea than by the swirl and fog of constant motion.

MIDDLE TENNESSEE

Refugees from slavery fled to the Union army the first chance they got in the western theater, just as they had in the East, but viable chances took a little longer to materialize. At Fort Monroe, General Benjamin Butler displayed few compunctions in deciding what to do about fugitive slaves who ran to his lines, but in the West General Henry Halleck, expert on international law and the rules of war—and perennial wor-

rier about maintaining the superiority of civil over military authority—
proved more hesitant. Halleck issued General Orders No. 3, barring
fugitive slaves from army camps, precisely to avoid giving military officers the responsibility for making decisions about slavery, or the opportunity to do so, which to his mind were necessarily questions that fell
to civil authority.[2] General Orders No. 3 did not prevent slaves in the
West from viewing the Union army as a conduit out of slavery, but it did
mean that they had to look a little harder for opportunities to reach it.
Opportunity arose in February 1862, when Fort Donelson on the Cumberland River and Forts Henry and Heiman on the Tennessee River
fell to Union forces. One of the largest slave owners in that region was
Woods, Lewis, and Company, an iron furnace corporation that owned
its laborers and housed them in barracks not far from the forts. When
the workforce bolted for Fort Donelson, the company wanted its laborers back, but instead the Union officer in command, Ulysses S. Grant,
issued orders for their employment "in the Quarter Masters Department for the benefit of the Government," and similar orders applied to
Fort Henry as soon as it fell.[3] Within the year, any early hesitation had
vanished, and Union men serving at the forts reported with satisfaction
"that if any officer refuse[d] to let the blacks come into our lines," he
would be dismissed.[4]

Slaves from the surrounding regions continued to come into the
forts, especially once churches from Michigan and Wisconsin began
sending books they could use to learn to read. One man who escaped
slavery and earned a living cooking for the Eighty-Third Illinois Infantry kept a spelling book next to his stove and studied it while he stirred
his pots. Another young boy who had made his own way to Fort Donelson from across the Kentucky state line looked his owner right in the
eye when the man came to try to lure him back to the Bluegrass State
with promises of paid employment and said he would not leave because
"I'm going to school."[5]

From Forts Henry and Donelson, Union forces moved on to occupy
Nashville, an important rail and river hub, in February 1862. As soon
as blue columns arrived, so did refugees from slavery, crowding into
houses, shops, and outbuildings abandoned by fleeing Confederates.[6]
Its convenience as a transportation hub also made Nashville an easy
place to attack, especially once General Don Carlos Buell removed

most of his army (which would later be named the Army of the Cumberland) to pursue the Confederate army into Kentucky, leaving behind only a skeleton force and orders to fortify the city with a ring of forts.[7]

Captain James Morton of the Corps of Engineers was charged with the duty of building Fort Negley in the summer of 1862. Morton began recruiting laborers by promising wages of $7 per month for workers living in army-provided housing on army rations and $12 per month for those sheltering and feeding themselves. Then came the threat of an imminent Confederate attack, and Morton dispensed with the niceties of recruitment. He sent gangs of soldiers through the streets of Nashville to impress laborers at all hours, including coming out of church on Sunday. Over the next eight months, 2,768 men in total (an average of about 1,500 at any one time) built the stockade structure stretching over fifty-one acres of St. Cloud Hill, often under armed guard, sleeping out in the open on the work site at night and subsisting on army rations. The Engineer Office meticulously kept track of wages due, to the tune of $85,858.50, but only $30,000 of those wages were ever actually paid.[8] Other commanders used more ethical methods. George L. Stearns, for example, listened when a group of black men told him, "We are willing to work, if the Gov't needs our services, with pay or without; but we don't like to be driven at the point of a bayonet. Let us know & we will volunteer." Stearns signed 257 men up to work for thirty days for $10 plus rations, and at the end of the thirty days he paid them. The following week, he raised another company of 300 workers on the same terms.[9]

Stearns aside, the habit of recruiting labor by dragnet died hard at Nashville. In the fall of 1863, the Nashville and North-Western Railroad performed emergency track maintenance on its lines in and around Nashville by impressing 240 men and boys. The coerced labor included eleven-year-old Charles Dotsin, sixty-eight-year-old Bob Ledwell, a skilled blacksmith named William Zelliner, a man named Mingle Pillow who had dashed to Nashville from Columbia, Tennessee, and hundreds of others whose names line the Nashville and North-Western Railroad's ledger. The distinction between slavery and freedom must have seemed elusive to them as they worked on the tracks.[10]

Others fared somewhat better, though none would have mistaken Nashville for the fulfillment of their dreams. Nashville proved one of the easier places for black men, women, and children to find work. They worked on the docks and rail lines, cooked for Union troops, and sold them berries in season by the quart. They nursed and laundered in the Union's hastily assembled hospitals for both soldiers and fugitive slaves.[11] They also attended schools whenever and wherever they could, practically from the moment they got to town.[12] Their numbers made it possible to create a social life and sense of community for themselves, for example when a group of freedpeople hosted a Christmas dance in the courthouse in 1863.[13] Some benefited from the ingenuity of Abigail Dutton, a grandmother from Massachusetts who went south to volunteer among soldiers and former slaves and astutely surmised that serving coarse army rations to the delicate stomachs of the sick and weakened was not the best nutritional route back to good health. In 1864, she began the Special Diet Kitchen, issuing fresh vegetables, broths, and ginger tea to the ailing and the recovering, at first as an experiment. Then, "mortality having decreased ever so many per cent," the "S.D.K." remained a fixture at Nashville, and the district superintendent of contrabands traveled to other camps in Tennessee and Alabama to encourage the adoption of similar dietary guidelines.[14]

Meanwhile, the Union army strove doggedly to take and hold territory, and especially to take control of the Mississippi River, which it would do by degrees and from multiple directions simultaneously. While forces pushed eastward over land from interior states like Tennessee, they also maneuvered for control of cities from both the northern and the southern ends of the big, muddy river. The most important city on the southern end was New Orleans, and it fell to the Union in the spring of 1862.

NEW ORLEANS

New Orleans prides itself on being unique, and during the Civil War that description would certainly hold true for the experience of exiting slavery in the Crescent City. Even before the war, New Orleans was exceptional in countless ways. It was a cosmopolitan metropolis still influenced by French and Spanish culture, thanks to its time in the not-so-distant past under each of those two empires. A large free black population lived in New Orleans, including an elite corps of free people of color who owned substantial amounts of property and sometimes slaves. The city's biggest profits came from sugar, a unique crop and product that also made things different anywhere it was grown, processed, or sold. Pro-slavery Unionism was uncommonly strong in the Deep South's largest city, bolstered by sugar planters and producers not eager to disrupt the federal government that had enabled the fabulous wealth their enslaved labor force produced growing sugarcane and converting it to cash through the capital-intensive refining process. To be sure, the city contained its passionate secessionists as well, but the warmth of their sentiment did not prevent New Orleans from falling to the Union with comparatively little struggle in May 1862 and becoming a magnet for slaves who dashed for the city from surrounding sugar parishes and from even farther up the Mississippi River. What refugees found when they got to New Orleans was ambivalence and uncertainty and not what they expected freedom to be. But it was not slavery, either. It was ad hoc, ambiguous, and made up a day at a time for rural freedpeople who fled to the city as well as for the men and women who had been enslaved in New Orleans before the war and never left.

For all of the city's distinctive qualities, some of the factors influencing what it was like to exit slavery in New Orleans resembled factors found anywhere slaves came into contact with the Union army. Leadership, for one thing, always made a difference, as did the attitudes of the particular Union soldiers whose paths black men, women, and children happened to cross. If and when the abolitionist general John W. Phelps got his way, freedom arrived the moment a former slave met the Union army.[15] Phelps was often superseded by General Benjamin Butler and then General Nathaniel Banks, neither of whom particularly cared to prolong slavery, but each of whom took the distinctly utilitarian approach of trying to woo wealthy, pro-slavery, recently Unionist sugar magnates back into the Union fold. Phelps responded by establishing Camp Parapet, about four miles north of New Orleans, as safe haven, and former slaves flocked there. The combination of Camp Parapet's presence, slaves' strengthened ability to challenge their masters by virtue of the demands of sugar cultivation and the presence of federal force, and changing war policy meant that by the end of 1862 nearly everyone had given up on the futile task of protecting the Union by coddling slaveholders. Still, before that point, what happened when a slave got to

Union lines depended in part on whether the soldiers there followed the dictates (and shared the outlook) of Phelps, Butler, or Banks. Any black men or women who fled to the lines of the Fourth Wisconsin Infantry in 1862, for example, found themselves tossed out or worse if they ran across General Thomas Williams, but if they encountered Colonel Halbert Paine (who cordially hated Williams and took perverse pride in being placed under arrest by him for defiance), they could count on shelter and a version of freedom.

The material circumstances encountered by former slaves in New Orleans to some degree resembled conditions wherever former slaves found the Union army. Factors like crowding and shortages contributed to living conditions similar to those found in any other wartime urban refugee camp, although stringent sanitary measures imposed by General Butler did, for all their unpopularity, ensure that New Orleans during wartime skipped the usual cholera and yellow fever epidemics that regularly punctuated the city's antebellum history.[16] Freedpeople worked for the Union army in myriad capacities, from drayage on the docks to teamstering to nursing to laundering to cooking to building fortifications to manning artillery guns.[17] They were also active as spies. Abraham Galloway accompanied Butler when the general left Fort Monroe for New Orleans and operated out of New Orleans for miles up the Mississippi River, until his mysterious disappearance into Confederate hands, from which he would somehow escape and return to North Carolina. Countless more black men and women lacked Galloway's swashbuckling fame but provided the intelligence on which Union efforts in the Gulf relied. Horace Bell, one of the Department of the Gulf's most industrious scouts, regularly filed reports full of the information he had garnered from slaves and former slaves, even at the cost of their own lives.[18]

Yet in other ways, New Orleans was genuinely unlike anywhere else. One such way was the presence and influence of the "colored elite." With their fragile social positions to maintain and much to lose, the elite free people of color in New Orleans had little choice but to calculate carefully at each step of the way from secession through war to eventual Reconstruction. When Confederates controlled New Orleans, some elite black men had offered to help guard the city as the Louisiana Native Guards. Their offers were declined, and the units extended the same offer to the Union army when it got to town.[19] On the one hand, the existence of a "colored elite" meant that African Americans, taken as a whole, had more wealth and power in New Orleans than anywhere else. But no group of human beings always acts "as a whole," no matter how many demographic features its members share, as the Union major John W. DeForest was reminded during his time in New Orleans. On one October evening in 1862, he attended a lavish dinner hosted by "the wives & sisters & friends of officers in the 1st Regiment of the Louisiana Native Brigade." At an exquisitely appointed table, DeForest sipped champagne, shared a "splendid supper," conversed in French, and learned that for some of the "intelligent & well informed & genteel" free *gens de couleur,* protecting their own tenuous place in New Orleans's exquisitely complex social structure meant "fighting for a position" and shunning former slaves. Others vigorously insisted that "they intend to elevate themselves and avenge their race," all members of it, and "they mean to give no quarter" to anyone who tried to stop them.[20]

That segment of the population formed a nucleus that could not only exercise economic power but also intensify that power by attracting aid from outside the state. The Northwestern Freedmen's Aid Commission, for example, identified the free black elite of New Orleans as a competent, on-the-ground conduit through which to siphon more and different kinds of assistance to the Crescent City. Whereas the commission typically concentrated on basic literacy efforts in most of the regions its agents worked, it looked to "the establishment of a seminary at New Orleans" for "colored girls" modeled "somewhat after the order of Mt. Holyoke."[21]

In contrast, newly freed people of color in New Orleans, especially those who had fled from hinterlands with nothing more than they could carry, needed basic material relief, and the distribution of supplies in New Orleans was even more complicated than it was everywhere else because of rampant corruption. Greed and fraud were certainly not absent elsewhere (or anywhere), but the sheer amount, proliferation, and audacity of corruption in the Crescent City was such that in practice it amounted to a difference in kind, not simply a difference in scale. It was so rife that in 1864, the adjutant general's office appointed the Smith-Brady Commission on Corrupt Practices in the South to investigate reports of corruption and malfeasance in New Orleans and surrounding areas.[22] Exiting slavery and searching for freedom in the largest city in the occupied South, in short, shared certain basic qualities with the experience of exiting slavery anywhere, but in many ways it was not quite like doing so anywhere else.

ARKANSAS

Finding freedom in Arkansas also operated according to its own distinctive rhythms. While Union forces occupied New Orleans and hunkered down in Tennessee, the Army of the Southwest under General Samuel Curtis moved from its starting point in the tenuously Union state of Missouri into Arkansas. When it did, black men, women, and children began "flocking to the army from every direction," gambling that the long columns of bluecoats offered a road out of bondage.[23] To the chiefly midwestern soldiers marching through Arkansas, facilitating slaves' escape from rebel masters was a commonsense matter of removing "a source of strength to the South almost equal to an army in the field," especially when fleeing slaves "every day bring in information" about where Confederate troops were and where valuable cotton and foodstuffs were hidden.[24] Far from discouraging the flight, General Curtis issued certificates of freedom, though he was also careful to stay on the right side of Halleck (and slaveholding Unionists in Missouri) by insisting that escaped slaves got to his lines by their own volition and without any "enticing" on his part.[25] Propelled by their own vision, former slaves needed little in the way of outside "enticement," and they continued to come in ever-growing numbers. "They appear to enjoy themselves at present," one soldier observed, "but what will be done with them when the army moves again, is more than I can see."[26]

As it turned out, Union forces stayed in Arkansas, but that soldier's worries were well-founded; how to provide safe shelter and basic subsistence for fast-growing numbers in a region where Union control over territory and especially supply lines was tenuous at best posed challenges that defied easy resolution. Within days of the army's arrival at Helena, the assistant quartermaster reported "a perfect cloud of negroes being thrown upon him for subsistence and support." Before long, large numbers of black men, women, and children were at work building fortifications.[27] They crowded into abandoned buildings, and even into a barn owned by the Sisters of Mercy (against the will of the nuns who demonstrated little of the quality that gave them their name), but they overfilled existing structures in short order. They turned to whatever they could find, "huddling together in huts" or even "caves, shelters of brush," or "cast-off tents" until they could forage enough materials to build cabins. Many of the hastily constructed shelters clustered together in a part of town christened Camp Ethiopia, which quickly became home to "between 3,000 and 4,000 men, women, and children."[28] Numbers continued to grow, and conditions continued to worsen in the first half of 1863. Helena was prone to flooding, and the fetid waters of the swollen Mississippi River that spring, along with overcrowding, poor rations, and compromised immune systems, contributed to shocking mortality rates.[29] "This is a terrible hole for niggers . . . They are sickening and dying very rapidly. What under the sun is to become of them I cannot tell," grumbled one unsympathetic officer in the fall of 1862.[30] Freedpeople's treatment at the hands of Union troops varied and seemed to depend not only on the regiment or the individual but on the day or hour that soldiers came into contact with refugees from slavery. In the most egregious of cases, surly soldiers assaulted or even killed black men or women who rubbed them the wrong way.[31] Consequences were even more likely to be dire for former slaves who fell into the hands of Confederate companies prowling around Helena's edges. Individual kidnappings were a constant threat, and in July 1863 a Confederate regiment consoled itself for losing the Battle of Helena by burning Camp Ethiopia's cabins and beating and killing many of the inhabitants.[32]

The army stepped up its guarding efforts by recruiting black soldiers, sometimes with invitation and sometimes with coercion. When the war began, the teenager Solomon Lambert continued to be hired out by his owners, as he had been his whole life. One time he and a gang had been driven as far as Texas to pick cotton, and on the way the driver had scared the workers into obedience by giving them a good look into a slave pen in Camden, Arkansas. The door swung open to the "big yard . . . tall and fixed so they couldn't get out," and the view of the penned-in yard "full of darkies. All sizes. All ages . . . the worst thing I ever seen or heard tell of in my life" continued to haunt Lambert. During the war, his master shuffled him around to make money where he could but also to keep him out of the hands of the Yankees. That strategy worked until August 1863, when Union soldiers started rounding up black men around Helena to fill out the Second Louisiana Battery of U.S. Colored Troops Light Artillery. Then "the Yankees run up on me and took me on," Lambert remembered, and he spent the rest of the war guarding Helena, duty that was tedious and often unpleasant but did help make Helena safer; only one member of the regiment was killed.[33]

Nothing at Helena remained static or unchanging—not safety, but also not even misery—which is not to say that conditions started out awful and got better, or the other way around, but rather to emphasize that Helena, like camps throughout the western theater, was in a constant state of instability and flux. Sometimes, for some freedom seekers in Helena, conditions did improve. When harvest time came in 1863, many black men, women, and children enjoyed a stretch where they were "comfortable and industrious," and by the following year many of them had managed to trade tents and lean-tos for cabins with gardens.[34] Sometimes improvements simply gave way to later deterioration or went in cycles. Beyond the aggregates, individuals experienced their own tragedies when children died, as well as their own triumphs of love when long-separated family members reunited or when a mother and her children filled a bushel basket with beans grown by themselves for themselves.

The one area that did demonstrate a reasonably steady trajectory in Helena was schooling, which became a subject of much focused attention in 1864 and stayed that way. The Northwestern Freedmen's Aid Commission and the American Missionary Association, along with a smattering of independent churches, began sending teachers to Helena and its environs in force in 1864.[35] William Allen, a Wisconsin teacher who had spent time in the Sea Islands before signing on to work as an agent for the Sanitary Commission, accepted an appointment as superintendent of freedmen's schools in September 1864, to better coordinate the work.[36] He dedicated immediate attention to physical structures, choosing sites for three new school buildings the following month, taking care to situate them on good plank roads traversable even amid Helena's frequent floods.[37] He also oversaw the work of teachers. He especially noticed Joanna Moore, a young Illinois woman whom he at first found too blond, "gushing," and enamored of poetry and other inessentials. Moore soon made clear that there was more to her than girlish "enthusiasms." She had sacrificed her own college education to work among freedpeople, first at Island Number Ten in 1863, before making her way farther down the Mississippi River. Through her travels, she remained refreshingly aware that she had as much to learn from her pupils as they did from her. In Helena, she taught at least twelve hours every day, at first in a drafty barn until a better structure could be fitted out, instructing both children and adults. She also joined forces with a black preacher to minister to the physical and religious needs of people for whom she grew to feel genuine love and spiritual kinship.[38] In another part of the city, freedpeople organized "a private school of their own" and "paid a teacher so much a month."[39]

Enthusiasm for learning mattered, but whether or not it bore results depended in some measure on security against Confederate attack, which was obtainable only with full Union control of the Mississippi River. Once Union forces held the Mississippi as far south as Memphis and Helena, and also controlled the mouth of the river by occupying New Orleans, that left the section of the river running through the state that gave the river its name: Mississippi. In 1862 and 1863, the Army of the Tennessee under the command of General Ulysses S. Grant pursued that objective, along with control of all adjacent territory and its railways and major tributary rivers. The efforts to do so were all consolidated within the Department of Tennessee, a department absolutely crucial to Union war strategy and within which tens of thousands of enslaved men, women, and children identified the Union army as their best escape route out of slavery. Despite the word "Tennessee" in its name, it was a department defined more than anything by the Mississippi River.

ON THE MOVE THROUGHOUT THE DEPARTMENT OF TENNESSEE

Everywhere the Army of the Tennessee went, fleeing slaves did, too, "like the oncoming of cities," as one officer described it. "There were men, women, and children in every stage of disease or decrepitude, often nearly naked, with flesh torn by the terrible experiences of their escapes . . . the women in travail, the helplessness of childhood and old age, the horrors of sickness and frequent death."[40] Sometimes they brought "horses, mules, wagons, cotton, oxen &c" that the army could use, and often they brought useful local intelligence. Sometimes they had time to gather personal possessions to sustain them on their journeys. But more often than not, they came with nothing in the way of material possessions other than what was on their person at the moment a chance for escape arose.[41]

Grant surveyed the arrival of freedom seekers from a different vantage point compared to his counterparts in the eastern theater, or even from General Samuel Curtis and his Army of the Southwest. Whereas General Benjamin Butler at Fort Monroe resided within a fortified stronghold surrounded by a moat, Grant and his armies remained on the move through perilous territory that switched from Union to Confederate hands and back again multiple times. In contrast to General Curtis, who had been quick to spot the benefits that black men and women might bring to the Union cause, the harried Grant at first saw only the problems associated with harboring freedom-seeking men, women, and children. Sick, malnourished refugees from slavery represented instant disease vectors that threatened the always precarious health of his troops. They were targets for attack by vindictive Confederates, which heightened the army's vulnerability. The challenges of addressing their needs diverted resources and mental energy from the military mission of winning a war. Neither pro-slavery nor passionately inclined in the abolitionist direction himself, Grant was foremost a soldier who followed orders, which by 1862 "prohibited the expulsion of the negroes from the protection of the army when they came in voluntarily." He was also a man with a conscience who could not simply throw freedom seekers out, because, as he put it, "humanity forbade allowing them to starve."[42] He needed a plan.

As it turned out, he went through several different plans. One was to get refugees from slavery out of harm's way and the army's path. In the late summer and fall of 1862, steamboats carrying war supplies down the Mississippi started heading back up it with hundreds of black men, women, and children on board, transported to the Midwest at government expense. Many disembarked at Cairo, Illinois, the southernmost tip of the state, where the Mississippi River, Ohio River, and rail lines all converged. Union forces had rushed to secure the spot as soon as war broke out.[43] Cairo dips down deep into slave territory: cross one river out of it and you find yourself in Missouri, or cross the other and you found yourself south of Paducah, Kentucky, so slaves began to run there almost as quickly as Shepard Mallory, Frank Baker, and James Townsend made a break for Fort Monroe in Virginia. The name "contraband" stuck at Cairo too, and by June 1861 post records for Camp Defiance, the Union army installation there, showed that at least some fugitives from slavery identified as "contraband of war" were at Cairo. A "contraband boy" named Pierson Cade found himself in the camp jail for a petty infraction on June 9 and 10, as did three more refugees from slavery listed only as John, Bill, and Ann.[44] Others got to Cairo when Union naval crews spotted them doing forced labor on Confederate fortifications, secreted them aboard ship, and brought them to Cairo.[45]

By 1862, a genuine labor shortage afflicted Camp Defiance and much of the Midwest, so in theory the arrangement of transporting a labor force out of army camps and up to Cairo made sense, or at least it seemed that way to Ulysses S. Grant.[46] There was certainly plenty of work. Refugees from Arkansas and Tennessee hauled on ropes and hefted cases of war supplies up and down gangplanks. They cooked and laundered. They maintained railroad tracks and loaded and unloaded railway cars. They lined up to collect the blankets and rations issued to them through the Quartermaster Department. And if they did not want to stay in Cairo, the army would pay their rail fare to Chicago or elsewhere in the state where employers were looking to hire.[47]

When Colonel Adolph Engelmann of the Forty-Third Illinois Infantry first heard of Grant's plan while commanding his regiment in Bolivar, Tennessee, he could see its logic, but he also had his doubts. Where he was in Bolivar, local slaves and their families had come in to help build fortifications, but that work was now substantially completed, and masters were clamoring for the return of their property, placing the army in what Engelmann drolly called "an unpleasant predicament." He knew "these negroes do not want to go back," but the children (and there were many) in particular were defenseless in the tenuously held territory. Moreover, Engelmann was not entirely confident in the treatment his own men were likely to mete out to the families. Still, Grant's plan to "send the women and children to the North" made him ask, "Does anyone want them there?"[48] Since Illinois attained statehood in 1818, its legislature had passed laws to prevent black migration into the state and to limit the rights and freedoms of African Americans living there. The heart of antiblack sentiment beat most strongly in the "Little Egypt" region in the southern part of the state, precisely where Cairo was located. Little Egypt had been settled chiefly by white migrants from the South who went on to elect state legislators like John A. Logan, who in 1853 led the charge for an even harsher Black Exclusion Law, which permitted the sale of black migrants into temporary servitude by public auction.[49]

Engelmann, in short, had good reason to worry. Response to early refugees from slavery who landed in Cairo was not uniformly hostile, but it was decidedly mixed. The men of the Eighty-Third Illinois were still in Cairo in the fall of 1862, awaiting orders to head south, when boatloads of "contrabands" began arriving from Tennessee. The soldiers particularly liked having the children around because it eased the pain of missing their own families. One lieutenant grew so attached to one child that he tried to persuade her mother to let him adopt "the little girl to raise but he could not get her consent," and one corporal admired the mother's determination to "make something" of herself and her family.[50] The *Chicago Tribune* took a utilitarian view of matters, observing that "colored refugees" were people "loyal" to the Union and capable of working. Spurning "the labor of these contrabands" for reasons of mere "prejudice," according to the *Tribune,* was "little less than suicide."[51] Still, Engelmann's worries about a vitriolic white response proved plenty well-founded in other quarters. The *Salem Advocate* bemoaned "a perfect inundation of this black element, disturbing all our social relations and threatening the complete overthrow of white labor." Its editor bitterly resented that "the Government would pay the expense of their transportation."[52] One difference between the *Chicago Tribune* and the *Salem Advocate* was geographic: Chicago was in the northern part of the state, whereas Salem was more than 250 miles south in the Little Egypt region. Another difference was partisan: the *Tribune* was a Republican paper, and the *Advocate* was a Democratic one, and 1862 was a congressional election year. President Abraham Lincoln's friend and political adviser David Davis warned that the combination of "the large number of Republican voters, who have gone to war" (and thus could not vote because absentee voting did not yet exist), and "the negroes, coming into the State," would "work great harm in the coming election."[53]

Elections were no small things to elected officials or to the army, and so the U.S. government's next move was to transport refugees from slavery out of Cairo to other locations in the Midwest on the Illinois Central Railroad, again at government expense. In addition, some Union officers in posts along the Mississippi River made their own arrangements to transport groups of fugitives to their home communities. When John Lewis Waller, his parents, eleven siblings, and nearly one hundred fellow slaves from near New Madrid, Missouri, made it to the encampment of the Thirty-Second Iowa Infantry, Captain John Scott found a way to get them to Tama County, Iowa.[54] Chaplain James B. Rogers of the Fourteenth Wisconsin Infantry similarly sent a large group of black men, women, and children by river and rail to Fond du Lac, Wisconsin, where he expected his parishioners at the Baptist church to help get the newcomers settled mere weeks before the fall elections. Similar efforts throughout Iowa and Wisconsin, and to a lesser extent Indiana, Minnesota, and parts of Illinois other than Cairo, continued as the fall harvest ripened.[55]

Newspapers roared with controversy. The antislavery *Fond du Lac Weekly Commonwealth* defended the in-migration somewhat weakly, arguing in terms of utilitarian benefit even as it insisted that once slavery was abolished nationwide, former slaves would prefer to stay in the South anyway. The Democratic newspaper the *Weekly Patriot* and its flamboyant editor, Samuel "Pump" Carpenter, threw all decorum to the wind and hoped that the influx would lead to such decisive Democratic victories that the Republican Party would be dead and buried under a tombstone reading, "Died with the nigger on the brain."[56]

Actual election results were mixed. Republicans swept Iowa and did well in Wisconsin, but they were crushed in Illinois and Indiana, states too large and politically powerful to be ignored. The results were enough to worry Republican leaders nationally about public support for emancipation, and the practice of shipping fleeing slaves north came to a halt.[57]

In the late fall of 1862, the army stopped transporting former slaves to the Midwest on Uncle Sam's dime, but the cessation did not stop

slavery's refugees from coming to the army. They hid in bushes trying to spot potentially sympathetic faces among enlisted men in blue
who went berry picking or watched foraging Union troops from roadsides on the lookout for soldiers who appeared as though they might
take fugitives along with them.[58] Once in camp, refugees from slavery
"offer[ed] their services" as "teamsters, etc.," and then in their free time
they used the relative safety of Union lines to conduct religious services
so devoutly that one Missouri private "felt ashamed that we white ones
do not praise the grace of God more sincerely."[59]

True to General Grant's practical bent and commonsense disposition, he came up with a new plan by melding the course followed in the
East with local circumstances and the initiative of the black men and
women who recognized an ally (however tenuous) in the Union army.
Former slaves had already established themselves in several locations
throughout the Department of Tennessee—Grand Junction, Tennessee, and Corinth, Mississippi, for example—when Grant implemented
his new system for imposing order in the autumn of 1862. He appointed
Chaplain John Eaton of the Twenty-Seventh Ohio Volunteers as superintendent of contrabands for the Department of Tennessee in November 1862. He ordered Eaton "to take charge of the contrabands" that
came into Union lines throughout the Mississippi valley and in Arkansas and central Tennessee, arrange "them into suitable companies for
working, see that they are properly cared for, and set them to work."[60]
Grant also extended free river and rail transport to all charitable donations and volunteers sent by Northern benevolent organizations to contraband camps within his command.[61]

Of all the camps in Superintendent Eaton's department, the one
most often cited as a "model camp" was at Corinth, Mississippi, partly
because of good freshwater supply, partly because of sympathetic leadership, and partly because of the security provided by the army's relatively strong hold on Corinth for part of 1862 and all of 1863.[62] Camp
population fluctuated, but it averaged in the high 3,000s, a figure three
times as large as the village of Corinth's prewar population of 1,200.[63]
By the spring of 1863, the majority of newcomers were women, and most
of them brought children.[64] Need outstripped resources at Corinth as
it did everywhere else, but the margin by which it did so was smaller.

One reason why conditions at Corinth were more favorable than in most other camps was that its superintendents enjoyed notably cordial relations with missionaries, aid workers, and freedpeople. Corinth's first superintendent was Chaplain James Alexander of the Sixty-Sixth Illinois, who had once lived in Mississippi and claimed to have had dealings with ten thousand refugees from slavery in the first year of the war, many of whose white owners he had contended with in his Mississippi days.[65] Alexander became colonel of the First Alabama Infantry of African Descent (later renamed the Fifty-Fifth U.S. Colored Troops) in May 1863. He was succeeded by John Phillips of the Fifty-Seventh Illinois, a Quaker whose antislavery and pro-Union principles trumped his pacifist ones to propel him into Union service. Superintendents Alexander and Phillips were both flawed, and neither could work the miracles it would have taken to prevent all suffering among thousands of displaced people buffeted by war, but each man felt a true interest in the work and compassion for freedpeople.[66]

The first order of business at Corinth was to attend to immediate material need. At first, incoming refugees took shelter in army tents, but they wasted no time before splitting logs and sawing boards to build cabins measuring twelve by sixteen feet, arranged along a pattern of streets named for Butler, Frémont, and other officers and kept in good order thanks to a campwide sweeping-out ritual conducted every morning before 9:00.[67] Along with a thriving built environment, freedpeople constructed a bona fide civil society, including a system of political wards, a self-governing police force, schools, and the Union Christian Church of Corinth.[68] The camp's success testified chiefly to the work and will of the black men, women, and children who constructed it, but work and will were present in other camps as well. What was different at Corinth was the luxury of greater security in which work, will, and hope could flower, a luxury also evident in the architecture of white Union troops, who constructed elaborate cabins with porches and gingerbread, architectural flourishes absent from the shelter that troops constructed in most places.[69]

Clothing proved to be a stubborn problem everywhere, but less so at Corinth than most other places. Superintendent Alexander reported that when refugees from slavery arrived, their clothing was "very poor, with exceptions," and Union soldiers and missionary aid workers all uniformly reported that black men, women, and children appeared in camp clad in insubstantial rags and sometimes next to nothing at all, but by 1863 the clothing of the people who had been in camp for any length of time was "good by their own earnings & by donations," especially of women's and children's clothing from Northern benevolent groups who recognized the unlikelihood of the army keeping on hand a stash of garments suitable for anyone other than men of military age.[70] The time lag between the arrival of new camp residents and new donation boxes made for periods of exposure and suffering, but in general the gap between need and resources where clothing was concerned was significantly smaller and more intermittent than was the case at most other camps.

Most slaves in the antebellum Cotton Kingdom (in whose heart Corinth was located) were underfed and malnourished, and that experience carried over to the camp at Corinth's early days, though with less intensity or permanence than at some other camps.[71] When the camp officially opened, residents were issued rations that matched the standard soldier's ration in everything except hominy and soap, both of which suffered from supply shortfalls. Amounts were adjusted in the months that followed (downward in the case of children, who were assumed to have lower caloric needs, for example), and if shipments were delayed or lost, it would be freedpeople who felt the lack before soldiers did, but in general inadequacies resulted less from too few calories than from the sheer monotony of bread, cornmeal, hardtack, salt beef, and salt pork that anyone who ever consumed Union rations complained about—rightfully. Particularly for the sick or those who arrived in camp in weakened condition, the coarseness of standard rations was too hard on enfeebled digestive systems to provide much nourishment, and no Abigail Dutton appeared to start a Special Diet Kitchen like the one at Nashville, so black men and women set to work to remedy the deficiencies.[72] By 1863, they made full use of the seeds and farm implements sent by Northern benevolent organizations to cultivate a 50-acre vegetable garden for their own use and a 175-acre one in which to grow food to sell to the army for extra cash.[73]

Produce improved diet, but poor health remained a constant specter. Missionaries established hospitals, and both the American Missionary Association and the Union army provided medical doctors, but "pnueumonia [*sic*], ... typhoid and congestive fevers" and "measles" remained endemic. Of the 3,637 refugees from slavery at Corinth in the spring of 1863, 900 were sick and 189 had died, 44 of them children.[74] New arrivals were especially vulnerable, often having withstood deprivation before arrival. Moreover, when large numbers arrived at once, the number in need jumped faster than new relief supplies arrived. In 1863, a Missouri sergeant matter-of-factly reported that newly arrived "negroes . . . on the Levee with no clothes on their persons and but a sheet or old Blanket to cover them" were "dying fast for want of something to eat and proper food and clothing and medical attendance."[75] Yet the incidence of dysentery and other intestinal maladies was lower at Corinth than in much of the western theater, and therefore mortality figures were not as catastrophic, partly because nearby Bridge Creek provided a clean, continuous water supply other than the Mississippi River, with its penchant for effluvia and its proneness to flooding.[76]

The atmosphere at Corinth was one of activity. From the moment they arrived, black men, women, and children worked for the army as teamsters, cooks, servants, laundresses, nurses, general laborers, and more, or else they farmed in either the vegetable patches or the hundreds of acres planted in cotton that they harvested and the U.S. government sold at a handsome enough profit to pay wages and bank a surplus. Wages were more generous than usual—fifteen dollars per month— but at Corinth as elsewhere the timing of payment could be sporadic at best. Even more than soldiers, black men and women laboring for the army were likely to go long months between paydays.[77] Learning happened in every corner of time and space that black men and women could snatch for themselves and their children. The American Missionary Association as well as specific Northern church congregations sent teachers and schoolbooks to Corinth, but even before they got there, freedpeople built a schoolhouse and elicited what instruction they could from Union soldiers and from any among their number who could read. By 1863, roughly three hundred children attended school regularly, and often their parents picked up whatever the demands of their workdays allowed. Religious services took place frequently, sometimes led by white missionaries with black participation in both preaching and singing and sometimes conducted exclusively by freedpeople. Black men and women sought to solemnize their unions with marriage ceremonies denied to them in slavery. On just one single Sunday in November, forty weddings took place "in and around Corinth," thirty of them in one large group ceremony. While practical benefits would flow from marriage, once the army authorized black enlistment and recognized some pecuniary obligation to soldiers' wives, wedding in 1862 (before black enlistment) sprang from different motives, partly religious and partly the reclamation of the basic right to family.[78]

Black enlistment changed the demographic makeup of Corinth. At first, black soldiers guarded the camp and conducted raids into northern Alabama to disrupt the Confederate general Braxton Bragg's supply lines. They invariably returned to Corinth with scores of black men, women, and children fleeing from slavery in northern Alabama. One was James Spikes, sometimes called James Spight. In May 1863, Adjutant General Lorenzo Thomas toured the Mississippi valley to recruit men into black regiments, and as part of that trip he and John Eaton paid a visit to Corinth. While Eaton and Thomas were there, James Spikes and most of the Alabama men he had come in with mustered into the First Alabama Infantry of African Descent, later renamed the Fifty-Fifth U.S. Colored Troops. Superintendent James Alexander served as their colonel.[79]

Between the quick response to Adjutant General Thomas's call for black troops, the camp's neat appearance, the thriving civil community, and the smaller-than-typical gap between need and available resources, it is not difficult to see why Corinth was so often and proudly pointed to as an exemplary camp, but if it provided a model of the transition from slavery to freedom at its smoothest, it also served as a cautionary tale of how the exigencies of war constantly threatened contraband camps and their inhabitants. Union forces were at Corinth because it housed a valuable rail junction, which the Confederates wanted back. The army's hold on the depot and encampments themselves was strong, but both regular and irregular Confederate forces prowled just outside lines. They were looking for opportunities to recapture or disable rail lines, and they were intent on "getting all the negars [sic] that they can find and sending them south," so setting foot outside the camp was endlessly perilous.[80] Robert Cartmell, a Confederate civilian who angrily sat out the war near Jackson, Tennessee, noted gleefully in his diary when a small Confederate detachment "stampeded" near Corinth and took some sixty "American Citizens of African Descent." He was just as jubilant half a year later, when he heard that "several hundred negroes has been captured by the Rebels."[81]

Yet Corinth's end came about not as a result of Union defeat or vulnerability but because of its military success. Once the entire length of the Mississippi River came into Union hands, Corinth's tactical value waned. By the beginning of 1864, Union forces controlled enough other miles of railroad track to turn the junction at Corinth from pivotal to peripheral. Determining that the soldiers encamped at Corinth could be more usefully deployed elsewhere, the Union general Stephen Hurlbut ordered the Union evacuation of Corinth on January 11, 1864. From January 23 to January 25, trains shuttled supplies, invalids, and freed-people to Memphis, and then Union forces burned the camp to deprive Confederates of any useful resources it might contain. Confederates came back anyway, re-enslaving any black people they could find and once again turning Corinth into slave country. What Union soldiers did not burn, Confederate ones did when they abandoned Corinth for the last time in January 1865.[82] Despite the military sense that the move might have made to Hurlbut, to the black men, women, and children who had created a thriving community at Corinth, shuttering the Union Christian Church and the school, watching homes built with their own hands burn to the ground, leaving Butler Street and Frémont Street to be trampled by Confederate guerrillas, and abandoning the parade ground and the vegetable patches to be overtaken by weeds were not tactics. They were tragedy.

When the men, women, and children of Corinth got off the train at Memphis, they joined thousands of others already displaced from the camps at Grand Junction, La Grange, Jackson, and Bolivar, which, like Corinth, had sprung up along the rail lines in western Tennessee.[83] In contrast to Corinth's stability and sturdiness (until January 1864), these camps always wore a makeshift aspect, and while they offered slaves escape from their masters, they provided less protection from war's many cruelties than Corinth did. Located in territory stripped so bare by both Union and Confederate armies throughout 1862 and 1863 that a Union officer's wife could not help but regret seeing "the orchards, farms, and houses once beautiful now all gone to ruin," these four camps never quite shook a desolate appearance that stood in contrast to Corinth's gingerbread cottages and flourishing gardens.[84] Camp residents at Bolivar built themselves cabins, but the other locations all remained tent cities, and sometimes there was not even enough canvas to go around. The tents at La Grange were so full that new arrivals huddled under nothing but blankets on their first night and then spent the next day fashioning improbable shelter out of green brush. Even at Bolivar, the flooding Hatchie River compelled freedpeople to dismantle their cabins and stack the boards in order to save the lumber from rotting or floating away.[85] Clothing remained as insubstantial as tents were drafty. Newcomers "dressed in all kind of clothes but mostly of the most ragged kind" might get along all right in August, but when winter came and aid society donations could not keep up with need, the "very indifferent" and "very destitute" state of clothing would mean suffering.[86] Diet was more meager, because these camps lacked Corinth's gardens to supplement the rations provided by the army, although in some cases freedpeople exercised the same resourcefulness they had exercised in slavery to add whatever they could in the way of meat or wildly growing plants. Precarious conditions showed in the state of camp inhabitants' health. One small mercy was that the incidence of dysentery and other intestinal disorders remained in check thanks to the availability of clean water, and another was that none of these camps except La Grange experienced a smallpox outbreak, but there the list of mercies ends. Diseases of exposure, particularly pneumonia, were depressingly prevalent, as were "crowd diseases" like measles.[87]

People moved in and out of these four camps with much more transience than at Corinth. One spring morning in the Tennessee countryside, an enslaved woman who reckoned her own age at "seventy-five or eighty" got up before light to milk the cows, as she did every morning. Crouched next to a cow with her eyes closed and her hands expertly performing their daily duty, she prayed to the sound of milk pinging against the bottom and then the sides of the bucket. When the substitution of soft whoosh for harsh ping told her the bucket was full, she leaned back, steeling herself to face the rest of the day. She opened her eyes and saw "Yankees' heads poppin' up above" the fence. Snatching the bucket of milk, she ran to the kitchen and hastily delivered it before heading out to the yard. There, she told the Union army captain all about "how dey had used us and how dey had 'bused us, all right

before massa's face." Meanwhile, other slaves rounded up four mules
to harness to a farm wagon and chose the four grandest bay horses
to hitch to the master's "fine carriage." As they did, the old woman
gathered children and grandchildren and supervised as they "fetched
out our old bags and old beds" and tossed them into the wagon. Then
she and thirty-one former slaves climbed into the carriage and rode
into the camp at La Grange, where they formed a semicircle around
the superintendent's tent "to have their names and ages registered." Yet
as much as the woman's "heart almos' jumped out of me for joy," she
couldn't have remained settled for long, because in a matter of weeks
the La Grange camp was closed for good. She might have ended up in
Memphis, which after the closure of Corinth in 1864 functioned as a
veritable hub for the area, or she might have shuttled back and forth
between Bolivar and Jackson, as escaped slaves from other plantations
in her region did. Jackson, in particular, was in need of repeated but
temporary labor through May and the first week of June 1863, sending
a flurry of requisitions to Bolivar for groups of "contrabands" to put to
work growing cotton, foraging, laboring on the railroad, or working
in the General Hospital there.[88] Any of them still in Jackson by June
7 probably found themselves in the middle of a blinding thunder-and-
lightning storm, standing with "thousands and thousands" in a long
"black line" waiting to get on a train to Corinth or to Memphis before
an anticipated Confederate raid burned them out.[89]

It is possible but less likely that the old woman and her family went
to the camp at Grand Junction, Tennessee, at least if she had anything
to say about it, for treatment of former slaves at Grand Junction by the
army was poorer than anywhere else in the area. As Grant explained to
President Lincoln, "negroes coming into our lines" met with "kind or
abusive treatment according to [the] peculiar views of the troops they
first came in contact with" in any given place.[90] While superintendents
of contrabands throughout the region reported either indifferent or good
relations between the army, aid workers, and refugees from slavery, the
superintendent at Grand Junction encountered "no cooperation—any
amount of opposition" and was "in some cases unable to procure suitable rations, quarters or guards." To make matters worse, former slaves
who brought oxen, yokes, wagons, chains, mules, or sometimes even a

coveted horse into Grand Junction generally found "much taken from them by officers and soldiers."[91] Things could also get dodgy at Jackson, because it lacked a designated camp superintendent to buffer the ill will of General John McClernand, the commander of the Thirteenth Corps until June 1863. McClernand was a Democratic politician with pro-slavery leanings and an inveterate opponent of anything that his superior officer, Ulysses S. Grant, did, including extending sanctuary, however haphazard, to refugees from slavery.[92]

Whatever their surroundings, freedpeople in these camps as elsewhere carried on with their lives: they bore children and buried children; they played marbles and held prayer meetings; they foraged through the countryside for food and furniture; they hid possessions from thieving Union soldiers and shared what they had with each other. Above all, they worked. By the summer of 1862, they were building fortifications at Bolivar and Grand Junction. They sought situations with the army as cooks, laundresses, and personal servants to officers. They cut hay and grew cotton on abandoned plantations. They repaired and maintained rail lines. They chopped wood and carried water. In these camps as at so many others, they kept the massive logistical undertaking that was the Union war effort afloat.[93]

Yet no amount of labor could shield Grand Junction, La Grange, Jackson, and Bolivar from the constant threat of Confederate attack. Both soldiers and freedpeople at Bolivar were so exposed in August 1862 that four hundred black men rushed to build fortifications out of the only materials readily at hand: dirt and confiscated cotton bales.[94] Threats to Grand Junction as the year 1863 opened drove John Eaton to order the evacuation of the entire population to Memphis for two months before returning to Grand Junction. Even then, no permanent guard was established, and camp residents remained vulnerable to "robbery and all manner of violence."[95] Sometimes former slaves got the better of would-be captors; once, a mounted band of Confederates galloped up to kidnap a group working in abandoned fields near La Grange, only to have one black man step coolly out from behind a fence to send a bullet "crashing through [the] ribs and heart" of the band's leader.[96] Many other refugees from slavery were not so lucky. More than once, Union soldiers found dead or dying freedpeople lying in ditches or by roadsides, abandoned after being shot by guerrillas.[97]

UP THE RIVER:
ST. LOUIS, CAIRO, AND COLUMBUS

To the enslaved, the Mississippi was like the circulatory system of the Cotton Kingdom, leading, for long years, deeper into slavery, but now they hoped to make it carry them in different directions. To flee bondage, they moved up and down it, sometimes seeking refuge with the Union army, sometimes moving from camp to camp, willing the river's throb and pulse to take them to where they could breathe the air of liberty. Sometimes, the river prevented them from breathing at all. In the winter of 1863, its waters swelled. On February 1, the men of the Thirty-Third Iowa had to cut a levee above Helena, and the high river "rushed through the narrow opening so fiercely as to flood" sections of Helena, including low-lying portions of Camp Ethiopia.[98] By spring, churning floodwaters washed more dirt, more disease, more catastrophe, and more suffering into Helena. A distraught general Benjamin Prentiss cried out, "Sickness rages fearfully among them in this unhealthy location" because of all the infernal flooding.[99] But those same rushing waters, he realized, might also provide a way out. "To better their condition and save their lives I sent a boat load of them north," he wrote.[100] Fifteen hundred sailed out of Helena on one day at the end of February, hundreds more at a time as the spring progressed.[101]

Plenty of freedpeople clambered onto steamers themselves, quite apart from orders from Prentiss. Charles Davis and his wife and two little boys, Willie and George, escaped Arkansas that way. They were part of a multitude who climbed aboard side wheelers, stern wheelers, paddle wheelers, flatboats, and mail packets, who rode the *Rocket*, the *Jesse K. Bell*, the *Keokuk*, the *Emma*, the *Bostona*, and dozens of others. Once Davis got his family settled near St. Louis, he went back to the river, earning a living aboard the steamer *Marble City*, a side wheeler owned by the Memphis and St. Louis Packet Line and hired to the army to operate chiefly between St. Louis and Cairo. The river swarmed with boats like the one on which Davis worked, as well as with steamers officially commissioned within the Mississippi River Squadron. The U.S.S. *Ouachita*, for example, churned up and down the river, fueled by the fire that John Wesly tended, kept in repair by the blacksmith Nolly Flenoy and the mechanic Peter Reason, and kept afloat by the labor of Nelson Boily, Martin McDermot, Maimnus Chisholm, and other men and boys who had fled Arkansas, Kentucky, South Carolina, and Tennessee to make their way to river towns like Cairo in search of work and a way out of slavery.[102] Sometimes the packets and steamers on which Davis, Flenoy, Boily, and countless others worked carried soldiers. Sometimes they carried crates stamped with "B.C." for Brigade Commissary, though everybody joked that "B.C." actually stood for the manufacturing date of the rations contained inside the crates. Sometimes ships transported sick and wounded for treatment at Northern hospitals. Sometimes they carried the remains of a dead soldier whose family was wealthy enough to afford a metal coffin and influential enough to persuade the Union army to ship the coffin home. Sometimes they carried hoes and seeds and schoolbooks for distribution among former slaves. In the flooding spring of 1863, they also carried black refugees fleeing slavery.[103]

Charles Davis would have seen plenty of such freedom seekers, because St. Louis and Cairo, along with Columbus, Kentucky, less than half a day's steamboat ride from Cairo, were major destinations that spring.[104] None of the three destinations was free from peril. As a steamer from Helena set out for St. Louis in February, General Samuel Curtis was anything but pleased. He had a war to fight and "prominent citizens" to placate while he did so. Some of those citizens remained loyal to both slavery and the Union, probably in that order, and he worried that threats to the former would shake the latter. Others in this deeply divided city dearly hoped slavery and Union *would* clash and the result would be no more slavery, but they worried that in the meantime liberty for anyone with black skin was too precarious to entrust to the locals and thought that former slaves' freedom would be safer farther up the river.[105]

By the time the sound of the steamboat's whistle rang on the St. Louis shore, Curtis put his worries about the delicate issue of slaveholder loyalty to one side and concentrated instead on the fifteen hundred former slaves about to dock at the city's edge. He hired out the Missouri Hotel on the corner of Main and Morgan Streets to serve as barracks, hospital, schoolhouse, and headquarters for the newly forming St. Louis Ladies' Contraband Relief Society. He placed Chaplain Samuel Sawyer in charge of relief. Immediate efforts focused on food, clothing, and medicine for the weary refugees who trudged from the dock to the hotel, holding children's hands, carrying fussy babies, lugging meager stores of bedding and clothing, and clutching sacks or packets or parcels containing any portable reminders of homes they had left behind. Within the month, most had found employment, working either for the army, for St. Louis County employers able to convince the good ladies of the Contraband Relief Society of their loyalty, or for farming families farther north in need of labor. Those still in St. Louis could attend the proper schoolhouse that the Ladies' Contraband Relief Society managed to scrounge up to take the place of the cramped hotel quarters; there they learned to read from two teachers commissioned by the American Missionary Association.[106]

While few individuals remained in the Missouri Hotel for long, new ones arrived frequently, and soon other locations were pressed into service as barracks. The following year, the army's superintendent of mechanics requisitioned "lumber, fencing, nails, roofing, brick, and lime, and labor" to construct a "building 400 feet long 32 feet deep 10 feet high in each story to be divided in 80 equal appartments of 20 × 16 feet," intended from the outset to house refugees from slavery.[107] But for men, women, and children seeking a route out of slavery, nothing in St. Louis, any more than anywhere else in the western theater, remained still or constant for long. Within months, Confederate sympathizers burned the new apartment building to the ground.[108]

The relocated Arkansas river man Charles Davis and his family had secured their own living arrangements by that time, so the arson did not uproot them, but Davis certainly saw the effects of constant resettlement as he continued to earn his living on the *Marble City*, chugging back and forth between St. Louis and the town that once again became a major destination for the displaced: Cairo, Illinois. In that soggy spring, Cairo was most notable for mud and rats, but freedpeople made the best they could of it.[109] By that time, hospitals and barracks were up and running under the jurisdiction of the conscientious if often overwhelmed superintendent, Chaplain James B. Rogers. Roughly four hundred black children attended schools.[110]

That spring, five women and three men gathered in Mrs. Maria Renfro's house on Fifteenth Street between Walnut and Cedar to form the American Methodist Episcopal Church of Cairo. They hosted a revival, to which the boatloads coming in from the South responded so generously that they swelled church membership beyond what Mrs. Renfro's house could hold. The congregation relocated to the corner of Sixteenth Street and Washington Avenue, part of what would grow into a corridor of black schools, churches, and community institutions all along Washington Avenue.[111] New arrivals needed all the support they could get from the church or anywhere else, because sickness continued to fester in a city so low-lying that Superintendent Rogers continually referred to Cairo as a "tub," and a medical inspector once reported "filth enough in many of its streets to poison all the population of New York City."[112]

Between disease, scarcity, and violence, life could be fragile in Cairo, as two toddlers named Ann and Millie learned to their sorrow. Their enslaved mother risked everything to get herself and her daughters out of slavery. She managed to escape and make it to Cairo. Once there, she worked in an army hospital under the supervision of the surgeon Simeon Bicknell. Yet even then, the determined young mother was not safe. According to one account, she died of whooping cough, and according to another source she was murdered by another refugee from slavery, but in either version she left behind two little girls under the age of four. Dr. Bicknell adopted Ann and took her home after the war to raise her as a sister to his own children but apart from the sister of her infancy.[113]

Ann and Millie were too young to have much say over their fate, but grown men and women who tired of the mud and rats of Cairo might ride a steamer half a day's journey to Columbus, Kentucky, and try their luck there.[114] In the war's early days, Confederates used enslaved labor to fortify the port town on the banks of the Mississippi but then abandoned it in 1862 in the wake of the fall of Fort Henry.[115]

Black laborers who could avoid evacuating with the Confederate army did so and were soon joined by black men, women, and children streaming in, drawn by the same hopes that drew the enslaved to Fort Monroe, Cairo, Hatteras Island, and anywhere else occupied by men with guns pointed in the direction of slaveholders. The Union quartermaster commandeered four frame-sided buildings near the corner of Clarke and Dabney Streets to turn into the Freedman's Hospital and ordered the construction of a "tenement" for "families of freemans and refugees" three hundred yards from the main depot on the banks of the Mississippi. By the end of the year, the "tenement" was overcrowded enough to necessitate the building of another one.[116] Everyone who lived in it worked. One benefit at Columbus was that pay came more regularly than at many locations, and there is no doubt it was earned. Black workers cut wood to fuel the incessant steamboat traffic. They tended livestock. They dug graves. They drove teams of horses. Full-grown men ditched constantly, although that particular form of labor was too heavy for children. Even very young children could and did take up shovels and brooms to clean up wood shavings around the goat pens to minimize the risk of fire.[117]

On Christmas Eve 1862, rumors of Confederate attack whirled into Columbus. Captain John C. Cox, the commissary, received orders to unload every government warehouse in Columbus and haul all contents "from storehouses onto wharf boats and steamers" so that government supplies could be shipped out of Confederate reach, if the rumored attack actually came. What followed was no silent night. Cox rounded up every ship or boat he could find. If it would float, it would do. He also sent to the tenement for every man, woman, and child to report to the docks. All night long, strong arms lifted crates of hardtack, bacon, boots, and ordnance, handed off coils of rope, and rolled hogsheads of flour out of the long, low government warehouses. Weary feet tromped from docks up gangplanks, stowing and stashing goods into every corner of every ship. Even children could scurry back and forth with armloads of order blanks and ledger books. By the time the first faint beams of light streaked the sky, every stick and stash and store was on board a boat in the Mississippi River, except for the very last sacks of flour and some bread, which were loaded in the Christmas dawn. All night long, former slaves worked, while a Union line from Jackson, Tennessee, to Columbus, Kentucky, blunted Confederates' strikes on the railroad tracks. The Union line held, but none of the black women passing heavy crates from arm to arm knew if an attack would come. None of the men hefting barrels knew. None of the children shimming and sliding crates into every available inch of space knew. What they knew that Christmas morning was exhaustion.[118]

They also knew danger, which stalked Cairo, Columbus, and St. Louis that day and every day, not only in the obvious ways like threatened attack, but also in the ever-present risk of kidnapping. A white man named Yocum thought he spied a golden opportunity, so he sought a job working for the superintendent of contrabands at Cairo. From that position, he could spot who was weak and vulnerable, and he could tell which former slaves were on their own and unlikely to be noticed if one day they did not return to the barracks. He had just the right contacts—friends like Frederick Huston, who worked as a clerk on the steamer *Armada,* and men like Jessie McComb and J. K. Gant, who knew how to sell and buy human beings without questions asked. For a while, Yocum kept his eye on a young boy named Morris, who worked in the Quartermaster Department and kept himself to himself. One night, Yocum pointed Morris out to McComb and Gant. They awaited their chance, then tied Morris up and got him ready to sell. If Yocum was feeling more ambitious and wanted to sell more than one person at a time, he might get in touch with John Atcher, known to move small bands in one go. And if he was worried about the "merchandise" being recognized in Cairo, he could hand a victim off to Huston to smuggle aboard the *Armada* on one of its regular runs to Columbus. At Columbus, Huston would wait for dark, then smuggle his captive off the boat and out of camp, to some slave traders who would share the profits with Huston and Yocum. One time, Huston bungled his part, and the boy he was supposed to sell got away and told his story to the Columbus post commander. Huston ducked back onto the *Armada,* cursing his lost profit but hoping to get back to Cairo and avoid detection. Instead, Brigadier General A. J. Smith wired ahead to have Huston arrested once the *Armada* docked at Cairo. Both Huston and Yocum were arrested by the provost marshal and held in jail until the end of the year, when they were transported to Washington, D.C., to face trial.[119] Meanwhile, authorities remained on the lookout for the ringleaders and masterminds of the scheme. Local authorities, and even the governor of Illinois, grew so alarmed, or possibly embarrassed, by the whole sordid mess that one of them even wrote to President Lincoln about it.[120]

St. Louis had its own problems with "rebels, speculators, & kidnappers," according to District Judge Advocate Lucien Eaton, who might just as well have added police and city officials to the list of participants in that city's distinctive kidnapping rings.[121] The Missouri senator Benjamin Gratz Brown testified in November 1863 that for a time freedpeople "taking refuge here [in St. Louis] were arrested and imprisoned, and sold for jail fees," generally by the police at public auction, although he maintained that by November that practice "has been entirely broken up."[122]

Whether or not the kidnapping threat had actually passed by late 1863, Union authorities intent on doing something about it authorized another surge of dislocation. From a safety perspective, orders to move seemed "palpably reasonable and necessary," but to those swept up in the directive, it still felt like one more instance of getting tossed around in the violent currents that accompanied slavery's end in western contraband camps.[123] Once spring came, Superintendent John Eaton ordered a subordinate to visit Cairo and Columbus, take note of conditions there, and then send Eaton his honest opinion "upon the necessity or expediency of removing the contraband camp at Cairo to some point out of the State of Illinois" to put a stop to the abduction rings.[124] When he got the report back, Eaton was convinced of "the great & imperative necessity of" resettling freedpeople "then at Cairo and Columbus" farther down the Mississippi River on Union-held Islands Number Sixty and Number Ten. Each island was "a military post & therefore secure from hostile attack and will remove them sooner also from kidnapping and many other difficulties." Moreover, the islands contained hundreds of acres of "rich arable lands," which would be perfect for conversion into what Eaton called "agricultural colonies" of black men, women, and children, kept safe from the twin evils of starvation and idleness by the honest toil of farming.[125]

In the waning days of March, Major General Stephen Hurlbut issued Special Orders No. 40, which accomplished precisely what Eaton advised—relocating freedpeople from Cairo and Columbus to Islands Number Ten and Number Sixty—for exactly the same purpose: to "cultivate the soil" in a place less vulnerable to abduction, which Eaton cited. That April, government steamers began transporting black men, women, and children to their next stop on the often baffling path out of slavery.[126]

Not everyone agreed to leave. Cairo might be full of mud, rats, and kidnappers, but it was also home to the AME Church and to a fledgling black community taking shape along the Washington Avenue corridor, and some African Americans preferred to take their chances there. In 1864, the Northwestern Freedmen's Aid Commission continued to ship clothes, shoes, books, and slates and still sponsored teachers.[127] Even at the end of the war, "freedmen and families in the employ of the Q [uarter] M[aster] Dept" at Cairo still lived in government barracks by the railroad tracks, which the quartermaster recommended "be given to the freedmen who have been in the employ of the department."[128] Still others had made their own living and working arrangements throughout the city. One former slave, Frank Price, worked as a police officer, which was saying something in a town whose jails almost always held one or more toughs locked up for beating or threatening black people.[129]

For many, what made the prospect of departure difficult was not so much the loss of barracks space or job opportunities as the prospect of yet more separation from loved ones. In the days before the government steamer's departure for Island Number Ten, Laura Haviland, an aid worker from Michigan, arrived in Cairo and accepted her first duty, which was to distribute clothing for the journey throughout the island and to help reassure the freedpeople about to be relocated that "they would never see the day again when they would be separated by being sold apart." Haviland's words were sweet but hollow to a mother whose eight-year-old son lay dying. The woman's husband and other children had been sold away years earlier, and now her only remaining child was far too ill to travel. Haviland accompanied her back to the child's sickbed, and "an hour later and the baby of eight years was in the spirit world." Time for the woman to stop delaying and get on board before the boat sailed at three o'clock. Still, she could not do it. She could not face the thought of her child buried hastily in the mud, where wharf rats were sure to gnaw his face. "I don't want to leave my chile on dis bare groun," she insisted to Haviland. Only the promise that Haviland herself would get a coffin made, and oversee the burial of the child in it, induced the woman to trudge, alone, up the plank and onto the steamer.[130]

Like the bereft mother, many went to Island Number Ten or Island

Number Sixty however heavy their hearts. The first boat left Cairo on April 7, 1863, stopped briefly at Columbus, and then proceeded onto Island Number Ten, loaded down with canvas for tents, crates of supplies, freedpeople, and whatever baggage they might tote.[131] Blossoms on hundreds of apple and peach trees greeted their arrival, offering a rare glimpse of beauty amid the usual mayhem of the emancipation process. Blossoms also reminded uprooted refugees that April was still early enough to get a crop in, but only barely, so it was straight to work with "plows, with harrows, hoes, axes, rakes, and garden and field seeds" donated by churches throughout Indiana and Ohio.[132] Later steamers carried lumber to build cabins, and one even brought Laura Haviland and her barrels of bedding, cotton shirts, wool socks, serge suits, and, most beloved of all, little girls' dresses, each with a pocket containing a two-inch-tall rag doll.[133] Paddle wheelers, side wheelers, and mail boats also carried more and more refugees from slavery. While waiting for crops to grow and peaches and apples to ripen, some of the men and older boys, and even some of the stronger women, worked in wood yards, reducing the island's forest cover into fuel for the voracious steamboat fleets that plied the Mississippi.[134] Even the extra employment could not slow the spring rains, or the pace of continued arrivals to the islands, and it did not take long to reduce the woodlands to "flat, almost treeless waste."[135] Overcrowding threatened within the month, and on the sixth of May, General Asboth recommended "a new contraband colony be established at the New Madrid Bend" because "Island No. 10 is already full."[136]

In that way, western emancipation continued its surging, swelling, uprooting motion, continually sweeping men, women, and children up and then setting them down elsewhere. They were certainly not the passive recipients of emancipation, driftwood caught up in an uncomprehended stream, that our comfortable versions of the Civil War and emancipation told us they were for so long. They did everything they could to get themselves to that river, and then they swam or paddled or rowed or took any number of heroic measures to keep afloat and make it to the high ground of freedom. Still, a river like the Mississippi is bigger than people are, especially when it is flooding, and the same was true of emancipation: there were times when no human effort could swim against all its crosscurrents, any more than human effort could swim against what one aid worker called "this broad, rushing, yellow flood" of the Mississippi River.[137]

PRESIDENT'S ISLAND, MEMPHIS

At the end of May 1863, Asboth established another new colony, this one on President's Island, a dollop of land in the Mississippi River adjacent to the city of Memphis.[138] Freedpeople who had taken refuge in the settlements and contraband camps throughout Tennessee and northern Mississippi found themselves swept back and forth with the Union army's shifting lines, much as refugees along the river found themselves swirled about by flooding waters, and many of them also landed in Memphis alongside evacuees from Cairo, Columbus, Island Number Ten, and Island Number Sixty. Tent cities called Camp Shiloh, Camp Bethel, and Camp Holly Springs burgeoned on a bluff of "clayey earth, gulleyed & scooped," and one formerly enslaved boy spent his days running a ferry the short distance from those settlements to President's Island. Another former slave, this one a grown man named Stephen Wright, oversaw the black police force that took shape on President's Island. Also nearby was "a neat camp, with spruce, orderly looking troops," the Sixty-First U.S. Colored Troops.[139]

The juxtaposition of several contraband camps and the encampment of black Union soldiers made for both joy and sorrow. The mingling of so many freedpeople from so many locations sometimes helped unite families. One day, amid the muck and the tents and the din of President's Island, a woman named Susie thought she heard her name called by a voice she recognized but had not heard in a decade and a half. Then she heard it again, and when she turned and looked, there stood the sister she had not seen since the day, fifteen years earlier, when her sister's lashed and broken body had been sold in punishment for the fierce and unstoppable grieving she had been doing since the sale of her sons, Susie's nephews, two years before. At first, the sisters could only clutch each other, not able to say a word, and then when fifteen years of distance and silence welled up, it broke out in a stream of feeling simply incapable of being contained by mere words. Finally, when Susie's sister could speak, she had even more joy to share: the two little boys sold seventeen years earlier, the boys she refused to kill off in her mind, were here, too, now almost grown.[140]

Along with reunions, the proximity of camps facilitated unions, and lots of them. Weddings happened twenty at a time, sometimes adding a legal gloss to unions years or decades old but denied legal marriage under slavery, sometimes reuniting spouses once separated by sale, and sometimes bringing young couples together in first marriages. Union officers were especially eager to solemnize marriages between black soldiers and their wives, partly to qualify the spouses for any benefits that marriage to a Union soldier might bring, and partly to impose order and Northern middle-class ideas about how society ought to be organized out of the disorder and chaos of a society transitioning out of slavery.[141]

At the same time, Union officers' chief priorities were to wage and win a war, which meant that the proximity of contraband camps and black soldiers sometimes led to the all-too-familiar heartbreak of family separation. In 1864 and 1865, a series of orders limited contact between black soldiers and freedpeople in contraband camps and the city of Memphis generally. Increasingly, former slaves not in the army were supposed to be on President's Island, and black soldiers were supposed to stay in camp on the mainland, except on specially designated visiting days. Officers insisted that military discipline and the health of their troops made such policies necessary for two reasons: the freedwomen who were genuinely the wives of soldiers distracted their husbands from military duty, and the freedwomen who were not wives spread disease and moral dissolution among the men through prostitution, according to white officers.[142]

Authorities exaggerated and overreacted to incidences of prostitution, but they did not make them up, for some freedwomen in Memphis were driven by the same age-old destitution that had pressed women in need since the dawn of recorded history. Most refugees from slavery who arrived at Union lines in Memphis got there hungry, even to the point of desperation. One man had not been sure if his mistress's tales about Yankees who boiled slaves to eat were true or not, and for a long time he had not wanted to risk it, but then she so thoroughly locked up all provisions that starvation was coming one way or another. Expecting that if they stayed put, he and his family would "die anyhow," the man resolved to "try de Yankees." On arrival, he found rations rather than boiling cauldrons and decided that Yankees were more likely to keep his family "alive, instead of killin'."[143]

The roll of the dice worked for that family but not for all. Rations sometimes went down to half rations for women and quarter rations for children, and Congress severely limited federal spending on freedpeople's medical care from the summer of 1864 to the fall of 1865. "Pnuemonia [sic], rapid in progress, sometimes terminating fatally twelve hours after the attack, typhoid, congestive fevers of a low grade, measles," and "gangrene" proliferated, often fatally.[144] Scarcity extended to more than just food and medical care. Missionaries came with supply barrels and schoolbooks, and doctors came with their well-intentioned but inadequate supplies of medicine, but the daily influx of people meant that shortages never abated. Neither did overcrowding. Freedpeople built cabins at the Holly Springs camp and on President's Island as fast as they could and as long as building supplies held out, but tents and lean-tos remained the only thin membranes that ever shielded many residents of Memphis's camps from the elements.[145] When William Allen visited President's Island one Sunday, he joined freedpeople in worship and listened to them sing a hymn about both death and survival. The hymn was fitting, because camps at Memphis held both death and survival in intricate choreography, neither one able to predominate over the other permanently, and neither disappearing, either.[146]

VICKSBURG

Death and survival also danced at Vicksburg, Mississippi, especially in the summer of 1863 following the Union army's capture of that riverfront city after a long siege that had reduced all the city's inhabitants, black and white, to near starvation. In the very last days before the city's surrender, small bands of Confederate troops, operating on the age-old military tactic of denying the enemy anything of use, had burned and destroyed crops, cotton gins, and buildings. They also ranged up and down the riverbank for miles, rounding up the most productive black workers to drive deeper into Confederate territory, out of the Union army's reach.[147] Two of those workers were six-year-old Matilda Bass's parents, who were forced to leave their daughter behind to face the mayhem without them.[148] From the Mississippi River, steamboat passengers witnessed "ascending columns of smoke rising from the burning ruins" and noticed that black "men, women, and children sick and well, in tattered garments which scarcely covered their nakedness were crouching in groups behind the friendly bank at the water's edge, in evident dread lest their pursuers should find them." Mothers tried to hush crying babies, and terrified children clung to their mothers' legs and skirts. Some of the refugees clutched tattered bags, others hugged ragged bundles to their chests, and a few held tight to "an old frying pan, bucket, pot, or basket, or such other article as could be hastily seized and carried." Most had absolutely nothing except grim determination to get away. One desperate group found an "old skiff" and climbed aboard, two or three at a time, to sail to a sandbar in the river and huddle under "sheds of brush."[149]

When Vicksburg came into Union hands just days later on July 4, so did control of the whole extent of the Mississippi River, and refugees streamed into the city. They looked to a Union-held Vicksburg as "the very gate of heaven" compared with slavery. Freedpeople were jubilant that Independence Day as they gathered along the levee "laughing and rejoicing with inexpressible delight." But they were also hungry and desperate. Overnight, the army found itself in charge of new camps and thousands of destitute refugees from slavery: 3,000 opposite Vicksburg, 8,550 at Young's Point, 2,800 at Paw Paw Island, 2,400 at the Yazoo River, and at least 1,000 at Goodrich's Landing. More followed in the successive months and weeks.[150]

The jubilation did not last long, for the merciless months of siege that preceded Vicksburg's fall scarred the city and its environs, even by wartime standards, and everybody suffered there. Quite simply, there was no food, medicine, or clothing to be had, and extended bombardment had destroyed block upon block of buildings that might have provided shelter. As John Eaton put it in a masterpiece of understatement, Union soldiers and officers "have had some new insight into the necessities of life."[151] Sick and wounded men of the Twenty-Seventh Missouri Infantry had lost their baggage on their long march to Vicksburg and now wore "only the remains of a shirt, and that as filthy as weeks lying in dirt could well make both it and the wearer." Most "were lying on oilcloths or blankets spread on the ground" with at least each other for company, but one dying infantryman, "literally besmeared with his own evacuations and sending forth a stench intolerable," had been dragged away some distance "as one who could not live and whose presence could not be borne longer," left to die alone with "a piece of ticking besmeared as his body, partially covering his filthy form."[152]

Yet if everyone suffered, freedpeople, especially "the poor colored woman and child," stood a singularly "small chance of special attention to their protection or comfort at the time of surrender," and they suffered most of all.[153] They huddled in churches, in caves, and "on the vacant lots and pavement." Occasionally, a soldier would share some "biscuit" from his own drastically reduced rations, but often there was just plain no food to be had. Whole rooms were filled with people simply waiting to die. Sometimes a man or woman would be able to summon enough final strength to crawl off into weeds to die alone, saving weakened survivors the job of removing another corpse, but often the ill and weakened simply died where they were.[154]

It did not take long for disease to maraud through the city, lingering longest and most mercilessly among former slaves. Within a month, at least four hundred were dead, and officer after officer assigned to work among the refugees sickened and died, too. Union authorities, fearing an epidemic among their troops, inaugurated a ruthless quarantine. Each day, soldiers prodded, forced, and hauled black men, women, and children into boats and sailed them across the Mississippi to the banks on the opposite side of soldiers' encampments. Whether or not the expanse of river prevented germs from traveling to healthy troops, it certainly made the task of getting rations to freedpeople even harder, and hunger drove former slaves to the desperate act of boiling mud in hopes of extracting some nutrient from it. With no chance to put a crop in so late in the summer, the year ahead looked even bleaker. By the end of the summer, some freedpeople even voiced the wish to be back home.[155]

Members of Northern benevolent organizations began packing their own travel satchels as soon as news of Vicksburg's fall reached Northern newspapers, and within weeks the first arrived to investigate conditions in and around Vicksburg. What they saw appalled them. "Camp life and few rations may be the best things that can be done at first for the freedman," wrote one agent of the Cincinnati-based Western Sanitary Commission, "but if the ostensible object was to kill him, nothing could be more effective."[156] Few wasted time on moral posturing. Officers of the Western Sanitary Commission wrote to President Lincoln, "not to find fault, but to seek for the remedy."[157] Meanwhile, Daniel Flickinger and Bishop Edwards, both members of the American Missionary Association, traveled from their homes in Ohio to the White House. A disheveled Lincoln, so "weary and care worn" that he could barely shuffle around "in his shirt sleeves," met them, and one of the men told the president, "I hope God will be with you." Lincoln flashed a quick smile and answered warmly, "It is much more important that I be with God, for He is always right."[158] The AMA missionaries and the Western Sanitary Commission agents requested free transit for aid workers and free shipping for donated supplies on army boats and on the railroads, and they got both, along with food rations when and where any were available.[159]

Enormous need never vanished from Vicksburg, but by the fall efforts to redress it began to make a dent, however inadequate and uneven. As soon as Daniel Flickinger got home, he put together a group of ten ministers and eight women to head to Vicksburg.[160] Churches around the country followed suit. J. H. Buchanan, pastor of Allegheny, Pennsylvania's Presbyterian church, headed straight to Vicksburg, established a home base, and then sent for parishioners to join him in what a church member described as "an opportunity . . . afforded to the churches of the nation to atone in part for the wrongs inflicted upon the African in this country."[161] African American members of a Cleveland voluntary association might not have thought in terms of "atonement," but they were just as quick to head to Vicksburg.[162] A stream of barrels packed with nonperishable food, bedding, shoes, and clothing flowed from every state in the Midwest, and by November sickness among the Union army ranks had abated sufficiently for a stable corps of officers to remain alive long enough to distribute the desperately needed relief.[163]

Stabilization in the army also opened up the possibility for paid work, and former slaves became "employees of the Government numbered by thousands."[164] A large group of black Methodists "who had been slaves in the city, and liberated by the results of the war," had "suffered at first" but were "laboring in the Commissary and Quartermaster's Departments . . . supporting their families" and were once again able to gather for worship by the fall.[165] By the end of 1863, hardship remained staggering—the Ladies' Contraband Relief Society of St. Louis still received "a great many urgent requests . . . and the need seemed to be greatest in and about Vicksburg"—but concerted and systematic, if still insufficient, efforts to alleviate suffering contrasted with the utter chaos that swirled around in the weeks immediately following Vicksburg's surrender.[166]

As 1864 began, medical care in particular garnered priority attention. Special Orders No. 114 established a network of hospitals and a system for running and supplying them identical to the one that applied to the Union army. The order also assigned surgeons, who varied widely in their competence and decency toward freedpeople but all of whom were regulated by the same requirements that bound doctors in army hospitals. Perhaps most important, the surgeon David O. McCord of the Sixty-Third U.S. Colored Infantry was appointed medical director for the Freedmen's Department of Mississippi and Arkansas, for McCord was genuinely dedicated to the work.[167] By the summer of 1864, Vicksburg's Freedmen's Hospital featured "large and well-ventilated" wards for men and women, as well as a maternity ward, and mortality rates there compared favorably with hospitals anywhere in the nineteenth-century United States.[168]

Conditions in general improved enough in the first half of 1864 for freedpeople to begin to rebuild life in the face of death. Relief supplies from the Western Freedmen's Aid Commission and the Northwestern Freedmen's Aid Commission flowed in fairly steadily, augmented by the proceeds from a large fair held in St. Louis over the last two weeks in May by the Ladies' Contraband Relief Society.[169] Comparative stability enabled more and more to find paid work in army wood yards and hospitals as well as for the Quartermaster and Commissary Departments. Others worked as servants, cooks, or laundresses, and still others found work apart from the army altogether (akin to working "on the economy" rather than on post at a military installation today). Enough freedpeople had enough money in their pockets to begin to strike entrepreneurial types (white and black) as a lucrative potential market, and the provost marshal began receiving multiple requests for permits to open dry goods stores specifically catering to freedpeople.[170]

Teachers arrived and so did schoolbooks. A superintendent coordinated a citywide educational system, and in a city where one year earlier former slaves had crawled into weeds to die or fought for life amid "filth and festering disease in wretched dog-kennels where the eye of humanity never penetrated," they now crowded into schoolrooms around shared books and slates.[171] Most vulnerable still were orphaned children, who at first huddled in hospitals or on the streets. By the spring of 1864, an orphan asylum offered shelter to hundreds of boys and girls left on their own, though it is doubtful that the conditions were particularly appealing.[172]

What did help children turn back toward life after all the dislocation and death was the stabilization in a growing number of adult freedpeople's circumstances, which allowed them to take in the orphaned, just as slaves had done when sale wrenched parent and child apart. By the summer of 1864, Josephine Johnston had gotten her feet under herself, at least a little bit. She even had a place to live, near the fire engine house on the Jackson Road, and so she took in five-year-old Julia and eight-year-old Jane, who had been sleeping at the Freedmen's Hospital, ensuring that whatever else the war took away, the two sisters had each other.[173] Sometimes such acts of kindness made miracles possible. They made it possible for someone like six-year-old Matilda Bass—who had been on her own since her owners had marched strong workers like her parents down to Texas—to remain alive, and after the war her parents came back and found her.[174] In short, one year after Vicksburg came into Union hands, Surgeon McCord was embroidering a bit, but he was not lying when he said of the condition of freedpeople in that city, "Order was brought out of confusion; what had been a disgrace to the Government was made to contribute to its honor."[175]

But time did not stop in the middle of 1864 any more than it had stood still in 1863. Black men, women, and children from the surrounding countryside continued to make their way to Union lines. They came in greater numbers than the army's "systematic efforts" and aid societies' benevolent donations could have succored, even if every soldier and officer bore goodwill toward former slaves, which not all did. As cooler weather approached, women and children once again lacked the warm clothing to make it through the winter. Approaching winter also sent more people scrambling for shelter among the bombed-out hulls of what once were Vicksburg's buildings. Left with few options, more

former slaves crowded into the wretched Refugees Home, hastily established in a building that had been so badly damaged during the city's
1863 bombardment that plaster lay in heaps on the floor, which itself was
pocked with treacherous holes. Windows were "shattered, the weath-
erboarding left in patches, and the fences torn away," and "every nook
and corner were saturated with human excrement."[176] To make matters
worse, the secretary of war, the surgeon general, and the Department
of the Treasury became embroiled in a scuffle over who should pay for
freedmen's hospitals, with the predictable result that for a while nobody
did, and desperate need and contagious disease came roaring back.[177]
And so it continued in Vicksburg, as throughout the Mississippi valley, and indeed throughout the western theater. Collectively, hardship
sometimes ameliorated and other times worsened, just as individuals'
own trajectories hurtled between grace and misfortune. Nothing—not
wretchedness, not relief, not liberty—remained static for long.

PLANTATION LEASING SCHEMES
IN THE MISSISSIPPI VALLEY

The most obvious factor influencing conditions in wartime contraband
camps like those in and around Vicksburg was the course of the war,
but another factor in the Mississippi valley was the plantation leasing
scheme, a method by which Union authorities hoped simultaneously to
alleviate camp overcrowding and make money. The practice of moving refugees from slavery out of disease-ridden contraband camps and
onto Union-held plantations helped even out excessive population density, but it also came with its own set of very definite drawbacks.[178]
The plantation leasing scheme in the western theater was akin to the
Home Farms that surrounded Suffolk, Virginia, but on a much larger
scale and generally operating on a wage-labor rather than shares system. In a nutshell, the U.S. government confiscated lands abandoned by
secessionist owners and leased them to Southern planters who claimed
loyalty to the United States, to Northern investors, or occasionally to
Southern free blacks and former slaves. Lessees then hired former slaves
to work for wages. Contracts between workers and planters stipulated
labor expectations, rates of pay, rations, and medical care and specified
basic working conditions including limits on punishment. They also

curtailed former slaves' newfound liberties, especially mobility, in ways reminiscent of the military discipline exerted by Toussaint-Louverture's army at the turn of the nineteenth century to keep formerly enslaved workers laboring on Haitian plantations while formerly enslaved soldiers revolted against France. Union army personnel were instructed to oversee the contracts with an eye to balancing the interests of planters and freedpeople and ensuring the productivity of the cotton fields.[179] Achieving "balance" between those competing interests would likely have proved difficult under ideal conditions; doing so in a deadly war zone was impossible. Taken on the whole, leased plantations, rather than resolving the many difficulties that accompanied slavery's demise, simply provided another backdrop against which the chaotic process of emancipation played out.

Yet trying to take leased plantations "on the whole" leaves out and obscures as much as it reveals, for the real stories of people's lives there played out not according to scripts of identical inevitability but in infinite variety, as a close look at even one small area like Goodrich's Landing, Louisiana, reveals. Located on the western banks of the Mississippi and watered by both the Father of Waters and Lake Providence, a lake created by an oxbow in the river, Goodrich's Landing's acres of rich, fertile soil yielded fortunes in cotton before the war. When war came, the planters who had benefited from those fortunes mostly fled rather than face the Yankees. In the summer of 1863, one Union general surveyed everything planters had left behind and reflected, "The sweep and progress of our Army has released the negro from his master and in the majority of cases driven away the owners of plantations. The negroes and plantations remained. The question was what to do with both."[180]

By the time growing season rolled around the following year, the army's answer to that question was already in place: on twenty-one leased plantations, 2,553 laborers grew cotton, 1,117 of whom were women and 802 of whom were children. The remaining 634 were men. All put their marks to contracts promising rations, housing, and medical care, plus seven dollars per month for the men and five dollars per month for the women and working children. An additional 350 people unable to work, chiefly very young children, lived and drew rations there. Most worked for white investors, but sixty-three black workers subleased the

L. D. Ballard plantation from an investment company and farmed it for themselves. A freedmen's hospital and a Union army surgeon were established there, and the Sixty-Sixth U.S. Colored Troops (stationed nearby at Lake Providence) guarded against Confederate attack and guerrilla raid.[181]

Greed and violence were everywhere. Opportunities for exploitation abounded, for cotton made money, and plenty of lessees "cared nothing how much flesh they worked off the negro provided it was converted into good cotton at seventy-five cents per pound."[182] Some overseers and lessees shorted rations, skimped on medical care, and pushed sick freedpeople off the premises if they grew too weak to work.[183] Often, they slithered out of paying wages, by either delaying payday until the very end of the year, docking wages for days lost to wet weather, or deducting wildly inflated amounts for time lost to sickness, damage to tools, or goods purchased in plantation stores.[184] Confederate guerrillas marauded throughout the countryside, burning fields and cotton gins, killing some former slaves, and kidnapping others to sell back into slavery. The Sixty-Sixth U.S. Colored Troops helped keep that violence partially in check, but its redeployment in the summer of 1864 left plantation workers virtually defenseless for nearly six months, until Special Orders No. 22 finally established a six-hundred-man 1st Regiment Plantation Guards to protect government-leased plantations and all who lived there.[185] Nor were Confederates the only purveyors of violence. Agents and lessees didn't wield the bullwhip of slavery days, a distinction of enormous significance to anyone whose flesh had been rent asunder by one or who had lived in fear of that fate, but neither did they always refrain from deadly force. On one occasion, an overseer point-blank shot a worker dead.[186]

Unsurprisingly, many freedpeople balked at these conditions, just as liberated slaves had done in Haiti. Some refused to work in the cotton fields and concentrated instead on subsistence crops and kitchen gardens. Others left the plantations entirely. If they did, they soon found themselves scooped up and set to work on the river levees for either half the amount they signed contracts for or sometimes nothing at all. If they had young children, sick loved ones, or anyone else who relied on them, those dependents were forced off the plantation, left with little recourse but to head back to densely populated contraband camps or "depots" whose overcrowded conditions were one reason why the experiment with government-leased plantations was begun in the first place. There were, in short, few reasons to believe that the wartime labor expedient would one day give way to a constitutional right to landownership, as Haiti's 1805 Constitution had done.[187]

Yet for all the undeniable abuse and expropriation, to flatten the story of the leased plantations into a two-dimensional tale of greed and oppression would tell something about what it was like to experience emancipation on a leased plantation at Goodrich's Landing, but it would miss much as well. There is no room in such an account, for example, for Sancho. Sancho, formerly an enslaved driver on a Goodrich's Landing plantation, knew how to grow cotton, and he knew how to win others' confidence. When his owner fled, Sancho emerged as the leader of a group of sixty or eighty freedpeople who had known each other in slavery and who decided to navigate their way out of it together. He sized up the attempts of newly arrived leasing agents, men who "knew nothing about raising cotton," to coax a cotton profit out of unfamiliar ground and noticed that one of the agents, a Mr. Field, seemed more sensible than most. Mr. Field and all the others were sent scrambling in the spring when guerrillas smashed plantation machinery and burned part of the first crop, but the raiders had not mown down the entire crop, so Field along with the others crept cautiously back to their fields. Sancho and his community bargained with Field for use of two-thirds of his plantation and settled on it in April. They brought in cows and mules, built cabins, and set their own crop. Then guerrillas tried to run Sancho off. He and four or five of the other men put up a fight long enough for the rest of the freedpeople to get away. Sancho was wounded in the fight but recovered with the help of his friends and neighbors. Together, the group managed to hold on to what they had built—the solidarity with each other as well as the cabins and fields— and they came back to cultivate and bring in their crop. Several of the men, including Sancho, also helped to defend neighboring leased plantations from further guerrilla raids. At harvest time, the group cleared sixteen thousand dollars in profit.[188]

Sancho's derring-do and stirring success story do not somehow make up for or counterbalance the suffering, disappointment, or maltreatment that abounded on leased Goodrich's Landing plantations; on the contrary, reflecting upon the small snippet of his life that comes down to us through the accident of record survival demands some measure of precision as we struggle to understand freedpeople's paths out of slavery in the Mississippi River valley. Sancho's months on a leased plantation do not lend themselves to easy tales of any kind, and certainly not to an insipid narrative in which some things were good, some were bad, but overall plantation leasing was either an irredeemable catastrophe or all for the best, take your pick. For one thing, Sancho's success and survival were not his alone but the product of sixty or eighty additional men, women, and children for whom the story of emancipation was not one of sweeping generalizations but rather one of making what they could of whatever each unpredictable day might bring, right on the ground where they stood.

And the same was true for men, women, and children laboring on government-leased plantations throughout the Mississippi valley, for while the leasing system almost always consisted of "strength contracting with weakness" and frequently "resulted in oppression," black men and women in the Mississippi River valley were by necessity experts at carving out lives for themselves despite asymmetries of power.[189] As far as asymmetries of power went, the current one was at least a moderate improvement over the one that pertained in slavery, in which powerful slaveholders' interests virtually always clashed with the interests of slaves. Now the powerful Union army's dual interests in winning the war and making a go of plantation leasing sometimes diverged from or even conflicted with freedpeople's interests, but sometimes—certainly more often than under slavery—the interests of African Americans and the powerful arm of the national government intersected.

In a few cases, former slaves managed to lease lands for themselves, most famously at the Hurricane plantation owned by the Confederate president Jefferson Davis's brother Joseph and leased directly to Davis's former slaves. The success of the resulting Davis Bend colony under the leadership of the freedman Benjamin Montgomery was legendary then and now and also reasonably representative of the handful of other black-leased plantations, which Union authorities described as having "done wonderfully well" even under difficult circumstances.[190]

More often, freedmen and freedwomen on leased plantations were to some degree at the mercy of white leasing agents, who varied widely.

Some did "care at least as much for the negro as for cotton." A man called Irish Nolan paid substantially more than the going rate—the men and women who worked for him earned between $12.50 and $18 per month—and he did not dock wages for sickness or wet weather, nor did he deduct for clothing.[191] Yet plenty of others were "mere adventurers" who displayed far more greed, incompetence, and racism than fairness.[192] Planters near Helena, Arkansas, quickly learned how corruptible Captain A. L. Thayer was. He could be counted on to turn a blind eye to—even encourage—shorting rations, extending work hours, and cheating workers of wages, as long as planters and lessees cut him a share of the cotton crop and of the undistributed rations to smuggle through lines and sell on the black market.[193] That kind of fraud stole lives as well as property. When Joanna Moore visited leased plantations near Helena, she found one plantation where seventeen orphans under the age of ten "were lying on beds of dirty straw," too ill to withstand the fields and without the care they needed to get well.[194]

Yet fraud could not steal all life. On that same plantation, Moore started a school by ignoring ridicule, persuading a soldier to build her an arbor, and then nailing a blackboard to a tree. She was not the same girlish ingenue who had first left college to work among former slaves. She was hungry and dirty, and she was weary from the heartbreak she saw day after day. Many of the children who gathered at her blackboard had lost at least one parent, and the women who collected the children at the end of the day were driven to exhaustion by their hours in the fields. Still, every night they sang, and Moore listened. Their songs were not Joanna Moore's hymns, and they certainly were not the tunes of the drivers who dictated their workdays, but songs of their own, whose meanings the women fiercely refused to allow others to appropriate or interpret.[195]

Time did not stand still on leased plantations any more than it did anywhere in the war's western theater. Conditions changed with the weather and the seasons as well as with overturn in leasing agents. The balance of power shifted constantly, not just between lessees and workers, but between the army and the Department of the Treasury, who fought bitterly over control of the plantation leasing scheme and whose "perpetual conflict" impeded "successful cultivation of the plantations" from Northern investors' points of view. Those same conflicts sometimes created bargaining space for black workers who, unlike outside investors or most Union soldiers, were the experts in growing cotton. At the White River, Hogan, DeSoto, Edwards, Coathill, and Bearfield plantations in Mississippi, freedpeople in March 1865 succeeded in getting the leases granted to white investors revoked and transferred directly to them by authority of "the Plantation Leasing Agency on the recommendation of the District Provost Marshal of Freedmen."[196] At the time, they could not know, of course, that within weeks the war would end and everything would shift once more, in directions nobody could predict.

THE INTERIOR OF MISSOURI AND KENTUCKY

Life was even less predictable in the western border states, with uncertainty and violence increasing in direct proportion to the distance from the Mississippi River and in inverse proportion to population density. Much of central and western Missouri consisted of no-man's-land, where scattered forces, Unionist slaveholders, and Confederate guerrillas made life catastrophically insecure for African Americans. Many bolted for any town where Union troops were, which helped a bit, but also turned into a form of virtual imprisonment. In places like Mexico, Missouri, it was "not safe to go out of town," because "secessionists ha[d] threatened to shoot every black."[197] In many places, pro-slavery sympathizers made good on those threats. In early spring 1863, the U.S. steamer *Sam Gaty* sailed the Missouri River carrying government property, Union soldiers, and black men, women, and children, when it was attacked by Confederate guerrillas who destroyed three hundred sacks of flour and forty-eight wagons, killed two Union soldiers and nine black passengers, and sold other black people who had been aboard into bondage.[198] That same year, three black men, one black woman, and two black children (a boy and a girl) were so desperate to escape to the free state of Kansas they followed the Fourth (Union) Missouri Cavalry *on foot* as the regiment advanced from Lexington, Missouri, to Independence. They began the desperate trek to Independence in the hopes that from there they would be able to get to the Kansas state line. For a day, the determined band kept up with the mounted soldiers, but on the second day Confederate bushwhackers ambushed the little party and killed all but one of the men, who escaped by playing dead and then hauling himself, despite his wounds, to a Union hospital in Independence.[199]

To make matters worse, loyalties were so divided in Missouri that refugees from slavery could not always tell who was on their side. In Ray County, a home guard unit of the Enrolled Militia was nominally Union, but under state rather than federal control. The militiamen so vehemently opposed the actions of Union forces who were sheltering slave runaways that they threatened to burn first the storehouse holding provisions for fugitives, then the bunks of the former slaves, and finally the quarters of the regular Union forces.[200] One way to inoculate Union forces in Missouri against the hostility of local slaveholding elites was to fill officer positions with other local slaveholding elites, a move that shored up shaky pro-slavery Unionism but proved disastrous for bond people seeking freedom. Slaveholders near O'Fallon, Missouri, were disgruntled and disgusted when Union soldiers commanded by Lieutenant Colonel Arnold Krekel harbored runaway slaves. Their enthusiasm for the Union cause only recovered when Colonel Odon Guitar succeeded Krekel and indiscriminately returned slaves to all owners, Unionist and secessionist alike, in 1863.[201] At the same time, Guitar's actions revealed the Union army to be an inconstant and unreliable ally for black Missourians in the turbulent center of the state.

Similar instability and tragedy unfolded in Kentucky. The town of Columbus, Kentucky, on the Mississippi River functioned more like a satellite of Cairo, Illinois, than a part of the Bluegrass State, but in regions more distant from the Mississippi the perils of pro-slavery Unionism operated much as they did in the interior portions of Missouri. General Speed Fry, the commander of the Camp Nelson contraband camp near Nicholasville, Kentucky, had no sympathy for former slaves and plenty for former slaveholders. By 1864, the bulk of black men in camp had been recruited into the Union army, and the freedpeople remaining were primarily women and children, or the old and the infirm, none of which stopped Fry from expelling them. He shut the camp down, in the middle of an unseasonable cold snap, in a state where former masters would wreak vengeance on runaways if they could get their hands on them. Before enlisting in October 1864, Private John Higgins of the 124th U.S. Colored Infantry lived in the camp.

Together with his wife, who worked for the army as a washerwoman, Higgins built his family a "small hut" in camp, where the family lived together. Higgins's wife and two children continued to live there for about a month after Higgins joined the army. Then, on the evening of November 24, the provost guard told Higgins's wife and children that they would be removed from camp the following day. The next afternoon, a guard rolled up to the hut with a wagon and ordered the Higgins family to get in. Mrs. Higgins was sick and implored the guard not to throw her out into the cold until she recovered. The guard replied, "If you do not get out we will burn the house over your heads," and so she left. Two days later, her husband found her and the children very ill and starving in nearby Nicholasville. Records do not indicate whether the members of the Higgins family survived or not, but several children froze to death in the expulsion, and at least one woman was beaten to death by her former master.[202]

Furthermore, because Kentucky did not leave the Union, civil authority remained paramount over military authority there, and civil authority favored the interests of slaveholders over those of men, women, and children seeking a way out of slavery. When General Don Carlos Buell's army held still in Kentucky in 1862, its members harbored and hired fugitives from slavery, but as soon as the army moved, local sheriffs rounded black workers up and sold them back into slavery for a quick profit.[203] We have known for a long time that the road from slavery to freedom was rarely clear or easy, but we have often assumed that it could ultimately lead in only one direction: inexorably, if sometimes slowly, out of slavery and toward freedom, with no return route. The experiences of freedom seekers in the western border states highlight a truth that was more obvious there than in some other places but actually held true everywhere. The path between slavery and freedom was no one-way road but rather a two-way street, and it could change direction at any time.

Sense of direction was profoundly difficult to retain as men, women, and children searched for ways out of slavery in the western theater of the Civil War. Nothing remained stable. Landmarks steady enough to navigate by were as difficult to spot as they are in the photograph with which this chapter began. To return to that scene, possibly in Baton Rouge on an unknown day, it is striking how utterly unglimpsable it could have been to Shepard Mallory, Frank Baker, and James Townsend, no matter how bright the moon over Fort Monroe shone on that May night in 1861. It is doubtful that Mallory, Baker, or Townsend could have known anything of the people whose likenesses would be captured years later and miles away. It is possible, by the middle of the war, that some of the people in the photograph had heard the names of Mallory, Baker, and Townsend, but it is not likely that they knew what the three men looked like. They did not necessarily have kin or friends or skills or songs or stories or basic biographical details in common. They might not have shared a single landmark by which to find their way. All the differences in what they knew, saw, thought, and felt surely mattered, for those differences determined what the sometimes awesome and sometimes awful experience of moving out of slavery was really like.

Yet in other ways, important ways, all those experiences—divergent and varied and even conflicting as they often were—were connected. They were part of a story that was even larger than the formidable sum of all its many moving parts.

Refuge Without Water

S ince 1861, there has been a compelling elegance, a satisfying sense of poetic justice, to the story of Fort Monroe. Jared Fuller noticed it and wrote about it to his wife back in Dubuque, Iowa. "It is here," he told his much-missed Sarah, "that the James River enter[s] Hampton Roads, on whose banks the first settlement of this country commenced, and it was within ½ mile of this camp that the first slaves were taken on shore from the Dutch ship." Two hundred forty-one years later, "it was here that Gen Butler declared the slaves of rebel masters to be counterband [sic]," and that same ground was "made famous" once again, this time by "large numbers of counterbands consisting of men, womun, and children" whose "future is yet to be written."[1] The Massachusetts soldier Edward Pierce noticed it, too, and shared his reflections in a widely read *Atlantic Monthly* piece that opened with

> In the month of August, 1620, a Dutch man-of-war from Guinea entered James River and sold "twenty negars." Such is the brief record left by John Rolfe, whose name is honorably associated with that of Pocahontas. This was the first importation of the kind into the country, and the source of existing strifes. It was fitting that the system which from that slave-ship had been spreading over the continent for nearly two centuries and a half should yield for the first time to the logic of military law almost upon the spot of its origin.[2]

The smooth narrative arc, the reassuring sense of all things coming right in the end, was and is so exquisitely symmetrical that we are tempted either to embrace it unreservedly or to go to the opposite extreme and reject it utterly as wishful thinking at best, hypocritical drivel at worst.[3] Yet neither of those two approaches will tell us much.

Better to reflect on Jared Fuller's sense of surprise and also uncertainty. Former slaves' "future," he pointed out, was "yet to be written." Fuller was, after all, talking about a landscape completely devoid of freshwater, a landscape where no amount of digging could ever find that most basic necessity of life, a landscape that should have been the last place on earth to turn for refuge, and yet a landscape where thousands fleeing slavery did exactly that. He was talking about a landscape where emancipation *might* unfold but at a time when nobody yet knew if emancipation *would* unfold for good. He was talking about a landscape that would repeat and recur, in many of its essentials, wherever fleeing slaves and the Union army met each other over the next four years. He was talking about a contraband camp, a landscape that brought to the surface powerful questions about human rights and about national belonging, questions for which nowhere in the world had adequate answers in 1861. Even now, with more than a century and a half to come up with better solutions, we do not have adequate answers, either.

Transcending the geographic variations, environmental influences, and local particularities, all contraband camps were, in essence, refugee camps. They, more than battle reenactments with no real fatalities or period clothing ordered on the Internet, shrink the distance between the world of the Civil War and our world. Today, donors to the UN's refugee agency, the Office of the United Nations High Commissioner for Refugees (UNHCR), receive a short DVD titled *Protecting the World's Most Vulnerable.* "When refugees flee their homes, it is often only with the clothes on their backs," the video explains. "They are searching for a way to survive." Images in the video make clear that the obstacles to refugees' survival consist not only of the violence they are fleeing but also of the absence of "basic tools for living" like "life-saving food, water, medical care, and the basic necessities for life." When donors make recurring donations, the categories under which they may choose to do so underscore that same basic point. So much a month will help dig wells for water. So much will provide canvas tents for shelter. So much will subsidize basic medical care. Images in the video—at once matter-of-fact and utterly haunting—drive home what the absence of these basic necessities means. Right now, not a century and a half ago, but right now, vulnerable people "stripped of their rights and of everything they own" bake in the sun as they did at Camp Parapet or shiver in the wind as they did on Craney Island. Right now, most of them (up to 80 percent, according to the UNHCR) are women and children, just as they were on President's Island outside Memphis, or at Columbus, Kentucky. In the video, a young woman who has lost her husband and seven brothers is so visibly depleted by the task of keeping her children alive in desperate circumstances that she can hardly raise her head high enough to look at the camera as she admits, "It is overwhelming. I am suffering." Women and children now sicken and die from lack of clean water at Dadaab, Kenya, the world's largest refugee camp, just as they did at Vicksburg, Cairo, and Fort Monroe.[4] The parallels forbid a posture of superiority and banish any comfortable notions that the world described in these pages is a lost and unrecognizable one or that we would have done any better by refugees fleeing slavery than Americans in the era of the Civil War did.

One big difference between then and now was that contraband camps were refugee camps before so much as the language to talk about refugee camps, let alone the institutional apparatus to mitigate the suffering, existed. As one emergency responder on *Protecting the World's Most Vulnerable* notes with pride, agencies like the UNHCR have "particular expertise in being able to bring *order* to the chaos" that characterizes any refugee situation. Nobody in 1861 had that expertise. There was plenty of chaos, but there was no such thing as organized, institutional aid to persons displaced by war, and would not be until the following century.[5] There were well-intentioned individuals. Voluntary organizations, benevolent societies, and churches tried to respond to the overpowering need in contraband camps, and their efforts certainly provided some relief, but no private efforts were or could be any match for the enormous, overwhelming, insurmountable scale of need faced by tens of thousands of refugees who arrived, often sick, usually hungry, and frequently with nothing more than what they could clutch and carry in the fleeting instant when an opportunity for escape arose.

The only organization with the infrastructure and geographic scope to reach all camps was the Union army, and so by necessity and default administration of the camps fell to the army, but there was absolutely no precedent in world history for armies—institutions whose purpose is to wage and win war—serving successfully as benevolent aid organizations. There are *still* no unreservedly successful examples of such a thing, for that is not what military forces are designed to do. Nobody, not even the army, had professional staffs numbering in the thousands dedicated solely to relief work, air fleets for dropping supplies, or financial instruments for collecting donations fast and channeling them efficiently. Such expertise and apparatuses do exist today, yet even all these innovations still only imperfectly address the needs of displaced men, women, and children looking to survive in circumstances and surroundings so unsettlingly similar to U.S. Civil War contraband camps.

More than 185 institutions across the globe, including many places in the United States, formally identify as members of the International Coalition of Sites of Conscience.[6] Although no sites of former contraband camps as of this writing are formally included on that list, contraband camps surely qualify as locations that cry out to be remembered in ways that thoughtfully choose deliberative reflection and tolerate a degree of discomfort and uncertainty rather than either prideful celebration or righteous condemnation. Contraband camps are no things to romanticize. They were not locations where anyone would want to be, any more than anyone would want to be in a refugee camp in Jordan, Pakistan, Djibouti, or Kenya today. Neither ought contraband camps to be sensationalized. They were not concentration camps, not part of some malevolent federal plot. They attest to moral muddiness rather than clarity. They were places where absolutely everybody was up against more than he or she could manage.

To be sure, identifying contraband camps as sites of conscience must be done carefully, so as to avoid the trap of presentism. The International Coalition of Sites of Conscience specifically and purposefully situates its sites within the context of "struggles for human rights," and historians have generally located the concept of human rights in the twentieth century, long after the U.S. Civil War.[7] A commonly cited starting point is 1948, when the UN issued the Universal Declaration of Human Rights, but Samuel Moyn opens *The Last Utopia:*

Human Rights in History by identifying the 1970s, decades after the UN declaration and more than a century after the Civil War, as the time in which a genuine human rights movement "that had never existed before" finally "coalesced."[8]

Yet something was changing in the nineteenth century. A different sort of conscience was beginning to stir, in the United States as elsewhere in the world. Leigh Webber, a private in the First Kansas Infantry, specifically worried that if the Union lost the war, "the hope of human rights is extinguished for ages."[9] Civil War contraband camps were not a cause or origin of that stirring, but they were a part of it.

In the first half of the nineteenth century, conflict was not the genteel affair of popular imagining, in which armies simply arranged themselves in formation and then sized up who was better armed; rather, after 1789, suffering in wartime worldwide *worsened* compared with earlier eras.[10] In 1859, Henry Dunant of Geneva witnessed the Battle of Solferino while traveling through what is now Italy and wrote a small book titled *Un souvenir de Solférino* to describe wounded left unattended, even buried alive.[11] He determined that no government or private philanthropic effort, however well-intentioned, could by itself adequately redress human need in wartime. Instead, Dunant called for "an international organization of national associations, in collaboration with their governments." He founded the International Committee of the Red Cross in 1863, and the Convention for the Amelioration of the Condition of the Wounded in Armies in the Field, better known as the First Geneva Convention, assembled for the first time in 1864. From 1864 to 1868, European states ratified the Geneva Convention, which at the time was something truly new under the sun.[12]

While Dunant organized, Francis Lieber wrote General Orders No. 100, also known as the Lieber Code, codifying wartime conduct unlike any U.S. document had ever done before.[13] Lieber took a close interest in Dunant's work and clearly saw his code as of a piece with it. In the summer of 1864, he wrote at length to Charles Sumner about the "congress of friends of humanity at Geneva." Lieber somewhat immodestly claimed that his own code "anticipated the Geneva Congress," but he also acknowledged that intolerable prisoner of war conditions and Confederate treatment of black Union soldiers at Olustee and Fort Pillow took place despite the Lieber Code. Faced with the inadequacy of his own work, Lieber realized "how necessary it is to establish international rules distinctly pronounced and adopted, in order to prevent, if possible, so fearful a relapse into barbarism."[14]

Yet it was not Francis Lieber who would, decades later, finally inspire the United States to ratify the Geneva Convention and found the American Red Cross; it was Clara Barton. Her wartime experiences—all of them—surely helped influence her to do so. Barton's work as an army nurse, her profound response to revelations of suffering in the Confederate prison at Andersonville, and especially her tireless work after the war to locate and identify Civil War dead are all well-known and easily identifiable as elements of the impulse behind her Red Cross work.[15] Yet the American Red Cross began its organized disaster relief in the United States not with aid to soldiers but with aid to noncombatants: specifically, victims of wildfire in Michigan and flooding along the Mississippi River. Barton's wartime experience with aid to noncombatants came in contraband camps. When smallpox "fell among and scourged" freedpeople at St. Helena in the Sea Islands, a year before the establishment of Dunant's Red Cross and long before anything like the World Health Organization, Barton was forbidden to travel between Beaufort (where she was) and St. Helena because of fears she would "expose our soldiers by going and returning." Despite the travel prohibition, Barton could not get images of newly freed women and children out of her mind, so she boxed up "tons of comforts such as I thought them most in need of, landing them silently from little boats up at the mouths of the creeks." At the other end of those creeks, a former slave named Columbus Simonds hauled the boxes of food, tea, and soft flannel out of the water and distributed the contents to the afflicted.[16] Later, Barton encountered more suffering in her work with "a large number of colored people, mostly women & children" who made their way to the Army of the James in Virginia. "In all cases they are destitute, having stood the sack of two opposing armies, what one army left them the other has taken," Barton reflected as she scurried to find food and paying work for mothers to support their children.[17]

Organized, international humanitarian aid capable of responding to needs of refugees displaced by war, in short, did some of its incubating in Civil War contraband camps. In saying so, we need to take pains to avoid a simple tale of progress. We cannot forget that the very first contraband camp occurred in a location that lacks freshwater, the most basic element for sustaining life. Contraband camps were no living springs, no founts of justice. But they did help to make it much harder to ignore need among the displaced, the uprooted, the most vulnerable.

Institutions designed for effective intervention now exist, but even the most technologically advanced, operationally sophisticated, generously resourced, and professionally staffed of them are designed to provide aid only temporarily. The UNHCR describes its purpose as ensuring respect for the basic rights of the world's "most defenseless people, men, women, and children," not all of the time, but when they "can no longer count on protection from their own country."[18] When refugees arrive in a camp, they are registered, fed, clothed, sheltered, and treated by a doctor if necessary, but none of those measures are intended to continue permanently. The UNHCR's ultimate goal is to repatriate and resettle refugees in places where their rights will be protected by the national state to which they belong, because under ordinary circumstances we expect most people's basic rights to be safeguarded by their national government. Before the Civil War, no enslaved man, woman, or child could have had any such expectation.

During the Civil War, that expectation changed, and contraband camps were part of why. When men, women, and children fleeing slavery arrived at a contraband camp, they met the Union army, a scenario with some obvious disadvantages given that armies do not typically make very good philanthropic organizations but with the one distinct advantage that armies do often serve as embodiments of and points of access to national governments. The Union army certainly did, and the response of the army—and the U.S. government—to the black men, women, and children who fled to it during the Civil War mattered. The urge to flee unquestionably originated with the people fleeing, but the response they met surely made a difference, as any Guatemalan child trying to reach her mother across the U.S. border in the summer of 2014, or any refugee seeking safe harbor anywhere, could attest. Courageous and self-motivated as all those who fled slavery were, they were no more so than the millions of men and women who had hated slavery since the seventeenth century but who had nowhere to run. Anyone who did run before the war encountered a U.S. government committed to protecting a slaveholder's right to property rather than a slave's right to self-ownership. Then came the war, and first at Fort Monroe, and eventually wherever former slaves and the Union army came into contact, black men, women, and children began to find troubled refuge in the U.S. government.

There was no freshwater at Fort Monroe, not one drop no matter how deep anyone dug. The refuge it could provide was and would remain troubled. Neither it nor any other contraband camp looked like a location for bringing slavery to its knees. They did not look like places for re-creating the relationship between the federal government and the individual. They did not look like venues for reinventing citizenship. But they were, and part II of this book looks more closely at how those things happened.

PART II

By the Sword

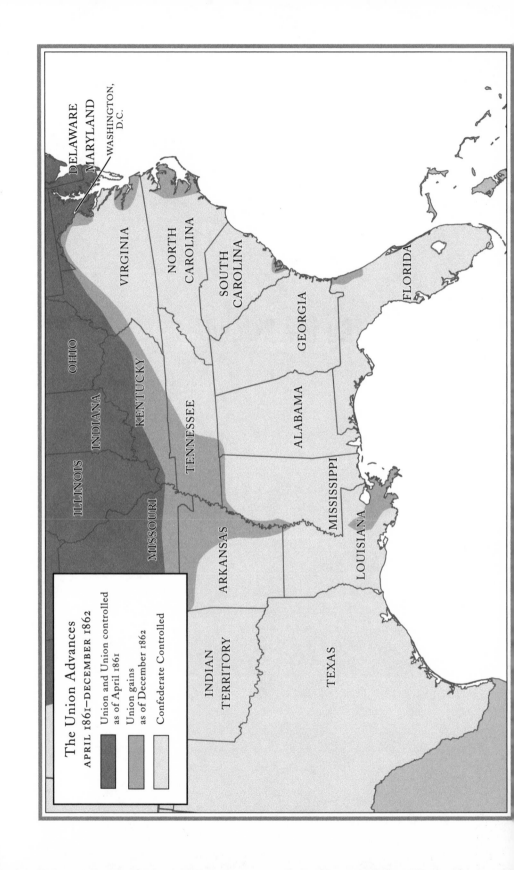

The Union Advances
APRIL 1861–DECEMBER 1862

Union and Union controlled
as of April 1861

Union gains
as of December 1862

Confederate Controlled

WASHINGTON,
D.C.

DELAWARE
MARYLAND

VIRGINIA

NORTH
CAROLINA

SOUTH
CAROLINA

GEORGIA

FLORIDA

OHIO

INDIANA

KENTUCKY

ILLINOIS

MISSOURI

TENNESSEE

ALABAMA

MISSISSIPPI

ARKANSAS

LOUISIANA

INDIAN
TERRITORY

TEXAS

THREE

Precarious Routes to Freedom

Wartime Emancipation in Contraband Camps

T he men, women, and children who fled bondage in the Civil War
ran to contraband camps seeking freedom. What they got at first
was military emancipation. Military emancipation was a process consisting of many, often contradicting elements, and it came in many vari-
ants, but despite all the discrepancies and variations it could be found
almost anywhere the Union army went in 1861 and 1862. One place to
look for it might be the jails of Nicholasville and Georgetown, Kentucky, which in quick succession held runaway slaves, white Kentuckians trying to catch them, noncommissioned Union officers willing to
kidnap them for cash, and an abolitionist Union colonel trying to free
them.[1] Another place to see the process in action might be the fields
of the Hoggatt plantation in Middle Tennessee, soggy from rain and
melted snow in the days after the fall of Fort Donelson. There, Union
soldiers shot hogs, burned fence rails, and gave black women and children like young John McCline their first "green backs."[2] At first glance,
the goings-on in Kentucky jails and Tennessee fields seem dramatically
different from, possibly even unrelated to, each other, like two scenes
on opposite sides of the cyclorama room, but both were part of military
emancipation's greater whole. In order to take place, military emancipation first had to overcome obstacles so large and serious that they
would have seemed nearly insurmountable before the war. Despite the

impediments, military emancipation began to take place quickly, and this chapter is in part about the difficult process of overcoming those obstacles in the war's first two years.

First things first: military emancipation happened because of war. The chaos of war on the one hand made new room for black families and communities to begin to build the autonomy they sought, but that same chaos also meant that they spent the entire war squarely in harm's way. Some dangers—infectious disease, for example—were impervious to human firepower, but other threats, particularly those posed by a Confederate army and citizenry intent on re-enslaving former bond people, were best combated by alliance with the Union army. The army had its own priorities, chief among them winning the war. The particular ways in which former slaves' aspirations and Union army objectives sometimes coincided and other times collided varied from time to time and place to place, but collectively they upended the relationship between slavery and authority and charted the unpredictable, rocky, and switchback-prone route out of slavery that was military emancipation.

The outbreak of the Civil War set the process of military emancipation in motion quickly but not automatically. In retrospect, it is easy to look back and see the arc of time bending unmistakably toward emancipation, but exactly how, and even whether, it would ultimately arrive at permanent abolition of slavery was neither inevitable nor obvious. Opposition to chattel bondage was nearly as long-standing as slavery itself, certainly on the part of the enslaved of course, but as the eighteenth and nineteenth centuries progressed, growing numbers of free black Americans and white Northerners wished to see legal slavery outlawed in the United States. Yet powerful obstacles had prevented them from doing so, and it was anything but a foregone conclusion that the obstructions would disappear with the outbreak of war. Many of the obstacles are best understood as structural forces, meaning forces beyond the power of individual humans to control. Obvious structural forces include economic, demographic, and political factors, all of which shored up slavery and defied the power of the institution's opponents to dismantle it. Sometimes prevailing ideas and assumptions can be so widespread that they, too, operate like structural forces, dictating individuals' behavior, facilitating some courses of action and foreclosing others. Historians sometimes talk about such prevailing ideas as "structures," or "sets of mutually sustaining schemas and resources that empower and constrain social action and that tend to be reproduced by that social action."[3] In plain English, widespread ideas so pervasive that they take on the power of structural forces are the unwritten rules that nobody needs to write down, because they are so ingrained in us that we can hardly even imagine breaking them. Some of them are minor, as when we instinctively leave space between ourselves and unfamiliar passengers on a bus. Others are major, with far greater impact. They are so binding that we rarely think about them until they are breached, but in those moments we see just how deeply embedded they are. Think about how uncomfortable you are if someone sits or stands right next to you on a bus when there are empty seats available. That discomfort illustrates how unsettling we humans find it when even a trivial unwritten rule is violated. Obstructing major structural ideas and assumptions is downright traumatic to our species, and that trauma can serve as a disincentive to change every bit as powerful and every bit as difficult to overcome as economic factors or the distribution of political power.

At the beginning of the war, three particular unwritten rules about slavery, race, and the national government were so widespread that they operated like powerful structural forces pushing mightily against the eradication of slavery. The first was that a black person was presumed to be a slave rather than a free person. Such a presumption was contested, especially by the new (but before March 1861 powerless on the national level) Republican Party, and most Northern states rejected it within their state boundaries, but it dictated the actions and position of the federal government, including the army, especially since the 1850 passage of the Fugitive Slave Law.[4] The second and third assumptions were not so controversial; in fact, they were so widespread as to be almost unthinking. The second was that slavery was a civil institution governed by civil authority, not military authority.[5] The third, though spiritedly disputed by elite Northern free blacks, reigned uncontested in the minds of almost all whites and certainly the wielders of federal power before the Civil War: it was that a direct relationship existed between the national government and white property owners, but no positive, direct relationship existed between the U.S. government and enslaved people.[6]

Obviously, these widespread ideas militated against the abolition of slavery, but even more precisely they dictated that the Union army have nothing to do with slavery at the war's outset, for several reasons. First, because the army was the embodiment of the U.S. government, it was supposed to operate from the presumptions on which the federal government operated, and that included the presumption of slavery rather than freedom as the normal status for black people. It also included the presumption that the national government could have no direct relationship with slaves as individual people but did recognize the civic personhood and property rights of white people, including slave owners. Moreover, the army represented military (not civil) authority, and therefore should exercise no jurisdiction over the civil institution of slavery. In sum, structural forces (not merely individual whim) seemed to make one point very clear when the war began: the army should have no business freeing slaves.

Undoubtedly, there were voices disputing that point. Free black Northerners and slaves themselves took a different view of that matter obviously, but so also did many Republicans, as well as some Union soldiers. World history is full of examples of armies manumitting the slaves of enemy combatants as a war measure. The British had done so in the American Revolution and the War of 1812, and one historian has looked closely at U.S. forces during the Seminole Wars and seen patterns that fit within this tradition. Numerous Republicans—Joshua Giddings, for example—tried to make the case right from the very outbreak of hostilities that such precedents illustrated the legality of military emancipation and urged Union forces to adopt it immediately. Not everyone saw things as clearly as Giddings and his allies did. The tangled back-and-forth in Congress and throughout Northern newspapers on the question of military emancipation demonstrates that the issue was thorny, complicated, and without clear precedent for any one definite course of action.[7]

The complications meant that Northern public opinion at the start of the Civil War regarded military emancipation with uncertainty and trepidation. Public opinion in 1861—and, very concretely, leaders elected by members of the public and the personnel of the Union army drawn from members of the public—were profoundly shaped by structural assumptions about blackness and slavery, civil rather than military authority's jurisdiction over slavery, and the possibility of a direct relationship between the national government and white people but not black people. Treaty negotiations surrounding the Seminole Wars were not nearly as familiar to Northern voters and potential Union army recruits as, say, "The Star-Spangled Banner," whose third verse celebrates how British troops but not American ones provided "refuge" to anyone trying to flee slavery in wartime.[8] Moreover, the actions of both the regular U.S. Army and militia units in the years leading up to the Civil War were clear. President James Buchanan called out U.S. forces against the antislavery settlers and any fugitives they tried to harbor in the Bleeding Kansas troubles of the 1850s and against John Brown and his small band (including Dangerfield Newby, trying to rescue his wife from slavery) in their raid on Harpers Ferry. Any direct military experience most Americans would have had when the war began would have come from serving in a state militia, and those units did not liberate either. They did things like put down Nat Turner's Rebellion. In fact, the single task that militias in Massachusetts were likely to get called out for more than any other in the 1850s was to enforce the Fugitive Slave Law.[9] Widespread presumptions so powerful that they amounted to structural forces, in sum, militated against a Union army freeing slaves when the war began.

Before military emancipation could proceed, structural assumptions would have to be overcome or at least breached. Structures are powerful, but sometimes they break, especially when human beings interact with each other in times of strain, such as wartime. Under those circumstances, structures can be disrupted. For example, a disruption happened when fourteen former slaves helped guide a boat from Fort Monroe through the tricky waters of Pamlico Sound and then manned one of the guns that captured Hatteras Island for the Union. Another disruption happened when a black woman gathered her children and grandchildren onto a Union army wagon to ride into camp at La Grange, Tennessee. In fact, a disruption happened every time refugees from slavery encountered the Union army, because these encounters placed slaves into direct contact with the national government. Moreover, wartime interactions exposed slavery as a state of war, and therefore properly subject to military authority.[10] Whether in Alexandria or Vicksburg, Corinth or the Sea Islands, countless real-life, on-the-ground, unpredictable interactions between black men, women, and children and members of the Union army placed mighty pressure on preexisting structures.

Members of the army could respond in one of four ways. Soldiers could cling to starting presumptions and continue to treat the refugees from slavery rushing into their lines as slaves. Another possible response was to yield one or even two of the structural assumptions but try to minimize the degree of change within the edifice as a whole by shoring up the others. The practical application of this second approach consisted of manumitting slaves, either individually or over large areas, while still upholding basic assumptions about the primacy of civil over military authority under normal circumstances and about the absence of any direct relationship between the government and black people. Taking this approach could answer the question of who black people reaching Union lines were not—they were not slaves—but it provided little clear guidance in determining who such people actually *were* and what their relationship to the national government ought to be. The third and fourth alternatives both involved more fundamental structural change. The third response was to emancipate slaves from bondage and to forge new relationships between them and the U.S. government via military authority. The fourth response was to emancipate and solidify those new, direct relationships with civil authority. It would be a mistake to place these four options along a clear timeline, as though they neatly followed one another as the war unfolded, because in truth the four options remained in tension with each other throughout and even after the war, but the response that increasingly predominated in 1861 and 1862 was the second one. That response, in essence, was military emancipation.

By the end of 1862, military emancipation had overcome the powerful forces militating against it and conclusively answered the question of who black people arriving within Union lines were *not* in the definition of the U.S. government: they were not slaves. At the same time, military emancipation in the first half of the war also opened up the even more difficult questions of *who* and *whose*, according to the U.S. government, newly emancipated black men, women, and children were. To put the point another way, military emancipation decided that any former slave who made it to Union lines no longer belonged to his or her former owner, and that decision marked a mighty change in U.S. history, but military emancipation did not decide where or even if a former slave belonged in the reconsolidating United States. The status of former slaves remained unknown, their inclusion within the national community unrecognized. Military emancipation as it unfolded in Civil War contraband camps was an astonishing achievement and also one with tragic shortcomings.

.   .   .

Wartime interactions between fleeing slaves and the national government began quickly. Even before hostilities broke out, four slaves presented themselves to Lieutenant Adam J. Slemmer, commanding officer of the First U.S. Artillery at Fort Pickens, in Pensacola, Florida. Flabbergasted to learn that the slaves "came to the fort entertaining the idea that we were placed here to protect them and grant them their freedom," Slemmer "did what [he] could to teach them the contrary." He took them to city marshals, who returned them to their owners. Additional slaves who made a similar attempt that same evening met with the same fate.[11]

This episode reveals that on the eve of the war, all three structural assumptions were firmly intact: the presumptive equation of blackness with slavery, the primacy of civil over military authority, and the existence of a direct relationship between the U.S. government and white but not black people. Take note of whom Slemmer saw, what he did, and what he did not do. Slemmer's report never named the people but referred to them as "four negroes (runaways)," because Slemmer immediately read their complexions as evidence that they occupied the status of slaves, not free men or women requiring individual identification. Slemmer did not return the slaves to their owners personally; rather, he took them to "the city marshal," a civil official, to do so, because civil rather than military authority governed slavery. Further, the dispatch relating the whole event opened with the sentence, "I have the honor to report that since my last report nothing has happened to disturb the peaceable relations existing between the U.S. forces and those opposing us." In that sentence, Slemmer reveals the assumption shared by the army, the U.S. government, and white Americans alike at the start of the war: "relations" existed between the United States and white people, like the slaves' owners and like the city marshal. The notion that "relations" might exist between the United States and black people struck Slemmer as so incongruous that it was nothing more than an "idea" that misguided slaves could "entertain."

So long as the three prewar structures remained in place, the least surprising, most logical answer to the question of who black people running to the Union army were was the one adopted by Slemmer: they were still slaves. That answer was indeed the one that animated the decisions and actions of some Union commanders in the war's early days, even including Benjamin Butler. Within days of the Confederate reduction of Fort Sumter and President Lincoln's subsequent call for troops, Butler and the Eighth Massachusetts Infantry arrived in Annapolis, Maryland, to reestablish communications between Maryland's capital and the nation's. While there, Butler assured Maryland's governor, Thomas Hicks, that he and the Bay Staters were "not here in any way to interfere with or countenance any interference with the laws of the state," which everyone knew meant slavery, and that they would even help put down slave rebellions, if it came to that.[12] The following month, General George McClellan assured residents of western Virginia that "not only will we abstain from all such interference" with "your slaves," but Union forces would also, "with an iron hand, crush any attempt at insurrection on their part."[13]

Some members of Congress opposed emancipation and backed efforts to block it. Before accepting a commission in the Union Army, John McClernand was a Democratic congressman from Illinois, the one free state whose state law shared the presumption (overtly stated by Southern state laws and implicitly accepted by the national government) that a black person was a slave. McClernand unabashedly announced, "I am for prosecuting this war for the purpose of vindicating the Federal authority and putting down rebellion and not for the purpose of subjugating the seceding States and holding them as conquered provinces; nor for the purpose of abolishing slavery."[14] The even more vitriolic (and later infamous) Democrat from Ohio, Clement Vallandigham, even proposed a law barring Union soldiers from "abolishing or interfering with African slavery in any of the States."[15]

Butler, McClellan, McClernand, and Vallandigham provide reminders of the not-very-surprising truth that many white Americans from the non-slave as well as the slave states were prejudiced against African Americans, but they also operated in keeping with precedent as most white Americans understood it. During the American Revolution, Lord Dunmore, the royal governor of Virginia, had infuriated the formerly ambivalent residents of the colony of Virginia into siding with their hotheaded New England counterparts in support of independence from Britain in very large measure by issuing a proclamation that announced complete abandonment of all claims to honor or even civility in the eyes of white Virginians: in 1775, he promised freedom to any slave that fought with the British against a rebellious master. In 1779, the British general Henry Clinton applied Dunmore's Proclamation to all thirteen colonies rebelling against the Crown.[16] Even George Washington lost slaves to Dunmore's Proclamation, which only intensified colonial indignation. Fugitives recaptured by American forces were usually remanded to slavery.[17]

In the negotiations surrounding the end of the Revolution, some American statesmen conceded or even embraced the legitimacy of military emancipation, but their voices were conveniently forgotten when the United States again battled Great Britain early in the next century.[18] As with the Revolutionary War, some individual slaves owned by Americans ran to the British in the War of 1812, and some did gain personal freedom in that way, but the institution of slavery as a whole was strengthened rather than weakened in the aftermath of the war, spreading across the North American continent and suffering no legal blows.[19]

In fact, after the War of 1812, Secretary of State John Quincy Adams, who personally hated slavery but was required to represent the views of the Monroe administration within which he served, advocated against the government of Great Britain on behalf of American slaveholders whose slaves had become free by running to the British army on the grounds that "the emancipation of enemy's slaves is not among the acts of legitimate war." In instructions to Henry Middleton, a diplomat negotiating the issue, Adams wrote, "As [military emancipation] relates to the owners, it is a destruction of private property nowhere warranted by the usages of war." The sticking point was not any sympathy for slavery on Adams's part. His diary for that year is full of his fulminations against slavery, and about the instructions to Middleton in particular he wrote that he was "not satisfied with them."[20] The sticking point was the conviction that *military* forces could not legitimately exercise authority over a civil institution like slavery. As Adams continued, "No such right is acknowledged as a law of war by writers who admit any limitation. The right of putting to death all prisoners in cold blood, and without special cause, might as well be pretended to be a law of war, or the right to use poisoned weapons, or to assassinate."[21] Northern readers of newspapers in the summer of 1862 were well acquainted with Adams's public pronouncements, because Northern newspapers reprinted them and vigorously parsed their meaning.[22]

To put the same point another way, some Union military and civil officials who resisted emancipation in the war's early days were just bigoted, but others were stymied by reluctance to take on the task of confronting deep-seated structural assumptions in the midst of a national crisis with no clear legal precedent for guidance. Major General John A. Dix, a veteran of the War of 1812, was the Free-Soil Democrat whose subordinates in eastern Virginia conceded to AFIC commissioners that Dix probably meant it when he claimed to champion the rights of refugees from slavery but that his professed principles translated into little concrete action to safeguard those beleaguered rights. Prior to his stint in Virginia, Dix had served in Maryland, where, like Butler, he followed a scrupulous policy of "declin[ing] to receive" slaves who ran to his lines, because he presumed that the U.S. government, in areas where its authority was not contested, could be in direct relationship only with "citizens" who had "rights of property." Enslaved men and women lay entirely outside the parameters of any relationship with the government, and his longtime loyalties as a Jacksonian Democrat, even one who opposed slavery, led Dix to oppose expanding the parameters of national government in any fashion.[23]

From the very beginning, some black and white opponents of slavery were willing to disrupt long-standing structural assumptions about civil rather than military authority over slavery and about the impossibility of a direct relationship between the U.S. government and black people. Mary Ann Shadd Cary, a black woman born in Delaware who moved to Canada and edited the newspaper *The Provincial Freeman* before returning to the United States during the Civil War, avowed in 1861, "We do not believe, and do not intend, that [black Americans] must always be as the substratum of the body politic."[24] Slaves who showed up at Fort Pickens, Fort Monroe, and anywhere else they could find the Union army announced their rejection of the status quo with their feet. Almost as soon as the Thirty-Seventh Congress convened in July 1861, the Illinois congressman Owen Lovejoy introduced a resolution declaring that "it is no part of the duty of the soldiers of the United States to capture and return fugitive slaves," and the resolution met with widespread Republican approval.[25] Some enlisted Union soldiers echoed that same spirit. From training camp even before he and his fellow recruits left their home state, one new recruit announced, "I am inclined to think that the ideas of the soldiers of Wisconsin will differ some what from those of Vallandigham of Ohio and others of his stripe, who consider it a part of the soldier's duty to return the 'contraband' to his master."[26] Voices like Shadd Cary's and Lovejoy's were real, as were the actions of fleeing slaves and the opinions of the Wisconsin infantryman, but at the beginning of the war they were offset by more conservative forces less inclined to go up against powerful structures.

But times were changing, and rapidly. Two months after Slemmer turned fugitives over to the marshal in Pensacola, one month after Butler's letter to Governor Hicks, and three days before McClellan's assurance to white western Virginians, Frank Baker, Shepard Mallory, and James Townsend ran to Fort Monroe, Virginia, and "delivered themselves up to" Union pickets. By that time, war had broken out (in contrast with the Slemmer incident, which preceded hostilities), and Virginia, unlike Maryland, was in rebellion against the United States. These differences created space for military rather than civil authority to play a role in determining what to do with the fugitives. Even then, they did not lead to any obvious or automatic course of action. Relevant wartime conduct manuals did not yet exist. Formal academic legal volumes were of limited use because most of the authoritative ones dated from the eighteenth century or earlier, whereas since the French Revolution a chasm had been growing between textbook theory and on-the-ground experiences of warfare in Europe and the United States.[27] The most applicable existing treatises, like James Kent's *Commentaries on American Law* (1826–1830), Francis Lieber's *Manual of Political Ethics* (1838–1839), and Henry W. Halleck's *International Law* (1861), not only failed to offer any clear guidance; they did not even consider the possible existence of such people as slaves fleeing to Union lines. The most popular book on law in the United States in the nineteenth century, Kent's *Commentaries,* meticulously considered the matter of fugitive slaves in times of peace but confined its discussion of fugitives in wartime to criminals and those charged with a crime (not runaway slaves). Despite its extensive treatment of "the general usage" of war regarding private property, Kent's *Commentaries* did not discuss slave property. Even Halleck's *International Law,* the most thoroughgoing treatment available, included sections on guerrillas, prisoners, enemy soldiers, enemy noncombatants, neutrals, and one's own deserters and fugitives found among the enemy, but it did not even mention slaves, and it did not have any category that could even remotely apply to fleeing slaves.[28]

On one level, what Butler did is well-known, as noted in the Prelude, but his actions are worth a closer look because they set in motion the precise and distinctive process by which military emancipation during the U.S. Civil War first began to overcome the structural presumptions militating against it. General Butler met with the black men on the morning of May 24, and once he ascertained that the Confederate army was using their labor in its efforts to wage war against the United States, he felt empowered to exercise military authority over slavery rather than defer to civil authority. He also saw no need to abide by the presumptive equation of blackness with slavery that would pertain in Virginia state law and in practical federal policy under normal circumstances. Instead, he "determined for the present and until better advised, as these men were very serviceable and I had great need of labor in my Quartermaster's Department, to avail myself of their services. I determined also that I would send a receipt to Col. Mallory that I had so taken them." An incensed Mallory sent an agent, Major John Baytop Cary, straight back to remind Butler of his "constitutional obligations to deliver up fugitives under the Fugitive Slave Act." Butler reminded Cary that Virginia claimed to be out of the Union, and therefore the Fugitive Slave Act was inapplicable. If Virginia was a loyal state, like Maryland, then Mallory would have a right to reclaim the men. Even with Virginia seceded, if Mallory himself "would come to the Fortress and take the oath of allegiance to the constitution of the United States," Butler would "deliver up" the men if Mallory insisted. Better yet, he would continue to use them in the Quartermaster Department and pay Mallory for their services in a very common practice known as "hiring out."[29] In either case, determination as to what to do about the men was a function of their owner Colonel Mallory's loyalty and his intentions for their use. It was with the white owner that the U.S. government had a direct relationship and therefore the attitude and inclination of the owner that would determine what to do about the three black men. As for the men themselves, Butler's approach focused on labor they could provide rather than their status as individuals, and thus avoided any consideration of a relationship between the U.S. government and the men as individuals.

These actions, which constituted Butler's much-touted "contraband policy," set aside one structure (the presumptive equation of blackness with slavery), sidestepped another (the jurisdiction of civil rather than military authority over slavery), and maintained a third one (the presumption of a direct relationship between the U.S. government and white masters, but not black slaves). An uneasy mixture of radical disruption and conservative brake application would continue to influence how military emancipation played out wherever the Union army and black people came into contact with each other.

Even at the time, both participants and onlookers recognized the uneasy coexistence of conservative assumptions and radical actions. Before Cary arrived, either Butler or a clerk on Butler's behalf had been dutifully writing out a report detailing staffing and supply levels in the meticulous Spencerian handwriting taught in nineteenth-century Northern schools. Cary's visit forced Butler to stop abruptly. When Butler returned to his desk after the meeting, the orderly, diligent penmanship gave way to a sprawling scrawl (unquestionably Butler's own) that explained, "I had written thus far when I was called away to meeting Major Cary." In a huge, looping hand that practically makes it possible to hear an agitated Butler trying to catch his breath, the general told the whole story to the War Department, underscoring the "questions which have arisen of very considerable importance both in a military and political aspect."[30] Even confined to antiseptic typeface rather than demonstrative longhand, the staid *New York Times* captured the tension when it noted that "the simple presence of a Union army in their neighborhood" changed *some* things for slaves but that even as Butler's bold move practically freed them from their masters, it still left them without "relations of any kind to society and the State."[31]

Maintaining one structure while skirting or subverting two others—all while carrying out practical, military emancipation—was tricky business, and it was not long before the precariousness of the whole enterprise was exposed by the actions of the most seemingly powerless of all actors in the nineteenth-century United States: black women and children. As soon as word got out that Butler had not sent Colonel Mallory's three men back, many more slaves started coming to the fort, only this time it wasn't just men. Just two days later, Butler wrote once again to General Winfield Scott to tell him slave escapes from their masters had now become "very numerous" and that "women and children" made up a chunk of the numbers. "Able-bodied men and women who might come within my lines" and who were owned by an enemy actively using them to wage war was one matter, and one that a little creative interpretation could find an answer for in international law's recognition of the legitimate right to confiscate as "contraband of war" property used by the enemy against you, as Butler noted.[32] Children too young to work, women too sick, weak, or encumbered by child care to work, and elderly slaves too feeble to work were a different story. Butler could turn to no precedent for how, as a representative of the U.S. government, he ought to regard these black women and children. The U.S. government did not recognize any direct relationship (let alone obligation) to enslaved women and children unmediated by white owners, whom the government did recognize as individuals with direct relationship to and claim upon the U.S. government. So what to do?

At first, Butler stretched the logic he had used so far a little further because the women and children entering his lines were the immediate family members of able-bodied workers whose labor he was expropriating from the enemy and channeling toward the Union cause. On May 28, he ordered that rations be served to the family members of all "able-bodied negroes" working in Union "trenches and on the works."[33] Butler had no doubts about the rectitude of his actions either militarily, because it made better sense to put black laborers to work building Union reinforcements than Confederate ones, or in "the humanitarian aspect" because as "a question of humanity, can I receive the services of the father and mother and not take the children?" Yet when it came down to the nitty-gritty question of exactly how he, as an agent of the U.S. government, should regard and classify black men, women, and children, he admitted that he was "in the utmost doubt what to do."[34]

In part, the out-of-character modesty might have been just for show, for nobody had ever accused Benjamin Butler of reluctance in making pronouncements whether he knew anything about the matter at hand or not. But Butler could also have been at least partly in earnest. As he surveyed the situation as an officer in the U.S. Army at Fort Monroe surrounded by black women and children taking refuge, he really was looking at a situation for which there simply was no ready-made script. In the months and years that followed, his counterparts in every theater of the war would similarly encounter not only robust black men arriving in camps to work or fight for the Union but also thousands of black women and children, sick and starving upon arrival and looking for safe haven from a government that had never recognized a direct relationship with them as individual people before.

Initially, the federal government sought to fortify one or two of the preexisting structural assumptions, even as it enabled limited, practical military emancipation. Secretary of War Simon Cameron responded to Butler's plea for direction in a May 30 letter "approv[ing]" Butler's "action in respect to the negroes who came within your lines from the service of the rebels." At the same time, Cameron's response buttressed preexisting structural assumptions concerning civil authority and direct relationships between government and individuals. "Persons held to service under the laws of any state" were still held to service under those laws if the state was loyal, and the Fugitive Slave Law was still the law of the land, Cameron affirmed. What was different was that "armed combinations" in select places within the Union, including Virginia, where Butler happened to find himself, made the setting aside of civil authority necessary, but only temporarily. Butler was to keep strict "account of the labor by [fugitive slaves] performed, the value of it, and the expense of their maintenance." That way, the "question of their final disposition" could be worked out later with owners, once the unnatural state of rebellion was no longer disrupting the ordinary relations that existed between the U.S. government and white slave owners.[35] It was not that Cameron or Butler secretly wanted to keep black people slaves.

Cameron in particular was all for military emancipation, but neither he nor Butler was yet prepared to overturn presumptions of civil over military authority, or of the U.S. government's direct relationship to white property owners rather than black men, women, and children held as slaves.[36]

New developments arose in Washington with the passage of the First Confiscation Act on August 6, 1861, and War Department instructions for the act's implementation, issued August 8. Section 4 of the act mandated that any slave owner who "employed" a slave "in any military or naval service whatsoever, against the Government and lawful authority of the United States . . . shall forfeit his claim" to the slave so employed.[37] Within two days, the War Department tried to explain to commanders in the field exactly what all of that meant. Because the legal question of whether slaves were or were not being used in the Confederate war effort was a matter for courts and not for military personnel, Union officers should not try to determine which fugitive slaves had and which had not been used in the Confederate war effort. Rather, they should accept all fugitive slaves within Union lines, employ them where possible, and keep careful records of the names of slaves and their owners so that after the war loyal owners could be compensated for their property loss minus the cost of food and other maintenance provided to slaves in camp. At the same time, Union forces were not to actively entice slaves away from owners.[38] The August 8 instructions, like the First Confiscation Act and like Butler's contraband policy, liberated certain slaves from certain owners while still recognizing the primacy of civil over military authority and while maintaining a direct relationship between the U.S. government and white people rather than black people.

Additionally, each of these actions left significant loopholes that created mass confusion on the ground, which would be sorted out piecemeal in response to local circumstances as the war progressed. Still, the early actions are important because Union lawmakers' and federal officials' attempts to uphold two key structural assumptions, even under pressure and even when willing or (like Thaddeus Stevens) eager to liberate slaves, demonstrate the power and endurance of preexisting structures.

Concerns about maintaining civil over military authority dated back even earlier than the very founding of the American republic; their longevity was one reason they were so difficult to overcome. Congress acted on those concerns in several ways over the course of the war, for example by establishing and actively empowering the Joint Committee on the Conduct of the War. Civilians outside Congress worried, too. One of the reasons that the naturally conservative Dr. George B. Loring approved of Butler's contraband policy was that its repercussions still made it possible after the war to sustain a "republic . . . on the same old principle [rather than] base it on military power."[39]

Francis Lieber, veteran and exile of Europe's Napoleonic Wars, truly dreaded the ascent of military power. "Nothing is more dangerous to modern civil liberty than a large democratic army," he worried to a friend in 1861, because such an army had both the force of public opinion and nearly limitless firepower on its side. With those two powers, there was no end to the liberties such an army could trample.[40] Lieber's misgivings about allowing too much military power, even to achieve an end of which he approved (military emancipation), were so pronounced that he toyed with truly odd ideas about what to do with confiscated or emancipated slaves. "Would not, perhaps the English, gladly take the Virginia run-away slaves and, at a later time, those we buy and emancipate, off our hands, and introduce them as free laborers into the We. Indies?" he wondered.[41] Eventually, Lieber returned to his senses and instead proposed, "Let Congress declare that all negroes coming into our lines are free," a move that would achieve emancipation via civil rather than military authority.[42] Similarly, the War Department's instructions for the implementation of confiscation expressly acknowledged civil primacy when they emphasized that "the substitution of military for judicial measures . . . must be attended by great inconveniences, embarrassments and injuries" and ought to be avoided.[43] These concerns explain why the Confiscation Act and instructions for its implementation left ultimate determinations up to courts and civil authorities, not soldiers, even as they enabled the radical, practical result of emancipation for some individuals.

More evidence that Butler's contraband policy, the First Confiscation Act, and the War Department instructions employed relatively conservative means to achieve the radical result of emancipating slaves is that all three upheld the third preexisting structure, namely the presumption that a direct relationship existed between the U.S. government and white people rather than black people. Butler, after all, used the actions of white owners rather than slaves themselves to determine the course of action the U.S. government should take regarding fugitive slaves. He also emphasized the benefits to the U.S. government of slaves' labor while eschewing the possibility of government ownership of slaves themselves, and he avoided any pronouncement on what a former slave's status was, if not the property of an owner. When the War Department approved Butler's actions, Secretary of War Cameron expressly noted, "The question of their final disposition will be reserved for future determination."[44] Similarly, the First Confiscation Act allowed for the effective emancipation of individuals, even as it avoided explanation of what if any alternative relationship existed between emancipated individuals and the U.S. government and even as it continued to look to masters' (rather than slaves') actions and intentions to determine the legitimacy of claims. The leading antislavery congressman Thaddeus Stevens pointed out as much when he noted that confiscation applied only to slaves "belonging to a rebel, recollect; I confine it to them."[45] The War Department instructions took precautions to respect "the substantial rights of loyal masters" by instructing army personnel to keep careful note of "the circumstances of each case" to ensure that "after tranquility shall have been restored . . . the just rights of all be fully reconciled and harmonized."[46] The sidestepping is not evidence of a reluctance to emancipate, especially on the part of congressional Republicans who had supported Lovejoy's resolution within days of convening. Rather, the avoidance grew from disinclination to go hurtling into a head-on confrontation with deep-seated structural assumptions, not least because such a collision could complicate the prosecution of the war. Actions like Butler's contraband policy, the Confiscation Act, and the War Department's instructions, therefore, all carried out practical emancipation to some extent while retaining civil over military authority and while recognizing direct relationships between the U.S. government and white rather than black people. So far, they amounted to one part radical change to two parts careful preservation, but that was just the beginning.

Butler's order, the First Confiscation Act, and the August 8 War Department instructions did not amount to total abolition, but they did begin freeing some slaves surprisingly early. Once war broke out, Colonel Harvey Brown assumed command of Fort Pickens from Adam Slemmer and informed the War Department, "I shall not send the negroes back as I will never be voluntarily instrumental in returning a poor wretch to slavery but will hold them subject to orders."[47] Similarly, even General George McClellan, among the most conservative on the slavery question, was, by the end of 1861, gathering testimony from escaped slaves who made it to the Army of the Potomac's lines, rather than turning them out of those lines. He might not like the August instructions, but for the most part he followed them.[48]

Sometimes in the war's early days, slaves gained their freedom singly or in small groups. Six black men stole away under a sliver of moon on the night of July 14, 1861, and took shelter in a lighthouse until they could catch the attention of the U.S.S. *Mount Vernon* the next morning. The crew picked them up and obtained permission from Secretary of the Navy Gideon Welles not to return them to their owners.[49] At other times, large numbers escaped slavery together. In a single night, more than two hundred black men, women, and children left Lowcountry plantations, crossed Skull Creek, and made their way to Union forces at Seabrook, near Hilton Head, South Carolina. There, they lit bonfires, sang, danced, and held a prayer meeting inside a captured Confederate fort to celebrate what they saw as their deliverance from slavery.[50]

To some Republicans, none of this emancipating was surprising. A founding principle of the Republican Party since its inception in the 1850s had been that God and the law of nations (rather than mere human effort) made freedom the natural state of all human beings, which could only be denied by positive state or local laws. In time of peace, the federal government could not interfere with positive state laws allowing slavery, but it could surround slave states with a "cordon of freedom," and it could put pressure on states to emancipate within their borders. In time of war, all bets were off, from the Republican point of view: no state or local laws were in effect in the so-called Confederacy because the act of secession revoked them. There, the freedom principle went back into effect, and so by some Republicans' lights military emancipation could begin immediately.[51] In a textbook case of preaching to the choir, Francis Lieber summarized basic Republican doctrine to the lead choirboy Charles Sumner in December 1861. Lieber explained that "negroes coming into our lines, must be and are by that fact free men; for on the one hand, the U.S. cannot become auctioneers of human beings, and on the other hand, our soldiers cannot see, in a human being anything but his humanity. To the being that flies to us, human being that is, does he talk, has he reason, is he, black or white, a Man, or is he a gorilla? If he is a Man . . . all the difficulty inherent in that institution [of chattel slavery] . . . ceases, I take it, by the inherent character of war."[52]

Lieber was not insincere, but he and many other Republicans were breathtakingly overconfident. Lieber's principles animated numerous Republican maneuvers, including Lovejoy's resolution and an amendment to the First Confiscation Act proposed by Lyman Trumbull, which would differentiate slaves from other "property" used by Confederates in support of the rebellion and explicitly sever anyone's claim to their labor rather than transferring that claim from the Confederacy to the Union.[53] Yet the legal foundations undergirding such maneuvers did not seem as firm to everyone as they seemed to Lieber, Lovejoy, and Trumbull. The "law of nations," for example, was no single, clear text, easily consulted and capable of dispelling all ambiguity. Rather, it was a capacious nineteenth-century term for an amorphous body of international law in an age predating any international institutions capable of adjudicating any such body of law. International law on slavery, particularly slavery in war, was far from an unambiguous rejection of slavery. On the contrary, in world history enslavement was a common *result* of warfare.

Moreover, the Republican view was far from universal among all Northerners, and it held no sway over national policy or the federal government before Abraham Lincoln was elected president. Lincoln's immediate predecessor, James Buchanan, succinctly articulated the exact opposite view (the view that had directed the actions of the federal government before 1861) when he chastised a group of Connecticut abolitionists who had the temerity to criticize Buchanan's support of a pro-slavery constitution for Kansas, despite the opposition of most Kansans to that constitution and to slavery generally. Because the Kansas Territory was part of the United States and, as a territory, lacked a state constitution specifically barring slavery, Buchanan argued, "slavery existed . . . and still exists in Kansas, under the Constitution of the

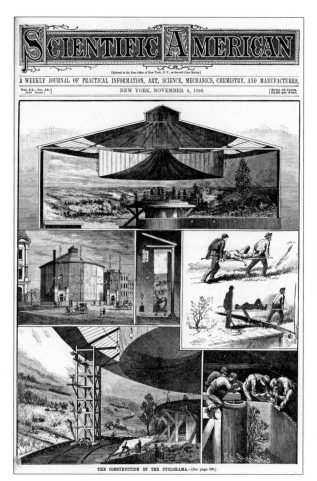

SCIENTIFIC AMERICAN

A WEEKLY JOURNAL OF PRACTICAL INFORMATION, ART, SCIENCE, MECHANICS, CHEMISTRY, AND MANUFACTURES.

NEW YORK, NOVEMBER 6, 1886.

THE CONSTRUCTION OF THE CYCLORAMA.—[See page 296.]

The 377-foot-long, 42-foot-high "Cyclorama of the Battle of Gettysburg" was painted by Paul Philippoteaux in 1883. This 1886 cover of *Scientific American* illustrating the construction of the Gettysburg cyclorama gives a sense of its all-encompassing feel. The detail shows one very small section of the painting as it looks today in the Visitor Center of Gettysburg National Military Park.

Engraving (1861) of Fort Monroe, Virginia. Note that the central figures are women and children.

Many refugees from slavery spent the war adjacent to Fort Monroe in Hampton, Virginia, shown here in 1861 after Confederates abandoned the city.

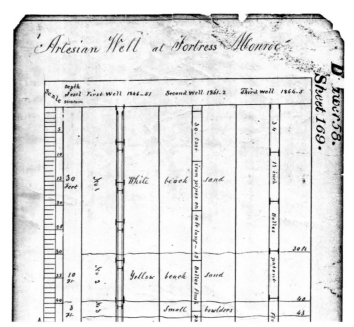

Soldiers tried digging wells at Fort Monroe, including the 900-foot artesian well shown in this 1866 engineers drawing. Despite the herculean effort and painstaking attention evident in the detail, neither this nor any other well has ever struck freshwater at Fort Monroe.

"Barricades on Duke Street, Alexandria, Va., Erected to Protect the Orange and Alexandria Railroad from Confederate Cavalry, 1861." Many former slaves who spent the war in Alexandria, including these men, worked for the Union army.

"Fugitive African Americans Fording the Rappahannock, August 1862." Union soldiers watch former slaves making their way out of slavery in August 1862, much as troops near Fredericksburg watched a group of more than eighty women and children escape in that same month.

"Arrival of Family in Union Lines, 1863." After the Emancipation Proclamation of January 1, 1863, even more men, women, and children ran to the Union army.

"Contrabands Escaping, 1864," by Edwin Forbes in *Frank Leslie's Illustrated Newspaper*

"Union Troops Removing the 'Hobble' from an Escaped Slave—a Scene on Otter Island, S.C., 1862," by Henry Stulen, a member of the regimental band of the Forty-Fifth Pennsylvania Volunteers, appeared in the *New York Illustrated News* on May 17, 1862.

"Bermuda Hundred, Va., African American Teamsters near the Signal Tower, 1864." These men worked for the Army of the James in 1864.

"Sweet Potato Planting, Hopkinson's Plantation, Edisto Island, South Carolina, 1862." After years of forced labor growing cash crops that enriched someone else, many former slaves preferred growing food crops for subsistence instead.

"Negro Quarters, T. J. Fripp Plantation, St. Helena Island, S.C." Near here, a Northern aid worker learned to respect the moral authority of women like "Old Peggy."

"Harriet Tubman (1823–1913),
Nurse, Spy, and Scout"

Clara Barton (1821–1912) at the time
of the Civil War

John Eaton (1829–1906),
shown here after the war

Joanna Moore (1832–1916). Shown here in 1867, Joanna Moore spent the rest of her life in the South teaching, working, and living with African American girls and young women.

"African American Soldiers Mustered Out at Little Rock, Arkansas, 1866." This illustration captures a moment when love of family, pride in contributing to Union victory, hopes, and fears all ran high.

United States." Then, just to make absolutely clear how obvious and widespread his position was, he added, "How it could ever have been seriously doubted is a mystery."[54]

With such an understanding of slavery as a nationally protected institution dominating the federal government until 1861, it is no surprise that regardless of how obvious the freedom principle or even the War Department's orders for the implementation of the First Confiscation Act appear in hindsight, or how clear they seemed in Republican parlors and among the books and papers of Lieber's study (which he called his Owlry), they created confusion rather than clarity when soldiers tried to apply them to real situations on contested and constantly shifting ground in 1861. "The policy of the Government on this question is as much a riddle and a mystery as the ancient oracles of Egypt," one Union soldier mused. "Secretary Cameron says something to please the North, which the President modifies to suit Reverdy Johnson and the Border States. So it goes. Each Commander of our volunteers follows his political predilection in regard to contrabands," and major disagreement between and even within regiments reigned.[55]

The Union general John C. Frémont stirred that disagreement even further by issuing a controversial proclamation on August 30, 1861, from his command in Missouri. A slave state, Missouri remained in the Union, as it turned out for the entire war, but in the summer of 1861 nobody knew that yet, and the fibers tying the border state to the United States were tenuous and frayed. Needing the support of Unionist slaveholders, Lincoln and congressional Republicans soft-pedaled the slavery issue in Missouri and tried to leave as much day-to-day running of the state in the hands of civil authorities as they possibly could. Frémont, on the other hand, threw all restraint to the winds in his proclamation by declaring martial law, transferring the "administrative powers of the State" to "military authorities," and, by military authority, freeing all slaves owned by Confederate sympathizers in the area under his command. In a stroke, Frémont's proclamation upended the presumptions that blackness equaled slavery and that military authority remained subordinate to civil authority in a state that retained a constitutional civil government. Unionist state officials howled in protest. President Lincoln showed remarkable restraint in his initial response, at first simply requesting that Frémont "modify" his proclamation to bring it in line with the First Confiscation Act, which had just as much ability to free slaves but would do so by civil rather than military authority. When Frémont refused first Lincoln's request and then Lincoln's subsequent order, even as he continued to blunder militarily, the president removed him from command.

Lincoln's purposes had more to do with Frémont's losing record in the field, and with upholding the primacy of civil over military law in a state not in rebellion against the United States, than they did with emancipation one way or the other, but removing Frémont still added to the muddle where the vexing question of what to do about slaves was concerned.[56] Francis Lieber, for one, found himself in such a pickle over the matter that he and Charles Sumner shivered on his doorstep one cold November night, unable to stop discussing the matter long enough to open the door and enter. Lieber harbored an absolute abhorrence of the dangers of subordinating civil to military authority in any way, but he also favored military emancipation. From his son Hamilton, then serving in Kentucky, he heard that "Frémont is worshipped by the army."[57] Hamilton Lieber did not speak for all soldiers, some of whom disapproved of Frémont's actions, but he was absolutely right that many of them believed, in the words of one Ohio volunteer, that Frémont's proclamation "has done more for to infuse energy into the Western Division of the service than all others together" and that only "*fogy* politicians" could be so dim as to interfere with the move.[58]

If Frémont reacted to the confusion by brushing aside the principle of civil over military authority in favor of immediate emancipation, General Henry Halleck, one of the few people in 1861 who was both well apprised of international law and actually on the ground where slaves were running, reacted quite differently. Halleck reminds us that the road to emancipation, even military emancipation, was a rocky, unsure path beset with detours rather than a swift, straight highway leading from the outset in one inevitable direction. Halleck's *International Law*, which he began writing just after the Mexican-American War and published in 1861, was as comprehensive as anything available at the war's outset, but the closest it came to discussing what to do about slaves who ran from an enemy was a section on "fugitives and deserters," by which Halleck meant fugitives and deserters from one's *own* side, not who ran from the enemy. Anyone running from the enemy was most likely to be a spy, according to Halleck's otherwise elaborate and precise classification scheme.[59] When General Halleck considered the phenomenon of slaves running to the Union army, he saw not a question of slavery or freedom but a question of potential spies and, even more important, of the relative weight of civil over military authority. On November 20, 1861, Halleck issued General Orders No. 3 for the Department of the Missouri. General Orders No. 3 directed that "fugitive slaves" in the department would not "be hereafter permitted to enter the lines of any camp or of any forces on the march and that any now within such lines be immediately excluded therefrom."[60] The order seemed the very opposite of Frémont's proclamation, and without question it caused tragedy, leading some Union officers to hand some slaves back to some masters.

Yet Halleck consistently explained that the purpose of the order was neither to further nor to frustrate slaves' hopes for freedom but rather to retain civil rather than military authority over slavery. In December 1861, Halleck criticized General Alexander Asboth when a soldier under Asboth's command returned a slave to his father-in-law, who claimed to be the owner. "The relation between the slave and his master is not a matter to be determined by military officers," Halleck chided Asboth, but "must be decided by the civil authorities."[61] Less than two weeks later, Halleck chastised another officer when the enlisted men of an infantry unit refused to deliver a fugitive up to his master. Superficially, the two reprimands look completely contradictory—one for returning a slave to an owner and one for refusing to do so—but Halleck's explanation the second time was almost identical. "I do not consider it any part of the duty of the military to decide upon the rights of master and slave," he again repeated in the second instance. "It is our duty to leave that question for the action of the loyal civil authorities of the State. This is accomplished by keeping all such fugitives out of our camps."[62] If no slaves were in camp, then civil courts, not military ones, would resolve conflicts between fugitives and their alleged masters, Halleck reasoned. Halleck's logic sounds tortured, unpersuasive, and positively immoral to us today (and must have sounded doubly so to the men, women, and children who ran to Union lines), yet the consistency with which Halleck repeated the logic, even under increasing pressure, testifies to just how tenaciously he believed that civil rather than military authority should govern slavery.

Stable though the presumption of civil over military authority regarding slavery was in peacetime, and clear though it remained to Halleck, when it met the chaos of war on the ground, turmoil resulted. Union soldiers in Halleck's department took the contradiction between the War Department's orders for the implementation of the First Confiscation Act and General Orders No. 3 as license to act according to their own lights, which in turn could set them at odds with their officers and with the local population. Slaveholding Unionists near Fort Holt, Kentucky, were so fed up with Union soldiers harboring their runaway slaves that they complained to Brigadier General Ulysses S. Grant, then commanding at headquarters in Cairo, Illinois. In response to a report that "negroes were found concealed in one of the huts at Fort Holt, and that the owner was forcibly prevented from recovering his property," Grant reprimanded the soldiers in question for "treating law, the orders of the Comdr. of the Dept. and my orders with contempt." Grant did not particularly want "the army used as negro catchers" (or, for that matter, "as a cloak to cover their escape"), but he reminded the men's commanding officer, "No matter what our private views may be on this subject, there are in this Department positive orders [that] must be obeyed." Most exasperatingly, from Grant's point of view, the whole mess could have been avoided, because "if Gen. Order No. 3, from Headquarters Dept. of the Mo., had been complied with, this would not have been necessary."[63]

But "ignore it and it will go away" was far too timid an approach to what was shaping up as a volcanic situation. Rather than taking matters calmly, enlisted Union soldiers howled in protest over Halleck's order. Heated conflict between officers enforcing it and men who hated it disrupted Union encampments throughout the department. The Illinois sergeant E. C. Hubbard, for example, dismissed what he saw as Halleck's weak excuse that slaves might be spies as "a mistake" that no "person conversant with the position of affairs in Missouri" could possibly have made if he had his wits about him. Moreover, he did not share Halleck's fastidiousness about the elevation of civil over military authority, at least under the obviously exceptional circumstances in which both the United States and former slaves now found themselves. Hubbard knew of "a dozen or more contrabands" hidden in camp. "To expel them from Camp is to expel them to starve," he recognized, and so he and his fellow soldiers would not do it, no matter what Halleck or anyone else said.[64] General Orders No. 3 also infuriated the Missouri sergeant John Boucher. "The better course I think would be to confiscate the property of all such nigger and all," he told his wife. "I am in hopes that this course will be carried out in the present Congress if so we may hope for a speedy conclusion to the war."[65]

Congress did, in fact, move to contain the chaos with law, beginning in March 1862, when both the House and the Senate passed a law banning Union soldiers and sailors from apprehending fugitive slaves and returning them to their owners, regardless of the owners' political loyalties. Its practical effect was to neutralize the Fugitive Slave Law or at least to relieve Union army personnel from playing any part in enforcing it. Lincoln signed the law on March 13.[66]

When combined with the First Confiscation Act and the War Department's orders for that law's enforcement, the March 1862 law effectively provided that enslaved men and women who made it to Union lines were no longer slaves, although some confusion in its implementation persisted. Throughout the spring of 1862, Louisiana slaves from New Orleans all the way to Baton Rouge ran to get to the Union army. Close behind them followed owners and agents claiming loyalty to the Union, and the responses that those agents met varied. Allegedly concerned about "the demoralizing and disorganizing tendencies to the troops of harboring run away Negroes," Brigadier General Thomas Williams issued orders to expel "fugitives in their camps or garrisons out beyond the limits of their respective guards and sentinels." Soldiers of the Eighth Vermont Infantry went right on hiding escaped slaves in their camps. Then, one day, their colonel, Stephen Thomas, sent a train with fifteen such discovered refugees forty miles outside camp "when the negroes were turned out and ordered to report themselves to their masters." What became of the fifteen freedom-seeking slaves disappears from the record, though three Union soldiers were killed when the train was ambushed on its way back to camp.[67] Colonel Halbert Paine of the Fourth Wisconsin, on the other hand, defied the orders. When challenged by Williams, Paine defended his actions by quoting the March 13 law in its entirety and arguing that turning black men and women out of camp with owners and bounty hunters lurking just outside "*in effect* requires nothing else" but "returning fugitives," which the law clearly prohibited. Paine's battle with Williams lasted for months before Paine eventually prevailed, but throughout that time and after, Paine's interpretation was in effect for all practical purposes, and local slaves knew it. They continued coming into camp, at first singly, then by the dozens, and by the end of June hundreds lived and worked with the Union army.[68]

The phenomenon was hardly confined to Louisiana but rather applied wherever Union troops were to be found. One year after the passage of the March 1862 law, Robert Cartmell, a staunchly Confederate Tennessean of status and property, marked its first anniversary by fuming about the inconvenience of having to prepare his own breakfast because his household was "without a *single* darkie now." The wretched (to Cartmell) state of affairs traced back to the year-old "law of Congress which prohibits any officer returning a fugitive slave." Now Cartmell scrounged around the cold larder for something to eat, while former slaves lived new lives "protected by the Federal Bayonets."[69] Cartmell's slaves, the fugitives who ran to the Fourth Wisconsin, and the thousands of others who fled slavery in the wake of the March 1862 law experienced military emancipation: their living conditions ranged from spartan to abysmal, and they enjoyed little security, especially if regiments sympathetic to their plight moved on, but as long as the Union army was around, they were no longer slaves.

Congress passed two more relevant laws that spring, one outlawing slavery in all U.S. territories and one ending slavery in the District of Columbia. While the impact of the territories law at first seems chiefly symbolic, it represented another step in the process of denationalizing slavery, which is to say, removing federal support for it and reducing it to a local oddity rather than the default status wherever the U.S. flag flew. The territorial law also delivered another blow to the presumption that the default status assigned to a black person by the federal government was slavery.[70] The District of Columbia Compensated Emancipation Act, signed by Lincoln on April 16, 1862, freed all district slaves immediately and also spelled out the civil process by which owners could request compensation: they had ninety days to file and submit a petition, consisting of a preprinted form, any supporting documentation such as a bill of sale or a will, and their own oath of allegiance to the United States plus two witnesses. A federal commission reviewed petitions and made decisions on compensation.[71] The D.C. Emancipation Law had obvious immediate results for enslaved people living in the district. Barbary, a "healthy, able-bodied woman, capable of performing as much labor as most *men*," finally received the legal right to command and benefit from that labor herself as a result of the D.C. Emancipation Act, as did her "sprightly, active" son, Robert, who worked as a waiter in city boardinghouses, as did approximately thirty-one hundred other black residents of the nation's capital.[72] The law also made a difference to slaves living in Maryland and northern Virginia, because slaves there could run to Washington in hopes of freedom. One newspaper reported that the resulting influx created "literally a substratum of negroes living in cellars and basements, from Georgetown to the Navy Yard," and another noted that "late proceedings in Washington relative to fugitive slaves, have created the impression in the surrounding counties in Maryland, that it is hardly worth while to make an effort to reclaim them."[73]

Yet even as military emancipation proceeded in its jerky, discontinuous spurts, resilient structural assumptions applied conservative brakes to the radical process, as General David Hunter learned in the spring of 1862. When Hunter tried to impose martial law and abolish slavery on his own military authority throughout coastal South Carolina, Georgia, and Florida in May 1862, President Lincoln declared Hunter's proclamation "altogether void." Lincoln's action in doing so generally gets trotted out to indict the president for acting too slowly on emancipation, and there is no question that Lincoln was personally more circumspect on the matter than Hunter, or than four million enslaved people would have liked him to be. Yet more was clearly at work in Lincoln's decision, as the rest of his counterorder makes perfectly plain. As Lincoln pointed out, earlier that spring "large majorities in both branches of Congress" had adopted a resolution pledging federal assistance to states abolishing slavery by civil authority. Because that resolution had been passed by elected representatives, it stood as "an authentic, definite, and solemn proposal of the nation to the States." The proposal carried the weight of civil authority, in other words, whereas "neither

General Hunter nor any other commander or person has been authorized by the Government of the United States to make proclamations declaring the slaves of Any State free." In attempting to do so, Hunter dangerously overrode civil authority with sheer military power.[74] Francis Lieber often fumed with impatience at Lincoln, but in this case he vigorously insisted "that the President could not act otherwise than he did regarding Gen. Hunter's Proclamation. A subordinate General has no right to issue a Proclamation of such vast import on his own account." Hunter could try all he liked to give his own unilateral action "a legislative character which it has not," but "if every general commanding a department were to issue his own legislative manifest," then civil government would be in danger and dictatorship would become a genuine threat, or at least so worried Lieber.[75]

Congress demonstrated a new way in which military emancipation could happen via civil authority in July 1862 with passage of the Second Confiscation Act. The new law expanded the category of masters who forfeited their rights to slaves to include all slave owners who gave their allegiance to the Confederacy, whether or not they actively employed their slaves in the Confederate war effort.[76] Lucinda Walker belonged to a man named Berry Prince who lived in Washington County, Mississippi, when she decided to run with her eight-year-old daughter, Alice, and twelve-year-old daughter, Winnie. The family made it all the way to St. Louis, where they procured from a Union army general official papers emancipating them "under the provisions of the Act of Congress of 17th July 1862."[77] They exemplified what it meant to be militarily emancipated: not yet thirty years old and single-handedly responsible for the care of her two daughters, Lucinda was four hundred miles up the Mississippi River from her home in a city where nobody knew who she was, but according to Congress and the Union army, she was no longer the property of Berry Prince, or of any other human being.

Meanwhile, as the Union army's camps filled up with men, women, and children in the summer of 1862, its ranks confronted a manpower crisis. Between April and June, the War Department, overconfident of imminent Union victory, suspended all recruiting efforts. As the end date of one-year enlistments approached and Richmond stubbornly refused to fall, the army suddenly faced a potential shortage of men to fight. Aggressive recruiting efforts on the part of the states, Congress, and the War Department launched into full swing, but it took time to attract, enlist, and train new soldiers, and the Confederacy was unlikely to wait politely until the Union got its house in order. Corps commanders everywhere demanded more men, more labor, more everything. Secretary of War Stanton needed solutions fast, and he turned to Francis Lieber to see if military emancipation could help provide any. Wherever slaves met the army, they immediately began to aid the war effort, sometimes in spite of the reception they received. Could those efforts be channeled, systematized, and harnessed to the war effort? Stanton wondered. Lieber, sure that his own breezy reading of the law of nations made the answer to that question an emphatic yes, dashed off his "Memoir on Military Use of Coloured Persons" to tell Stanton so in August 1862.[78]

The "Memoir on Military Use of Coloured Persons" gathered together thoughts that Lieber had already published in lectures and newspaper columns, and in turn it was publicized and circulated in the late summer and the fall of 1862. In places, the memoir simply rehearsed familiar Republican logic, such as when Lieber reminded readers, "The Commander in Chief has lately declared that, in war, no general can distinguish between free and slaves persons, who offer themselves as fugitives from the enemy," and that anybody who made it to the Union army "shall never be returned into slavery." Yet the memoir moved beyond simple reiteration to suggest a way in which on-the-ground reality might be harnessed to meet war needs. In contraband camps and behind Union lines everywhere, former slaves were contributing vital labor and intelligence to the war effort, as anybody who read the newspaper could scarcely fail to notice. Lieber proposed an elaborate scheme of organizing black freedmen into work parties who would help the war effort in two ways: "by positive increase of our ranks and by weakening the enemy." In some ways, Lieber was behind the times.

Black Northerners were already agitating vigorously for the enlistment of black men into the Union army as full-fledged and equal Union soldiers, whereas Lieber proposed service as "servants, cooks, shoemakers and tailors, blacksmiths, carpenters, ditchers, and agriculturists, wagoners, and boatmen" for pay, but not equal status as soldiers. Moreover, an equal or even greater number of women and children lived in camps and served, cooked, sewed, nursed, built, dug, labored, and grew, but Lieber only saw utility in the labor of men, so while anybody (including women and children) who made it to the Union army ought to be regarded as free, in Lieber's view only black men offered "essential benefit" rather than "greater and greater embarrassment to us." The conservatism and restraint of military emancipation as espoused by Lieber and enacted in law and policy in 1862 are easy to spot from this distance and must have seemed intolerable to the men, women, and children fleeing slavery. Still, the radical potential awakened by practical emancipation had begun to be glimpsed—dimly, partially, but glimpsed all the same—by powerful white men with hands near the levers of governmental power.[79]

The classic example of military emancipation policy, of course, was the Emancipation Proclamation. Issued by President Lincoln on September 22, 1862, the preliminary Emancipation Proclamation promised to free all people held as slaves in areas still in rebellion against the United States as of January 1, 1863, and the final Emancipation Proclamation carried out the promise on the first of January under the logic of military necessity. Even before the ink in the president's signature was dry, observers argued over whether the proclamation amounted to a shining moment ending slavery with a stroke of the pen or a cramped, meaningless bit of verbiage wrung from a reluctant racist who only cared about the Union, and they have continued to do so to the present day. The combined result of both caricatures has been to obscure some basic truths about a document that took an important—not first, not last, not single, but important—step in a crucial process.[80] For one thing, the proclamation continued to shower blows on the two structural assumptions that the Confiscation Acts and wartime actions had begun to pummel, namely the presumption of slavery as the default status of any black person and the inviolate jurisdiction of civil rather than military authority over slavery.

For another thing, both the preliminary and the final proclamations ushered more people out of slavery. News about the preliminary proclamation spread far and fast, and combined with the impact of the First and Second Confiscation Acts and the March 1862 act prohibiting soldiers from serving as slave catchers, it spurred even more black men, women, and children to dash for Union lines. In October 1862, the anti-abolition *Chicago Times* complained that so many black people had fled slavery "during the six weeks past" that if the trend continued "for a few months to come as briskly as it has been carried on," the result would be to "Africanize" the state of Illinois. Robert Cartmell, another hostile witness in Tennessee, groused the following month that "Federal camps are swarming with negroes" lured by the proclamation's promise.[81] As December drew to a close and the first of January waited just around the corner, numbers continued to climb. More than two hundred black men, women, and even tiny children "walked as though they was tired most to dith," but weariness did not stop them from making their way to the Union army at New Bern, North Carolina, on December 27.[82] Meanwhile, as refugees from slavery continued to flee, Union war news looked so bleak that Lincoln finally sacked General George McClellan once and for all and then suffered the fallout of yet another Union defeat at Fredericksburg, a defeat so humiliating and ignominious that observers throughout the United States (and even European onlookers) wondered if Lincoln would retract the promise made on September 22. As night fell on the last day of December, free blacks, slaves still in bondage, and refugees from slavery in wartime contraband camps gathered in "watch meetings" to see if a final proclamation would materialize.[83]

It did. Not all Union soldiers welcomed the proclamation, but most recognized the move as militarily necessary to win the war, many recognized it as morally necessary to win the war justly, and all knew that whatever their personal feelings, they now literally marched as enforcers of the proclamation that they carried on one-and-a-half-inch slips of paper to distribute "among the blacks while on the march."[84] Black slaves knew it, too, and the numbers fleeing slavery continued to rise, spurred by the final Emancipation Proclamation even in areas exempted by the text of the document itself. Perennially incensed Robert Cartmell grumbled about how exceptions in the proclamation were "no use," for even though "Mr. Lincoln's emancipation proclamation did not embrace Tennessee . . . every bodies' [slaves], as mine, are riding about the streets of Jackson . . . refusing to return."[85] Wherever the army was on the day the proclamation went into effect, slaves came from radii extending hundreds of miles, by land, water, and any imaginable form of conveyance. Hundreds of occupants of the camp at Suffolk, Virginia, for example, "came here from North Carolina[,] know all about the Proclamation and they started in the belief in it."[86] Steamers like the *Jesse K. Bell* and the *Rocket* sailed up the Mississippi River filled with hundreds of men, women, and children who fled slavery in Helena, Arkansas; Lake Providence, Louisiana; Yazoo Pass, Mississippi, and countless other points where word of the proclamation emboldened slaves to reach for freedom.[87]

What slaves grasped when they reached for freedom via the Emancipation Proclamation was a stalk growing in the same nettle patch as the Confiscation Acts, War Department orders, and law prohibiting military personnel from enforcing the Fugitive Slave Law: the nettle patch of military emancipation. Like the medicinal value of stinging nettles, the efficacy of military emancipation in specific circumstances was clear. John Eaton specifically endorsed a "military in preference to civil form" of emancipation in the midst of war "because martial law must prevail over the regions during the war; because more simple, avoiding undesirable questions & complications; and because more easily adjusted to all necessities & changes."[88] Military emancipation meant that the bonds defining men, women, and children as property and shackling them to owners were broken by power conferred by war and wielded by the Union army and navy. That the bonds were broken at all by a national government that had up to that point protected and even helped to forge them was without question revolutionary, and few men or women born into slavery confused military emancipation with continued slavery, any more than someone treated with nettle tincture for asthma, bronchitis, or pneumonia would confuse clear breathing with chronic coughing. Yet stinging nettles come by their name rightly; just as surely as they sting and burn, military emancipation came with clear drawbacks and shortcomings.

For one thing, armies are military forces whose purposes are to fight and win wars; they are not humanitarian organizations, and they often bring "heartbreak as well as liberation."[89] There was heartbreak aplenty in Civil War military emancipation, especially when the same military necessity that enabled the Emancipation Proclamation also enabled orders that contributed to war strategy but cut against the best interests of refugees from slavery or even outright harmed them. Men and women seeking freedom from their masters by running to Union forces in Middle Tennessee, for example, did escape their masters, but they also ran smack-dab into a demanding war effort that could pluck them from schoolrooms or jobs in hospitals and plunk them back down where the army needed them most, such as in grinding manual labor on Fort Negley in Nashville. One woman named Margaret and another named Dilla Best were among the hundreds of former slaves who fled from as far away as Huntsville, Alabama, to Union lines at Murfreesboro, Tennessee, in hopes that a securely held Union city would help them consolidate their hold on freedom. Margaret found work as a servant to the Union army surgeon William Eames, and Dilla found work in Eames's hospital, but both watched as the young men and boys among their connections and acquaintances were shepherded onto railroad cars and impressed into Fort Negley labor. Dilla herself remained at the hospital but while there contracted an illness that killed her in a mere thirty-six hours.[90] Wartime conditions worsened the ever-present crowding, exposure, and poor sanitation in contraband camps and contributed to towering mortality rates everywhere former slaves ran. By December 1, 1862, for instance, typhoid and especially "Small Pox—This terrible disease" were so "prevalent in [Alexandria, Virginia], especially among the 'contrabands,'" that an epidemic claimed 185 victims by the time the U.S. government constructed a specially designated hospital.[91]

Military emancipation's impact on slave states that stayed in the Union was even more unpredictable. It is not the case that slavery skated through the war untouched in the border states; those states, like all others, were affected by both Confiscation Acts and by the March 1862 law prohibiting Union soldiers from returning slaves, as black men and women well knew. Hundreds, and eventually thousands, made their way to a Union-guarded contraband camp at Cape Girardeau, Missouri, located on the Mississippi River. From that protected location, freedpeople who wanted to liberate "any of their family" were able to "arm themselves, go with a few soldiers and take them" from locations throughout southeastern Missouri and southwestern Kentucky. Two black men walked the ten miles to Jackson, Missouri, on a cold February night, insistently knocked on the door of the Davis farm, and "said they wanted Caroline." Caroline decided not to go, but another black woman, Matilda, decided to take her chances at "the Cape." Earlier in the month, five male slaves acted even more boldly by heading to "the Cape" in "open day light." With spring just around the corner in

Cape Girardeau County and in the adjoining counties of Fulton, Hickman, and Carlisle in Kentucky, it became clear that "men who hitherto farmed extensively [would] do nothing in that line," because so much of the labor force had escaped to the Union encampment.[92]

Border states were exempted from the Emancipation Proclamation, not that the legalities stopped black men and women or Union troops from acting on news of the proclamation. Colonel William Utley and the men of the Twenty-Second Wisconsin Infantry found themselves in Kentucky in the fall of 1862. Every time the Twenty-Second moved camp, fugitive slaves accompanied them, disguised as soldiers, hidden with baggage, or concealed in any other way the black men and women and the soldiers from Wisconsin could devise to spirit the slaves away from their owners. Slaveholders complained to Brigadier General Quincy Gillmore, who ordered Utley to turn all fugitives out of camp. Utley "coolly tore [the orders] in two in the presence of the messenger," claiming that the March 1862 law of Congress superseded any such order. Gillmore disagreed, arguing that the law did not apply in states still in the Union. The longer the regiment stayed in the state, the more slaves it sheltered, and the more local enmity it aroused, to the point where armed civilians of Georgetown, Kentucky, lined the streets hoping to get the chance to shoot at the regiment as it marched through town. When the regiment sheltered a slave belonging to George Robertson, former chief justice of the Kentucky Supreme Court, Robertson tried to arrest Utley, but no soldiers would cooperate, and the War Department sustained Utley.[93]

If the exemption of border states from the Emancipation Proclamation did not extinguish local slaves' hopes for freedom, it could nonetheless frustrate them, often tragically. Nat Leonard, a Unionist slaveholder in Ravenswood, Missouri, commiserated with his friends Judge Walker and J. M. Nelson about the prospect of a shorthanded harvest season, thanks to all the slaves who, emboldened by news of the preliminary proclamation, bolted their owners. Already, Leonard and Nelson had lost two good workers each, Walker had lost one, and neighbors in nearby Boonville lost "some 7 or 8" in a single night. On the other hand, another neighbor managed to recapture one of his escaped slaves and "gave him a round whipping" before setting him back to work.[94] In short, when refugees from slavery grasped the stinging nettle of military emancipation in the border states, the sting could be even sharper, but most disconcerting, the nettle could prove elusive or temporary, disappearing the moment a seeker thought it was within reach.

Moreover, even outside the border states, military emancipation provided a workable path out of slavery only when the Union army was around to enforce it. When Confederate forces briefly recaptured Murfreesboro, Margaret, the woman who escaped slavery and became a servant to the Union surgeon Eames, narrowly avoided re-enslavement by running ten miles and hiding in the wilderness for a week. Not everyone she was with got so lucky. One person was shot, and two more were caught and "unmercifully flogged" by owners who clapped them right back into bondage.[95]

Beyond individuals' daily risk of personal re-enslavement, the institution of slavery itself had displayed considerable resilience in the aftermath of most other wars in world history, including some that appeared to weaken slavery during the war itself but in the long run inflicted only reversible, not permanent, damage. Because we know that the Civil War ended slavery, it is all too easy to assume that once slaves began leaving their masters, slavery was doomed because no earthly power could reinstate it. Republicans in the 1860s brimmed with that optimism, but emancipation was not an onrushing or irreversible tide. It did not somehow erase a former master's desire to re-enslave, nor did it neutralize the former master's willingness to use force to realize that desire, as world history so clearly demonstrated. During the American Revolution, some of the slaves who escaped to the British gained permanent freedom, but others were sold in the Caribbean after the war. Meanwhile, Northern states in the newly independent United States began gradually abolishing slavery at the exact same time that some Southern states strengthened it. North Carolina, for one, had been swept up in revolutionary fervor, much like Connecticut, Pennsylvania, or any of the other states we now think of as "Northern" states, but the moment not only passed; it reversed course. In the 1780s, the North Carolina state legislature made manumission more difficult and "even authorized the re-enslavement of those who had been freed."[96] When the War of 1812 came, Americans held in bondage once again ran to the British, but after the war's conclusion slavery actually spread and grew stronger in the United States.[97] During the Napoleonic Wars, military emancipation abolished slavery in numerous Caribbean locations, such as Guadeloupe, but reestablishment of slavery followed the end of conflict.[98] More recently, military emancipation during revolts and independence movements in Latin America throughout the first half of the nineteenth century freed slaves in wartime, but there, too, abolition gave way to re-enslavement, sometimes after as much as a decade of freedom.[99] Only in Haiti, commonly identified as the only successful slave rebellion in history, did military emancipation lead eventually to permanent abolition of slavery, but not without a period of reestablished slavery first, even there.[100] There was no a priori reason why military emancipation in the United States in the nineteenth century would be immune from any of those outcomes once it lost the authority it held only in time of war.

Another shortcoming to military emancipation was that despite its effectiveness at weakening two prewar structural assumptions (the presumption of slavery as the default status of all black people, and the elevation of civil over military authority where slavery was concerned), it left one (the presumption of a direct relationship between the U.S. government and individual white people but not individual black people) largely untouched and intact. *The New York Times* recognized as much when it described the "thousands of negroes collected about" Fort Monroe as lacking "relations of any kind to society and the State." All agreed that "they cannot and will not be sent back into Slavery," but that resolution still "leaves the whole question of title," meaning status or rank, not certificate of property ownership, "in abeyance."[101] To put the point another way, military emancipation could answer the question of what at least some former slaves were *not:* in specified areas, for as long as a state of war existed, they were not slaves. But military emancipation could not answer the logical follow-up question of who, in relation to the national government, they became.

Confusion over the status of the militarily emancipated was almost guaranteed by the negative rather than positive language predominant in the first half of the war. The Confiscation Acts and even the Emancipation Proclamation stipulated that slaves were freed *from* "their servitude" and could "not again [be] held as slaves." The March 1862 law prohibiting Union army enforcement of the Fugitive Slave Law told soldiers what *not* to do, but nothing stipulated what, precisely, former slaves were freed *to,* nor did anything instruct soldiers in what *to* do.[102] The vagueness manifested itself everywhere. When Colonel Robert J. Rombauer wrote from Pacific, Missouri, to consult the department provost marshal on what to do about a local man demanding the return of his alleged slaves the month *after* the March 1862 law, the provost marshal restricted his response to what Rombauer and his men should *not* do, answering that "the U.S. forces will leave negroes and their owners to settle their affairs by civil process and will not engage in the restoration of fugitives nor will they take negroes from their masters." Even after that response, Rombauer had no idea what to do, and the former slaves in question had no idea where they stood.[103] As late as the following year, the district judge advocate Lucien Eaton remained so flummoxed that even though he recognized former slaves in Union camps as "presumptively free," he also admitted that inconclusive direction from Washington made "systematic provision by the military authorities for the freed people of color" well-nigh impossible, because he had no idea what their relationship to the national government was.

·   ·   ·

These examples, and countless more like them wherever former slaves and the Union army came into contact with each other in the first half of the conflict, make the point that there is a big difference between emancipating slaves and changing the relationship between the national government and the institution of slavery. Without a doubt, Civil War contraband camps served as the venues in which tens of thousands of black men, women, and children took their first steps out of slavery, and in that way they weakened the institution of legal, state-supported slavery in the United States. As two agents sent by Congress to investigate conditions in contraband camps in Alabama, Tennessee, and Kentucky reported, the very existence of a contraband camp "by its moral influence ... greatly weakened and almost broke the bonds of the slave" because "the master knows his slave has the power to leave him and to reach this camp, where he will be secure, and consequently the tasks and punishments he has been accustomed to exact, or to inflict, are greatly reduced and ameliorated."[104] Specifically, contraband camps, the interactions between slaves and the Union army that transpired there, and the response of the executive and legislative branches of the U.S. government to those interactions set the process of military emancipation in motion by disrupting two deep-seated prewar structural assumptions, one equating blackness with a presumption of slavery and one presuming civil rather than military authority over slavery.

Yet for permanent abolition of slavery, first tentative steps, even if taken by tens of thousands of pairs of feet, were not enough. Instead, a fundamental break in the relationship between the national government and slavery needed to take place. The Civil War began severing the relationship between the national government and slavery with the sword of military authority. Doing so had required the overcoming of enormous obstacles, and it marked a dramatic, even radical accomplishment, but also an incomplete one. Past precedent clearly showed that breaks between nations and slavery were not always clean and that even when slavery had appeared to be eradicated in other times and places, it had come back, much in the manner of communicable diseases like smallpox and measles if immunizations stop taking place. One step absolutely vital to ensuring the permanent destruction of slavery was to seal it with civil authority, which would have to wait until after the war.

Full and permanent freedom also required a new relationship between the national government and former slaves. Emancipated slaves not incorporated into the body politic of the national government could not ensure that they would remain free, because they lacked recourse to a power strong enough to defend their freedom against potential re-enslavers. The way to gain access to a sufficiently robust source of power in the Americas in the nineteenth century was to be incorporated into a national state as part of the body politic. For former slaves to do so in the U.S. Civil War, the third structural assumption, the one presuming a direct relationship between the U.S. government and white but not black people, would need to fall, but it stood fast in 1861 and 1862. Even with military emancipation well under way, it was more "midnight in the exodus," as John Eaton put it, than it was the dawning of a new day, because what former slaves had really been emancipated into was statelessness. Eaton feared that in their liminal phase, newly released from slavery but not yet incorporated by the national government, freedpeople's "road may be rough and perilous, clouds may thicken and lower."[105] In the course of traveling that rough and perilous road from 1862 to 1865, black men, women, and children would dramatically weaken presumptions of black statelessness, and they would begin pointing the way toward a new relationship between the federal government and former slaves. The process by which they did so was sometimes unintentional and often haphazard, and it almost always occurred amid thick and lowering clouds.

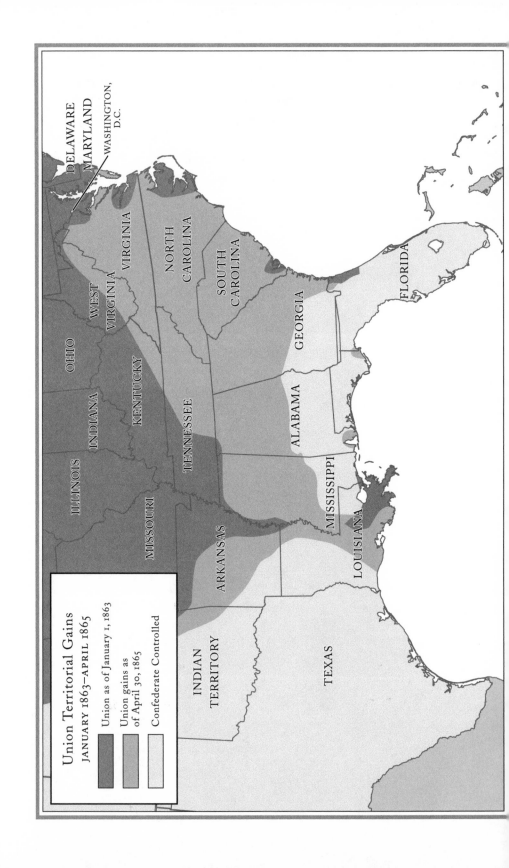

Union Territorial Gains
JANUARY 1863–APRIL 1865

Union as of January 1, 1863

Union gains as
of April 30, 1865

Confederate Controlled

DELAWARE
MARYLAND
WASHINGTON, D.C.

VIRGINIA
WEST VIRGINIA
VIRGINIA

NORTH CAROLINA

SOUTH CAROLINA

GEORGIA

FLORIDA

OHIO

INDIANA

KENTUCKY

TENNESSEE

ALABAMA

ILLINOIS

MISSOURI

ARKANSAS

MISSISSIPPI

LOUISIANA

INDIAN TERRITORY

TEXAS

FOUR

Uneasy Alliances

Wartime Citizenship in Contraband Camps

L uther T. Collier, T. R. Bryan, W. W. Woodward, and J. B. McDonald were all substantial men who did not see any reason why the war churning around them as 1862 drew to a close should interfere with the obligation of the U.S. government to help them protect their property. Much of their wealth consisted of slaves, but they lived in Chillicothe, Missouri, not in a state that had openly rebelled against the United States, and so they expected the sword of military emancipation to remain sheathed where they were concerned. In some ways, it did. The Emancipation Proclamation set to take effect in just a few weeks did not apply to them. The Twenty-Seventh (Union) Missouri Infantry operating where the four men lived consisted of their friends and neighbors, who they thought could be trusted. Consequently, they were at first merely annoyed when some of their slaves ran to the Twenty-Seventh Missouri. A simple note to Lieutenant Colonel Augustus Jacobson, or, if he proved tiresome, a quick visit to camp, ought to restore their slave property to them. Instead, soldiers refused to turn refugees from slavery out of their encampment, and Lieutenant Colonel Jacobson claimed he neither would nor could return slaves. Collier, Bryan, Woodward, and McDonald were shocked. They, after all, were white. They were men. They owned property. In other words, they were "citizens . . . entitled, as we believe, to protection from this wholesale system of robbery." Their claim on the U.S. government and its armed forces was clear, and it was simply inconceivable to them that black men, women, and children could have any competing claim. Next, they wrote to Jacobson's superior, General Samuel Curtis, for redress, but Curtis sided with Jacobson and the regiment, sending back nothing more than a wry reply about how "war opens a wide door."[1]

Right from the beginning of the war, black men, women, and children had exited slavery through war's wide door, but they knew that dangers like re-enslavement and death could follow them through that door, just as Collier, Bryan, Woodward, and McDonald tried to do. If former slaves were to arrive at the destinations they sought, they would need access to a power strong enough to help them combat slaveholders' violent opposition. The chief sources of that kind of power in the Americas in the mid-nineteenth century were national governments. The most promising route to former slaves' hoped-for destinations coursed not through the dangerous no-man's-land of statelessness into which military emancipation initially released them but rather through national belonging.

Questions of national belonging and its opposite, statelessness, were everywhere in the mid-nineteenth century. In fact, Americans so often point to the U.S. Civil War as their nation's bloodiest war that it is easy to lose sight of how, in many ways, it fit right into a nineteenth century characterized worldwide by state building and the florescence of romantic nationalism. A series of revolts and revolutions rocked Europe. Empires shifted and new nation-states fought their way into existence in South America. One of the deadliest conflicts in human history, the Taiping Rebellion, eviscerated China from 1850 to 1864. All over the world, it seemed, places were tearing themselves apart over questions of national inclusion and exclusion. Those themes animated diplomatic negotiations, columns of newsprint, public debate, and even literature.[2] One of the most influential short stories of 1863 was Edward Everett Hale's "Man Without a Country," which tells the story of Philip Nolan, who renounces the United States and as punishment is banished from it for the rest of his days. While Nolan's tragic exile most clearly chastised secessionists and their Northern sympathizers (the "Copperheads"), Nolan's growing inability to meet life's hazards without the protection of a national government also warned of the dangers of statelessness.[3]

The fictional Nolan experiences personal statelessness as punishment for his individual renunciation, but for large numbers of real people throughout the Atlantic world in the mid-nineteenth century emancipation resulted in statelessness, or at least brought their formal statelessness to the fore. Such was clearly the case for a group of African captives who sparked an international incident known as the Christie Affair. Named for the British minister to Brazil, William Christie, the Christie Affair took place from 1861 to 1865, the exact years in which the United States was tearing itself apart. Briefly, British patrolling vessels enforcing the international ban on the transatlantic slave trade had intercepted captives being illegally exported from Africa to Brazil, and now the question was what to do with the so-called *emancipados*. Because the slave trade was illegal, the captives could not be sold as slaves. At the same time, they were not recognized as free Brazilians by the national government of Brazil. Instead, they were relegated to an awkward "not-slave, not-Indian, not-foreigner" category. With the government of Brazil designating the former captives as permanent outsiders, William Christie maintained that the *emancipados* were beholden more to the British Empire than to the Brazilian national government for whatever thin shadow of freedom they might enjoy. Some of the captives, in contrast, insisted on a direct relationship between themselves and the "bureaucracy of the Brazilian state" as the guarantor of their emancipation and even went so far as to join in widespread Anglophobia sweeping Brazil as a way of laying claim to Brazilian identity.[4] Diplomatic relations between Britain and Brazil formally ruptured in 1863, demonstrating just how destabilizing the issue of statelessness could be, even when the numbers concerned were relatively small. The U.S. government, fighting for its survival, could not afford the destabilizing influence of a sizable stateless population.[5]

Yet thanks to wartime emancipation, the United States suddenly had a large and growing stateless population on its hands, and no real idea of where or how former slaves fit within the national community. Antebellum courts had held that "manumission confers no other right than that of freedom from the dominion of the master and the limited liberty of locomotion . . . It does not and cannot confer any of the powers, civil or political, incident to citizenship."[6] The highest court in the land, the Supreme Court, agreed. In 1857, the *Dred Scott* decision insisted point-blank that African Americans "are not included, and were not intended to be included, under the word 'citizens' in the Constitution, and can therefore claim none of the rights and privileges which that instrument provides for and secures to citizens of the United States."[7] Emancipation in other slaveholding and formerly slaveholding societies, with the exception of Haiti, had not led straight to national belonging, either. The Reverend A. D. Olds had ministered to former slaves in Jamaica at the time of West Indian emancipation three decades earlier and reflected on that experience as he worked among freedpeople in the Corinth contraband camp in 1863. In Jamaica, Olds remembered, "the transition from a state of absolute subjection" to "a state where each is to control the disposition to his own time & to choose freely his own course" within the "community" had not happened all at once but rather had passed through a liminal "apprenticeship" state, which neither amounted to full independence nor equated to national belonging.[8] If the status of the *emancipados* in Brazil was not confusing enough, the post-manumission status of Brazilian-born slaves was not much clearer. Enslaved Brazilians could only be emancipated by a multistep process consisting of original liberation, a waiting period of several years spent in an indeterminate state, and then submission of a petition for "Full Freedom," which might or might not have been granted. In short, the world as nineteenth-century Americans knew it was full of possible relationships that might exist between a government and a liberated slave, not one of which clearly paralleled the circumstances of refugees from slavery during the U.S. Civil War.

Francis Lieber grappled with this dilemma and what it meant for army dealings with former slaves while and after he wrote the Lieber Code. Written at the end of 1862 and issued as General Orders No. 100 in 1863, the code made quite plain in Articles 32, 42, and 43 that "fugitives escaping from a country in which they were slaves" were no longer slaves upon reaching the Union army, but that was as far as it went. Nowhere could it clearly state what former slaves' new status was, which may be one reason Lieber was looking to exchange ideas with someone from Brazil in early 1864.[9]

Congress authorized the American Freedmen's Inquiry Commission in 1863 in part to investigate and recommend what to do about the large stateless population that emancipation was suddenly creating within U.S. borders. One of the agents specially chosen by Secretary of War Edwin Stanton to lead the AFIC was Samuel Gridley Howe, a man acutely attuned to questions of national belonging, inclusion, and statelessness. Among his many other pursuits, Howe had participated in the Greek War of Independence from Turkey (1821–1829) in his youth. He knew Edward Everett Hale, and he read widely about world events.[10] In 1863, he was also reading letters sent back to him from a friend whom he had sent to collect "all the evidence we have conc[ernin]g the colored race in Jamaica & in the Honduras."[11] Meanwhile, Howe himself set off to do the same thing in Ontario. While he was there, *Macmillan's*, a popular British periodical circulated widely in Canada, reprinted "Our Relations with Brazil" by William Christie, which served as a reminder of how statelessness created problems for national governments.[12] Howe, in short, was in Canada looking for alternatives to freedpeople's statelessness.

Freedpeople were doing much the same thing throughout the occupied South, for even more urgent reasons. Former slaves needed, and knew they needed, access to the power of the U.S. government, and so they sought a combination of inclusion and rights protection that they explicitly called citizenship. The trouble was how to get it, for emancipation alone certainly did not provide it. The *Dred Scott* decision recently and emphatically made clear that African Americans could *not* be U.S. citizens. Collier, Bryan, Woodward, and McDonald certainly knew of the *Dred Scott* decision, and they took it for granted that the soldiers of the Twenty-Seventh Missouri knew and would abide by it as the year 1863 dawned. When the war began, many soldiers probably would have, but as the war progressed, black women and children who aided the Union army in contraband camps (every bit as much as black men who enlisted in the Union army) compelled soldiers to reconsider. Time and again, ordinary white farmers and clerks serving as provost marshals or picket sentries in the Union army had good reason to question why the U.S. government should help a master who wanted his slaves back, if the Union could benefit by extending protection to black nurses, laborers, and laundresses instead. Freedpeople's labor on behalf of the Union war effort forged a distinctive definition of citizenship not merely as payback for fighting but as a direct, reciprocal relationship with the U.S. government involving the exchange of individuals' useful service to the national government for positive protection of rights by that government. In contrast to the expectations of white men like Collier, Bryan, Woodward, and McDonald, war-forged citizenship was citizenship founded not in who people were but in what they did for the national government. The hard-struck bargain between freedpeople and Union soldiers widened access to citizenship, made the federal rather than the state government the arbiter of inclusion, and folded rights protection into what had formerly been a relationship chiefly of membership and obligation.

Wartime citizenship was a passageway to national power built largely by the formerly powerless. Like a passageway, wartime citizenship arrived at a particular destination, but also like a passageway it proved to be more narrow than the broad vistas originally envisioned by former slaves when war first opened its wide door to emancipation. Moreover, it came at a very high cost. Yet alongside its serious shortcomings, wartime citizenship marked a notable turnaround. Before the war, the national government had served as the reliable ally of slaveholders and a powerful denier of black people's rights, even the most basic right of personhood. During the war, wherever former slaves came into contact with the Union army and especially in contraband camps, they used their loyalty and their labor to turn the federal government from *slaveholders'* ally into *their* most efficacious—if often wary and tragically imperfect—ally in the pursuit and protection of the basic rights that gave their lives meaning.

· · ·

Freedpeople and members of the Union army were keenly aware of the need for some clarity in matters of national belonging and rights protection each time black men, women, and children entered Union lines. Chaplain Samuel Sawyer, the railroad agent J. C. Hanford, and a group of former slaves trying to get to St. Louis ran smack into the confusion and obstruction that resulted when such clarity was lacking. In the winter of 1863, General Benjamin Prentiss ordered the Reverend Samuel Sawyer, then serving as chaplain to an Indiana regiment, to accompany a group of fifteen hundred black men, women, and children from Helena, Arkansas, to St. Louis, where the Ladies' Contraband Relief Society awaited their arrival. The chaplain and the former slaves made their way to Jefferson City, Missouri, where they hoped to board the train and take the Pacific Railroad the rest of the way to St. Louis. Sawyer carried orders for the government-funded rail transport of "contraband teamsters and their families," which, to Sawyer and his traveling companions, made it perfectly plain that they should board the cars and be on their way. At the Jefferson City depot, the railroad agent Hanford refused to let the group board. How could he know for sure that these people were entitled to rail transit? First, didn't the passage of the Second Confiscation Act and the Emancipation Proclamation mean that if the black people standing in front of him were really from Arkansas, then they were actually free people and therefore not "contrabands," whatever that had meant? Second, if the order was for the "families" of teamsters, what was he to do about the unmarried women in the group? They were unlikely to be teamsters themselves, Hanford assumed, nor, if they were single, could they be wives of teamsters. In fact, local slaveholders claimed that some members of the group assembled with Sawyer were actually their slaves trying to escape. As citizens loyal to the Union, the alleged owners insisted, they were entitled to army protection of their property. Third, how could Hanford allow these prospective passengers to ride at the expense of the U.S. government when he had no way of knowing what their relationship to that government actually was?[13]

Chaplain Sawyer eventually had to board the train to report for duty, leaving the group of former slaves behind in Jefferson City, their status still undefined. He complained furiously to Union command, and the provost marshal went after Hanford and his superiors in the Pacific Railroad. Meanwhile, Lucien Eaton, district judge advocate in St. Louis, wrote to Major General John Schofield emphasizing that "the faith of the Gov't has been pledged by the Proclamation" to former slaves but that "villainy" persisted in the slave state of Missouri "owing to the severity—the barbarism—of our state laws." For the time being, Eaton reported, the provost marshal general in St. Louis did his best to oversee the movement of refugees from slavery into and out of St. Louis, but his efforts could only provide stopgap measures. A system and an authority higher than the state of Missouri were clearly called for, and they needed to come from the federal government.[14]

But what could the federal government use to determine eligibility for national belonging? As early as the summer of 1862, freedpeople's actions were beginning to make it clear that obvious markers like race or customary ones like property ownership would no longer do. To take one example from that summer, five slave women escaped and made it to Union lines in Jackson, Tennessee. There, they went to work at an army hospital alongside the Union army surgeon Dr. James D. Strawbridge. One day, a white man claiming to own the women showed up at the hospital, tied up one of the women, and started dragging her out of the hospital by her neck. Dr. Strawbridge punched the owner, forcibly released the woman, and "started to drive [the owner] from the Hospital grounds," when he was stopped by the provost marshal. As it turned out, the slaveholder had applied to the provost marshal for permission to reclaim his property and had received an ambiguous (perhaps purposely so) response. Strawbridge would not budge, so "the Provost then declined taking them away" while Strawbridge appealed to Major General John McClernand to have the women officially detailed to hospital duty on the grounds that "their services are absolutely necessary and could scarcely be dispensed with at the present time." They, far more than a secessionist with a fair complexion and a substantial amount of property, deserved the protection of the U.S. government, because they were aiding the Union cause while the slaveholder, an "undisguised secessionist," sought to subvert it.[15]

By no measure does this incident qualify as a happy story—the woman ended up back in the hands of her owner—but it does show how the war blew the cover off previously unexamined notions and forced officials to wrestle with the formerly far-fetched possibility that a black woman might have a stronger claim on the U.S. government than a white man did. McClernand, a lifelong Southern-leaning Democrat and personal friend to many slaveholders, ordered Strawbridge to report to him immediately. He cursed the doctor furiously and tried to "squash" him by throwing a chair at his head. McClernand was intent on his course of action—he would send those women back by hook or by crook—but he was livid, because even though his own opinions on the matter were strong and clear, and even though he was unquestionably the ranking officer whose word would be final with or without justification, he recognized that Strawbridge and the women made too compelling a case for even him to refuse without giving a reason. So he came up with one. Because other people could perform the same service, the general rationalized, those *particular* women were not militarily necessary to the Union cause and should be returned to their owner. McClernand did not craft this convoluted justification because he liked being made to explain himself, especially by a subordinate and by black women! He had to make a case, however ridiculous, that the women were not personally and uniquely useful enough to the Union cause because the stern logic of war made the women's utility to the nation too important to ignore.[16]

Clashes between former slaves and white slaveholders set Union troops and government officials to arguing over whose side the U.S. government should be on throughout the occupied South. At exactly the same time that Strawbridge was punching a slave owner, McClernand was throwing chairs, and black women were tending to the wounded, Colonel Halbert Paine was quarreling with General Thomas Williams near Baton Rouge, Louisiana. Williams insisted that the army's first duty was to loyal Unionists who owned slaves. Paine disagreed and continued to harbor refugees. All spring and summer in Baton Rouge, General Williams alternated between clapping Paine into jail for harboring slaves and releasing him to fight whenever the regiment was needed in battle. The arrangement afforded Paine plenty of time to make the absurd scenario known to lawmakers back east. In July 1862, Senator Timothy Howe of Wisconsin raised the matter in Congress, where he insisted that all former slaves who made it to Union lines "ought both to be employed and protected." Moreover, he continued, "I do not hesitate to say that no officer ought to be employed for an instant . . . who does not feel it to be his solemn and his bounden duty to furnish protection to every woman and every child who appeals to him for protection from the authority or control of those who are now in arms against it." Say what one would about property rights or about the relative merits of race and rank, there was a war on, and "I would rather have the Negro than the brigadier [Williams]," Howe thundered, because "he is worth more to the service; he is worth more to the government; he is worth more to mankind." That was true of women. That was true of children. That was true of anyone willing to contribute to the Union war effort. Howe's emphasis on usefulness to the Union neatly echoed the dispute between Strawbridge and McClernand, only this time it led to the opposite conclusion from the one McClernand had drawn.[17]

In fact, momentum in that dispute had already begun shifting right under McClernand's nose in Jackson. He might have thought he had heard the last of the women, but "great dissatisfaction" was brewing in the Union ranks toward "officers in authority" (like him) who stubbornly persisted in "guarding Rebel property." The very same week that McClernand hurled furniture at Dr. Strawbridge and returned slave women to their owner, Corporal James Jessee of the Eighth Illinois Infantry (stationed in Jackson) grumbled, "Soldiers are getting tired of fighting the Rebels and guarding and protecting them at the same time." Jessee and his messmates had a better idea, one that transferred the protection of the federal government away from people fighting against it and toward people aiding it: "No protection of [slaveholders'] person or property. No returning of negroes to their master. But allowing them to remain in camp as cooks."[18] Hardheaded realism, not sentiment, inspired Jessee's recommendation, and before long he and the men of his regiment started to put it into action. Throughout the fall of 1862, his diary reported more and more slaves from throughout the county coming to work and spy for the Union army, and he also noted ways in which the army reciprocated by exercising its power for the protection of former slaves rather than masters. For example, when a slave woman informed the men of the Eighth Illinois Infantry that her master was a Confederate and had guns hidden in his house, Corporal Jessee did more than just refuse to return her. He found the owner, marched straight up to him, and gave him a piece of his mind and his fists for the poor treatment meted out to the woman over the years.[19]

In 1863, similar momentum continued picking up back in the eastern theater. It was obvious in coastal North Carolina, where the Confederate civilian James Rumley complained that "the scoundrels in authority here know very well that the African race is the only one whose loyalty they can trust." Black North Carolinians had given authorities plenty of reason for that trust, building forts, loading and unloading ships, building bridges, and making themselves "invaluable and almost indispensable," as one Union authority put it, in countless other ways. That spring, a young boy named Charley went on scouting missions more than forty miles in radius, at great risk to himself. On one mission to assess Confederate strength and position at Kinston, Charley and a friend made it right into enemy lines before being discovered by

Confederate pickets and a pack of bloodhounds. Cornered, they shot two dogs and a horse from underneath a soldier before taking off on a thirty-six-mile run back to the nearest Union sentry posts, slogging much of that distance through a foul swamp in hopes of throwing dogs off track. With twelve miles left to go, dogs once again picked up their scent. As Charley and his companion tried to blend into the scenery by flattening their backs against trunks of trees, a Confederate soldier rode into view. The boys shot and wounded three of the dogs and used the cacophony of their howls as cover while they tore off their coats, pants, and caps and raced back to camp with little other than shirts, revolvers, and valuable military intelligence. Meanwhile, as black men and women acted "as spies and informers," white property owners (who had formerly assumed that their rights to property were what the army should be protecting) found themselves enduring a "reign of terror" in which their "private property [is] seized, often upon information of negroes."[20]

To disgruntled white Southerners, it seemed that the army regarded "any mark of African blood [as] a passport to favor with that government," which was saying something in a land that had so recently refused to issue actual passports to black people. On board a boat on the Beaufort Inlet Channel one spring day in 1863, a black man decided he had had quite enough of being bossed around by the boat's white owner. Outraged, the white man strode into the provost marshal's office to complain "that a negro boy had behaved with great insolence toward him and had threatened him with personal violence, while on board the white man's own boat." The provost marshal "gave the citizen no satisfaction," and as if that officer's laconic bemusement were not insult enough, another federal officer who happened to be present "openly advised the negro, when a white man molested him, to use the weapons god had given him," namely his fists. At the same time, when a black man went to the Union commandant William B. Fowle Jr. to press charges against a white man who owed him money, Fowle ordered the white man to pay the bill.[21]

The momentum was even apparent in the nation's capital, the seat of the very federal government that before the war had been slaveholders' reliable ally but now was unmistakably switching sides. A Virginia slave owner not yet fully cognizant of the shift persuaded his Episcopal minister to travel to Washington with him one day to testify to his good character so that Union army officials would help reclaim some of his black female slaves who had escaped and were now in the District of Columbia working for the army. The women were among a group of "177 women over the age of 14" who made their labor as laundresses "available for the use of the government," according to the D.C. superintendent of contrabands, D. B. Nichols. To the slave owner's surprise, the best he could get was a carefully supervised meeting with the women in Superintendent Nichols's quarters. During that meeting, the white Virginian reminded the women of the generosity he had shown them. "Haven't you had your pig? And didn't I let you go to meeting?" he pleaded. Somehow, the women remained unpersuaded by pigs or prayers. Rather than agree to return to Virginia, one of the women handed Nichols a butcher knife and told him to "let the wicked blood out of that man who has come to take my daughters." As a privileged white property owner, the master had expected aid from the U.S. government in regaining his property, but instead Nichols protected the women's right to refuse to go with their former owner. The women who turned to him for that protection most likely did so not because of who he was personally or because they had reason to expect unusual kindness from him; in fact, Nichols would land himself in trouble later in the war for unkindness to freedpeople. Rather, they turned to the U.S. government that he represented.[22] They had gained access to that government thanks to their wartime contributions. The national government would prove to be an imperfect ally at best, as Nichols's own mercurial behavior demonstrated, but it was the most effective ally available to the formerly enslaved women.

In the Mississippi valley, as Superintendent John Eaton noticed the wary alliance taking shape in 1863, he gathered data for systematic analysis. Coming out of the antebellum tradition of understanding the relationship between the individual and the national government chiefly in terms of duty and obligation, and embroiled as he was in a war for the nation's survival, Eaton naturally recognized that a key factor in determining the relationship between the U.S. government and slave refugees had to be "Can this people aid us in subduing the rebellion?" To find the answer, he sent a series of interrogatories to the superintendents of contraband camps throughout his department, seeking hard evidence from "witnesses of widely different opinions, having under their observation all the diversities of the black race, in great numbers, from all the possible conditions of slavery." He sent his questionnaires to Memphis, La Grange, Grand Junction, Bolivar, and Jackson, Tennessee, to Providence, Louisiana, to Cairo, Illinois, to Columbus, Kentucky, and to Corinth and Holly Springs, Mississippi. Pages of inquiries asked about the clothing, food, and health of refugees from slavery when they first arrived in camp and after some time in residence. They asked about shelter, hospitals, mortality, and relations with Union troops as well as hostile local whites. They asked about intelligence, skills, aptitudes, morals, ideas and values, and attitudes toward former owners, the Confederacy, the Union, and the army. The interrogatories also asked the very direct question, "What of the work done for individual or Government, by men, by women?"[23]

Eaton, in other words, was directly inquiring about former slaves' (male *and* female) usefulness to the U.S. government, and he got answers that went beyond the anecdotal; they constituted hard data about how black men, women, and children in 1863 directly contributed to the nation. Superintendents up and down the Mississippi River valley wrote back to say that black men, women, and even children directly contributed their own labor and resourcefulness—their digging, ditching, weeding, hoeing, harvesting, hauling, distributing, cooking, nursing, scouting, and more—to Union forces in ways that brought direct strategic and financial benefit to the Union war effort. Eaton noted the service of black men as soldiers in the Union army, but he also totted up acres throughout the Mississippi valley under cultivation thanks to women "both married and unmarried." He noted property "converted from disloyal to loyal use" by women and children and credited black women's nursing, sewing, laundering, and baking with sustaining Union troops. He compiled tables enumerating laborers in camps throughout the Department of Tennessee in 1863. The table for Corinth showed 750 women cooking or laundering for Union troops and 464 men working as carpenters, blacksmiths, teamsters, or cooks. Data from Grand Junction testified to 58 women cooking or laundering for troops and 46 men carpentering, blacksmithing, or driving teams. At Memphis, 69 women cooked or laundered, and 36 men plied their skills as carpenters, blacksmiths, or teamsters. And Eaton well knew, with hard-and-fast numbers almost impossible to come by, that those figures seriously understated reality on the ground. In short, the answer to his original question, "Can this people aid us in subduing the rebellion?" was an indisputable and resounding yes.[24]

The language and idea of usefulness were everywhere in 1863. Vincent Colyer returned to New York that year to write an account of his time among former slaves in North Carolina, which he titled *Brief Report of the Services Rendered by the Freed People to the United States Army in North Carolina, in the Spring of 1862, After the Battle of Newbern*.[25] When General Benjamin Prentiss wrote from the contraband camp at Helena, Arkansas, in June to ask Major General John Schofield for permission to transport "disabled men, women, and children" away from "this unhealthy location" at government expense, he couched his request in terms of returning the sick former slaves to "a source of usefulness instead of a mere source of encumbrance."[26] In that same month, the AFIC published its *Preliminary Report*, which in its very first paragraph identified former slaves as "auxiliaries to the government in its prosecution of the war."[27] At the same time, the AFIC sent questionnaires about "the colored population of your town" to towns and cities throughout the North explicitly asking (among other things), "Do you consider them, upon the whole, as valuable members of the community or not?"[28] A war correspondent in Nashville, Tennessee, told conservative-leaning Northern readers that "everywhere, where hard useful work is to be done, you will find the descendant of Ham cheerfully bending himself to his tasks, and helping forward the grand movement which is to result at no distant day in the complete success of a long-struggling Government to maintain itself and its integrity, in spite of rebel venom and fury, and by the process, elevating himself."[29]

John Eaton, along with many Union authorities, thought hard in 1863 about what black people's usefulness to the U.S. government should obtain for them in return. Altogether, Eaton concluded, "the interests of humanity [and] the demands of justice" made it obvious that the government of the United States was in the debt of freedpeople.[30] But a debt consisting of what, and to be paid how?

One possibility suggested by some historians is that Eaton and other Union authorities saw African Americans' contributions as a "way of paying back the favor of freedom."[31] At first glance, that explanation seems plausible, because later generations of historians did look back and write erroneously about emancipation as a sort of favor handed to passive African Americans. One 1927 biography of Ulysses S. Grant, for example, mischaracterized former slaves in the United States as "the only people in the history of the world, so far as I know, that ever became free without any effort of their own."[32] In the 1860s, however, such a view would have made no sense. To Republican soldiers like John Eaton, the law of nations made freedom the natural state of all human beings, which could only be denied by positive local laws, and no state or local laws were in effect in the so-called Confederacy because the act of secession revoked them. In Eaton's particular case, his Republican beliefs were reinforced by his deep faith, as a Presbyterian minister, in the efficacy of grace over works: there were some things that simply came from God or they did not come at all, but no human effort could "earn" them, and for Eaton freedom was one of those things. Therefore, nobody in Union lines could "pay" for the "favor" of freedom because it was already inherently theirs.[33] By the mid-nineteenth century, one need not be a Republican or a minister to concede the same basic point, for it had become a commonplace in middle-class white Northern culture. The Democratic general Benjamin Butler did not embody anybody's idea of devout piety, yet he shared the assumption that black men, women, and children who made it to Union lines in 1861 immediately "assumed the condition, which we hold to be the normal one, of those made in God's image," namely "free."[34]

Instead, the labor and other useful contributions of the men, women, and children who fled from slavery to the Union army earned them, not the unearnable gift of freedom, but rather a new, direct relationship with the U.S. government. Not immediately, not completely, and certainly not easily, yet unmistakably, the actions of freedpeople in contact with the Union army forged a relationship between African Americans and the national government. Inclusion within the national community had long been advocated by Northern free blacks, but throughout the antebellum era it had been rejected, ignored, or denied by the leaders of the U.S. government. Now, more than two years into a terrible war, the national government found itself fighting for survival and aided in that struggle by black men, women, and children.

As the year 1864 began, signs of an altered relationship between the national government and black people were cropping up across the landscape, rather like a digital time-lapse map showing bird spottings or weather phenomena, in which a dot appears in one locale, followed seconds later by dots in other locales, not directly related to one another, but demonstrating similar phenomena unfolding in more than one place at the same time. By the end of 1863, Martha and Albert Pool and their eight-year-old son, Benjamin, had escaped enslavement in Elizabeth City, North Carolina, and made their way to Union forces at New Bern, about a hundred miles away. As 1863 drew to a close, smallpox tore through New Bern, and the Union army established a smallpox hospital to quarantine and treat former slaves afflicted with the contagious—and deadly—disease. On the first day of the New Year, Martha and Albert each entered into a contract with the U.S. government to work as nurses in that hospital for set wages. So did Sarah Dowell, Sara Faber, Susan Grimes, Mathew Ircott, Zachary Johnson, and a dozen other former slaves, whose names a Union army clerk meticulously recorded in a register on January 1, 1864. More nurses would sign (or mark with an *X*) similar contracts with the U.S. government at New Bern until the epidemic finally abated in June. The U.S. government entered into similar contracts with freedpeople working at government hospitals in Baltimore, Alexandria, Hampton, Norfolk, and indeed so many places that the War Department began to keep the multivolume *Register of Colored Nurses Under Contract.*[35]

The Pools, and all the former slaves working as nurses under contract in New Bern, spent their days trying to alleviate suffering, sorrow, and the stench of death. The work was hard, risky, and often tragic thanks to contagion and mortality rates. By no means did it offer an easy path to anything, but entering into a contract to do that work was significant. For one thing, it marked a specific and protected legal relationship between the federal government and a former slave who, very recently, had no ability to enter into any kind of relationship at all with that same government. In addition, it was a contract for federal employment, which marked a remarkable turnaround from the antebellum United States, where federal law had outright prohibited black federal employment so completely that African Americans were not supposed to drive the mules that pulled U.S. mail wagons.[36]

Moreover, a contract did more than just spell out the terms of a former slave's employment; it was serious constitutional and legal business connoting a deep citizenship right, because a contract articulates in writing that both parties are giving written consent and they have mutual and reciprocal obligations to abide by the contract's terms. Legal historians often call the nineteenth century the age of contract, in which the notion of "contract became a dominant metaphor for social relations and the very symbol of freedom." The heart of a contract consists of agreement and consent rather than force or coercion, at least in theory. Actual contracts regulated two distinct realms in the nineteenth century: the world of work through labor contracts and the domestic sphere through marriage contracts. When former slaves exited slavery and entered into labor contracts, agreement and exchange replaced coercion and domination. When former slaves married, they entered legal contracts permitting and governing a legal relationship— marriage—that had been off-limits to them in slavery. For many anti-slavery advocates, in sum, once former slaves could enter into contracts, the very culmination of emancipation had been reached.[37]

In retrospect, contract as replacement for enslavement seems like a very narrow gain, because we see contract through a postbellum lens that differs a bit from the perspective available to former slaves during the Civil War. In later decades, the habit of describing emancipation as the transition from bondage to contract *did* narrow and limit freed-people's gains, because after the Civil War powerful white Americans came to associate contracts increasingly—almost exclusively—with the marketplace. More than mutual promises, contracts became crabbed statements of the limits of what one party will do for another: exactly what this document says and not one whit more. They described a relationship that the postbellum social scientist William Graham Sumner identified as "realistic, cold, and matter-of-fact" rather than expansive or idealistic.[38] But William Graham Sumner's concept (which was the dominant postwar one) drew on the idea of contract as part and parcel of classical liberalism, acquisitive individualism, and nascent industrial capitalism, which is not where the idea had originally started. The idea went back at least as far as Puritan covenant theology, in which God and God's people entered into compact and agreed to live in love for one another, working foremost for the good of the whole. Contract was not so much bill of lading as it was Kingdom of God and Body of Christ.[39]

Early modern political thinkers like Thomas Hobbes and John Locke added Enlightenment rationalism to arrive at a notion of a social contract, in which individuals offered their free consent to governments in exchange for protection.[40] These understandings of contract predated the heavy influence of classical liberal economic theory, which would overpower older notions after the war.

When formerly enslaved men and women like Albert and Martha Pool made X marks on contracts with the U.S. government, they knew much less Adam Smith than they did the book of Exodus or Paul's First Letter to the Corinthians. They were not merely swapping a master's whip for the promise of meager pay, and they were not acquiescing in tenets of liberal individualism.[41] They were entering into a new relationship with the national government that they understood to be predicated upon membership, reciprocity, and interdependence.

Far from the war's front lines, powerful white Northerners also grasped the need to redefine and codify the relationship between former slaves and the U.S. government, though they often differed on what the content and nature of that relationship should be. From his New York study, Francis Lieber corresponded with members of the AFIC in the winter of 1864, at exactly the same time that he was composing a pamphlet to be published by the Loyal Publication Society expressly to combat Northern opposition to the Union war effort.[42] Lieber could plainly see that interactions between former slaves and the Union army contrasted sharply with Copperhead efforts to impede the war effort, and the contrast unevenly but inexorably made presumptions of black statelessness untenable. In writing the Lieber Code, Lieber had sidestepped the question of former slaves' status within the national community, but by 1864 he knew he had to tackle that question head-on, and so he contemplated how best to define the U.S. government's insiders and outsiders in this tumultuous moment of state expansion. To Lieber, "best" meant systematically and with indisputable authority. Nothing less than the Constitution would do. Through the cold and gradually lengthening winter evenings, he wrote his pamphlet recommending seven constitutional amendments. As Lieber explained to Senator Charles Sumner, the point of all seven proposed amendments was to ensure "that the integrity of this Country and our Nationality shall not be given up." To secure the national government, Lieber explained, "the Taney principle must be wiped out." To that end, the very first of the recommended amendments stipulated, "Every native of this Country (except sons of aliens whom the Law may exempt and Indians not taxed) and every native citizen owes plenary allegiance to the government of the United States and is entitled to and shall receive, its protection at home and abroad due by every government to its citizens or subjects." The next three proposed amendments addressed treason, sedition, and their punishment. The fifth abolished slavery and undergirded the legitimacy of military emancipation by stating, "So soon as a person is within the limits of the United States or has found shelter under the Flag of the same of whatever condition or race that person may be, he or she shall cease to be the property of any one . . . whether at war or in amity with the United States." The sixth criminalized slaveholding and slave trading. The seventh admitted legal testimony from any "human being" regardless of "race or colour."[43]

A number of interesting features about these proposed amendments stand out, not the least being the sheer number of them. To us, the logical starting place seems to be what Lieber called "Amendment E," the amendment abolishing slavery, which also explicitly legitimized and made permanent the military emancipation of slaves who made it to the Union army. Using no less an instrument than the U.S. Constitution to make the case for military emancipation's legitimacy showed both that Lieber recognized how contested military emancipation was and that he worried about its reversibility. In fact, just days later in a letter to Sumner, Lieber feared that "some states . . . the day after readmission . . . will turn on their heels and re-establish forced labor of some sort—slavery in fact" if the national government did not act.[44] Lieber's worries were not far-fetched. Reestablishment of slavery had happened in many other places, even briefly in Haiti, generally thought of as the world's most successful slave rebellion. Yet so preoccupied with establishing abolition's permanence was Lieber that the emancipation amendment concerned itself solely with the former slave no longer being someone else's property and not with who or what the former slave became after liberation. The amendment, in other words, underscored the reality of statelessness following emancipation.

The final amendment about testifying in courts is especially interesting in light of Lieber's conviction that courts should allow testimony from all people, free or slave. It testifies to Lieber's somewhat idiosyncratic view that access to courts did not depend on a person's status or relationship to any government. In late March, Lieber again tried to contact the Brazilian minister to the United States to "put some four or five questions to him" about if and how Brazilian courts admitted "the evidence of coloured free persons, and of slaves." Testifying in courts, as Lieber saw it, was not about rights and not even really as much about the testifier as about legal process, for Lieber's logic was that courts should make use of all available evidence no matter where it came from, just as courts admitted objects as evidence even though objects had no legal standing.[45]

The first four of the proposed amendments had to do with defining the state's insiders and outsiders in terms of reciprocal relationships. Those who opposed the state through crimes of treason or sedition, Lieber posited in the second, third, and fourth amendments, placed themselves outside its protection and liable to trial by it. The first proposed amendment, in contrast, expressly identified who *was* "entitled to and shall receive" the "protection" of "the government of the United States": everyone who demonstrated "plenary allegiance" to the U.S. government. That "protection" derived partly but not entirely from birth, because both Indians and the children of exempted foreign residents (diplomats and the like) were born in the United States but did not automatically merit the protection of its government. It grew more clearly out of demonstrated "allegiance" than birth alone and in that way extended to African Americans. Yet to Lieber, such "protection" was not necessarily citizenship, because it extended to "every native of this Country" *and* to "every native citizen," suggesting that those were two separate populations, not one and the same thing.

In sum, Lieber's ideas about what citizenship was and who qualified for it differed quite notably from the version of citizenship that freedpeople were forging in contraband camps, but his treatise demonstrated that the contest over citizenship was going strong in 1864. It had been for some time. No less an authority than the attorney general, Edward Bates, waded into the waters when he was asked point-blank in 1862 whether black people could be citizens. Months passed before he published his answer, *Opinion of Attorney General Bates on Citizenship*, and even then it proved infuriatingly noncommittal on some points.[46] The precise catalyst for the opinion was a letter to Bates from Secretary of the Treasury Salmon P. Chase inquiring, "Are colored men citizens of the United States, and therefore competent to command American vessels?" Chase needed to know because a U.S. schooner commanded by a black man had been stopped by a revenue cutter on the grounds that only citizens could command U.S. vessels. Chase, who would soon go on to become the chief justice of the Supreme Court, was no legal slouch himself, so the very fact that he had to ask demonstrates how unknown the answer was.

Bates knew that Chase needed the cutter captain back in command of his vessel so he had better come up with an answer of yes, but in order to do so, he answered on the narrowest possible grounds. First, he shifted the question from whether or not black people *were* citizens to a more specific question of whether someone is "legally incapacitated to be a citizen of the United States by the sole fact that he is a *colored*" person. From that narrow starting point, he demonstrated that nothing in the U.S. Constitution said in so many words that a black person could not be a citizen. From that absence, Bates reasoned that a black person born in the United States was, "at the moment of birth," a citizen, unless that person was a slave, a category he deliberately excluded from consideration in the *Opinion*. On the one hand, the answer seems perfectly clear, but Bates spent most of the pamphlet emphasizing that nobody knew what citizenship actually meant. "I have often been pained by the fruitless search in our law books and the records of our courts, for a clear and satisfactory definition of the phrase *citizen of the United States*," he wrote. Despite all his looking, he could "find no such definition." He was left to conclude, then, that citizenship "means neither more nor less than a member of the nation." Membership, of course, was not insignificant, but it was also not, as he took pains to clarify, a guarantee of rights. In fact, Bates went out of his way to emphasize, "Rights enjoyed and the powers exercised have no relation whatever to the quality of citizen."[47] The version of citizenship that refugees from slavery were crafting in Civil War contraband camps, in other words, was not one fashioned by leaders and then conveyed down to them but one that they assembled themselves from their experiences and then sent back up the chain of command through the soldiers and officers they encountered in camps.

The frequency with which the words "citizens" and "citizenship" appeared among members of the Union army began taking a noticeable uptick in 1863. In the aftermath of the Battle of Chancellorsville in May of that year, Corporal John Fife of the First New Hampshire Battery declared, "I believe" that "the colored people that are now being made free . . . have the right of citizenship."[48] John Eaton concluded his exhaustive analysis of freedpeople in the Mississippi valley with the recommendation "that these people may be introduced the most speedily to the knowledge & practice of all the duties & amenities of citizenship."[49] Even General Nathaniel Banks, widely criticized by soldiers and members of the AFIC for being more sympathetic to Southern whites than to former slaves, insisted in 1863 that by virtue of their labor former slaves deserved the "privileges of citizenship," not as "a boon conferred, but a right conquered."[50]

War brought new possibilities of belonging, inclusion, and rights protection within African Americans' grasp, but it could also yank those things out of reach again, especially when the war went poorly on the battlefield. The Union's military fortunes for the first two-thirds of 1864 seemed to range from the merely disappointing to the outright catastrophic, such as when the Army of the Potomac lost more than six thousand men in a single morning at Cold Harbor on June 3 and then continued to slug it out with the Army of Northern Virginia for the rest of the summer, with no visible advantage to show for its efforts. Meanwhile, western campaigns bogged down, chief among them the campaign to take Atlanta. In those months, official attention focused chiefly on the battlefield and the upcoming presidential election. Army officials in the field, pulled in multiple directions and sick of the war, began to note "helpless freedmen dependent on the government" at least as often as they acknowledged former slaves' contributions to the war effort.[51] Meanwhile, African American Union soldiers confronted the hard and lingering reality of inequality when the paymaster finally appeared and brought them three dollars less per month than white soldiers *and* charged them for their own uniforms. Strenuous protest on the part of black troops (and even some white ones) eventually nudged Congress toward equalizing soldier pay with a law passed in June 1864, but not before the protests of the men of the Third South Carolina

Volunteers—former slaves turned Union soldiers—were labeled a "mutiny" and resulted in the execution of Sergeant William Walker.[52]

Then, in the fall, Union armies began to realize key victories, and the newly emerging version of citizenship once again gathered strength. Delegates to the National Equal Rights Convention, a meeting of free black leaders from all over the North held in Syracuse, New York, in October, gave speeches, affirmed resolutions, wrote a declaration of wrongs and rights, and issued a petition, all of which emphasized citizenship rights for black Americans.[53] When the AFIC published its *Final Report* in 1864, it expressly argued, "We need the negro not only as a soldier to aid in quelling the rebellion, but as a loyal citizen to assist in reconstructing on a permanently peaceful and orderly basis the insurrectionary States."[54] As the tide of war turned steadily in the Union's favor in 1865, the reciprocal relationship in which African Americans' service to the Union merited protection of basic rights by the U.S. government continued to solidify, and former slaves proved useful to the Union in ever more ways. Throughout the Mississippi valley, freedpeople continued to labor for the army; they also helped populate Union-held territory with loyal Unionists to prevent hostile Confederates from reclaiming it. In recognition of the contributions of former slave women near Vicksburg, General John Parker Hawkins granted them government land confiscated from secessionists. The new proprietors of the land, black women described in army records as "citizen negroes, not more than 5 of [whom] were soldiers' wives," built houses, which they owned under title protected by the U.S. government. Even after the war, when the land reverted to its secessionist owner, the owner could neither evict the women nor claim their houses but had to settle for the compromise measure of collecting rent for the land under the watchful eye of government authorities.[55]

When former slaves and members of the Union army spoke about citizenship in return for useful service to the Union war effort, they meant no empty trope. They meant that "the emancipated population have secured to them their civil and political rights by national authority," as the AFIC commissioner James McKaye put it. The "fundamental rights of citizenship in a free government" that former slaves had earned by their service to the Union war effort consisted of protection by the national government of certain specific rights.[56] The rights themselves were not so much what citizenship consisted of, nor was citizenship the source of the rights, which could have their origins in any number of places; former slaves and Union soldiers would probably have been about as likely as anybody else to say that there were certain things that a person ought to be entitled to regardless of his or her relationship to any particular government. But what citizenship meant was that if the ability of someone who aided the Union government to exercise certain specific rights was threatened, then the national government of the United States was obligated to protect the exercise of and access to those specific rights. Certainly, many white Northerners at the time and historians since would dispute whether citizenship really meant what former slaves and their wary and sometimes reluctant allies in the Union army said it did. Even if you are a gambling sort, you would want to be a little careful before wagering too much on the proposition that the definition of citizenship articulated in contraband camps would win the full approval of legal scholars then or now, but legal scholars were not the audience that black men, women, and children in contraband camps were trying to convince.

Rather, when a group of formerly enslaved Louisianans told Superintendent of Negro Labor George Hanks that they "have a right to demand the protection of the Government," they sought to convince the army, and the national government more generally, for very practical purposes.[57] For those practical purposes, they achieved some notable wartime success. A *New York Times* reporter noted a group of "stout-limbed and stout-hearted women [who] marched for two days" with Brigadier General Hugh Judson Kilpatrick's cavalry from central to coastal Virginia, "aid[ing] the expedition in various ways" like finding fodder for horses and helping tear up railroad tracks. The formerly enslaved women "were finally rewarded by reaching Gen. Butler's lines, where they have some rights that white men are bound to respect."[58]

What rights, specifically, did black men, women, and children claiming citizenship expect the Union to protect? The most basic involved personal safety and mobility: the ability to move about or stay put as one wished, even (especially!) when a white person claiming to own a body had other ideas. The Union army protected that right each time one of its members sheltered a fugitive from a slave owner who demanded that soldiers either return a slave or not interfere while the slave owner took care of that sordid business on his own. Beyond simply preventing black people from being taken places they did not want to go, the Union army increasingly safeguarded the ability of former slaves to go where they pleased. The federally protected right to personal mobility was evident in Vicksburg, Mississippi, in January 1865, when black women (including unmarried ones) who worked for the army were eligible for more liberal passes to travel than other people and were exempt from surcharges on permits to remain in Vicksburg that were imposed on all other adults except Union soldiers and their wives.[59] Indeed, one of white Confederates' recurrent complaints was that the Union army permitted more freedom of movement among blacks than whites.[60]

Closely connected was protection for the bonds of marriage and family, which slavery had expressly denied. Everywhere the army went, black couples called on its members to legally marry them. Corporal Austin Andrew (Twelfth Illinois Infantry) wrote to his sister about thirty-nine weddings "in and around Corinth" the previous Sunday, while Private William Hinshaw of the Eighth Illinois performed the "mariage seremonay" to "ner thiarty coples" requesting it near Marshall, Texas. The famous Spotswood Rice incident, in which a Missouri slave turned Union soldier promised his daughters' owner that the Union army stood by his right to his children and that she would "burn in hell" if she interfered with his right, dramatically illustrates the expectation that the U.S. government protected black people's family rights. Non-soldiers like Lavinia Bell also acted on that expectation when she turned to Union authorities for help in her quest to protect her daughter from the sexual advances of an owner.[61] Rose Herera, a formerly enslaved Louisianan who turned to the Union army to charge her former owner with kidnapping Rose's three children and to restore her children to her, appealed directly to General Stephen Hurlbut with a straightforward claim: "Petitioner further shows that herself and her aforesaid three children are free and entitled to the rights of American citizens, and to the protection of the government of the United States, to which she now appeals."[62]

In addition, citizenship meant access to education. Former slaves everywhere insisted "that their children shall reap those advantages of instruction which were denied to themselves," and they looked to the Union army to safeguard their children's ability to attend school.[63] A group of black Chicagoans fighting for access to schools plainly and publicly stated its case with the following pronouncement: "We are recognized citizens by the government fighting for our rights that have been denied."[64] Throughout the South, former slaves staked their claims by building and attending schools, sometimes even before they built houses.[65] By the end of the war, so many former slaves had flocked to Union-run schools in Vicksburg that the provost marshal scurried to find buildings big enough to hold them, and his dilemma was not unique.[66]

Citizenship also meant access to courts as plaintiffs, defendants, witnesses, and jurors. Former slaves, all the way from William Sherman in Florida to black Canadians like Thomas Smallwood who had fled U.S. slavery in the antebellum era, all brought up the importance of courts.[67] It was not that African Americans had never set foot in a courtroom before. Even as slaves, some black men and women had found their way before judges; Francis Lieber's position that anybody ought to be able to provide evidence was not confined solely to him. Also as slaves, black Southerners had devised substitute forums to carry out their own legal business.[68] The difference was that as citizens African Americans could rightfully expect the U.S. government to protect their use of courts and the legal system on their own behalf. Near Hampton, Virginia, Anthony Bright and other former slaves had been cultivating acreage deserted by white owners since 1862. Incensed by the sight of African Americans independently farming the land, some local whites turned to the court to put the farm in their hands. At the trial, which was presided over by the Union provost judge Major William Bolles, Anthony Bright stepped briskly into the witness box to testify to his right to work the land and reap its harvest. A local official balked at admitting testimony from a black man, but Bolles ignored him, and Bright seized the chance to use the courtroom to secure the fruits of his own labor.[69] The formal U.S. legal system did not wholly displace former slaves' extralegal adjudicatory forums, but, as Anthony Bright vividly understood, federally protected access to courts as witnesses, jurors, and plaintiffs could yield tangible benefits.[70]

Finally, citizenship explicitly meant that the U.S. government ought to ensure equality before the law. "The laws is the principal thing that trouble us," a Kentucky freedman told AFIC agents. Laws governing fair employment did not constitute the totality of citizenship for him, but they were an important component of it, which black people had clearly earned with their contributions to the Union cause.[71] Albert Butler, a former slave born in Tennessee and living in Canada by 1863, agreed that laws made all the difference. Because Canadian law treated black and white equally, black people in Canada "can have recourse to the law, and, as a general thing, we get more justice than in the States." It was not that white Canadians felt any more warmly toward blacks than white Americans did, Butler emphasized. The difference was "that class of persons who would be disposed to blackguard and interrupt people do not do it so much here as in the States . . . because the law is enforced more rigorously."[72]

It goes without saying that Confederates violently resisted the new version of citizenship that slaves and the army were hammering out in Civil War contraband camps, but some white Northerners also objected. One disgruntled white Indianan complained to Governor Oliver Morton, for instance, that "the Negro, is not a citizen of these united states . . . any more than a horse or a cow."[73] By and large, Union soldiers were among the quickest of white Northerners to recognize black citizenship, which they tended to do in rather matter-of-fact fashion. When a black woman named Nancy Drake was brought before the provost marshal in Huntsville, Alabama, for illegally selling whiskey to soldiers, the provost marshal filled in his logbook as he would for anyone else: Drake was a "Cit[i]z[en]," and she was formally charged and then released on the same terms as all the other accused brought before him.[74] Similarly, Lieutenant Colonel R. S. Donaldson set one steady price, $2.50 per cord, for any wood "cut for sale by citizens, white or colored" in Davis Bend, Mississippi.[75] Even still, some Union soldiers also resisted. On August 4, 1864, E. P. Cartwright was arrested at the Cairo, Illinois, contraband camp for drunkenness. The army clerk who recorded the incident in the camp's record of arrests at first identified Cartwright as a "citizen" but then crossed out "citizen" and wrote "colored" instead.[76] Beyond matters of word choice, in some instances, Union troops did not protect the rights of black people who helped them but rather ignored or violated those rights. At Yorktown, for example, two inspectors were appalled by the "gross violation of [freed-people's] rights, and the claims which they have upon us as a people and a nation."[77]

To combat white resistance to black citizenship, wartime propo-nents of black citizenship often focused on disproving assumptions of dependence, a quality that limited or precluded usefulness and was "deemed antithetical to citizenship" in conventional antebellum Amer-ican thought.[78] As one former slave turned soldier spelled out, "It has been said that a black man can not make his own living, but give us opportunities and we will show the whites that we will not come to them for any thing . . . The colored people know how to work, and the whites have been dependent upon them."[79] AFIC commissioners, relief workers in contraband camps, and Union army personnel insisted that refugees from slavery were not irredeemably dependent on the govern-ment or anyone else. "The people are helping themselves," one Pine Bluff aid worker boasted to his brother back home, while the AFIC's *Final Report* (May 1864) repeated over and over that worries about freed slaves becoming "a burden on the community" were groundless and that the "ability of colored populations, when emancipated, to take care of themselves" was obvious.[80] Not content with generalizations, Union army personnel marshaled hard evidence to make the same point. Gen-eral John Dix reported that women and children at Fort Monroe "cost the Government at this time little or nothing; at most only a few extra rations," while the superintendent of contrabands at Norfolk similarly emphasized that the freedpeople under his jurisdiction received no clothing from the government because "my aim has been as far as pos-sible to make the labor of the negroes support them[selves]."[81] From New Orleans, General Benjamin Butler reported that the army pro-vided food for "thirty-two thousand whites" but "only ten thousand negroes."[82] Vincent Colyer pored over ledgers and supply lists of flour, beef, coffee, sugar, soap, and beans, calculating that even though there were "over 4 times as many poor blacks in the district" of New Bern, North Carolina, "they asked for and drew only 1/16 as much in food and rations" as white refugees did, while at the same time the labor, horses, forage, and sheep that former slaves "obtained for the Government" in North Carolina "far exceed[ed] in value all that was ever paid to the blacks."[83]

Of course, some former slaves were dependent—they were war refugees, after all—but their advocates made the case that needy individuals were exceptions made that way by circumstances, and so would become independent and useful as circumstances changed. As the numbers of refugees from slavery entering Union lines jumped dramatically after the Emancipation Proclamation, John Eaton observed to Senator Henry Wilson that time and proper government response would show that if African Americans were "down indeed in the scale of civilization, [they were also] susceptible of improvement, capable of coming up, of industry, of honesty, of courage, of piety or every social, civil & intellectual, moral & religious attainment, not an expense to Government or charity but a profit."[84] He put that conviction into practice time and again. For example, when the Contrabands' Relief Commission of Cincinnati sent bolts of cloth for the use of refugees from slavery in Memphis, Eaton assured the secretary of the society that when he distributed the yards of fabric, he would show "a preference for those most ready to do for themselves" because "the elevation of unfortunate persons" depended on avoiding the appearance of "idleness & beggary."[85] Eaton and others who echoed those same points sound astonishingly cold and callous to us, and no doubt to desperate women who needed clothing for their children. Yet there was a logic and purpose to what they said, for if they could convince white lawmakers and the voters who elected them that freed slaves contributed to rather than siphoned resources from the war effort and the national government, then they had a better chance of convincing skeptics that "the Government must protect" the basic rights of former slaves, "positively, unequivocally, by forces clearly defined, [and] strong orders from the U. States Government through the War and Navy Department."[86]

That kind of protection mattered to former slaves, not because it represented the sum total of their hopes for freedom, but because they aptly recognized it as necessary to achieving their aspirations for themselves, their families, and their communities. It was not for the mere sound of the words "American citizen" that black men, women, and children braved enormous risks to get to Union lines or suffered staggering hardships in contraband camps. They risked and suffered for the love of their children, or yearning for control over their own lives, or longing for "collective autonomy" for their kin and communities, or desires all their own. They knew that white slaveholders enjoyed legally sanctioned power to deny all of those things and were not about to relinquish that power without a fight.[87] Obtaining what former slaves cared about required a direct line to an alternative source of power strong enough to overcome slave owners' hitherto-unchallenged monopoly on the use of force. Refugees from slavery who ran to Union lines identified the Union army and the central state that it embodied as a potential source of just such power, and they offered labor, resources, local intelligence, and goodwill. Those contributions contrasted so sharply with the hostility of local white people that they made a compelling case for the obligation of the U.S. government to protect the rights of black people on the grounds of useful service, instead of white people on the grounds of race and property ownership. They crafted a distinctive alliance between former slaves and the U.S. government, and they called the exchange of useful service for federal protection of basic rights "citizenship." This version of citizenship was not the only version in the ongoing national argument over what citizenship meant, but in the crisis of wartime it gained currency, traction, and influence that no other version of U.S. citizenship inclusive of black people had been able to gain before the war.

Still, citizenship as the reciprocal exchange of useful service for rights protection came with drawbacks. It was not a version of citizenship that recognized much federal government responsibility for human welfare, and therefore did little to alleviate "suffering too harrowing to be named in sensitive ears, which only governmental interference could prevent."[88] It was not a version suited to the attainment of economic justice. Its basis in useful labor created plenty of room for exploitation. It did not address suffrage, a right now taken for granted as citizenship's defining hallmark, but not as critical to refugees from slavery as a version of citizenship more immediately attuned to their urgent wartime needs. And it did not last forever, for the meaning of citizenship continued to change after the war.

The wary alliance forged between former slaves and the Union army was nothing short of a turnaround. It dramatically reversed the status quo antebellum, in which the U.S. government had been the reliable ally of white slaveholders and a potent force for denying black rights. The standard answer to how the United States could go from *Dred Scott* to black citizenship in less than a decade is "the Civil War," but by itself that answer is vague and unsatisfying. Times of war and crisis are just as likely to lead to narrowing eligibility requirements, restriction of rights, and exclusion rather than inclusion. The difference was that in Civil War contraband camps, the unleashed forces of war blew apart what had previously seemed to be intractable borders around who could be citizens, and black men, women, and children grasped the opportunity to refashion the relationship between the U.S. government and black people and to change what citizenship meant. They contributed their labor, cunning, property, and resourcefulness to the Union war effort, and they compelled army personnel to decide on the spot what *really* made a citizen: being white and owning something, or making oneself useful to the survival of the United States.

The clock did not stop in the spring of 1865 when armies surrendered, for defining citizenship is not a "once and for all" sort of task. Wartime had created new possibilities for inclusion and rights protection, but there was no guarantee that inclusion would continue or rights would be protected once the war ended. Civil authority would eventually have to replace martial law. The presence of the Union army as a visible source of power to counter the power of former slaveholders would have to shrink. Opportunities for black men, women, and children to contribute directly to the survival of the United States would not be so readily apparent or visible. Horace James captured the uncertainty well as his tenure as superintendent of Negro affairs in North Carolina came to an end. "The fact is," he reflected in the last *Annual Report* he would write from New Bern, "that nothing can be relied on in this District, except the certainty of change."[89] War had opened a wide door, just as General Samuel Curtis had observed in 1862. It remained to be seen whether the resumption of civil authority would keep the door propped open or start to close it up again.

Into the Wilderness

In the spring of 1865, Fort Monroe bustled as busily as ever. Over four years of war, the Union army had never left, and there was still no source of freshwater within the fortress, but in other ways things were utterly changed. Four years earlier, the city of Hampton had relied on slave labor to scrub its homes, move its trade, grow its food, and build and maintain its railroad. Now there was not a slave in or around the fort, but there were freedpeople everywhere. Many of those freedpeople still scrubbed, ferried, grew, and built. Frank Baker and James Townsend, two of the three men who first ran to the fort in May 1861 and prompted Butler's famous "contraband decision," worked as day laborers and would for the rest of their lives in and around Hampton Roads. Others did things that few people could have predicted in 1861. Shepard Mallory, the third of the three men who presented themselves to Butler, worked as a carpenter and was on his way to owning his own home at 260 Lincoln Street.[1] Some worked as nurses in government hospitals under the supervision of Harriet Tubman, who had been appointed "Matron at the Colored Hospital" by the surgeon general of the United States.[2] Others served in the army. Gaston Becton and the black men who had joined the Thirty-Sixth U.S. Colored Infantry in North Carolina (after Abraham Galloway extracted a series of promises from Union army recruiters) filed into the fort at the end of May.

The way was far from smooth for anybody. Harriet Tubman found so many abuses in the hospitals that she marched off to Washington, D.C., in July to advise the surgeon general personally about them. Becton, still in his teens, went on a growth spurt and outgrew his uniform by several inches. Many of his married comrades-in-arms were outraged to learn that back home on Roanoke Island authorities were cutting off rations, leaving the men's families to go hungry because the regiment's wages were delayed (as usual) and the soldiers could not send pay home to buy food. To top it off, the Thirty-Sixth U.S. Colored Infantry was heading to Texas, the last place the men had expected to go when they signed up in 1863.[3] As the United States prepared to move from war to ostensible peace in 1865, things looked much different from how they had looked in 1861; they also looked different from how anyone had expected.

Richmond, Virginia, erstwhile capital of the Confederacy, certainly looked different. Explosions had rocked it on April 3, when the retreating Army of Northern Virginia blew up an ironclad and torched ammunition stockpiles on its way out of town. The city was rocked once again when black Union troops entered. The Thirty-Sixth U.S. Colored Infantry, the Twenty-Ninth Connecticut Infantry, the Fifth Massachusetts Cavalry, and more marched and "rode in triumph along the streets" while black Richmonders "cheered and cheered." Back on Roanoke Island, when family members of the men of the Thirty-Sixth U.S. Colored Infantry learned of Richmond's fall, one woman rejoiced, "I shall see my chil'en before I dies!"[4]

While some troops remained in Richmond to secure the city, the Thirty-Sixth U.S. Colored Infantry helped chase the remnants of the Army of Northern Virginia south and west and was among the forces that boxed the army in, a maneuver that forced General Robert E. Lee's surrender at Appomattox Court House. That surrender did not single-handedly conclude the fighting, but it did spell the impending end of the Confederacy. More than any other single event, it signified a turning point to those who lived through the war. Just out of reach of Union forces (and therefore still enslaved) in Appomattox County, Fanny Berry and her kith and kin "knew dat dey were free" as soon as they heard that General Lee had capitulated. When Berry and her newly freed neighbors heard that black soldiers were among the Union troops who extracted the Army of Northern Virginia's surrender, they began to sing.[5]

All that spring, the very atmosphere seemed to shimmer with

expectation as the Confederacy crumbled. In Mobile on Alabama's Gulf coast, African Americans young and old hurrahed when they heard of Lee's surrender from the soldiers of the Thirty-Third Iowa Infantry parading through their streets.[6] Even earlier, something different in the way that the city of Charleston coughed irregular bursts of smoke into the air that February had inspired black Union soldiers on nearby Morris Island and freedpeople from surrounding Sea Islands to jump into boats or cobble together rafts or find any way at all to sail into Charleston. When they got there, they found churches riddled with bullet holes, battered houses with doors rattled off, shops with shot-out windows. Everywhere they looked, they saw crumpled newspapers, battered lamps, trampled drapery, torn books, and ruined furniture strewn promiscuously about the streets. They found a mess, but still they wanted to be there when the cradle of secession fell to Union forces. As the sun rose the first morning after Charleston's fall, men and women gathered in praise, hope, and expectation. A tall black man climbed up on a bench and, shaking with the intensity of his emotion, reached his hands out to his fellow freedpeople surrounding him and said, "Come at last, come at last!"[7] In the war, he saw God's hand, which he knew meant transformation was sure to follow.

Neither the man in Charleston nor any of the cheering freedpeople in Richmond, Roanoke Island, Appomattox County, Mobile, or anywhere else thought that all their struggles were behind them. As gratifying as news of Richmond's fall and the Army of Northern Virginia's surrender was to former slaves in Vicksburg, Mississippi, for example, they still had to contend with a housing shortage, a flooding Mississippi River, and the frustration of seeing churches in which they set up schoolrooms commandeered as hospitals to cope with the rising number of sick thanks to unsanitary conditions spread by the floodwaters.[8] On Roanoke Island, families awaiting soldiers' pay, as well as laborers working for the army in and around New Bern who had also not seen a paycheck in months, were turned away from the commissary by Assistant Superintendent Holland Streeter.[9]

Moreover, news of the fall of Richmond and the surrender of Lee's army was followed so swiftly by news of President Lincoln's death that many people experienced those things less as separate events than as a single milestone in which victory, tragedy, and violence all conjoined. Just four days after the freedpeople of Roanoke Island had ignored their hunger pangs and made the sea and sky ring with victory shouts, a "dispatch boat, with drooping flag, shrouded in mourning" pulled in to the wharf. Guns began to boom once again, this time in sorrow. "I cant see light anywhere," confessed one formerly enslaved woman, who looked only to the "Good Lord, to have pity on us" now.[10] At Pine Bluff, Arkansas, freedpeople, missionaries, and soldiers got even less "opportunity to rejoice." Less than half an hour elapsed from the time they "heard of the fall of Richmond" until "the sad information" of Lincoln's death arrived by telegraph. Fearful that the assassination would incite black Union soldiers at Pine Bluff to violence against local whites, army officers prohibited African American troops from leaving their quarters, even to visit their families in the adjoining contraband camp. Pushed over the top by both the killing of Lincoln and the tyrannical restrictions on their movements, several black soldiers "fixed bayonets & loaded & cocked muskets." They were not about to countenance a return to the days when a white person decided if and when they could see their families, although they also knew never to be too sure that such days were gone for good.[11] Former slaves of all people knew better than to believe in simple happy endings.

But they also knew that things were different. Newly married to her first husband, Union soldier Edward King, Susie Butler King, her husband, and a group of friends returned to Savannah after the Confederacy's collapse. They were sure that "a new life was before us now, all the old life left behind."[12] Too quick a reading of that sentence might make the young bride seem deluded or naive, and there is no question that in later years she would know sorrow, would grow disappointed, even disillusioned. In fact, Edward would die before the birth of their first child, leaving the widowed Susie to raise the baby on her own until her later remarriage. Yet in the spring of 1865, what Susie King knew was that she was married, in a state that before the war had not recognized slaves' marriages. She knew that she traveled freely to Savannah, a city in which once she could not have taken a step without a pass signed by a white person. She knew that she returned with a "group of friends," in a city where before the war it was illegal for black people to congregate without direct white supervision. She also knew that she would be teaching school, in a state where African American literacy used to be a crime.

From our vantage point in the twenty-first century, we can see what was coming, but neither Susie King nor four million formerly enslaved men, women, and children knew the future, and we need to stop and recognize that they saw themselves in a moment real and distinct, not merely in a fleeting prologue to what we know came later. Four million of them had been defined solely as the property of another human being in 1860 by a national government that, in all its international dealings as well as interstate transactions, functioned as a slaveholding nation. By 1865, that same national government had delivered a series of blows, none of which had single-handedly killed the beast of slavery but which had unambiguously announced that in the eternal state of war that was American slavery the power of the U.S. government had switched from the slaveholders' to the slaves' side. The institution of slavery, which had been in thriving demographic, financial, geographic, political, and economic health in 1860, and had even made it through the war largely unscathed in the areas most distant from the Union army, was now in a state of health that varied by location but ranged from weakened to terminally ill to thoroughly dead. And lest we indulge in condescension, we should remember that from former slaves' vantage points there were many things about that change that they saw better than we do now. The former slaves Albert and Martha Pool, to take just one example, saw the difference between a U.S. government that barred black employees and a U.S. government hospital in which both worked as nurses under contract with the government, earning wages that allowed them to support their son, Benjamin, who could not be sold away from them as he approached his tenth birthday.[13]

If freedpeople in 1865 would have been quick to remind us not to mistake 1865 for 1861, they would be just as quick to remind us that God's ways are not our ways, so if they knew that whatever came next would not be like what came before, still they did not know what it *would* be like. Nor did anyone else. Never in U.S. history, and only rarely in world history, had war resulted in permanent abolition. Still less had it resulted in permanent citizenship—or clearly defined status of any sort—for the formerly enslaved. Whether or not it would in the

United States in the latter half of the nineteenth century was anything but clear. Perhaps the only definite in 1865 was that it was a time of momentous transition, characterized by multiple, simultaneous conversions. Freedpeople were exiting slavery and seeking membership within the national community as citizens at the same time as the United States was transforming from a slaveholding to a non-slaveholding nation and the country was transitioning out of a state of high-intensity warfare to low-level conflict that everyone wanted to call peace. Each of those passages would influence how the others unfolded.

In particular, the transition from martial law back to civil authority raised unsettling questions, because so far martial law had made it possible to press for emancipation and citizenship, whereas civil law had proved ineffectual or even obstructionist to former slaves' efforts to gain those things. Would wartime gains last? Most basically, would freedpeople remain free? Could wartime destruction of slavery translate to permanent emancipation? The Confiscation Acts and the Emancipation Proclamation pertained only in time of war, and slave societies in the past had shown themselves to be remarkably adept at reimposing bondage once armed conflict came to a halt. Not only the Emancipation Proclamation's pertinence as a war measure but also its author's death at war's end raised additional questions about what former slaves—and the entire nation—could expect next. In his final report as superintendent of Negro affairs in North Carolina, Horace James might have overemphasized freedpeople's views of Lincoln, but he did not exaggerate their uncertainty when he observed that they remained in a "transition state, scarcely knowing whether they were or were not free—a point made still more uncertain to them by the untimely death of their great Deliverer, Abraham Lincoln."[14]

Beyond emancipation, what legitimacy did *any* acts carried out under military authority in time of war retain if war ended? How secure, for example, were former slaves' titles to lands they now occupied, which had been confiscated from Confederates during the war? As one of the tax commissioners sent by the Treasury to the Sea Islands to report on land use in 1863 had observed, "A mere military title furnished no security, no permanence" once a state of war had passed.[15] As military authority once more bowed to civil authority, would all, some, or any of the tasks accomplished by military authority continue to be carried out? That question was no mere abstraction for the sick men, women, and children trying to recuperate in the Prentiss House Freedmen's Hospital in Vicksburg, Mississippi. During the war, when a handyman was needed, the surgeon T. J. Wright simply sent for somebody from the Quartermaster Department, but when he asked for help after the Confederate surrender, the assistant quartermaster replied that he no longer had authority to use military resources for the repair of a civilian institution.[16]

And what would become of the uneasy alliance that African Americans had forged with the government of the United States, now that the government was no longer fighting for its existence? In the spring of 1863, Abraham Galloway had been able to secure promises of equal pay, education, a basic degree of sustenance, and equal protection of the law for African American families by holding a gun to a Union recruiter's head. The recruiter could agree because war put extraordinary power at the disposal of the national government and the Union army. Now that the nation's survival was no longer in jeopardy, the U.S. government had no gun to its head anymore. Neither could it marshal the same power or resources. What kind of alliance would be possible as war's flames subsided into embers and then cooled to ashes?

PART III

Time in the Desert

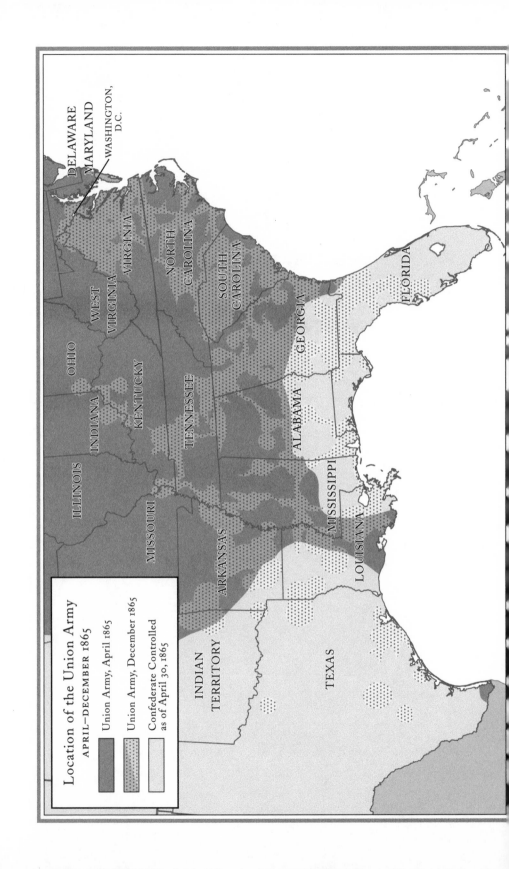

Location of the Union Army
APRIL–DECEMBER 1865

- Union Army, April 1865
- Union Army, December 1865
- Confederate Controlled as of April 30, 1865

DELAWARE

MARYLAND

WASHINGTON, D.C.

WEST VIRGINIA

VIRGINIA

NORTH CAROLINA

SOUTH CAROLINA

OHIO

INDIANA

KENTUCKY

TENNESSEE

GEORGIA

ALABAMA

FLORIDA

ILLINOIS

MISSOURI

ARKANSAS

MISSISSIPPI

LOUISIANA

INDIAN TERRITORY

TEXAS

FIVE

Imperfect Plowshares

From Military to Civil Authority,
April–December 1865

By the late fall of 1865, with harvests gathered on the Georgia coast and islands, local people were eager to travel and trade, and given the region's geography the best way to do so was often by boat. Lieutenant J. M. Daughty of the U.S. Navy spent a lot of time patrolling and monitoring seafarers, as Southern whites who had fled for the war began to return and as former slaves began to resettle in the wake of the quick postwar dispersal of most contraband camps. During the war, the army had confiscated secessionists' boats, some for its own use and some for use by freedpeople. Now one white man by the name of Frashior pestered Daughty "as a U. States officer, to return him his property." With the rebellion over, Frashior considered that the U.S. government and its armed forces resumed the duty to protect white men's claims to property and owed him his boat. Freedpeople and William Eaton, a former Union army soldier turned Freedmen's Bureau agent to whom Daughty appealed for guidance, disagreed: that boat rightfully belonged to people who had helped save the Union. In this instance, the objectives of the national government and of formerly enslaved people remained aligned, as they often had during the war when soldiers and African Americans joined forces to defeat the Confederacy and the army possessed the authority under martial law to advance shared goals.[1]

Yet even during the war, the aims of the army and of freedom-seeking former slaves had not always coincided perfectly, and once the Confederate States of America no longer existed, visions began to diverge more openly. Freedpeople's hopes varied from person to person, but by and large many shared aspirations of permanent emancipation, education, mobility, access to courts, family rights, land, and the right not to be whipped. Some actively sought voting rights, though such aspirations were not so urgent to others. The army and the Freedmen's Bureau prized wage labor, education, family rights, access to courts, limits on punishment, and the permanence of emancipation. Military personnel and Freedmen's Bureau agents were even less unanimous on the matter of political rights than freedpeople themselves were. Some championed black voting rights, while others opposed them and still others simply did not give them much thought one way or the other. In other ways, the army and the Freedmen's Bureau diverged even further from the visions of former slaves, for most did not share freedpeople's emphasis on land and mobility and placed less store by black autonomy than former slaves did.

The simultaneous congruence and divergence in goals was evident many times over in William Eaton's typical workweek. In the same harvest season he deflected Frashior's complaints about his boat, he also mediated several conflicts between former slaves and returning white landowners. In the broadest sense, Eaton favored the causes of loyal former slaves over disloyal former slaveholders, who as far as he was concerned deserved "an iron hand and a rod of steel." Eaton defied white resistance and installed a windmill to generate power for former slaves to mill their crops, for example. He sympathized with freedpeople's desires to farm for themselves rather than work for their former owners. Yet he also insisted that those who had agreed to work for wages or shares, however reluctantly, do so, and he had no patience for former slaves' desires to trap or visit rather than work in the fields at all hours when the demands of the harvest were at their height. He also gave in to pressure to rein in the political organizing being carried out by Tunis Campbell, a free black man from New York who went south to work among freedpeople, lest former slaves allow politics to distract them excessively from the necessities of work.[2]

Moreover, even where the views of the armed forces remained congruent with those of freedpeople—both, for example, still clearly recognized recent secessionists as an ongoing threat—the conclusion of the war also meant subjection of military authority to civil authority. That transition was fully in keeping with the political tradition of a country whose founding principles included suspicion of standing armies and martial law, but it had serious drawbacks for former slaves, for whom freedom and rights were most likely to be real if the army was within earshot.[3] What would happen when soldiers went home? Would it be possible to enjoy and exercise basic rights once soldiers left? Would, for that matter, freedom even last?

By the time Confederate armies surrendered, Congress had passed a constitutional amendment abolishing slavery, but the requisite number of states had not ratified it, and so it was not yet the law of the land. To emphasize, former slaves faced the spring and fall of 1865 without the Thirteenth Amendment yet in effect. Its pending ratification was enough to safeguard the liberty of freedpeople located near Union army troops, but it was not enough to make freedom real for black men, women, and children distant from the military. With Union forces nearby in coastal Georgia, Frashior tried to regain ownership of his boat but not of human beings. John M. Ingram, in contrast, lived inland, farther from the army's reach. When one of his former slaves returned home, Ingram ordered her about, just as he always had, and sent her sprawling to the ground when she defied his directions. Acting on the freedom she had found during the war, the woman got up off the floor. Ingram knocked her down again, tied her up, suspended her from the ceiling beams, and lit a pine torch directly above her so that its boiling pitch would drip onto her back while he lit another torch at her feet to burn her legs. His aim was clear: to show her that she was still a slave. Tied up, with her flesh burning and nobody to come if she cried out, the woman at that moment knew (with an urgency that standard accounts of the Civil War often miss) that re-enslavement could genuinely happen.[4] For her, and for many others, the end of war threatened to make things worse, not better, for there was no way to know for certain if emancipation would remain permanent or if slavery would revive, as it had after every other conflict in U.S. history. There was no inevitability in 1865: re-enslavement was an all-too-real possibility.

The wartime collaboration (sometimes purposeful, sometimes unwitting) between the Union army and former slaves, which had produced distinctive versions of both emancipation and citizenship, had developed under two specific conditions: the first was an atmosphere of chaos in which congruence between army goals and freedom seekers' desires outweighed divergences in their objectives, and the second was martial law. Neither of those two conditions should be romanticized. Chaos made it easier to overlook the real differences in the army's and freedpeople's priorities, but it also made for horrific material conditions and genuine humanitarian crises. Throughout human history, martial law has led to reigns of terror, and it certainly runs counter to the deep-seated American founding principle of subordinating military authority to civil authority. Yet the fact remained that in 1865 the liberty and rights of former slaves had so far been more effectively furthered and protected amid wartime flux and under martial law than they had in well-ordered peacetime under civil authority. Too hasty a return to the antebellum order, and specifically too rapid a shift from military to civil governance, especially with neither emancipation nor freedpeople's civic status yet protected by the Constitution, could place emancipation and black rights in danger. By the end of 1865, the risk of re-enslavement had been averted and emancipation had been rendered permanent, but freedpeople's citizenship and protection of their basic rights remained vulnerable.

·   ·   ·

Former slaves and free black leaders assembled in conventions throughout the South to express their hopes for freedom practically from the moment that armies surrendered. In the first weeks and months after the war, former slaves differed widely from each other on the details of what freedom would mean, but they shared a persisting confidence that some fundamental aspirations to autonomy for themselves, their loved ones, and their community would be realized. Black Louisianans gathered in the African Methodist Episcopal Zion Church of New Orleans in May.[5] Freed Virginians met in Norfolk in June and then again in Alexandria in August, the same month that "Colored Men of Tennessee" convened in Nashville.[6] North Carolinians participated in the State Convention of the Colored People of North Carolina in Raleigh in September.[7] As November gave way to December, former slaves in Little Rock participated in the "Convention of the Colored Citizens of the State of Arkansas."[8] Even more ambitiously, the National Equal Rights League brought black leaders from many states together at its first annual meeting in Cleveland in October.[9] In each of these conventions, African Americans hashed out visions of a renewed American national community that included them and in which they enjoyed legal equality, security, protection of basic rights, and full participation as members of the body politic, often (though not always) through equal access to the vote.[10] They had good reason to be optimistic. They had, after all, just witnessed the defeat of slaveholders whose death grips on slaves' hopes had seemed unshakable a mere four years earlier, and they knew that the efforts of former slaves in collaboration with the Union army had helped bring about that defeat. It seemed only reasonable that continued collaboration would help freedpeople attain their aspirations and actualize their hoped-for rights.

One of those rights was mobility, a right former slaves immediately began to exercise. A young man named Gus had first taken his future into his own hands when the columns of Sherman's army marched by Louisville, Georgia, in 1864. Gus accompanied Captain J. G. Randall of the Twenty-First Wisconsin Infantry on the rest of the march and then, after the war, to Randall's hometown of Mukwonago, Wisconsin, where Gus reinvented himself as August Cowen, farmworker and local hero for rescuing two young brothers from drowning in 1870.[11] In the fall of 1865, more than four hundred freedpeople decided to start over in the North and accompanied Annie Hager of the Western Freedmen's Aid Commission from Camp Nelson, Kentucky, to Ohio.[12] So many former slaves left North Carolina for Worcester, Massachusetts, in the months following the war that an employment office for former slaves opened there, and over the course of the 1860s the city's black population doubled, enabling the creation of a small but thriving African American community in that city.[13]

Yet for all who set off for distant and unfamiliar locales, many more set out to search for family members lost through the slave trade, hoping to remake their world and their lives as freedpeople right on the ground they had known all their lives.[14] A young man named J. H. Holmes had once watched his sister poked and prodded, turned and examined, and eventually sold in one of Richmond's infamous holding pens, Lumpkin's Jail, where slaves marked time between sale and purchase in the interstate slave trade. In days when war's rubble still lined the streets of the former Confederate capital, Holmes returned to the jail, desperate for any leads that might help him locate his sister. He never found her, but he helped turn the jail into a school and church. In the very quarters where he had seen women "taken down and whipped on one side, then kicked over and whipped on the other," he now heard sermons of hope.[15] In Darlington District, South Carolina, where slaves caught sneaking food to Union prisoners of war had recently been beaten and tortured by Confederate captors, now men, women, and children gathered to mark the first post-emancipation harvest by raising a liberty pole and singing "Kingdom Coming" as they danced around it. Then they ran a U.S. flag atop the pole, while a formerly enslaved man vowed, "When we sell our cotton we put de money in OUR pocket" and use it to care for "wife and babies."[16]

The hopes of J. H. Holmes, of the black Carolinians dancing around the liberty pole, and of former slaves everywhere were the same hopes cherished during centuries of slavery and remained just as bitterly opposed by former slaveholders as emancipation had been. During the war, when military leadership had shared or championed former slaves' aspirations, military authority had helped freedpeople overcome opposition to emancipation. Whether civil authority would continue to serve as a counterweight to white Southern resistance depended in part on civil leadership. With the death of President Abraham Lincoln, much civil authority passed into the hands of Lincoln's successor, Andrew Johnson.[17]

A Jacksonian Democrat before the war, a Tennessean, and a staunch white Unionist in the face of his state's secession, Johnson governed in a notably different key from Lincoln. He had been serving as military governor of the Union government in Tennessee when the Republican convention of 1864 tapped him as Lincoln's running mate because his Southern identity and Democratic credentials shored up the ticket's claim to being a true Union party.

At first, abolitionism's enthusiasts assumed harmony between Johnson's priorities and freedpeople's aspirations. In the new president's first week in office, he emphasized that "treason must be punished and impoverished" and secessionists' "social power must be destroyed," and he continued to sound that refrain in several of his speeches and other public utterances.[18] He also met with radicals like Chief Justice Salmon P. Chase and General Carl Schurz and dispatched them on fact-finding missions throughout the former Confederacy.[19] In short, Johnson's views on emancipation seemed sound enough when he said things like "Slavery is dead, and you must pardon me if I do not mourn over its dead body." Johnson called slavery the "disturbing and dangerous element" that had brought secession and war in the first place, and he wanted to "hurry it out of sight" and reassemble state governments and the Union using "only those parts of the machinery which will move in harmony." Those machinery parts definitely did not include slavery.[20]

As the months of 1865 passed, Johnson's words and actions increasingly revealed that as far as he was concerned, freedpeople's citizenship, rights, and aspirations did not count as "parts of the machinery which will move in harmony," either. Determined to restore civil government and subordinate military authority to it throughout the Union as quickly as possible, Johnson immediately recognized provisional state governments set up in Louisiana, Arkansas, and Tennessee as full-fledged state governments. Before May was out, he did the same for Virginia and North Carolina. In two proclamations issued on May 29, 1865 (aimed specifically at North Carolina but widely understood as templates for other states to follow), Johnson extended all civil and property rights "except as to slaves" to almost any former Confederate who took an oath of future loyalty to the United States, regardless of participation in secession or rebellion. Fourteen categories of elite secessionists were exempted from Johnson's blanket absolution, but even these special cases could appeal to the president for individual pardons, which Johnson went on to grant with breathtaking speed in the summer and fall of 1865. Additionally, Johnson recognized a state government in North Carolina and specifically subordinated military forces there to the will of Governor William Woods Holden and the new state government.[21] Over the next six weeks, Johnson named provisional governors for the remaining six states of the former Confederacy and applied similarly lenient terms.

Quick recognition for a state's government had real consequences for national policy and serious drawbacks for former slaves. Recognition would allow a state to send a delegation to Congress when it convened in December. Johnson's amnesty permitted Confederate leaders to hold office and return to Congress. During the war, Congress had emerged as a branch of the federal government that, like the president, had increasingly functioned as a powerful ally of refugees from slavery against shared enemies. It did not bode well for the continuation of that alliance if the members of Congress drafting national legislation were the same people who had so recently fought for slavery.

Johnson's insistence on speedy restoration had even more direct influence on former slaves' daily lives because of amnesty's impact on the local level. For one thing, restoration meant that antebellum state laws went back into effect, with dire consequences for the recently emancipated. In the states of the former Confederacy, antebellum state laws actively discriminated against blacks in a host of ways ranging from treatment before the law to allowable punishment to a prohibition against black literacy. Discriminatory laws could have been circumvented if President Johnson directed governors or state legislatures to set aside prejudicial laws or if he permitted provost marshal courts rather than civil courts to continue to function, because army courts during the war, unlike civil ones, treated African Americans with relative equality. Instead, the president made no move to do the former and actually hastened rather than delayed the resumption of civil courts.[22] In sum, Johnson's actions in his first months as president threatened and undermined the tenuous alliance that had developed between freedpeople and the federal government during the war.

Northern travelers in the South noted an immediate change in tone. In April and May, observers found erstwhile rebels who knew they were beaten and so longed for peace that they were sure to "acquiesce in any mode of reorganization."[23] Those traveling in the summer and fall, once speedy restorations had begun, found much more hostility and defiant determination to resist any elevation in status for former slaves. When the German immigrant and former Union general Carl Schurz toured Georgia, Alabama, Mississippi, and Louisiana, he found whites quick to beat and shoot black workers, mock the U.S. government and Union army, and insist on restoring local affairs as closely as possible to what they had been before emancipation. He had no doubt that Johnson's leniency was to blame for the turnaround, telling his wife, "I have come to the firm conviction that the policy of the government is the worst that could be hit upon."[24] J. W. Shaffer of Illinois had served as chief quartermaster in New Orleans during part of the war and traveled down the Mississippi to visit afterward. By the end of 1865, he was stunned by the quick change in tone. "It has become very much more rabid than it was at the close of the war," he testified. "Immediately after the surrender of the southern armies their officers and men came back completely subdued," but as soon as the U.S. government pardoned them, restored their land, and "put them into power" with "entire control of political affairs," former Confederates' "malignant dispositions" flared.[25] It was not only visitors who thought so. The Nashville Unionist William Driver lamented that the moment "when *Richmond fell*" was a "Golden hour" when "the South lay [a] helpless conquered thing at our feet, ready for such terms as we might offer" but "Andrew Johnson" had betrayed "our duty" and instead "nailed to the Cross of national imbecility the last hope of a Race whose unnumbered wrongs are before the Throne of God."[26]

For black Southerners, the change in tone had all-too-real repercussions as waves of antiblack brutality and aggression crashed across the South in the latter half of 1865, renewing rather than washing away the violence that the enslaved had endured in slavery. In Alexandria, Louisiana, a group of former Confederate soldiers met clandestinely to hatch a plan to "kill all the colored soldiers as soon as they were discharged from the Union army for taking up arms against their masters." Meanwhile, in the Gulf Coast parishes of St. Mary and Terrebonne, local whites tore down or burned down freedpeople's schools.[27] A woman in rural Alabama heard that the Yankees were in nearby Choctaw County and set out with her three young children to get closer to the soldiers and the safety they might provide. When she got to a river, she was stopped by a white man named Bill Odam, who demanded to know if the woman and her children planned on sailing down the river. When she said yes, he promised to "show you the way through hell." He cut her throat, slashed her two older children across their necks, and then threw the baby, still alive, in the river.[28] Such instances were "lamentably frequent," as the Union general Wager Swayne acknowledged. He knew, because with his own eyes he saw "the incontestible [*sic*] evidence of negroes who present themselves at the military agencies [in Alabama] having been shot, stabbed, or otherwise severely injured."[29]

The violence was convulsive and turns the stomach of anyone reading accounts of it, however dispassionately relayed, but it was anything but senseless. On the contrary, it had a clear purpose: to undo emancipation. Military emancipation had been necessary to *begin* the process of eradicating slavery, for nothing—no efforts of black or white abolitionists, no fruits of antislavery politics, and none of the accumulated hatred of and resistance to the institution of slavery on the part of generations of slaves—had prevented slavery from growing into a larger, stronger, and more lucrative institution in 1860 than it had ever been. It took the brute force of the Union army to land the first real blows. But emancipation by military authority would never be enough to *complete* the legal eradication of slavery on its own, because it was reversible as soon as the army left, a truth demonstrated by world history and by the experiences of emancipated slaves when Confederates recaptured territory or people. For example, a North Carolina man made his way out of slavery in 1863 by dashing to Wilmington and working for Union troops, but then he got recaptured. He tried to escape again by setting out to float to Union blockading vessels on a plank of wood, only to be fished out of the water by a Confederate soldier who dragged him onto the beach, administered "bars and stripes" across his back, and forced him back into slavery.[30]

Soldiers and civilians who had sometimes hesitantly and sometimes eagerly allied with freedpeople during the war realized that safeguarding freedom for good would require nothing less than a constitutional amendment. As the AFIC commissioner James McKaye explained in a special report to Congress after months of sifting through testimony, the only way "to secure, beyond any possible peradventure or doubt, the civil right of the colored man to personal freedom" was "by placing that right in the new order of things, on the same broad basis as that of the white man." That "broad basis" needed to be the strongest source of civil authority of all: the U.S. Constitution. In other words, McKaye and the AFIC argued for a constitutional amendment prohibiting slavery.[31]

Congressional Republicans agreed and had been working toward a constitutional amendment abolishing slavery for over a year. When the Thirty-Eighth Congress convened in December 1863, James M. Ashley, congressman from Ohio, proposed an amendment to the House of Representatives, while the Missouri senator John Henderson did the same in the Senate. Both proposals went to the Judiciary Committee, out of which Senator Lyman Trumbull reported the text for the Thirteenth Amendment on March 28, 1864. "The only effectual way of ridding the country of slavery, and so that it cannot be resuscitated," declared Trumbull, was by constitutional amendment "forever prohibiting it within the jurisdiction of the United States. This amendment adopted, not only does slavery cease, but it can never be reestablished by State authority, or in any other way than by again amending the Constitution." Without an amendment, Trumbull warned, "there is nothing in the Constitution to prevent any State from reestablishing it."[32] The Senate overwhelmingly approved the amendment, and a majority of members of the House voted for the measure on June 15, 1864, but in the House the proposed amendment did not receive the necessary two-thirds supermajority required for a constitutional amendment. Repeal of the Fugitive Slave Law later that same month helped blunt the danger of re-enslavement a little bit, but Republicans knew that nothing less than a constitutional amendment could really do the job in the long run.[33] The reelection of Lincoln and Republican gains in congressional races in the election of 1864 put the force of public opinion behind the amendment. Meanwhile, the state legislatures of Missouri and Maryland abolished slavery within their states. In response, some House members changed their "no" votes to "yes," resulting in a 119 to 56 vote in the House (and therefore passage by the Thirty-Eighth Congress rather than waiting for the Thirty-Ninth) on January 31, 1865.[34]

As soon as the vote total was announced, "loud and continuous cheering arose spontaneously from the crowd on the floor and in the galleries," and the nation's capital rang with "a salute of one hundred guns" and "a jubilant feeling throughout the city."[35] The next day, a choir regaled the White House with a congratulatory serenade. As the news spread, celebrations small and large erupted throughout the Northern states and among Union soldiers and refugees from slavery in Union-occupied territory throughout the South.[36]

The only problem was that the amendment was not yet in effect when armies surrendered in the spring of 1865. Momentous a milestone as the January vote was, twenty-seven states (three-fourths of the total) still needed to ratify it, either by voting in their legislatures or by holding a special convention. Within a week, Congress sent the amendment to the states, and six states ratified it almost immediately. Before the month was over, that total was up to seventeen, and ratification continued to proceed at a steady pace throughout the spring. The ending of the war, paradoxically, slowed the process down as states turned to the immediate needs of transitioning out of wartime. In fact, in Delaware and Kentucky, the two border states that had neither left the Union nor abolished slavery by state law, slavery remained legal.[37]

Ratification of the Thirteenth Amendment, in sum, was in full swing when formal hostilities came to a halt, but because it was not yet complete, the war ended before abolition was fully secured by civil authority. That possibility had worried proponents of emancipation during the war, like one Vermont clergyman who had cautioned that permanent freedom "depends on *how* [the war] ends," because if Confederates got their way, "*all [slaves] that can* be, will be restored to the 'benign sovereignty' of their old masters."[38] What he meant was that emancipation brought about by military authority during the war was good as far as it went, but if its effects were to outlast the fighting, a constitutional amendment needed to be in place. Francis Lieber made the same point when he worried that without a constitutional amendment "we shall have back some states in a condition that the day after re-admission they will turn on their heels and re-establish forced labor of some sort—slavery in fact."[39]

With ratification not yet complete, the rash of antiblack violence encouraged by Johnson's leniency toward former Confederates came dangerously near to fulfilling Lieber's gloomy prophecy in the summer and fall of 1865. In coastal South Carolina, a judge from Maine noticed how often local whites threatened and assaulted black men and women harvesting crops for their own rather than a white master's benefit. Bereft of the food they had grown, former slaves would be forced to turn to their former owners for enough sustenance to survive the winter, ex-Confederates reasoned. Once that happened, former owners could impose conditions that mimicked slavery.[40] That same logic prevailed throughout the former Confederacy as the first harvest began to ripen. In August 1865, a freedwoman named Caroline prepared to gather in the crop she had spent months growing in northern Alabama, but a white man named Parson Bowen and his son, Philip, beat her and drove her off the land in order to prevent her from reaping the fruits of her own labor.[41] Elsewhere, African Americans suffered re-enslavement in name as well as fact. Incidents of owners blatantly kidnapping former slaves and fleeing for Cuba, where slavery was still legal, were so rife that even the U.S. Senate and the State Department got involved in investigation and prosecution.[42]

Slavery was also still legal in Kentucky, which made violent re-enslavement there an especially acute threat. Wartime emancipation had freed black people who had made it to the army or who were owned by secessionists, as well as black Union soldiers and their family members, but those wartime measures still left roughly sixty-five thousand black Kentuckians legally enslaved to owners who appeared determined to wrest all the mastery they could out of the last few months of legal bondage. Often white Kentuckians did not even bother to determine if a former slave was already legally freed but instead operated on the assumption that as long as legal slavery persisted, "all negroes were presumed to be slaves."[43] As the wife of a member of the 119th U.S. Colored Infantry, Mary Wilson was legally free, but that didn't stop police in Lexington from forcing their way into her house, abducting her, stripping her, tying her to a beam in a slaughterhouse, and beating her with their fists and a leather whip before delivering her to her former owner, who also kidnapped her child.[44]

Finally, on December 6, 1865, the state legislature of Georgia ratified the Thirteenth Amendment as a condition of reentering the Union, and the Thirteenth Amendment was officially part of the U.S. Constitution.[45] For Delaware and Kentucky especially, ratification dealt the final legal blow to slavery. By that time, the number of slaves in Delaware had dwindled into the low hundreds, and the state legislature's retention of slavery amounted chiefly to symbolic sullenness, so the impact was less dramatic there than it was in Kentucky.[46] In the Bluegrass State, ratification's impact was much more than symbolic. On December 7, John M. Palmer, the Union general still in command of the Department of Kentucky, released Circular No. 6, which unambiguously stated, "Whatever doubts may have heretofore existed on the subject, Slavery has now ceased to exist in Kentucky."[47] Slavery, at last, was legally dead throughout the United States.

Ratification of the amendment set the Civil War apart from other American conflicts, which had temporarily disrupted slavery but not destroyed it and sometimes even strengthened it. The Civil War, in contrast, yielded the Thirteenth Amendment, which changed the fundamental nature of the United States. Since the adoption of the Constitution, pro-slavery and antislavery political leaders, no matter how bitter their differences, had agreed or at least accepted that only states could touch slavery. Meanwhile, the U.S. government had operated as a slaveholding nation in its international affairs, and in domestic affairs the federal government had grown more rather than less activist on behalf of the institution of slavery and the interests of slaveholders over the course of the nineteenth century. Now the Constitution conclusively abolished legal ownership of one human being by another in the United States and secured emancipation by civil authority.[48] Small wonder, then, that *The Right Way*, a weekly periodical that went into publication for and by white and black New England abolitionists as final ratification approached, dedicated its Last Words column to ratification of the amendment for much of December.[49]

Yet nationwide response to the final ratification of the amendment was oddly muted, and *The Right Way*'s title unwittingly helps indicate why, for a "way" indicates a direction but not a final destination.[50] Indeed, *The Right Way*'s weekly publication schedule did not finish up with ratification but rather was just getting started, which helps remind us exactly what emancipation did and did not do. While the elimination of legal slavery meant a great deal for the United States, it was hard to know for sure what it meant for the individuals actually emancipated. As one legal historian explains, "Emancipation produced a legally naked individual, stripped of any status or protection of law, almost totally devoid of legally enforceable rights."[51] Just as military emancipation during the war determined that a refugee from slavery who made it to the Union army was no longer a slave but emancipated that former slave into statelessness rather than unambiguous national belonging, so, too, the Thirteenth Amendment affirmed that bond people were not slaves, but it did not confer standing within the national community, either.

The Thirteenth Amendment made former slaves free, but it did not make them citizens. Congressional debate in fact made clear that emancipation and citizenship were not the same thing. In the process of debating the amendment before its passage, the Senate considered including language stating, "No negro or person whose mother or grandmother is or was a negro shall be a citizen of the United States and be eligible to any civil or military office, or to any place of trust or profit under the United States."[52] In the end, no such language was included, but the spirited discussion surrounding it demonstrated that the amendment as passed did not contain the citizenship status that freedpeople in contraband camps claimed in exchange for their labor on behalf of the Union war effort. Some states emphasized that same point at the time of ratification. The Alabama state legislature, for example, attached the condition that neither the amendment nor any act of the U.S. Congress said anything about "the political status of freedmen in this State."[53] The black rights advocate John Mercer Langston might not have agreed with the Alabama legislature about much, but he also recognized that even with "the abolition of chattel slavery, the question of our right to full citizenship is not yet defined."[54] Similarly, the African Methodist Episcopal minister John Lynch noted that the "status" of former bond people was "not yet fixed."[55]

The point is not that the Thirteenth Amendment was meaningless—far from it—but rather that we need to be ruthlessly precise about both what emancipation accomplished and what it left undone, because *both* what it did and what it failed to do profoundly shaped the real lives of former slaves. We may want emancipation to be all or nothing—either a splendid triumph or a tragic failure—but people who lived through emancipation, people like Steve and Anna, knew that their experiences did not fit into any such unambiguous schemes. When war broke out, Steve was owned by one family but usually spent his time hired out to Carr Waller Pritchett, a white Unionist living in the Confederate-leaning interior of the deeply divided state of Missouri, who paid Steve's owners for the use of Steve's labor. Worried that his loyalty would get him killed, Pritchett fled 150 miles to St. Louis, leaving his wife and family behind to get by as best they could by working out a makeshift partnership with Steve and his wife, Anna, who would also remain behind. Bettie Pritchett and her children moved into the town of Fayette and earned cash by cooking for federal soldiers. Steve, Anna, and their children stayed on the Pritchett farm, trying to limit the damage that Confederate guerrillas inflicted, while Steve worked for a Union officer for wages of ten dollars per month. Neither Steve's family nor the Pritchetts gained complete satisfaction from the arrangement, but all were resigned to it as a matter of expediency while war raged and former bond people remained "in a transition state."[56]

When the Missouri state legislature enacted abolition by state law in January 1865, some big changes resulted for Steve and Anna's family. Steve kept the ten dollars per month he earned from the army rather than conveying it to Bettie Pritchett, and Anna negotiated for a share of the crop that the family managed to wrest from the war-torn Pritchett farm. But emancipation did not solve everything. Steve and his family lacked personal security, because they still lived in terrible danger from Confederate guerrillas. They lacked economic security, because Carr Pritchett still owed nearly a year's worth of back wages for Steve's labor before Pritchett fled, and there was no way to know if those wages would be paid to Steve's antebellum owner (from whom Pritchett hired Steve) or to Steve himself, if, of course, they were ever paid at all. Steve lacked the assurance that he could turn to the courts for redress. In fact, Steve and his family lacked fundamental security of identity, because they did not even have a legally recognized surname. As even Bettie Pritchett recognized, it would take putting some of the "gas expended in speeches and glorification" into "solid form" to figure out what came next for former slaves.[57]

If the ten-dollar wages saved Steve and his family from complete "nakedness," to borrow legal historians' metaphor for emancipation, they still left them ill-clad and highly vulnerable to the elements when the bitter wind of white Southern resistance blew away the garments with which they sought to clothe themselves. That wind blew hard throughout the South in the summer and fall of 1865, not only in the waves of violence unleashed by white individuals, but also in the actions of the Southern state governments reconstituting themselves according to Johnson's conciliatory methods. As these state legislatures grudgingly ratified the Thirteenth Amendment (a condition for readmittance to the Union), they also turned state laws to former slaveholders' purposes. Throughout the region, statehouses fortified prejudicial antebellum laws, which had been aimed chiefly at the relatively small population of free blacks, with even more sweepingly discriminatory state laws designed to keep the much larger population of former slaves in check.

Collectively, these 1865 and 1866 laws have come to be known as the Black Codes. The Black Codes included "vagrancy" laws to prohibit black mobility without white permission and to limit African Americans' freedom of choice as to where and for whom they worked. They included "apprenticeship" laws that permitted the state to take black children away from their parents. They prohibited blacks from testifying against whites in courts, renting or leasing (let alone owning) land, or possessing firearms. At the same time, these new state laws specifically permitted whipping and other forms of corporal punishment for blacks but not whites.[58] Once the U.S. Congress convened in December, it would begin to dismantle the Black Codes, and none would remain in effect past 1867, but nobody knew that yet in 1865. Plainly, the end of formal hostilities did not instantly transform former slaveholders into willing respecters of African Americans' rights, as the black abolitionist Phillip Bell pointed out when he cautioned against leaving former slaves "to the tender mercies of their former oppressors, full of hatred and rebellion as ever."[59] If former bond people like Steve, Anna, and millions of others were to turn their rich visions of equal standing, civic personhood, and rights protection into lived reality, they needed access to a source of power strong enough to overcome violent ex-Confederate opposition to those visions.

Former slaves and their wartime allies insisted that African Americans' wartime contributions to the nation's survival merited an ongoing partnership with the national government to protect freedpeople's hard-won freedom and rights from attacks by ex-Confederates. George Grubbs, a white Union soldier from Indiana who spent the summer of 1865 in Tennessee waiting to be mustered out, celebrated Independence Day in Chattanooga at a "celebration, and a very creditable one, too," mounted by local "colored people" in cooperation with the "bands of the four Colored Regiments." Grubbs especially admired "a procession of Soldiers and *Citizens*, men, women and children and numbering not less than two thousand or more."[60] He placed a double underline beneath the word "Citizens" to emphasize his view of black men, women, and children as contributors to the nation's survival and rightful beneficiaries of its strength and protection. While Grubbs watched a parade in Chattanooga, Abraham Galloway participated in one in Beaufort, North Carolina, and he concluded it by delivering a passionate address about former slaves' equality before U.S. law as the logical outcome of the interdependent relationship between the U.S. government and former slaves that had developed during the war.[61] One month earlier, a group of black Richmonders had gathered at the home of the community leader Peter Matthews to compose an address to the president of the United States. Their remarks reminded President Johnson that "during the whole of the Slaveholders' Rebellion, we have been true and loyal to the United States Government," supporting it not only with prayers but also by giving "aid and comfort to the soldiers of Freedom (for which several of our people, of both sexes, have been severely punished)." Now former masters continued to "seek not only to oppress our people, but to thwart the designs of the Federal Government and of benevolent Northern associations in our behalf." The mayor of Richmond was an unrepentant Confederate, as were members of the civil police force, and the Black Codes hardly inspired confidence. "We cannot appeal to the laws of Virginia," the address continued, and so "we have nowhere to go for protection and justice but to that power which made us free." From that power, freedpeople of Richmond asked for "protection" of their right to choose their own clergy, walk freely about the city, seek their own employment, and search for lost family members. In exchange, the U.S. government could expect the continued "loyalty of our hearts and the power of our arms [on which] you may ever rely with unbounded confidence."[62] Moreover, the national government *needed* people of reliable loyalty throughout the states of the former Confederacy to counteract rebels who might otherwise renew their efforts to destroy the Union.[63]

In 1865, many white Northerners, including those in the army and the federal government, shared freedpeople's expectation that citizenship as a rights-protecting relationship between African Americans and the U.S. government would outlast the war. "As it is well known," explained the Northwestern Freedmen's Aid Commission *Annual Report*, "the nation [owes] . . . obligations to victims whom it has despoiled for two hundred years," while at the same time "the real interest of the nation [resided] in the well-being of the National Freedmen."[64] The Pennsylvania congressman William D. Kelley made a similar point when he told an audience gathered in the Concert Hall of Philadelphia that "the Almighty has so inextrically [*sic*] interwoven our duty of justice to [freedpeople] with our own welfare, that in pleading with you to extend justice to them, I plead with you to promote your own peace and happiness." Fulfilling that duty of justice required the U.S. government to protect specific, concrete rights of the "four millions of laboring people at the South," including "the right to testify in open court, . . . the right to make a contract . . . [and] the right to public education." Kelley's speech was reprinted in black newspapers around the country, and it also circulated as a pamphlet.[65] As the *Iowa State Register* summed things up, Congress retained "a solemn obligation to protect and shield the freedmen from oppression, injustice and revengeful inflictions prompted by their participation in and profit by the great National triumph. In other words, it feels bound to secure to them the rights and immunities, not merely of freedmen, but of freemen."[66]

During the war, the Union army had served as a somewhat irregular—but still the most effective—guarantor of freedpeople's rights, and even after Confederate surrender military authority remained the most readily effective source of power for asserting and protecting those rights. As soon as word of the surrender at Appomattox reached Alexandria, Virginia, General John Slough promised "full protection to the persons and property of these colored" and ordered that "all local laws, drawing a distinction between whites and blacks, upon the subjects of punishments and testimony, be repealed."[67] That same summer, when Mayor B. F. Pullen of Paris, Kentucky, embarked on a scheme to deport all black people from the city, he was stopped in his tracks by the Union major general John M. Palmer, who criticized the "morally unjust and politically tyrannical . . . policy of persecution" and vowed to protect "the rights of the colored people to the enjoyment of their personal freedom."[68] Former Confederates, in fact, never tired of commenting on the alliance between former slaves and the army. J. L. Kirkpatrick, the president of Davidson College in North Carolina, had managed to ride out most of the war with little disturbance to slavery because Union forces came nowhere close to Mecklenburg County, where Kirkpatrick and the college were located. Yet in the fall of 1865, "private soldiers who mingle with the negroes on terms of equality" did come, which, complained Kirkpatrick, "upturns our society upon its foundation."[69]

The army had been an imperfect and uneven ally during the war, sometimes aiding freedpeople's aspirations and other times outright mistreating former slaves, but the departure of Union troops made former slaves even more vulnerable. In Norfolk, Virginia, in the summer of 1865, the only thing worse than the presence of New York soldiers was their absence. During the war, some members of the Ninety-Ninth New York had kidnapped and sold fugitive slaves, and now that the war was over, some persisted in terrorizing freedpeople, much to the disgust of Lucy Chase. But when "civil power is established here, and the military command is restricted," Chase fretted, things got even worse. "The bullying street-cry of the returned rebel soldiers" echoed through city streets as men brandishing knives and pistols threatened to "kill every nigger, or drive 'em all out of town." In nearby Portsmouth, "the divided, and somewhat obscurely defined, responsibilities resting upon the associate military and civil authorities" similarly allowed violence and confusion to reign.[70]

A shift to civil authority, however perilous to former slaves, had to happen for several reasons. First, the Union army demobilized astonishingly quickly. Once formal hostilities ceased, Northern soldiers and civilians were impatient to get troops home (a common response recognizable in our own time). By the end of 1865, the Union army that had numbered 2 million men over the course of the war was down to fewer than 125,000 troops scattered throughout the South. The army had not disappeared entirely, but numbers like that simply could not exert authority effectively even if they were evenly distributed over the 750,000 square miles of the former Confederacy, which they were not. A disproportionate segment of the troops that remained under arms were black soldiers, partly because most had enlisted in the latter half of the war and so were further from the end of the three-year period they signed on for than white soldiers who had enlisted in 1862 or earlier were. The bulk of them were, like Gaston Becton and his fellow soldiers in the Thirty-Sixth U.S. Colored Infantry, transferred to duty in more sparsely populated Texas, remote from the more concentrated populations of Southern civilians, white or black. At the same time, contraband camps were dispersed as rapidly as possible in the summer of 1865, so freedpeople went from being concentrated within a finite area that could theoretically be guarded to dispersed throughout the countryside where they could not.[71] Finally, the subordination of civil authority to military authority, however expedient in time of war, came into question after Confederate surrender ended because civil authority must eventually supersede military authority in any government other than despotism.

As military authority faded, freedpeople needed direct access to manifestations of the U.S. government other than the army, and one of the first available was the Freedman's Savings and Trust Company, usually called the Freedman's Savings Bank, or just the Freedman's Bank. The precedent for the Freedman's Bank came from military savings banks established by Union commanding officers in New Orleans, Norfolk, and Beaufort, in which black soldiers could deposit their pay and bounties. In 1864, the Congregational minister John Alvord saw the Beaufort bank in action when he met with freedpeople in the Department of the South. After returning to New York, he convinced a group of bankers and businessmen to organize a bank for former slaves and then persuaded Senator Henry Wilson to introduce a bill to incorporate the bank in the Senate. President Lincoln signed legislation authorizing the Freedman's Savings and Trust Company on March 3, 1865. The bank would be overseen by philanthropically minded trustees who could not borrow against the deposits and who were required to invest in U.S. securities. Congress could monitor the bank by inspecting the books at any time. Before the year was out, seventy-two thousand depositors lodged funds in ten branches located in New York City, Washington, D.C., and throughout the South. By 1872, thirty-two branches of the banks operated, chiefly in the states of the former Confederacy. Deposits over $1 earned 6 percent interest semiannually, and by January 1, 1873, the bank had paid out $262,379.82 in interest to depositors. The Freedman's Savings Bank, like many other banks, did not survive the panic of 1873 and so was eventually disbanded, but depositors' later losses were not yet evident in 1865.[72]

While not a government agency in the exact same straightforward way as the army or the Treasury, the Freedman's Savings Bank nonetheless connected the economic well-being and advancement of African American families with the U.S. government and its symbols. Former slaves concretely invested their hopes in a visible, tangible representation of the national government, which they in turn expected to protect the aspirations they harbored for themselves and their loved ones. When a new depositor opened an account, he or she walked into a branch and offered a series of personal details such as address, occupation, place of birth, regiment and company, and family members. Bank employees filled out a deposit record, often using the generous amount of space after a "Remarks" blank to trace family relationships in some detail. Sam Fobs, who opened an account in Tallahassee, Florida, provides a typical case in point. Fobs's deposit record not only lists the names of his wife and children but also notes the names of his dead parents and siblings and lists the names of nieces and nephews whom Sam "has in charge."[73] Depositors then recorded deposits and gains in a passbook decorated with pictures of Abraham Lincoln, General Ulysses S. Grant, General Oliver O. Howard, and the U.S. flag.[74] In her patriotically decorated passbook, Susie King kept track of what remained of her husband's enlistment bounty after his death left her a young single mother struggling to care for a new baby.[75] Besides the material benefits to individual African American depositors and investors, the bank served collective purposes as well. About half of the bank's employees were African American, and prominent black leaders also served on its board. Moreover, any interest unclaimed by heirs of depositors who died was to be invested in education for freedpeople. In these ways, the Freedman's Savings Bank bolstered the sense of the U.S. government as the ally of former slaves.[76]

The most well-known evidence of a persisting relationship between the U.S. government and formerly enslaved African Americans was the Bureau of Refugees, Freedmen, and Abandoned Lands, better known as the Freedmen's Bureau. When the AFIC reported to Congress in 1864, one of its strongest recommendations was for the establishment of a federal agency to oversee the transition from slavery to freedom. That recommendation grew from commissioners' clear-eyed recognition that former slaves would continue to live in proximity to people who had just fought a bloody war to keep them enslaved, which made a formidable federal presence necessary to ensure that former slaveholders did not find new ways to reinvent slavery. In response, Congress established the bureau as a temporary agency of the War Department on March 3, 1865, with legislation stipulating that the bureau would last for one year after the end of the war.[77] The Freedmen's Bureau coordinated direct material relief, opened schools, managed lands confiscated from

Confederates by the Union army, oversaw labor contracts, and protected freedpeople's civil rights in the face of continued ex-Confederate hostility.

In many ways, the Freedmen's Bureau marked a breathtaking departure. It was the first U.S. government agency ever dedicated to humanitarian purposes, and it was also the first U.S. government agency predicated explicitly on the assumption that a direct relationship existed between the national government and African Americans, the very people who the *Dred Scott* decision had stipulated could *not* occupy a civic status that put them in direct relationship with the U.S. government. The bureau's supporters were well aware of its momentous novelty and hopeful regarding its efficacy. Just days after Congress passed the bill creating the bureau, Clara Barton, who had put herself in the thick of war's misery in South Carolina and Virginia, welcomed what she called the "*Bureau of Liberty*" as the best way to secure the "results and objects of this war" and the only way to "sound the key notes of human advancement." Rufus Saxton likewise anticipated "that it shall be a power in the country and a blessing to those in whose interests it was established."[78]

Alongside its novelty, the bureau represented some continuities with the wartime Union army, for both good and ill. When a freedwoman walked into a bureau agent's office, she put herself in direct contact with the U.S. government, just as refugees from slavery during the war had put themselves into direct contact with the U.S. government by fleeing to contraband camps. Both army and Freedmen's Bureau, in other words, offered direct points of contact between the national government and formerly enslaved people. Such a point of contact often served freedpeople's needs and hopes when the goals of former slaves and the bureau converged, just as the army had proven itself an ally to former slaves during the war when its aims matched those of black men, women, and children escaping slavery. But just as the army disappointed freedpeople's hopes and even worked against their interests when military mission departed from former slaves' needs and desires or when particular officers disdained black people, so too could the bureau disappoint when its priorities diverged from freedpeople's or when leadership lacked affinity with former slaves.

One readily apparent reason for so much continuity between the

Union army and the Freedmen's Bureau was that very often the same people were involved in both. The Union army general Oliver O. Howard was appointed to lead the bureau with the assistance of General Rufus Saxton as second-in-command and with ten assistant commissioners, each with direct supervisory authority over a specified district. At first, many of the on-the-ground employees were either Union soldiers or former slaves, often the same men and women who had labored for the Union in contraband camps or by accompanying the Union army. Samuel Riddick, for example, had fled his North Carolina owners during the war, made it to Portsmouth, Virginia, hired himself as a servant to General Nelson Miles, and then after the war returned to North Carolina, where he worked for the Freedmen's Bureau in Raleigh.[79]

Like the Union army, the Freedmen's Bureau continued to cooperate (sometimes uneasily) with Northern benevolent societies. The American Missionary Association, the Freedmen's Aid Commission, and other philanthropic organizations sent material goods, monetary donations, and volunteers to help in the work of "succoring the needy, caring for the sick, . . . affording relief and employment . . . [and] attending to [freedpeople's] intellectual and spiritual wants."[80]

Bureau agents also commonly picked up where the Union army left off "as a means of protection" for former slaves, to borrow the words of the bureau agent Clinton Fisk.[81] Much as fleeing slaves had identified the Union army as potential counterweight to their owners' hitherto-unchallenged power, so too did freedpeople regard the Freedmen's Bureau and its agents as potential sources of power that could be drawn upon to pursue their own aims and protect their own priorities in the face of ex-Confederate opposition. Sometimes Freedmen's Bureau protection amounted quite literally to a shielding from coercion and violence. At the close of the war, the teenager Maggie Westmoland was too cut off from kin or economic opportunity to defend herself when her former mistress married a man who beat Maggie, forced her to work, denied her necessities like shoes and decent clothing, and prevented her from going to school. Maggie escaped after neighbors reported the man to the Freedmen's Bureau.[82] When a formerly enslaved woman in Savannah found herself in a standoff with former owners, she marched straight to "the Bureau, and very soon had things made right."[83] In Mississippi and Texas, where one ex-Confederate tactic in the effort to reimpose slavery was a harsh apprenticeship system that effectively stole children from their parents, black mothers and fathers turned to the bureau to find "a sympathetic ear" and for help "to reclaim members of their families who were being detained by force."[84]

The Freedmen's Bureau also protected some freedpeople's access to basic life necessities, at least to a limited extent. Formal hostilities ceased in the spring of 1865, at the very tail end of (or even, in some locales, after) the planting season, which meant that a productive year depended on getting crops in fast and tending them assiduously. Robert Smalls and the *Planter* continued their remarkable career by ferrying seed, farm tools, and the parts to build a windmill—all supplied by the Freedmen's Bureau—to colonies of freedpeople establishing themselves on the islands off the Georgia and South Carolina coasts.[85] In the meantime, freedpeople needed to eat during the lean months while crops matured in the fields, and in many locales the Freedmen's Bureau filled that gap with dull but adequate rations.[86] As harvest approached in Fayetteville, Tennessee, members of three black families appealed to the nearest Freedmen's Bureau agent when a white farmer tried to "defraud them of the present crop" of corn and cotton, as well as of the land and fodder they needed to succor their "70 head of Hogs Large and small."[87] The Freedmen's Bureau often provided access to hospitals and barracks.[88] The urgent need for clothing, especially for women and growing children, did not suddenly diminish. One Union soldier in Baton Rouge wrote home to Wisconsin to say that if any Badger Staters wanted to help Louisiana's freedpeople make it through the winter, the best thing to do was "to consign [clothing] directly to the Hd Qrs of La. Freedmen's Bureau."[89]

Freedpeople and the Freedmen's Bureau shared a belief in the importance of education and generally agreed that the national government, acting through the bureau, should protect former slaves' access to it. In this endeavor, the Freedmen's Bureau picked up exactly where the army left off. By the end of May 1865, 1,261 former slaves studied five and a half hours a day in Vicksburg's schools, some as beginning "alphabet scholars" and others studying arithmetic, grammar, and geography.[90] Partly in response to the clear preference expressed by black learners, and partly out of recognition that the bureau was only a temporary agency, Freedmen's Bureau personnel quickly centered their efforts on training black teachers who would remain long after the dissolution of the bureau. Institutions still with us today—Fisk, Howard, and Hampton Universities, for example—are the most famous manifestations of this initiative, but countless smaller ones also abounded. H. R. Pease, the superintendent of freedmen's schools in Louisiana, for example, worked with the AMA in New Orleans to "assist in the establishment of a Normal School to prepare colored persons for teachers—more acceptable to their people & on many acc'ts better than white teachers."[91] Black Marylanders who had built their own school turned to the bureau for assistance in rebuilding it after angry whites burned the original structure to the ground on November 11, 1865.[92] By 1870, the bureau had spent five million dollars building some forty-three hundred schools in almost every county of the former Confederacy and transporting aid workers and missionaries to teach in them.[93]

Another way in which the Freedmen's Bureau maintained continuity with the Union army was in the matter of courts, because bureau courts, like provost marshal courts during the war, came closer than civil courts did to "guarantee[ing] freedmen both equal rights and unbiased legal forums in which to vindicate those rights."[94] The ability to testify, to tell one's story and seek legal redress, was a right that refugees from slavery had claimed and embraced again and again when they recounted events to provost marshal courts throughout the war, which whites in the occupied Confederacy had rarely failed to note with disgust. As several scholars have demonstrated, the ability to testify about violence committed against oneself in a court of law carried tremendous symbolic import and cemented bonds between the power of the U.S. government represented in those courts and black men, women, and children who sought those courts out, often at personal risk and expense, to make their testimony heard.[95] Yet the importance of courts went well beyond the symbolic. Courtrooms could become places where former slaves turned to put their families back together again, as Rose Herera demonstrated by enlisting the aid first of provost marshal courts in Louisiana and later of the State Department itself in recovering her children from Cuba after their former owner spirited them away to keep them enslaved.[96] Under the Freedmen's Bureau, courts also served practical material purposes. Throughout the former Confederacy, black workers whose wages were not paid or whose property was interfered with turned to provost courts and Freedmen's Bureau courts to give clout to their self-advocacy in everything "from a pig to a plantation," as one provost judge described his typical day at the office.[97]

When and where freedpeople's aspirations aligned with Freedmen's Bureau priorities, in sum, the bureau represented a first attempt at translating the wartime relationship between the army and refugees from slavery into a postwar context. In the summer of 1865, New Orleans's black elite gave "our cordial approval to [the Freedmen's Bureau commissioner] General [Oliver O.] Howard's policies" and praised the "energetic and bold" actions of specific agents in their newspaper, the *New Orleans Tribune*, because the bureau provided the most direct evidence that a rights-protecting relationship between the U.S. government and black men, women, and children would continue.[98] Taking a panoramic view, a Washington, D.C., African American newspaper, the *New Era*, described the bureau as "the first friend of the freemen, as their champion and defender under military rule, and after the reestablishment of civil authority, as their advocate."[99]

Yet friends occasionally fail each other, and such was sometimes the case with the Freedmen's Bureau in 1865. The former slave Philip Joiner and the black clergyman Robert Crumley contrasted the "buoyant" and "hopeful" outlook that Freedmen's Bureau agents inspired among former slaves in the spring and summer of 1865 with the much grimmer state of affairs that followed the "transfer of the power of the Freedmen's Bureau from military to civil agents" later that year.[100] An ex-slave from North Carolina similarly remembered both early hopefulness and hard limits when he recalled, "Freedmen's Bureau helped us some, but we finally had to go back to the plantation in order to live," because "our masters had everything and we had nothing."[101]

Some bureau failures were the products of glaringly obvious reasons, like the persistent racism among some agents who never had freedpeople's best interests at heart in the first place. Throughout his short-lived tenure as bureau agent in Chicot County, Arkansas, for example, Thomas Hunnicutt remained intent on controlling and exploiting African Americans. He forcibly moved free black workers to the plantations of former owners who paid him for the service, sexually exploited freedwomen, and in general convinced former slaves that they and the bureau were natural enemies.[102]

Yet many reasons for the bureau's shortcomings stemmed from causes less simple and contained than the individual failings of people who worked for it. As a wholly new type of federal agency in U.S. history, the bureau operated under some distinct structural disadvantages. It never had anything close to the funds or an adequate number of agents to cover the 750,000 square miles of the former Confederacy. To make matters worse, President Andrew Johnson, motivated by his desire for quick restoration of state governments and distaste for centralization as well as his own racism, exacerbated already formidable structural challenges. He cut appropriations and undermined agents. In the fall of 1865, he went even further and began forcing out the most abolitionist-leaning agents (for example, Rufus Saxton on September 22, 1865) and replacing them with local Southern whites who shared their neighbors' insistence on reimposing a white supremacist social order. At the same time, Johnson persisted in pardoning ex-Confederates and restoring their confiscated and abandoned lands to them, including lands inhabited and cultivated by former slaves. Johnson also hastened the transition away from military and Freedmen's Bureau courts toward local civilian courts, which did not permit black testimony, explicitly treated whites and blacks differently, and were presided over by ex-Confederates.

Sometimes, the Freedmen's Bureau floundered because for all the aims its agents shared with former slaves, in other key ways its priorities veered sharply away from those of freedpeople. This divergence was especially apparent in the matter of land. In the spring of 1865, the Union army controlled approximately 850,000 acres of land abandoned during the war by Confederates, which a clause of the bureau's enabling legislation authorized it to "set apart, for the use of loyal refugees and freedmen."[103] At the time, former slaves and free black leaders—along with many Republicans, army personnel, and bureau agents—understood that section of the Freedmen's Bureau Bill as essentially enshrining in civil law the military expedient that General William Sherman had established with his Special Field Orders No. 15 issued in January 1865. By June 1865, roughly ten thousand black families from Charleston, South Carolina, to Jacksonville, Florida, had received "possessory title" to over 400,000 acres under Special Field Orders No. 15. Those families had put in crops and fully expected to own their forty-acre plots for good. Elsewhere, some former slaves did in fact realize their hopes for land. Most famously, the ex-slave Benjamin Montgomery led a self-governing colony of former slaves at Davis Bend, the plantation of Joseph Davis, the Confederate president Jefferson Davis's brother.[104]

More often, the Freedmen's Bureau focused on labor management instead of black hopes for landownership, not always out of malevolence so much as the fact that land use was the area in which the specific mandate and authority entrusted to the bureau were least clear.[105] In large swaths of the occupied Confederacy during the war, the Union army oversaw not direct distribution of land to refugees from slavery but rather plantation leasing, whereby whites loyal to the Union leased confiscated lands from the U.S. government and paid former slaves to labor on them in either wages or shares of the crop. Analogous arrangements proliferated in 1865 and beyond, as did many instances of exploitation and abuse.[106] More labor ombudsmen than land officers, Freedmen's Bureau agents often spent their days overseeing and enforcing the terms of contracts that specified how former slaves would earn a living working on land controlled by someone else. Bureau regulations established basic wages and working conditions and checked planters' most egregious attempts at exploitation. Freedmen's Bureau agents in Memphis, for example, aided 7,280 former slaves in negotiating labor contracts "at good remunerative wages" in just three weeks.[107] When planters violated regulations by cheating on wages, stretching hours, using violent punishment, or curtailing the rights and privileges of freedpeople, black workers took their grievances to the bureau. White employers were then "brought before the commissioner & either heavily fined or incarcerated for an indefinite period."[108] At the same time, former slaves were often held to long days of hard labor growing crops under the direction of someone else, which, if not exactly a continuation of slavery, was not what they hoped or expected freedom would mean, either.

Sometimes, gaps between freedpeople's goals and Freedmen's Bureau objectives grew out of stubbornly persistent ideas about dependency. The same urge to disprove prevailing notions about black people's incapacity for self-support that animated so much of the AFIC commissioners' investigations also coursed through the early Freedmen's Bureau, leading agents to militate overzealously against the stigma of dependency. As a sub-assistant commissioner in Virginia put the point, "No greater harm can be done the negro, than supporting those who can support themselves."[109] We are hardly free from this sort of thinking in our own day and age; a June 2013 NBC News/*Wall Street Journal* poll found that more Americans identified "too much welfare that prevents initiative" as the source of poverty than any other cause.[110] That dynamic was heightened for bureau agents because they worked for an agency that was made temporary by law, and so the goal of freedpeople's long-term self-sufficiency often predominated in agents' thinking over immediate relief. Moreover, the bureau never received funding from Congress but relied on collecting rents, selling crops, and otherwise generating income necessary to carry out its many duties. As a result, agents could seem—and sometimes were—callous and insensitive to urgent material need, particularly when it came to cutting off rations and closing down contraband camps so hurriedly after Confederate surrender.[111]

Edisto Island, South Carolina, provides a case study in the checkered fate of the Freedmen's Bureau in 1865. May mornings on Edisto Island began cool and full of promise. The full, oppressive heat of the summer had not yet descended, and instead warm sun and temperate breezes coaxed the first buds to appear on cotton plants while the leaves on cornstalks unfurled.[112] At first glance, the sun, soil, fields, and gardens might have looked much as they did in any year, but for the freedpeople who lived on Edisto, there were unmistakable differences. Families lived in cottages unoppressed by the constant fear they'd be broken up by sale, and they tended those promising new crops on land they believed had been declared their own by Sherman's Special Field Orders No. 15. Some took on additional work for the Union army and set the wages they earned by or deposited them in the Freedman's Savings Bank in Beaufort to save up for a future truly their own. To be sure, they still knew hunger and want. There was never enough clothing or medicine. And some families would never be reconstructed because of death or distance or the passage of time. Edisto freedpeople surely knew of the glowers—and worse—of the former owners who began trickling back, but they also knew that the army and the Freedmen's Bureau agents were nearby, preventing ex-Confederates from acting on most of their malevolent designs. They did not, in short, live in utopia, but they did live in hope.

It was that sense of hope that Mary Ames and Emily Bliss noticed when they stepped off a boat and onto Edisto in May 1865. Guns had no sooner been stacked at Appomattox than Ames and Bliss, two young white women from Massachusetts, had applied to go south to teach in Freedmen's Bureau schools. In a few short weeks, their zeal (and a government steamer) landed them on Edisto. They moved into an abandoned mansion and hired the services of Jim and Sarah, two former slaves from the interior of the state who had followed Sherman's army that winter. Jim, Sarah, and their six young children all shared the mansion with Ames and Bliss.[113] Later that spring, Sarah had another baby, this one born free, whom she named Mary Emily, not out of any sense of deference, but because the women had genuinely become friends.[114] They admired one another and they relied on each other, and they knew it. Mary Ames was far from perfect, and she knew that, too. She sometimes struggled to overcome her own unthinking prejudices and automatic assumptions. Her better self did not always win those struggles, but it was usually willing to at least face them. One day, when Ben (one of Jim and Sarah's little boys) asked if the reason she had never kissed him was that he was black, she gathered him into her lap and held him close, with genuine love, until he fell asleep.[115] At nine o'clock in the morning on May 15, 1865, Mary Ames opened the doors of an old church repurposed as a Freedmen's Bureau school, and dove into teaching the alphabet to anywhere between 70 and 150 eager learners a day.[116]

Yet the Freedmen's Bureau on Edisto, as elsewhere, could not banish tragedy and sometimes contributed to it. As fervent as Mary Ames was about teaching her scholars to read, write, and calculate, she also saw it as her duty to instill Northern middle-class habits of personal hygiene. So rigid were her convictions about cleanliness that she unwittingly sent a fourteen-year-old boy named John to his death. John and his sister Eliza walked five miles to attend Ames's school, and by the time they arrived, Ames found John to be so dirty that she sent him "into the creek to bathe," not pausing to consider if he knew how to swim. He did not, and the shifting of the tide pulled him out to sea, where he drowned.[117] John's tragic fate anticipated more heartbreak for the island. Before the year was out, Jim, Sarah, and all but two of their children had sickened and died.[118]

Heartbreak had struck the whole island on an even larger scale by the end of the year. As late summer began to mature into fall, families prepared to harvest the crop that should have been their own. Then, in September, the Union general George Gordon Meade toured South Carolina, where ex-Confederate landowners regaled him with tales of the woe that would befall them, the state, and the entire nation if Rufus Saxton and the Freedmen's Bureau carried on with the radical program of distributing the Sherman Reserve land to freedpeople. Former plantation owners wanted it back for themselves, and they won Meade over to their side. Meade had no trouble convincing the president, who ordered the complete restoration of all lands to prewar owners.[119] On October 9, Johnson directed the Freedmen's Bureau commissioner Oliver O. Howard to visit the "tracts of land . . . set apart by Major-General W. T. Sherman's Special Field Order, No. 15" and "effect a satisfactory arrangement by which the lands might be returned to the former owners." Howard would have to undo much of what his comrade-in-arms Rufus Saxton had done, which would be anathema to Howard the soldier. Worse, Howard, the sincere advocate for the rights of former slaves, would have to personally tell black farming families that everything they had worked for had been betrayed.[120]

Families met Howard and Saxton at the landing when the two arrived on Edisto and then crowded into a church to listen to Howard deliver the painful news that they were to give up the homes, fields, and gardens they had purchased and cultivated, and return to working for the very people who once claimed to own them. Flabbergasted black men and women vowed that they had no intention of working "for the Secesh." One man explained that before freedom he might have lived his whole life with a basket on his head—a basket full of someone else's profit—but "now that it had been taken off and air and sunlight had come to him, he could not consent to have the basket over him again."[121] Howard appointed a three-man committee consisting of Henry Bram, Ishmael Moultrie, and Yates Sampson to consult with the people of Edisto and report back to him.

Days later, the committee addressed Howard "with painfull Hearts" to explain why Edisto families could neither consent to Howard's plan nor comply with his request to forgive their former masters. "You only lost your right arm in war and might forgive them," committee members pointed out to Howard the amputee, but "the man who tied me to a tree & gave me 39 lashes & who stripped and flogged my mother & sister" had far more than an arm to answer for. The wealthy man who had extorted and tortured and "who will not let me stay In His empty Hut except I will do His planting & be Satisfied with His price & who combines with others to keep away land from me well knowing I would not Have any thing to do with Him If I Had land of my own—that man, I cannot well forgive."[122]

The committee argued in terms of more than just grievance and poignancy, moving as those terms were; its members also argued in terms of the wartime relationship forged between the U.S. government and African Americans. In both the response to Howard and a letter to President Andrew Johnson, the committee laid out a straightforward case. Before the war, slaves had been stateless and invisible in the eyes of the national government, but then war came and that national government had needed them. Former slaves, and not just soldiers, helped to defeat a "common enemy" when the Union's very existence had been threatened by secession and rebellion. Everybody had played a part, including women and children, not as auxiliaries to soldiers or dependents of men, but as themselves. "Plenty whidow & Fatherles" children had stepped forward to "serve you," the central government, as "allies In the war." In return, black men and women secured from the government "promises . . . to observe the principle of common faith between Its self and us Its allies." Now that the U.S. government's survival was assured, thanks in no small measure to the efforts and actions of former slaves, the freedpeople on Edisto did not consent to undoing the very relationship that had helped bring about the Union's success. They had "not been treacherous," nor had they acted from "selfish motives." Instead, they had earned inclusion within the national community, and they had legitimate claims on the U.S. government for the protection of basic rights to land, security, family, and livelihood, without the interference of people who had once claimed to own them.[123]

Along with principle, there was necessity. The members of the committee knew with merciless clarity that they *needed* a direct relationship with the national government if their aspirations for freedom were to amount to anything in the face of violent ex-Confederate resistance. Absent a direct and explicitly rights-protecting relationship between the federal government and former slaves, "there is no rights secured to us." Rather than "law . . . which our Hands can reach," black men, women, and children would find themselves living under laws purposely designed by the states of the former Confederacy to leave them "landless, Homeless, Voteless." Placed back at the mercy of powerful former slaveholders and subject to laws made by them, without land and without the advocacy of an active federal government on their behalf, "we . . . cannot feel our rights Safe," argued the people whom Bram, Moultrie, and Sampson represented. Surely, Howard must "see this Is not the condition of really freemen."[124] Howard did, but he was powerless to do anything about it, and in the end antebellum owners got their land back, and former slaves lost it.

The tragedy of Edisto Island makes it seem that the hard-fought bargain struck by refugees from slavery and the army during the war— citizenship as a reciprocal exchange of useful service to the Union for a direct, inclusive relationship with the national government that protected individual rights—would not outlast the war that forged it. There is no question that the alliance between freedpeople and the U.S. government was under siege from many sides. It was not as successful at procuring freedpeople's hoped-for ends after the war as it had been during the conflict. As Rufus Saxton recognized, "the Freedmens Bureau," the most tangible postwar manifestation of the alliance between former slaves and the U.S. government, "is but just starting on its mission and we have no past experience to guide us in the performance of the peculiar and delicate duties which pertain to it." The newness and lack of precedent proved to be genuine drawbacks in a climate shaped in part by many Americans' (including the president's) desire to get back to normal.

Yet despite the pressure and even with the lost ground, the bargain did not simply crumble. The bureau's most committed supporters and the former slaves who availed themselves of its services still had plenty of energy in 1865. Since President Johnson's proclamations of May 1865, the Union general Carl Schurz had worried that federal relinquishment of control would undo the results of the war, for freed slaves and for the Union. Pointing to both world history and persistent Southern attitudes, Schurz's November *Report on the Condition of the South* repeatedly stressed the related dangers of re-enslavement and renewed rebellion and warned the federal government against abandoning its black Southern allies. Schurz insisted that "the future of the republic" depended on "continuing the control of the national government in the States lately in rebellion."[125]

Even the most loyal of Andrew Johnson's confidants who toured the former Confederacy affirmed that the U.S. government and former slaves still needed each other. Suspicious of Schurz's reforming inclinations, Andrew Johnson authorized simultaneous fact-finding missions on the part of people he expected to be more sympathetic to his approach. One was General Ulysses S. Grant, and another was Johnson's former private secretary, Benjamin Truman. Grant's and Truman's reports were more critical of former slaves and sympathetic to Johnson than Schurz was, but even their missives made the need for continued partnership abundantly clear. Grant considered the continuation of both the Freedmen's Bureau and a Union military presence to be "absolute necessity," and even Truman, who admitted that he was "strongly on the side of these [white] Southern people," nonetheless conceded, "A Freedmen's Bureau must exist."[126]

If enemies of the bureau and proponents of restoring antebellum white supremacy thought that its supporters would meekly step aside, they had another think coming. As reports on conditions in the former Confederacy generally and on race relations specifically began to circulate, proponents and creators of the wartime bargain fought back with renewed effort and passion. As the year 1865 waned, they looked with vigor ahead to 1866. Although the bureau's enabling legislation authorized it for only one year, its supporters began a campaign to extend its lifetime. Howard's visit to Edisto and other Southern states in October and November convinced him that, as he explained to the chair of the Senate's Military Affairs Committee, "the time has not come for the Government to surrender authority in any state I visited."[127] When he returned to Washington, he wrote a report for the entire Congress, met with numerous individual members, and invited senators and representatives to bureau headquarters to read letters and reports coming in from bureau agents serving throughout the former Confederacy. Howard specifically wanted to transfer authority for hearing cases involving freedpeople back to either provost marshal courts or what he called "Freedmen's United States courts," and he wanted to discourage Congress from readmitting states to the Union (and congressional representation) on the basis of the provisional governments organized that summer under the influence of President Johnson's leniency and overt support for the maintenance of white supremacy.[128]

Howard's report, missives from Schurz, Grant, and other travelers, newspaper coverage of atrocities against former slaves, November elections, and the urging of black men, women, and children all influenced the Thirty-Ninth Congress when it convened in December to reinvigorate the alliance between freedpeople and the U.S. government so that it would remain strong enough to combat ex-Confederates' resumption of power. Because 1865 was an off year, fewer elections took place than the preceding or following years, but in those Northern states where contests were scheduled for state as well as national office, Republicans soundly defeated Democrats running in support of Johnson's program of lenient self-reconstruction for the seceded states. When a group of supporters gathered outside the Indiana Republican Schuyler Colfax's Washington residence to congratulate him on his party's victories, he responded with a speech vowing that Congress would not readmit states to the Union (or to Congress) on the basis of the provisional state governments constructed that summer and fall precisely because of treatment of freedpeople in those states. Mistreatment made clear to him that Congress, as protector of black Americans' basic rights, needed to take a firmer role in Reconstruction, and it would do so. Congress would throw out hastily reestablished state governments and reimpose military authority over much of the former Confederacy until such time as loyal, reliable state governments could be organized.[129] Further, provost marshal courts and Freedmen's Bureau courts would regain authority throughout the states of the former Confederacy and fight back against the forces threatening to erode the alliance between the federal government and freedpeople.

Black Southerners recognized the necessity of a continued relationship with the national government to make their freedom real and to help prevent future rebellions, and they assessed their ongoing alliance with both hope and realism. They knew better than anybody that the U.S. government and the people who represented it and wielded its power were flawed and full of human failings. There were plenty of soldiers, Freedmen's Bureau agents, and provost judges whom they (with good reason) flat out despised, but they plainly recognized the federal government and its agents as the best available allies, and they drew on them as resources.

The success of the continued alliance between black Americans and the federal government was uneven in 1865, yet even the failures served a purpose. Rather than inevitably dooming the fate of Reconstruction, early failures made clear that a continued relationship between freedpeople and the national government was necessary for both parties and emboldened Congress to shore up the relationship, at least for the immediate future.

. . .

For former slaves, and for the U.S. government, 1865 was neither anticlimactic footnote to the four years preceding it nor inconsequential prelude to decades of later disappointment; instead, it stood as its own moment, brimful of expectation, possibility, and conflicting purposes, and shot through with violence. The year had brought real but limited gains for former slaves. In defiance of genuine threats of re-enslavement, permanent abolition was secured by civil authority with the passage of the Thirteenth Amendment. Black inclusion within the national community and freedpeople's enjoyment of basic rights, in contrast, seemed less assured, for the Thirteenth Amendment did not address civic status, and so did not invest the weight of civil authority into the version of black citizenship as a direct, rights-protecting relationship between the federal government and black men, women, and children, which had developed during the war.

So freedpeople and their allies faced a dilemma. As 1866 dawned, they confronted the simultaneous necessity and inadequacy of civil authority to preserve African American inclusion within the national community and protect black rights. Throughout world history, reasonably well-regulated military forces serving as counterweights to local populations accustomed to persecuting the marginalized have proven more effective than civil authority at safeguarding the rights of vulnerable populations. In East Prussia in 1919, for example, German civilians were more lethal to Poles, Latvians, and Jews than the German army had been. The same dynamic was evident in South Asia in 1947 and even to some extent in tumultuous locales in our own day. Yet a combination of practical, political, structural, and ideological factors made long-term martial law for the states of the former Confederacy an unviable, and undesirable, option. Freedpeople needed some form of civil authority to take the army's place. The Freedmen's Bureau constituted a first step but not a completed journey in that direction. In addition to the bureau's inherent shortcomings, its enabling legislation made it a temporary rather than permanent institution. Could gains secured in wartime and safeguarded by martial law survive under civil rather than military authority, once the army demobilized and the Freedmen's Bureau went away?

Violence across the South made it very clear that if freedom were to have any meaning for ex-slaves, then freedpeople needed direct access to a source of power strong enough to counteract white resistance and protect their efforts to act on their own aspirations and priorities. They continued to look to the U.S. government as a source of precisely that power, an imperfect source, to be sure, but the best prospect available despite its many failings. Neither white Southern intransigence nor President Johnson's hostility to black rights suffused the latter half of 1865 with the sense of doom and failure that in retrospect we associate with the long story of Reconstruction. Instead, those developments invested the question of black citizenship with a sense of urgency. The gloomy story of the so-called nadir of race relations in the late nineteenth and early twentieth centuries was not indelibly written in 1865; in fact, no story yet was, for in 1865 much still remained in flux and multiple long-term outcomes remained possible. As satisfying as a clear and tidy conclusion would be, there is simply no tenable way to close an account of the Civil War or emancipation with a tidy, satisfying "The End."

Conclusion

The Gettysburg cyclorama portrays a single day, but a cyclorama depicting emancipation and citizenship would extend well beyond the 1860s. It might include a scene that took place on September 15, 2011, when a red and gold garrison flag slipped gracefully down a flagpole. As Colonel Anthony Reyes folded and cased the colors, the U.S. Army presence at Fort Monroe, the third-longest continuously used fort in the nation, came to an end after 188 years of active duty.[1] Fort Monroe's closure had been coming since 2005, when the Base Realignment and Closure process (BRAC) identified the fort as one of many installations nationwide to be closed or consolidated, in ongoing efforts to adapt today's military to current needs. Soldiers and their families, local leaders, and residents of Hampton, Virginia, attended the dignified deactivation ceremony. Before it began, a member of the grassroots organization, the Contraband Historical Society, reflected, "Today is a bittersweet day with the military leaving, but it's sweet in terms of what's coming in the future."[2] Six weeks later, President Barack Obama signed an executive order designating Fort Monroe a national monument. Thanks to the efforts of the Contraband Historical Society in Hampton, and descendants of Fort Monroe freedpeople nationwide, "Freedom's Fortress" would not be razed to make room for private development, but would become the property of the National Park Service.

The designation of Fort Monroe National Monument was without question a triumph for descendants of the men, women, and children who sought freedom there, but its passage from military to civil authority elicited not so much uncomplicated celebration as sober reflection and considerable concern. Competition for ownership of its historical legacy was, and remains, fierce. As a young army engineer in the 1830s, Robert E. Lee lodged in Building 17, and the Confederate president, Jefferson Davis, was held in quarters in the Fort Monroe casemate after his capture by U.S. authorities at the end of the Civil War; on these grounds, the United Daughters of the Confederacy and their allies sought to hold the fort as a shrine to Confederate memory. Local Hamptonites saw natural beauty and recreational opportunities on the peninsula that houses the fort and wanted to ensure public access to them. Experts in engineering and military history wanted attention drawn to the fort as a surviving example of the coastal fortification system instituted under President James Monroe after the War of 1812. Archaeologists and those with an interest in precolonial history, as well as people of Native American heritage, wanted reminders that people lived in coastal Virginia before the English arrived in the seventeenth century. The continued presence of the federal government (through the National Park Service) aroused suspicion and hostility in some quarters. And the members of the Contraband Historical Society and their supporters nationwide wanted to be very sure that the story of ten thousand freedom seekers and their part in the emancipation process would be told with clarity, honesty, dignity, and due attention to suffering and sacrifice, not simply lighthearted or triumphal celebration.[3]

The National Park Service took (and takes) these concerns seriously. It convened an extensive series of public meetings and comment sessions and sought substantive input from professional historians. One of the great joys of my professional life was the privilege of taking part in one roundtable in May 2013. For two days, a group of historians, bringing collective decades of extensive research and scholarship, stayed at the fort and engaged in serious dialogue with park personnel, who brought intensive expertise in the specifics of the fort, and with members of the Contraband Historical Society, who brought wisdom and deep local knowledge. The members of the Contraband Historical Society greeted all us interlopers with eminent graciousness but also with a bit of reserve or even wariness. I had no trouble understanding why. Beyond the understandable concerns about outsiders missing or misrepresenting what local people knew to be true about their place, the fort's transition from the army to the National Park Service was rife with allegory. In a way, the transition is reminiscent of the transition to civil authority at the close of the Civil War.

As the presence of the Union army in the former Confederacy shrank, freedpeople looked to civil authorities to honor and continue the alliance they had built with the army. One of those authorities was Congress, which convened in December 1865, a time when newspapers throughout the North reprinted samples of the Black Codes passed by Southern state legislatures and reported widespread violence against freedpeople throughout the South. Freedpeople's conventions sent petitions and Northern free black communities sometimes even sent lobbyists to Congress, urging federal guarantees for former slaves. Republicans in Congress needed little prodding. Recognizing the need for legal mechanisms to turn the liberty promised by the Thirteenth Amendment from abstraction to reality, Senator Lyman Trumbull introduced "An Act to Protect All Persons in the United States in Their Civil Rights, and Furnish the Means of Their Vindication." Better known as the Civil Rights Act of 1866, the law declared that people born in the United States were entitled to citizenship "without regard to race, color, or previous condition of slavery or involuntary servitude" and established that all citizens enjoyed equal legal rights (such as access to courts and right of contract) and property rights. President Andrew Johnson vetoed both the Civil Rights Act and a law extending the life of the Freedmen's Bureau, but on April 9, 1866 (one year after the surrender at Appomattox), Congress overrode the veto and enacted the Civil Rights Act as federal law. It was by no means all that former slaves and other proponents of equal rights hoped for, but it still upheld the federal government as a source of power to which African Americans could turn. Like the Union army in wartime, Congress proved to be an imperfect ally, but the very existence of an alliance between African Americans and the U.S. government still marked a turnaround compared with before the war.[4]

Johnson's veto of the Civil Rights Act did not stop the passage of the law, but it did heighten Republicans' awareness of the need for a measure even stronger than a federal law, and the strongest measure available was constitutional amendment. In fact, the debate over what would become the Fourteenth Amendment to the U.S. Constitution was already well under way. The conversation focused on several points, including not only African Americans' rights in the abstract but also the specific roles that the state and federal governments should play in rights enforcement. The amendment as it passed on June 13, 1866, was a compromise taking all those concerns into account. In essence, it imported the substance of the Civil Rights Act into the Constitution while upholding the antebellum principle that states retained first authority over citizenship. At the same time, it allowed for the activation of the federal government as recourse when a state government discriminated. The final section explicitly conferred upon Congress the power to pass laws needed to enforce the amendment.[5] After passage by Congress, the amendment functioned as a key issue in the 1866 midterm elections, with Republicans supporting and Democrats opposing it. In the House of Representatives, Republicans maintained a 143 to 49 majority over Democrats, and in the Senate Republicans maintained a 41 to 11 majority. Meanwhile, the amendment went to the states for ratification, which it received from the requisite twenty-eight states in July 1868. On July 28, 1868, Secretary of State William Seward certified that the Fourteenth Amendment was now a part of the U.S. Constitution.[6]

In some ways, the Fourteenth Amendment clearly grew out of the experiences of the Civil War. Most urgently, it secured the Thirteenth Amendment, because it is far more difficult to enslave a citizen than a noncitizen. In so doing, the Fourteenth Amendment helped to ensure the permanence of emancipation in the United States, in contrast to most instances of wartime emancipation throughout world history, which more often resulted in re-enslavement or the perpetuation of slavery. Looking backward from the present makes it easy to miss the significance of that accomplishment, but to former slaves facing the genuine danger of re-enslavement in the months following the war's end, that achievement was no small thing. In addition, the Fourteenth Amendment looked forward as well as backward. One historian has even called the Fourteenth Amendment "the centerpiece" of "a positive-law program spelling out in considerable detail exactly what rights accompanied emancipation."[7] Legal scholars and Fourteenth Amendment specialists differ as to exactly how much the framers of the amendment intended it to protect freedpeople's rights. In any interpretation, the Fourteenth Amendment sustained the relationship first forged during the war between former slaves and the national government, making an attempt, however faulty, to translate their wartime alliance into peacetime relationship.[8]

In other ways, the Fourteenth Amendment broke from the experience of the Civil War. The amendment did not completely revert to the antebellum status quo, in which state governments alone determined citizenship, but it did dial back the role of the federal government to one of safety mechanism if states failed to perform their duties adequately. That function differed from the primary and direct role that the federal government assumed for former slaves who came into contact with Union forces during the Civil War. In addition, the grounds for citizenship shifted, from the wartime bargain of an exchange of labor and loyalty for rights protection to birthright citizenship. On the one hand, that modification widened access by not making citizenship contingent on what a person did. On the other hand, it narrowed and limited what the national government owed to citizens in return. Fourteenth Amendment citizenship, in other words, asked less of all parties than the wartime alliance between former slaves and the national government did.[9]

One unforeseen consequence was that the shift away from a labor and loyalty basis to a birthright basis helped erase the centrality of black labor to the Union war effort and the survival of the U.S. government. Amnesia on that point was already apparent by the 1870s, when a new federal agency, the Southern Claims Commission, began conducting investigations into the claims of loyal Southern Unionists who had lost property at the hands of the Union army during the Civil War. The SCC provided forms—longer ones for white claimants, shorter ones for black claimants—for people seeking redress for lost property to complete. On the basis of the answers that claimants provided in the preprinted blanks on the forms, the SCC determined whether and how much compensation was due. Questions seven through fourteen on the white forms asked claimants to describe their service and wartime contributions to the Union, but those questions did not appear on the forms administered to black claimants. African Americans were quite literally left with no space to remind the national government of their critical efforts on the Union's behalf.[10]

The content of the Fourteenth Amendment also triggered a quick pivot in freedpeople's and equal rights advocates' focus from citizenship as protection for an array of rights to a more exclusive concentration on suffrage. The amendment itself did not guarantee black suffrage, a goal that had long been important to Northern free blacks and appeared as one of several goals articulated by freedpeople directly after the war. It did try to encourage states to extend suffrage to black men by apportioning representation in Congress on the basis of number of registered voters in a state rather than raw population, but Southern state legislatures quickly signaled their willingness to forgo congressional representation rather than enfranchise African Americans.[11] As the amendment's inadequacy as an avenue to voting became clear, male-dominated civil rights organizations (among both Northern free blacks and former slaves) trained their sights on voting rights and argued almost exclusively in terms of black soldiers' military service as reason for black citizenship and suffrage. Pennsylvania provides a case in point. Equal rights organizations from towns and cities all over Pennsylvania sent representatives to statewide conventions in the years immediately following the war. In 1865, several municipalities, including Philadelphia, Harrisburg, and Pittsburgh sent women's organizations called Ladies' Union Associations to the convention. In addition, one delegate sent by the Hollidaysburg Equal Rights League was a woman, Mrs. W. Knox. The report of the Business Committee at the August 1865 annual meeting explicitly used the language of "the people of this State, without distinction of sex or color." Yet no women's organizations or female delegates appear in the list of participants at conventions held in 1866 or later, and those same conventions focused much more exclusively on black Union soldiers' army service as grounds for black male voting.[12] That strategic shift, along with the absence of queries seven through fourteen on the SCC forms, obscured the centrality of black women's labor to the war effort and undercut black women's ability to keep their priorities alongside black men's emphasis on suffrage.

The version of U.S. citizenship as alliance and exchange of labor and loyalty for protection, which had been forged by former slaves— women as well as men—and Union soldiers in Civil War contraband camps, then, can be understood as incomplete in terms of all that it did not accomplish, but it can also be understood as incomplete in the sense of one stage of the unfinished and ongoing project of defining citizenship. Later events like the Fifteenth Amendment, the *Civil Rights Cases,* Henry Cabot Lodge's Federal Elections Bill, and *Plessy v. Ferguson* and new forces like economic change, an evolving women's rights movement, and increasing immigration would ensure that the unceasing work of determining U.S. citizenship's meaning continued. And continue it has, sometimes expanding the definition and other times restricting it. Recognizing the reinvention of U.S. citizenship during the Civil War as a crucial, but not the final, stage in the process of defining citizenship serves as a reminder that the meaning of citizenship is neither inevitable nor unchanging but rather is always a work in progress. Responsibility for any weaknesses, shortcomings, or disappointments in the current state of that work rests as much with us as with the long-dead Civil War generation.

The work of the Civil War generation had its own share of failings to be sure, most obviously the disproportionate share of war's suffering and violence borne by the men, women, and children exiting slavery. To acknowledge and grapple with the violence, cruelty, and death that attended the passage out of bondage requires real caution, and it also takes a certain willingness to stand in the cyclorama room a few moments more, despite feeling eager to get out and move on. There are at least two tendencies into which it is easy to fall but which hinder rather than help to come to terms with emancipation. The first is to minimize discomfort by sanitizing suffering with an "all for the best" outlook. To take this approach is to look at the whole painting with genuine goodwill but then to dash into the lobby to construct a narrative that can make sense of all the overwhelming detail only by selectively omitting the most troubling parts of it. In this telling, a straight line exists from the struggles of the 1860s to the civil rights movement of the 1960s, and the appalling violence that African Americans endured along the way is regrettable, but to some degree counterbalanced by the assurance that all came out right in the end. But do the living have the right to make those kinds of "all is well that ends well" determinations about suffering endured by people in the past?

Sometimes trying to avoid this first pitfall leads to the equal and opposite one of getting stuck in the violence and pain, unable to see any meaning at all in it beyond utterly senseless, gratuitous suffering. It becomes easy to take a condemnatory stance toward the past, which prevents coming to terms with how emancipation happened, for if the story is one only of gratuitous violence, cruelty, and pain, then suffering becomes spectacle.[13] In this scenario, a cyclorama viewer becomes transfixed by a disturbing segment of the whole and stays rooted in place, admirably willing to engage with the wrenching subject matter portrayed in that section but unable to take in that segment's inextricable relationship to the whole. When that happens, it is too easy to separate violence out and treat it like some tangential freak show, rather than as chillingly central to a contest for legitimacy between rival governments, carried out by whole populations, in which the participants were black and white, male and female. Separating violence out also obscures the truth that violence was inherent and inescapable in slavery itself, no less at the time of slavery's painful death than during its long and poisonous life. Slavery sickened, tortured, maimed, and killed people during its long centuries of profitable life, and it did in its death throes, too, like a beast crushing whatever has the misfortune to be underneath it when it finally comes crashing to the ground. The death of slavery was violent, but slavery, not the act of exiting it, was the killer.

Without a doubt, the suffering that attended the death of slavery was sometimes mitigated and sometimes worsened by the actions and decisions taken by individual people, just as every brushstroke in a cyclorama contributes to its sum total. The reasons for actions that made things worse include personal shortcomings or racist sentiments of individuals in the army, U.S. government, Freedmen's Bureau, or Northern public, but the reasons do not end there, any more than even the most intricately rendered detail can stand in for the entire cyclorama. Coming to grips with emancipation requires confronting the bigger reasons as well as the individual failings. There were bigoted soldiers, leaders, and government agents, and there were also conscientious, well-intentioned, and even heroic ones. *All* of them were up against much more than their limited capacity as human beings could handle. Stunningly rapid demobilization, enabled and exacerbated by President Johnson's massive cuts in appropriations, left too few Freedmen's Bureau agents, scattered too far apart, facing too much violence and hostility from recently defeated former Confederates, to carry out even the best of intentions, as recent scholarship has shown with great insight and sensitivity.[14]

The point is not to whitewash, to minimize suffering as somehow inevitable, or to sink into resigned nihilism. The point is that even in U.S. history, which is so often told as a story of people who can do anything they set their minds to, human beings are not all-powerful. They run up against forces bigger than themselves sometimes. Sheer will cannot always make the universe bend in its direction. People can try; they can do their best. At Fort Monroe, soldiers collected water in cisterns for much of the nineteenth century, but the taste made the water undrinkable. In the 1890s, engineers designed a system to pipe water in from elsewhere, and to this day the fort relies on water from outside to sustain life, because at Fort Monroe itself there is simply no freshwater to be had. The U.S. Army dug nine hundred feet into the ground, but none of that digging could make freshwater appear where it just plain does not exist.[15] Human beings act on their surroundings and with their given circumstances, and those efforts make a difference, but they also sometimes run up against the immovable. Fort Monroe could never have furnished life-giving water by itself; without massive intervention, the refuge it could provide to former slaves, or anyone else seeking shelter there, could only ever be troubled.

Taking the measure of emancipation and wartime citizenship—the refuge that former slaves found first in the Union army and ultimately in the U.S. government—requires a willingness to "hold success and failure in the one hand," as Lena Deevy, a very wise and indefatigable nun I know, is fond of saying. Nobody living through the war had the option of neatly categorizing it as all success or all failure. Nobody living through emancipation could indulge in the luxury of choosing triumph or tragedy. They had to live in both, so if we would understand war and emancipation, we need to do so, too. The task of living with both triumph and tragedy is entirely different from a noncommittal "some of each" approach that allows us to duck the full implications of either. On the contrary, it means accepting "all of both" and confronting the full implications of both triumph and tragedy, no matter how uneasily they sit together. It means staying put in the overwhelming cyclorama room long enough to remain truly present to all the individual contradictory scenes and to the disorienting panorama at the same time. Coming to grips with the Civil War, emancipation, and citizenship demands that we not step to one detached side or hold ourselves bemusedly above labels like triumph and tragedy, but rather that we live right in the unbearable but essential tension between them.

Acknowledgments

If I could carry a tune (which I cannot), there are two different versions of the song "Hallelujah" by Leonard Cohen that I would sing all the time. The first contains the line, "Even though it all went wrong, I'll stand before the Lord of Song, with nothing on my tongue but Hallelujah." My favorite line in the second version goes, "Love is not a victory march; it's a cold and broken Hallelujah." This book has been one very long march, with extended stretches where all went wrong, and there was a lot more that was cold and broken about it than there was victory. It has been, in that wholly unsentimental and unglamorous sense, a labor of love that many people have helped me carry out, and I am grateful for the opportunity to say thanks.

Historians begin with sources. Because most of the sources I used in this book were located in archives, I begin with the librarians and others who helped me in those wondrous repositories. The entire reading room staffs at the Huntington Library, Massachusetts Historical Society, and Tennessee State Library and Archives were especially gracious and hospitable, and they made the time spent at each of those locations sheer joy. Chris Meekins at the North Carolina Division of Archives and History was so generous with his expertise and goodwill that he requires individual mention. Harry Miller of the Wisconsin Historical Society told me that a century ago, the director summed up the goal of the State Historical Society of Wisconsin (as it used to be called) as "we aim to be useful." Miller himself more than lived up to that aspiration and made the reading room in Madison one of my favorite places, not counting Fenway Park. Until I traveled to the State Historical Society of Iowa in Des Moines, I did not think the generosity of Meekins or Miller could be rivaled, but then I met the matchless John Zeller of Des Moines. John is not an archivist, but a fellow researcher and peerless expert on all things Iowa. He shared with me some data on the 1870s as well as a research aid that he had created, and one of my few regrets about deciding to conclude this book at the end of 1865 is that in so doing, I robbed myself of the ability to do justice to John's precise and rich resources. Zeller truly is a gem.

Working on this book pulled me back into the world of public history, which I had known in my National Park Service ranger days. I could not have asked for a warmer "welcome back" than the one I received from Chris McDaid, cultural resources manager at Fort Monroe when it was still an active U.S. Army installation; Kirsten Talken-Spaulding, the first superintendent of Fort Monroe National Monument, along with Eola Dance and Aaron Firth, interpretive rangers there; Josh Gillespie and Robert Kelly of the Fort Monroe Authority; the members of the Contraband Historical Society in Hampton, Virginia; Audrey Davis of the Alexandria Black History Museum; the Friends of Freedmen's Cemetery in Alexandria, Virginia; and the members and staff of the Alexandria Archaeology Museum, fearlessly led by the recently retired Pam Cressey.

My day job while writing this book was teaching at Georgetown University, and as teachers everywhere know, students teach us a lot. Sometimes the sheer enthusiasm of Danny Aherne, Bridget Ansel, Ethan Chess, Emma Thompson, Kari Nelson, and Will Redmond kept me afloat, as did the exceptionally good cheer of the students in the spring 2015 History of Baseball class. Chris Howard Miller and I decided to use the Georgetown Undergraduate Research Opportunities Program as a chance to learn the intricacies of the downtown branch of the National Archives, and we found some great stuff together. Georgetown History Department graduate students—including Paul Adler, Chelsea Berry, Carrie Crawford-Swenson, Kyra Daniel, Ben Feldman, Zackary Gardner, Jessica Hower, Joe Hower, Luke Jackson, Adam Sikes, Jordan Smith, Kate Steir, Larisa Veloz, and Cory Young—have listened, questioned, and taught me a lot. In particular,

Elena Abbott, Brian Taylor, and Tom Foley have been constant sources of joy. Their forthcoming work will enrich us all. Tom also created this book's maps, which is fortunate for everyone involved, because the relationship between maps and me can most charitably be described as adversarial.

The metaphor I used constantly in the classroom for teaching and learning history was conversation, and one of the reasons I insisted to students that we teach and learn history in conversation with others is that I have been the fortunate beneficiary of so many helpful chats. Especially key in this regard have been Abby Cooper, Thavolia Glymph, James Oakes, Aaron Sheehan-Dean, Silvana Siddali, Amy Murrell Taylor, and Mike Vorenberg. Bill Blair and Tony Kaye provided welcome encouragement at a very early stage. Thanks to them, portions of chapters 3 and 4 originally appeared in different form in *The Journal of the Civil War Era*, Vol. 4, Issue 2 (172–204 Copyright © 2014 by University of North Carolina Press. Reprinted by permission of University of North Carolina Press). I am also very grateful for conversations about craft and process with Suzy Smith and Rosie Zagarri.

Writing history depends on the goodwill of others every bit as much as teaching and learning it do. Ari Kelman, Aaron Marrs, Aaron Sheehan-Dean, and Silvana Siddali all read the entire manuscript. It would be impossible for me to exaggerate how vital Ari's encouragement was at the moment that it arrived. Aaron Marrs offered a suggestion that was so completely spot-on that I now cannot imagine this book without it. Aaron Sheehan-Dean saved me from using a phrase with an unfortunate double meaning that I had utterly failed to notice, and he also displayed his distinctive knack for grasping what I mean. Silvana, who consistently proved able to reignite my enthusiasm for all things nineteenth century, accompanied me through multiple drafts of both the introduction and the conclusion, patiently coaxing what I was trying to say out of the early murk. Speaking of patience, my Knopf editor, George Andreou, displayed a bottomless well of it, because this book took much longer than anticipated, and for that I am deeply grateful. Terezia Cicelova, Cassandra Pappas, Victoria Pearson, and Ingrid Sterner all helped to copyedit, design, and shepherd this book through production with a delightful and much-appreciated blend of minimalism and precision. Sandy Dijkstra is the only agent I have known, and I cannot imagine that there is a more tirelessly supportive one. Matthew Christensen helped with images on a short timeline with good cheer and great grace. To all of them, many thanks.

This book is a Georgetown book, and while it cannot repay the many debts I owe that incomparable institution, I hope it can at least indicate my deep gratitude and affection. A quick glance at the list of archives on which this book relied pays homage to the Georgetown University Pilot Research Project Grant and the Georgetown University Senior Faculty Research Fellowship, which helped make trips to all those locations possible. The offices of the college dean and the provost, and especially the History Department chair extraordinaire Carol Benedict, were exceptionally gracious in making an impromptu semester of unpaid leave possible, which enabled me to write at a time when other matters urgently needed my attention. In doing so, Carol acted out of her own infinitely kind nature, as well as out of a tradition of absolutely wonderful Georgetown history department chairs, exemplified by her immediate predecessor, Aviel Roshwald, and by the utterly inimitable John Tutino. These chairs set the tone for the most collegial and collaborative department on the planet, where there was never enough office space but always an abundance of companionship. Tommaso Astarita is the rock without whom we all would founder. Katie Benton-Cohen, Marcia Chatelain, David Collins, Maurice Jackson, Amy Leonard, and Meredith McKittrick have all been staunch allies, as has Joe McCartin, but I will save him for later. Michael Kazin was always willing to talk about baseball. Alison Games's constancy as advocate and friend knows no bounds; neither does John Tutino's. Adam Rothman and I share a birthday and a propensity for terrible puns, which goes to show that the fates were in a mischievous mood the day we both entered the world. Where this book is concerned, Adam saved me from inadvertently changing Nathaniel Banks's political allegiance and encouraged me to write the interludes in a different register, and I thank him for both interventions. One tradition that sets the department as a whole apart is the book manuscript seminar, at which, under the dauntless leadership of John McNeill, colleagues read and comment on each other's near-finished books. By attending my seminar, John McNeill, Tommaso Astarita, Katie Benton-Cohen, Michael Kazin, Amy Leonard, and John Tutino made this book much better. All remaining shortcomings are mine alone, but any lift this book achieves is thanks to all of them.

In many ways, this book is the product of thinking I did while feeling lost in the dark. Joe McCartin insisted calmly that I was not lost. (The shortness of that sentence is in inverse proportion to the magnitude of the contribution.) So, at different times, did Kate Baker-Carr, who many years ago defined a true friendship as one that bore unpredictable fruit in the world; by her definition, our friendship remains one of the hardiest perennials ever grown, and its yield continues to sustain me. Rosie Zagarri was willing to be lost with me, and her companionship made it possible to keep putting one foot in front of the other. Mary Novak reminded me that we all come with a compass, and she taught me how to use mine. Now, anyone who knows me will know that I cannot navigate to save my life, but that was precisely what I needed to do, so I am grateful to Peter Folan, S.J., Kevin O'Brien, S.J., and Isa Helfgott (not S.J.), who each at different times told me that I was on the right track. Brian MacDermott, S.J., helped me to see many things in the dark, including the beginnings of light's return.

Others who have no obvious connection to this book were pivotal to its completion because they provided encouragement at the times that this book came closest to the trash heap. Chief among them are my friends Audrey and Ciaran Rynne, John Jenkins, godfather to my older son, and all the teachers of Holy Trinity's Shepherd's Flock class in Washington, D.C., especially Becca Brusseau and Kelly Rogers. I am grateful beyond words to each of them for their willingness to set aside presumptions about how children are supposed to be and see who my sons *are* instead. They inspire me to work for a world that will do the same for every person. Nobody in the Boston Red Sox organization has the least idea who I am, but the Red Sox actually also helped me see this book through to completion. Win or lose, and even in the seasons full of lineup and rotation decisions that led me to suspect that management consisted of saboteurs on the New York Yankees payroll, for at least 162 games a season, the Red Sox are always there. No matter what, there is a box score in the morning paper. Even when a season ends, after a period of grief, they come back. The day I submitted my doctoral dissertation years ago, my husband and I went to see Pedro Martinez pitch at Fenway. When I sent off my first book manuscript just before my first son's birth, we drove from our home outside Washington, D.C., to Baltimore to see the Sox play the Orioles. Tomorrow, I will mail this manuscript, and the following day my husband, sons, a family friend, and I will go to Fenway Park to see the Sox take on the Tampa Bay Rays.

As the previous sentence indicates, above all else, there are the boys in my life, two little and one big. Many times, I thought that they meant that this book would never get done. In fact, the book I at first envisioned did not get done, but *this* quite different book did, precisely because of who my boys are. Aidan—fiery light, luminous being—was an infant when this book began, and by the end he was big enough to "play detective" by sitting next to me and using his astonishing eye for detail to help spot names we had seen before on long, long lists. He will also always talk about baseball with me. The way he encounters the world is radically different from the way that most of us do, and every time I decided to try to approach the evidence in the way that his brain would, I saw something I had not noticed before. That dynamic holds true for much more than this book. Kieran came to us in the research stage of the book, bringing with him joy and more. Like his brother, he brought much that only he could teach, including his own particular brand of resilience and resourcefulness. Above all, Kieran has taught me how very much one learns by not talking. Now he has plenty to say for himself—usually loudly—and although these days we occasionally ask ourselves *why* we thought that spending all those hours on the floor doing speech therapy with him was such a great idea, the truth is that his voice is sheer unearned and unearnable gift. When I worked on my first book, Derek Manning cheerfully built a bookcase to contain overflowing photocopies shipped home from archives. For this book, he built me an office. That he did so with neither desire nor intention to read what I would write there makes the gift even more deeply generous, as does his forbearance in never once lamenting the decision to build that office when the time came for us to move away and leave it behind. From the start, Derek and I have thought of ourselves as a team that specialized in pulling off the impossible. We have grown much more humble—both in the content of the "impossible" that we are pulling off each day and in our estimation of our own efficacy in doing so—but we have also grown ever more sure that the key, even when all goes wrong, is standing before all of it together. None of it is a victory march. Hallelujah.

Abbreviations Used in the Notes

AFIC   American Freedmen's Inquiry Commission

AMA   American Missionary Association Archives, 1839–1882, accessed via *Slavery and Anti-slavery: A Transnational Archive*, pt. 4: Age of Emancipation, www.gale.com /DigitalCollections

DU   Special Collections, Perkins Library, Duke University

FSB   U.S. Freedman's Bank Records, 1865–1874, Freedman's Savings and Trust Company, National Archives and Records Administration, Washington, D.C., http:// familysearch.org

FSSP   Freedom: A Documentary History of Emancipation, 1861–1867, ser. 1, vols. 1–3; ser. 2, vol. 1; and ser. 3, vols. 1–2, edited by Ira Berlin et al. New York: Cambridge University Press, 1985–2013

INSL   Indiana State Library

HL   Henry E. Huntington Library, San Marino, California

ISHL   Illinois State Historical Library

LOC   Manuscripts Division, Library of Congress

MHS   Massachusetts Historical Society

MOHS   Missouri Historical Society, St. Louis

NARA   National Archives and Records Administration

NCDAH   North Carolina Division of Archives and History

NL   Newberry Library, Chicago

NWFAC   Northwestern Freedmen's Aid Commission

OR   *The War of the Rebellion: A Compilation of the Official Records of the Union and Confederate Armies* (Washington, D.C.: Government Printing Office, 1888–1922)

RG 15   Records of the Department of Veterans Affairs
(the "Pension Records")

RG 92   Records of the Office of the Quartermaster General

RG 94   Records of the Adjutant General's Office, 1790–1917

RG 94 M619   Records of the American Freedmen's Inquiry Commission,
Letters Received by the Office of the Adjutant General
(Main Series), 1861–1870, 1863-328-0, Microfilm Collection
619, reels 199–201

RG 105   Records of the Bureau of Refugees, Freedmen, and
Abandoned Lands (the Freedmen's Bureau)

RG 105 M1914   Records of the Bureau of Refugees, Freedmen, and
Abandoned Lands (the Freedmen's Bureau), Office
of the Assistant Commissioner, Bureau of Refugees,
Freedmen, and Abandoned Lands, the "Pre-Bureau
Records," 1863–1865, Microfilm Collection 1914

RG 110   Records of the Provost Marshal General's Bureau
(Civil War)

RG 217   Records of the Accounting Officers of the Department of
the Treasury

RG 233   Records of the U.S. House of Representatives at the
National Archives, Chapter 6, Records of the Claims
Committees

RG 393   Records of U.S. Army Continental Commands, 1821–1920

SHSI   State Historical Society of Iowa, Des Moines

SHSW   Wisconsin Historical Society (formerly known as the State
Historical Society of Wisconsin)

TSLA   Tennessee State Library and Archives

WHMC   Western Historical Manuscripts Collection, University of
Missouri

WPA Narratives   *Born in Slavery: Slave Narratives from the Federal Writers'
Project*, 1936–1938, http://memory.loc.gov/ammem/snhtml
/snhome.html

Notes

INTRODUCTION

1. Private Constant Hanks (Twentieth New York Militia) to his mother, Aug. 8, 1862, Fredericksburg, Va., Constant Hanks Papers, DU.

2. Lieber's third son, Guido Norman, also served in the Union army. For biographical details about Lieber as well as his sons' actions during the war, see Frank Freidel, *Francis Lieber: Nineteenth-Century Liberal* (Baton Rouge: Louisiana State University Press, 1947). For Lieber's musings about what should become of slaves who ran to Fort Monroe, see Francis Lieber to Charles Sumner, June 1, 1861, Francis Lieber Papers, box 42, HL. For a brief account of his trip to Fort Monroe, see Freidel, *Francis Lieber*, 307–8, and Matthew J. Mancini, "Francis Lieber, Slavery, and the 'Genesis' of the Laws of War," *Journal of Southern History* 77, no. 2 (2011): 333. For Lieber's accounts of his trip to look for Hamilton, see Lieber to Edward Allibone, March 17, 1862, Lieber Papers, box 22, and Lieber to Edward Bates, April 8, 1862, Lieber Papers, box 23. For evidence of former slaves in Paducah, Cairo, and Mound City by the winter of 1862, see RG 393, pt. 2, entry 1106, District, Division, and Post of Cairo, Misc. Records 1862–1865, NARA.

3. Asboth to Mrs. V. C. Taylor, April 10, 1863, Columbus, Ky.; Asboth to General Hurlbut, April 12, 1863, Columbus, Ky.; Asboth to Henry Brinmore of the Sixteenth Army Corps, June 22, 1863, Columbus, Ky., RG 393, pt. 2, entry 986, Letters Sent Oct. 1862–July 1864, NARA.

4. Yoni Appelbaum, "The Great Illusion of Gettysburg," *Atlantic Monthly*, Feb. 2012; National Park Service, "The Gettysburg Cyclorama," http://www.nps .gov/gett/historyculture/gettysburg-cyclorama.htm; Boston Center for the Arts, "History of the Cyclorama," http://www.bcaonline.org/aboutthebca /history.html. Newspaper quotation from *Watchman*, Feb. 19, 1885, quoted in Boston Center for the Arts, "History," http://www.bcaonline.org/aboutthebca /history.html.

5. For a recent interpretation of slavery as just such a state of war, see Sven Beckert's analysis of "war capitalism" in *Empire of Cotton: A Global History* (New York: Knopf, 2014).

6. A list of important works on emancipation could easily run to several pages and still omit many important works. A good place to begin is Adam Rothman, *Slavery, the Civil War, and Reconstruction,* a 2012 pamphlet in the American Historical Association's American History Now series. A sampling of important works includes the interpretive essays at the beginning of each section of each volume in Berlin et al., *Freedom: A Documentary History of Emancipation* series; Ira Berlin et al., *Slaves No More: Three Essays on Emancipation and the Civil War* (New York: Cambridge University Press, 1992); Barbara Fields, *Slavery and Freedom on the Middle Ground: Maryland During the Nineteenth Century* (New Haven, Conn.: Yale University Press, 1984); Louis Gerteis, *From Contraband to Freedman: Federal Policy Toward Southern Blacks, 1861–1865* (Westport, Conn.: Greenwood Press, 1973); Stephen Hahn, *A Nation Under Our Feet: Black Political Struggles in the Rural South from Slavery to the Great Migration* (Cambridge, Mass.: Harvard University Press, 2005); John Rodrigue, *Reconstruction in the Cane Fields: From Slavery to Free Labor in Louisiana's Sugar Parishes, 1862–1880* (Baton Rouge: Louisiana State University Press, 2001); Julie Saville, *The Work of Reconstruction: From Slave to Wage Laborer in South Carolina, 1860–1870* (New York: Cambridge University Press, 1996); Leslie Schwalm, *A Hard Fight for We: Women's Transition from Slavery to Freedom in South Carolina* (Champaign: University of Illinois Press, 1997). For caution against overemphasizing slave "agency," see Edward Baptist, *The Half Has Never Been Told: Slavery and the Making of American Capitalism* (New York: Basic Books, 2014); Walter Johnson, "On Agency," *Journal of Social History* (Fall 2003): 113–24; Walter Johnson, *River of Dark Dreams: Slavery and Empire in the Cotton Kingdom* (Cambridge, Mass.: Harvard University Press, 2013).

7. For one statement of the argument that the actions of slaves destroyed slavery in spite of Lincoln, see Vincent Harding, *There Is a River: The Black Struggle for Freedom in America* (New York: Harcourt, Brace, Jovanovich, 1981). For a defense of Abraham Lincoln's chief role in emancipation, see James McPherson, "Who Freed the Slaves?," *Proceedings of the American Philosophical Society* 139, no. 1 (March 1995): 1–10.

8. FSSP; Eric Foner, *The Fiery Trial: Abraham Lincoln and American Slavery* (New York: Norton, 2010); James Oakes, *Freedom National: The Destruction of Slavery in the United States, 1861–1865* (New York: Norton, 2013); Silvana Siddali, *From Property to Person: Slavery and the Confiscation Acts, 1861–1862* (Baton Rouge: Louisiana State University Press, 2005); Michael Vorenberg, *Final Freedom: The Civil War, the Abolition of Slavery, and the Thirteenth Amendment* (New York: Cambridge University Press, 2001).

9. For a recent, authoritative case for emancipation's quick beginnings, see Oakes, *Freedom National.* The slow, reluctant emancipation interpretation was common from the 1980s to the first decade of the twenty-first century. For a classic formulation of it, see Harding, *There Is a River.*

10. Orlando Patterson, *Slavery and Social Death: A Comparative Study* (Cambridge, Mass.: Harvard University Press, 1982).

11. See, for example, Vincent Brown, "Social Death and Political Life in the Study of Slavery," *American Historical Review* (Dec. 2009): 1231–49.

12. This view of slavery is long-standing, and its pedigree is efficiently covered in James Oakes, "The Right Versus the Wrong of Property in Man," in *The Scorpion's Sting: Antislavery and the Coming of the Civil War* (New York: Norton, 2014),

although Oakes disagrees with the conclusion I draw, that if slavery consists in being the legal property of another person, emancipation from it consists in ceasing to be property but does not automatically lead to citizenship.

13. Edward L. Ayers and Scott Nesbit, "Seeing Emancipation: Scale and Freedom in the American South," *Journal of the Civil War Era* 1, no. 1 (March 2011): 17. See also Glenn David Brasher, *The Peninsula Campaign and the Necessity of Emancipation: African Americans and the Fight for Freedom* (Chapel Hill: University of North Carolina Press, 2012); Robert Hunt, *The Good Men Who Won the War: Army of the Cumberland Veterans and Emancipation Memory* (Huntsville: University of Alabama Press, 2010); Anthony Kaye, *Joining Places: Slave Neighborhoods in the Old South* (Chapel Hill: University of North Carolina Press, 2007), esp. chap. 6; Chandra Manning, *What This Cruel War Was Over: Soldiers, Slavery, and the Civil War* (New York: Knopf, 2007); Amy Murrell Taylor, "How a Cold Snap in Kentucky Led to Freedom for Thousands: An Environmental Story of Emancipation," in *Weirding the War: Stories from the Civil War's Ragged Edges,* ed. Stephen Berry (Athens: University of Georgia Press, 2011).

14. For recent emphasis on the violence and suffering of emancipation, especially but not only in contraband camps, see Thavolia Glymph, *Out of the House of Bondage: The Transformation of the Plantation Household* (New York: Cambridge University Press, 2008); Thavolia Glymph, "'The Liberty to Be Free': The Problem of Freedom as a Problem of American Exceptionalism" (talk delivered at "Beyond Freedom: New Directions in the Study of Emancipation" conference, Gilder Lehrman Center, Yale University, Nov. 12, 2011); Thavolia Glymph, "'This Species of Property': Female Slave Contrabands in the Civil War," in *A Woman's War: Southern Women, Civil War, and the Confederate Legacy* (Richmond: Museum of the Confederacy, 1996), 54–71; Jim Downs, *Sick from Freedom: African American Illness and Suffering During the Civil War and Reconstruction* (New York: Oxford University Press, 2012); Hannah Rosen, *Terror in the Heart of Freedom: Citizenship, Sexual Violence, and the Meaning of Race in the Postemancipation South* (Chapel Hill: University of North Carolina Press, 2008), and her work in progress on Helena, Arkansas; Leslie Schwalm, "Between Slavery and Freedom: African American Women and Occupation in the Slave South," in *Occupied Women: Gender, Military Occupation, and the American Civil War,* ed. LeeAnn Whites and Alecia Long (Baton Rouge: Louisiana State University Press, 2009). For readers in search of more general information on contraband camps, secondary works are usually about specific locations, such as Cam Walker, "Corinth: The Story of a Contraband Camp," *Civil War History* 20, no. 1 (March 1974): 5–22, and Patricia C. Click, *Time Full of Trial: The Roanoke Island Freedmen's Colony, 1862–1867* (Chapel Hill: University of North Carolina Press, 2000).

15. Robin Blackburn, *The American Crucible: Slavery, Emancipation, and Human Rights* (New York: Verso, 2011); Peter Blanchard, *Under the Flags of Freedom: Slave Soldiers and the Wars of Independence in Spanish South America* (Pittsburgh: University of Pittsburgh Press, 2008); Robert Conrad, *The Destruction of Brazilian Slavery, 1850–1888* (Berkeley: University of California Press, 1973); Eric Foner, *Nothing but Freedom: Emancipation and Its Legacy* (Baton Rouge: Louisiana State University Press, 1983); Steven Hahn, *The Political Worlds of Slavery and Freedom* (Cambridge, Mass.: Harvard University Press, 2009); Maya Jasanoff, *Liberty's Exiles: American Loyalists in the Revolutionary World* (New York: Vintage, 2012); Cassandra Pybus, *Epic Journeys of Freedom: Runaway Slaves of the American Rev-*

olution and Their Global Quest for Liberty (Boston: Beacon Press, 2007); Rebecca Scott, *Degrees of Freedom: Louisiana and Cuba After Slavery* (Cambridge, Mass.: Harvard University Press, 2008); Rebecca Scott, *Slave Emancipation in Cuba: The Transition to Free Labor, 1860–1899* (Pittsburgh: University of Pittsburgh Press, 2000); Arthur Zilversmit, *First Emancipation: The Abolition of Slavery in the North* (Chicago: University of Chicago Press, 1977).

16. Jasanoff, *Liberty's Exiles;* Pybus, *Epic Journeys of Freedom;* "Liberty and Union, Now and Forever, One and Inseparable: Views of John Quincy Adams," *New York World,* Sept. 2, 1862, reprinted in *Washington Intelligencer;* Francis Lieber, "Notebook on Slavery," Sept. 1862, Lieber Papers, box 23; Adam Rothman, *Slave Country: American Expansion and the Origins of the Deep South* (Cambridge, Mass.: Harvard University Press, 2007); Laurent Dubois, *A Colony of Citizens: Revolution and Slave Emancipation in the French Caribbean, 1787–1804* (Chapel Hill: University of North Carolina Press, 2004); Blanchard, *Under the Flags of Freedom;* Conrad, *Destruction of Brazilian Slavery;* Spencer Leitman, "The Black Ragamuffins: Racial Hypocrisy in Nineteenth-Century Southern Brazil," *Americas* 33, no. 3 (1977): 504–18; Daniela Vallandro de Carvalho, "Praças de frágeis destinos: Serviços e sociabilidades dos 'escravos libertos' da revolução farroupilha na corte imperial (séc. XIX)" (paper presented at the conference "Quinto Encontro Sobre Escravidão e Liberdade no Brasil Meridional," Porto Alegre, 2011, brought to my attention by Bryan McCann); Laurent Dubois, *Avengers of the New World: The Story of the Haitian Revolution* (Cambridge, Mass.: Harvard University Press, 2004); Carolyn E. Fick, *Making Haiti: The Saint Domingue Revolution from Below* (Knoxville: University of Tennessee Press, 1990); Maurice Jackson, "'Friends of the Negro! Fly with Me, the Path Is Open to the Sea': Remembering the Haitian Revolution in the History, Music, and Culture of the African American People," *Early American Studies* 6, no. 1 (Spring 2008): 59–103.

17. I use "autonomy" here in a much different way from the sense of acquisitive individualism embedded within a liberal framework. I mean the ability of freedpeople to order their own lives, families, and communities and pursue shared ends; the sense is an alternative to, not unthinking acceptance of, acquisitive liberal individualism. For another work that uses the concept of autonomy in a similar way, see John Tutino, *Capitalism and Community, Patriarchy and Revolution: The Mexican Heartland in the World, 1500–2000* (Stanford, Calif.: Stanford University Press, forthcoming). I thank John Tutino for sharing this important work with me while still in manuscript form.

18. On antebellum visions of black citizenship, see Stephen Kantrowitz, *More Than Freedom: Fighting for Black Citizenship in a White Republic, 1829–1889* (New York: Penguin Press, 2012). On antebellum and wartime black claims making, see, among others, David Cecelski, *The Fire of Freedom: Abraham Galloway and the Slaves' Civil War* (Chapel Hill: University of North Carolina Press, 2012); Hahn, *Nation Under Our Feet;* Martha Jones, *All Bound Up Together: The Woman Question in African American Public Culture, 1830–1900* (Chapel Hill: University of North Carolina Press, 2007).

19. "Address for the Promotion of Colored Enlistments," Philadelphia, July 6, 1863, quoted in David Blight, *Frederick Douglass' Civil War: Keeping Faith in Jubilee* (Baton Rouge: Louisiana State University Press, 1991), 161; Mary Frances Berry, *Military Necessity and Civil Rights Policy: Black Citizenship and the Constitution,*

1861–1868 (Port Washington, N.Y.: Kennikat Press, 1977); Joseph Reidy, "The African American Struggle for Citizenship Rights in the Northern United States During the Civil War," in *Civil War Citizens: Race, Ethnicity, and Identity in America's Bloodiest Conflict,* ed. Susannah Ural (New York: New York University Press, 2010), 213–36; Christian Samito, *Becoming American Under Fire: Irish Americans, African Americans, and the Politics of Citizenship During the Civil War Era* (Ithaca, N.Y.: Cornell University Press, 2011); Brian Taylor, "'To Make the Union What It Ought to Be': African Americans, Military Service, and the Drive to Make Black Civil War Service Count" (Ph.D. diss., Georgetown University, 2015).

20. Carole Emberton plays off DuBois's insights in *Black Reconstruction* to critique the soldier-to-citizen narrative on these grounds in "Only Murder Makes Men: Reconsidering the Black Military Experience," *Journal of the Civil War Era* 2, no. 3 (Sept. 2012): 369–93.

21. Reidy, "African American Struggle for Citizenship," 231 ("pin[ning] their own hopes on the soldiers" quotation); Amy Dru Stanley, "Instead of Waiting for the Thirteenth Amendment: The War Power, Slave Marriage, and Inviolate Human Rights," *American Historical Review* 115, no. 3 (June 2010): 732–65; Stephanie McCurry, "War, Gender, and Emancipation in the Civil War South," in *Lincoln's Proclamation: Emancipation Reconsidered,* ed. William Blair and Karen Fisher Younger (Chapel Hill: University of North Carolina Press, 2009), esp. 122, 143–45.

22. The "voting and earning" interpretation comes from Judith Shklar, *American Citizenship: The Quest for Inclusion* (Cambridge, Mass.: Harvard University Press, 1991). Shklar *is* convincing that slavery influenced what citizenship meant. Michael Vorenberg, "Citizenship and the Thirteenth Amendment: Understanding the Deafening Silence," in *The Promises of Liberty: The History and Contemporary Relevance of the Thirteenth Amendment,* ed. Alexander Tsesis (New York: Columbia University Press, 2010), 62.

23. James Kettner, *The Development of American Citizenship, 1608–1870* (Chapel Hill: University of North Carolina Press, 1978), 8–10.

24. Rogers Smith, *Civic Ideals: Conflicting Visions of Citizenship in U.S. History* (New Haven, Conn.: Yale University Press, 1999). Between 1789 and 1830, eleven new states wrote new constitutions, and many of the original thirteen revised theirs. Then, from 1830 to 1861, eight more new states wrote state constitutions, and seventeen existing states revised theirs. See Alexander Keyssar, *The Right to Vote: The Contested History of Democracy in the United States* (New York: Basic Books, 2009), table A4, 349–53.

25. David S. Bogen, *Privileges and Immunities: A Reference Guide to the United States Constitution* (Westport, Conn.: Greenwood Press, 2003), esp. 12–13. The notion of usefulness as precondition is a very old one connected to ancient understandings of republicanism. See, for example, J. G. A. Pocock, "The Ideal of Citizenship Since Classical Times," *Queen's Quarterly* 99, no. 1 (Spring 1992): 35–55.

26. Delegate Pettit's Speech, *Debates and Proceedings of the Convention for the Revision of the Constitution of the State of Indiana,* 1850, 461–62, accessed Dec. 2008, http://indiamond6.ulib.iupui.edu/cdm4/document.php?CISOROOT=/ISC& CISOPTR=6357&REC=10. State constitutions are available at the NBER /Maryland State Constitutions Project, http://www.stateconstitutions.umd.edu /index.aspx. The proceedings of state constitutional conventions are available

for researchers to read at the relevant state historical societies (I read Wisconsin's at the Wisconsin Historical Society in Madison, for example), and sometimes in hard copy, such as Benjamin Franklin Shambaugh, ed., *Fragments of the Debates of the Constitutional Conventions of 1844 and 1846* (Iowa City: State Historical Society of Iowa, 1900). Finally, proceedings (including Indiana's, from which the Pettit quotation was taken) are increasingly available online. See, for example, Illinois at http://www.archive.org/stream/journalishso6illiuoft#page/n373 /mode/2up. See also Daniel J. Elazar, *Exploring Federalism* (Huntsville: University of Alabama Press, 1987), esp. 88–90, and Silvana Siddali, "Race, Prejudice, and Citizenship in Old Northwest State Constitutions" (unpublished paper, annual meeting of the Society for Historians of the Early Republic, Baltimore, July 2012).

27. It was that emphasis on perceived usefulness that helps explain the preoccupation with former slaves' alleged indolence and potential dependency long noted by scholars like Kate Masur in "A Rare Phenomenon of Philological Vegetation," *Journal of American History* 93, no. 4 (2007), among others. For a different view on antebellum citizenship that emphasizes "voting and earning," see Shklar, *American Citizenship*.

28. Henry Clay, Speech on "The Fugitive Slave Rescue in Boston" Resolution, Feb. 18, 1851, *Cong. Globe*, 31st Cong., 2nd sess., 597; "The Dred Scott Decision: Opinion of Chief Justice Taney," available from the Library of Congress Web site, accessed July 2013, http://memory.loc.gov/cgi-bin/query/r?ammem/llst :@field(DOCID+@lit(llsto22div1)):#0220002.

29. Jeanne Boydston, *Home and Work: Housework, Wages, and the Ideology of Labor in the Early Republic* (New York: Oxford University Press, 1990); Nancy Isenberg, *Sex and Citizenship in Antebellum America* (Chapel Hill: University of North Carolina Press, 1998); Linda K. Kerber, *No Constitutional Right to Be Ladies: Women and the Obligations of Citizenship* (New York: Hill and Wang, 1998), esp. chaps. 2 and 3; Susan Zaeske, *Signatures of Citizenship: Petitioning, Antislavery, and Women's Political Identity* (Chapel Hill: University of North Carolina Press, 2003). The same dynamic also appeared in discussion surrounding women's rights in the French Revolution. See, for example, Joan Landes, *Women and the Public Sphere in the Age of the French Revolution* (Ithaca, N.Y.: Cornell University Press, 1988).

30. William Novak, "The Legal Transformation of Citizenship in Nineteenth-Century America," in *The Democratic Experiment: New Directions in American Political History*, ed. Meg Jacobs, William Novak, and Julian E. Zelizer (Princeton, N.J.: Princeton University Press, 2003), 85–119; Akhil Reed Amar, *The Bill of Rights* (New Haven, Conn.: Yale University Press, 1998). On the Fourteenth Amendment specifically, see Raoul Berger, *The Fourteenth Amendment and the Bill of Rights* (Norman: University of Oklahoma Press, 1989); William Nelson, *The Fourteenth Amendment: From Political Principle to Judicial Doctrine* (Cambridge, Mass.: Harvard University Press, 1988); Michael Vorenberg, "Abraham Lincoln's 'Fellow Citizens'—Before and After Emancipation," in Blair and Younger, *Lincoln's Proclamation*, 151–69, and Vorenberg, "Citizenship and the Thirteenth Amendment," 58–77.

31. On wartime growth, the classic account is Richard Bensel, *Yankee Leviathan: The Origins of Central State Authority in America, 1859–1877* (New York: Cambridge University Press, 1991). On the recent American Political Development

turn emphasizing a more active antebellum state, see Brian Balogh, *A Government out of Sight: The Mystery of National Authority in Nineteenth Century America* (New York: Cambridge University Press, 2009); Gary Gerstle, "A State Both Strong and Weak," *American Historical Review* (June 2010): 779–85; Richard John, "Governmental Institutions as Agents of Change: Rethinking American Political Development in the Early Republic, 1787–1835," *Studies in American Political Development* (Fall 1997): 347–80; William Novak, "The Myth of the 'Weak' American State," *American Historical Review* (June 2008): 752–72.

32. David F. Ericson, *Slavery in the American Republic: Developing the Federal Government, 1791–1861* (Lawrence: University Press of Kansas, 2011); Don E. Fehrenbacher, *The Slaveholding Republic: An Account of the United States Government's Relations to Slavery* (New York: Oxford University Press, 2001); Rothman, *Slave Country*.

33. Drew Gilpin Faust, *This Republic of Suffering: Death and the American Civil War* (New York: Knopf, 2008); Stephanie McCurry, *Confederate Reckoning: Power and Politics in the Civil War South* (Cambridge, Mass.: Harvard University Press, 2010); Donald Nieman, "From Slaves to Citizens: African Americans, Rights Consciousness, and Reconstruction," *Cardozo Law Review* 17, no. 6 (May 1996): 2115–39.

34. FSSP; Berlin et al., *Slaves No More;* Hahn, *Nation Under Our Feet;* Masur, "'Rare Phenomenon of Philological Vegetation.'" See also Susan Eva O'Donovan, *Becoming Free in the Cotton South* (Cambridge, Mass.: Harvard University Press, 2007).

35. See Owen and McKaye to Howe, March 19, 1863, Washington, D.C., AFIC Papers, box 2, folder 76, Houghton Library, Harvard University, and AFIC Records, RG 94, M619, reels 199–201, NARA. Additional correspondence to and from James McKaye can be found in the James Morrison MacKaye Papers at the Library of Congress. McKaye is a little tricky, because sometimes his surname is spelled "McKaye" and sometimes "MacKaye," even by him! For consistency in this book, I have used "McKaye" in the text. In the notes, I retain whichever spelling is used in the source or collection, so for example, "MacKaye Papers" when citing from the James Morrison MacKaye Papers at the Library of Congress. The AFIC awaits its historian, but for a recent, primarily descriptive article see Matthew Furrow, "Samuel Gridley Howe, the Black Population of Canada West, and the Racial Ideology of the 'Blueprint for Radical Reconstruction,'" *Journal of American History* (Sept. 2010): 344–70.

36. I have listened very carefully to conversations about exactly this subject among members of the Contraband Historical Society of Hampton, Virginia, and members of the Contrabands and Freedmen Cemetery Memorial committee of Alexandria, Virginia, both consisting of descendants of people known during the Civil War as contrabands.

37. See, for example, Schwalm, "Between Slavery and Freedom," 140, 225n14.

PRELUDE

1. Butler, *Butler's Book,* Table of Contents. An 1866 drawing titled "Artesian Well at Fortress Monroe" meticulously documents the nine hundred feet that soldiers dug in pursuit of freshwater, showing soil content and other details at each depth. The drawing appears in an engineer report on various wells experimen-

tally (and futilely) drilled at Fort Monroe, the original of which can be found in RG 77, drawer 58, sheet 169, NARA, College Park; I saw the copy in possession of the Casemate Museum at Fort Monroe, courtesy of the Fort Monroe Authority.

2. Butler, *Private and Official Correspondence,* 1:105–7. For the original handwritten copy, see Benjamin F. Butler, May 24, 1861, Benjamin F. Butler Papers, Manuscript Division, LOC.

3. Solomon Bradley Testimony to AFIC, AFIC Records, file 3, reel 200, frames 275–76, NARA. Bradley later learned that the woman's offense had been that she had burned the edges of waffles she had been cooking for breakfast.

4. As told to the AMA missionary William King and relayed in a letter from King to S. S. Jocelyn of the AMA, April 11, 1863, Craney Island, Va., AMA H1-4717, accessed July 25, 2013.

5. The best single-source estimate of numbers can be found in FSSP, ser. 1, 3:77–80, which counts at least 475,000 former slaves in direct contact with the Union army in contraband camps, working for the army, or serving as black soldiers (most of whom first went to contraband camps and enlisted from there) in the spring of 1865. That number does not count the thousands who had been in contraband camps at an earlier point and died.

6. See Anderson, *Brokenburn;* Coffin, *Reminiscences,* 619; John C. Inscoe and Gordon B. McKinney, *The Heart of Confederate Appalachia: Western North Carolina in the Civil War* (Chapel Hill: University of North Carolina Press, 2003); Walker, "Corinth."

7. Hahn, in *Nation Under Our Feet,* 72, points to one post near Jackson, Tennessee, where men accounted for nearly 90 percent of all fugitives arriving within one six-month period. That proportion was anomalous in both space (other camps did not replicate those proportions) and time (a much higher proportion of the total refugee population in and around Jackson over the whole course of the war consisted of women), but it does demonstrate that there were many more fit men of prime age in camps early in the war than there were later in the war.

8. Nancy Fraser and Linda Gordon, "A Genealogy of Dependency: Tracing a Keyword of the U.S. Welfare State," *Signs* 19, no. 2 (Winter 1994): 309–36, esp. 312–15, quotations from 313 and 315; Gordon S. Wood, *The Radicalism of the American Revolution* (New York: Knopf, 1992). Gregory P. Downs, in *Declarations of Dependence: The Long Reconstruction of Popular Politics in the South, 1861–1908* (Chapel Hill: University of North Carolina Press, 2011), makes the case that the old notion of dependence as a normal state for most people, and one entitled to make its own particular demands on the independent, was still alive and well in North Carolina during and after the Civil War, but Union officials and Northern aid workers appear to have fully absorbed the modern notions of dependence and independence that Fraser and Gordon detail.

9. On the lack of any direct relationship between enslaved people and the national government, see Don E. Fehrenbacher, *The Dred Scott Case: Its Significance in American Law and Politics* (New York: Oxford University Press, 2001), and Fehrenbacher, *Slaveholding Republic;* Hahn, *Nation Under Our Feet.* On passports, see Oakes, *Freedom National,* 264; Craig Robertson, *The Passport in America: The History of a Document* (New York: Oxford University Press, 2010), esp. chap. 2 and Appendix p. 254. Passports are a little complicated because in the first half of the nineteenth century, the State Department issued them to *residents* of the

United States, not just citizens. Consequently, instances of African Americans holding U.S. passports did exist in the early antebellum period, just as instances of non-naturalized immigrants did, until 1847, when the secretary of state clarified that African Americans would be issued a special certificate, not a regular passport. The combination of the *Dred Scott* case and an 1856 law passed by Congress restricting the issuance of passports only to citizens led the State Department to even more strictly forbid passports for African Americans.

10. On Union soldiers' changing attitudes toward slavery and race, see Manning, *What This Cruel War Was Over.*

11. Moore, "Reminiscences," 291.

12. Julia Wilbur to Amy Post, Nov. 5, 1862, Alexandria, Va., Isaac and Amy Kirby Post Family Papers, 1817–1918, Rush Rhees Library, the University of Rochester, transcribed by Alexandria Archaeology Museum, Alexandria, Va.

ONE · GRIT AND LIMITS

1. Photograph reference: "Gwine to de field," Hopkinson's Plantation, Edisto Island, S.C., Henry P. Moore 1862, William Gladstone Collection of African American Photographs, LC-DIG-ppmsca-11370, LOC.

2. Willcox, *Forgotten Valor,* 267–68. On Price and Birch, see Robert H. Gudmestad, *A Troublesome Commerce: The Transformation of the Interstate Slave Trade* (Baton Rouge: Louisiana State University Press, 2003); Janice G. Artemel, Elizabeth A. Crowell, and Jeff Parker, *The Alexandria Slave Pen: The Archaeology of Urban Captivity* (Alexandria Archaeology, Office of Historic Alexandria, Alexandria, Va., 1987); Lisa Kraus, John Bedell, and Charles Lee Decker, *Joseph Bruin and the Slave Trade* (prepared for Columbia Equity Trust, Inc., June 2007, available at Alexandria Archaeology, Office of Historic Alexandria, Alexandria, Va.).

3. Wilbur to Amy Post, Nov. 5, 1862, Alexandria, Va., Post Family Papers, 1817–1918.

4. Ibid.

5. Harriet Jacobs, "The Freedmen at Alexandria," *Evening Post,* April 29, 1863, in Yellin, *Harriet Jacobs Family Papers,* 481, also letter on 400.

6. Wilbur to Anna Barnes, Feb. 27, March 10 and 18, 1863, in Yellin, *Harriet Jacobs Family Papers,* 451, 470, 478.

7. J. R. Bigelow to AFIC, May 8, 1863, Alexandria, Va., James Morrison MacKaye Papers, LOC. For another instance, this one in Nashville, perpetrated by Captain Ralph Hunt of the First Kentucky Volunteers in May 1864, see Bostwick and Hood, *Report upon the Condition and Treatment of Colored Refugees in Kentucky, Tennessee, and Alabama,* 3–4.

8. J. R. Bigelow to AFIC, May 8, 1863, Alexandria, Va., MacKaye Papers.

9. Harriet Jacobs to J. Sella Martin, April 13, 1863, in Yellin, *Harriet Jacobs Family Papers,* 478; Jacobs, "Freedmen at Alexandria," 481.

10. Jacobs to Lydia Maria Child, March 23, 1864, in Yellin, *Harriet Jacobs Family Papers,* 558.

11. Samuel May Jr. to the editor of the *National Anti-slavery Standard,* Oct. 30, 1864, in ibid., 586; Report to the Executive Committee of New England Yearly Meeting of Friends, upon the Condition and Needs of the Freed People of Color in Washington and Virginia, Nov. 10, 1864, in ibid., 589.

12. *Alexandria Gazette,* Jan. 12, 1863.
13. Shephard, "Excavations at the Contrabands and Freedmen's Cemetery and the Concept of the Proper Coffin in the Mid-19th Century." On the scant responsibility shown even to soldiers at the start of the war, see Faust, *This Republic of Suffering.*
14. See, for example, "Broke Jail," *Frederick (Md.) Examiner,* May 20, 1863.
15. FSSP, ser. 1, vol. 2, p. 487.
16. Commandant of Contraband Camp to all whom it may concern, April 11, 1863, Contraband Camp, Point Lookout, Md., MacKaye Papers, LOC.
17. For an excellent introduction to western Maryland and its connections to Harpers Ferry during the Civil War, see Catoctin Center for Regional Studies, "Crossroads of War: Maryland and the Border in the Civil War," http://www.crossroadsofwar.org/; "Fort Frederick in the Civil War," Maryland Dept. of Natural Resources, www.dnr.state.md.us/publiclands/western/fortfrederick civilwar.asp.
18. On the *Pearl,* see Josephine F. Pacheco, *The* Pearl: *A Failed Slave Escape on the Potomac* (Chapel Hill: University of North Carolina Press, 2005).
19. D. B. Nichols Testimony, AFIC Records, file 1, reel 200, frame 117, NARA.
20. On numbers, see ibid., frames 106 and 120–21, NARA. For more on location and especially Lincoln's daily route, see Matthew Pinsker, *Lincoln's Sanctuary: Abraham Lincoln and the Soldiers' Home* (New York: Oxford University Press, 2003), map 1, p. 6, and pp. 16, 66–68.
21. "Plan of Contraband Camp" and Lieutenant Colonel Edward P. Volume to Brigadier General D. H. Rucker, Sept. 23, 1863, Washington, D.C., and ensuing related correspondence, "Constitution, Ft. through Contraband Camp (1863)," Consolidated Correspondence file, RG 92, NARA. Freedmen's Village lasted long after the war, although the federal government began the process of disbanding it in the 1880s and finally completed the closure in 1900 by compensating residents for the appraised value of their homes plus the amount collected into a so-called contraband fund tax from African Americans working for the federal government during the Civil War. See Joseph P. Reidy, "Coming from the Shadow of the Past: The Transition from Slavery to Freedom at Freedmen's Village, 1863–1869," *Virginia Magazine of History and Biography* 95, no. 4 (Oct. 1987): 403–28.
22. Leach to Samuel Gridley Howe and James Morrison McKaye, April 28 and 29, May 1 and 6, 1863, and Leach to Chapman, May 8, 1863, MacKaye Papers, LOC.
23. Lieutenant M. G. Raymond Testimony, AFIC Records, file 1, reel 200, frame 133, NARA. For numbers in D.C. contraband camps (4,939 in spring of 1863) and for testimony about black men guarding D.C. in anticipation of the Stonewall Jackson raid, see Nichols Testimony, reel 200, frames 106 and 120–21, NARA.
24. New England Freedmen's Aid Society Records, MS N-101, box 1, MHS; *Freedmen's Record,* May 1865, 80, American Antiquarian Society, Worcester, Mass., http://www.americanantiquarian.org/digitalaas.
25. For more on the black elite of Washington, D.C., and Washington, D.C., generally, see Kate Masur, *An Example for All the Land: Emancipation and the Struggle over Equality in Washington, D.C.* (Chapel Hill: University of North Carolina Press, 2010), chap. 1.
26. Lockwood, *Mary S. Peake,* 24, 27–28.

27. Butler to Simon Cameron, July 30, 1861, *Private and Official Correspondence,* 1:185–88; Pierce, "Contrabands at Fortress Monroe."

28. Report of Major General Benjamin F. Butler, June 10, 1861, Fortress Monroe, Va., in *OR,* ser. 1, 2:77–80; Report of Major General Benjamin F. Butler, Aug. 8, 1861, Fortress Monroe, Va., in *OR,* ser. 1, 4:567–68; Butler, *Butler's Book,* chap. 6; Lockwood, *Mary S. Peake,* 25.

29. Butler to Lewis Tappan, Aug. 10, 1861, Fort Monroe, Va., AMA H1-4336. LeBaron Russell of the Boston Educational Commission (later renamed the New England Freedmen's Aid Society) was appointed a special commissioner to investigate conditions at Fort Monroe, and he confirmed that rations were "generally sufficient" but that "the principal deficiency is in clothing of which many are in want." Russell to Secretary of War Stanton, "Report on the Condition, Necessities, and Capacity of the Colored Refugees from the Enemy in Fortress Monroe and the Vicinity, in Regard to the Unpaid Wages of Their Labor for the Government," Dec. 25, 1862, AFIC Papers, box 3, folder 91, HO.

30. Kathryn Shiveley Meier, for example, characterizes the experiences of both Union and Confederate soldiers in Virginia in 1862 as a "continuing health crisis in the ranks" and a "health crisis larger than the medical directors were willing to admit." See *Nature's Civil War: Common Soldiers and the Environment in 1862 Virginia* (Chapel Hill: University of North Carolina Press, 2013), 80, 95.

31. Lockwood, *Mary S. Peake,* 27–29; AFIC Records, file 2, reel 200, NARA; Pierce, "Contrabands at Fortress Monroe."

32. Lockwood, *Mary S. Peake,* 29–39.

33. On Galloway, see Cecelski, *Fire of Freedom.*

34. Captain C. B. Wilder Testimony, AFIC Records, file 2, reel 200, frame 146, NARA.

35. "What Shall We Do with the Slaves?," *New York Times,* Dec. 14, 1861. See also Pierce, "Contrabands at Fortress Monroe." For work in hospitals, see MacKaye Papers, LOC.; correspondence between McKaye, LeBaron Russell, and Samuel Gridley Howe in AFIC Papers HO; RG 393; AMA; Testimony of Edward Whitehurst (former slave from Hampton who nursed at Newport News from May to Aug. 1861 and after that at Hampton and Fort Monroe), July 31, 1877, Elizabeth City Co., VA Case Files, Approved Claims, ser. 732, Southern Claims Commission, RG 117, cited in FSSP, ser. 1, 2:128. Corporal Jared Fuller to wife Sarah, May 19, 1862, Portsmouth, Va., Jared and Sarah Fuller Papers, SHSI. Fuller served in Company A of the Eleventh Pennsylvania, which consisted of Iowans who had enlisted in Dubuque on Sept. 21, 1861, into what had begun as an independent company but was then attached to the Eleventh Pennsylvania Cavalry to fill that regiment.

36. Sergeant Luther Furst (Signal Corps, Thirty-Ninth Pennsylvania), Diary, May 11, 1862, York River, Va., Harrisburg Civil War Round Table Collection, U.S. Army Military History Institute, Carlisle Barracks, Pa. For more on escaped slaves' contributions to the Peninsula Campaign, see Brasher, *Peninsula Campaign and the Necessity of Emancipation.*

37. Russell to Stanton, "Report on the Condition, Necessities, and Capacity of the Colored Refugees from the Enemy in Fortress Monroe and the Vicinity, in regard to the Unpaid Wages of their Labor for the Government," Dec. 25, 1862, AFIC Papers, box 3, folder 91, HO.

38. Suthey Parker Affidavit, Sept. 2, 1865, "Negroes: Employment," RG 92, Consolidated Correspondence file, NARA; also cited in FSSP, ser. 1, 2:110–11.
39. Fuller to wife Sarah, Feb. 8, 1862, Fort Monroe, Va., Fuller Papers; Sergeant John England (Ninth New York) to fiancée Ellen, July 24, 1863, Fort Monroe, Va., Union Army boxes, John England Letters, Manuscripts and Special Collections, New York Public Library.
40. Lockwood, *Mary S. Peake,* and Lockwood to Senator Wilson, Jan. 29, 1862, in FSSP, ser. 1, 2:112–14.
41. Wilder Testimony, AFIC Records file 2, p. 10, reel 200, frame 145, NARA.
42. On Wool, see Edward Coffman, *The Old Army: A Portrait of the American Army in Peacetime, 1784–1898* (New York: Oxford University Press, 1986); Robert E. Ficken, *Washington Territory* (Pullman: Washington State University Press, 2002); *Olympia Pioneer and Democrat* for most of 1856; and *Dictionary of American Biography.*
43. John E. Wool, General Orders No. 5 (Jan. 30, 1862), No. 6 (Feb. 4, 1862), and No. 21 (March 15, 1862), Department of Virginia, RG 393, pt. 1, entry 5078, NARA; *OR.,* ser. 2, 1:809, 812; *House Executive Documents,* 37th Cong., 2nd sess., No. 85; Testimony of John Wilder (assistant to Captain C. B. Wilder), AFIC Records, file 2, reel 200, frame 142, NARA.
44. Return of two-tier wage scale: John Wilder Testimony; verified by C. B. Wilder's Testimony, AFIC Records, file 2, reel 200, frame 144, NARA. Dix acknowledged Russell's arrival in a letter to Stanton, Nov. 22, 1862, RG 393, entry 5046, NARA; Russell to Stanton, "Report on the Condition of Colored Refugees at Fortress Monroe and the Vicinity, in Regard to the Unpaid Wages of Their Labor for the Government," Dec. 13, 1862, AFIC Records, box 3, folder 90, HO; and Russell to Stanton, "Report on the Condition, Necessities, and Capacity of the Colored Refugees from the Enemy in Fortress Monroe and the Vicinity"; Russell to Tucker, Nov. 23, 1862, Boston, MacKaye Papers, LOC.; Russell to Stanton, Jan. 2, 1863, Boston, MacKaye Papers, LOC.; Russell to Tucker, Jan. 11, 1863, Boston, AFIC Records, box 3, folder 92, HO; Russell to P. H. Watson (assistant secretary of war), Feb. 20, 1863, Boston, MacKaye Papers, LOC.; Russell to Samuel G. Howe, Aug. 12 [1863], MacKaye Papers, LOC.
45. C. B. Wilder Testimony, AFIC Records, file 2, reel 200, frame 145, NARA.
46. Dix to Corcoran, Nov. 26, 1862, Fort Monroe, Va., RG 393, pt. 1, entry 5046, NARA.
47. Ibid.; Corcoran's response, Nov. 26, 1862, RG 393, pt. 1, entry 5063, NARA. For more on Corcoran's background, see Samito, *Becoming American Under Fire.*
48. For continued depredations by Corcoran's men and especially the Ninety-Ninth New York (and other soldiers' contempt for such actions), see Palmer Letts and C. P. Day to AFIC commissioners, Aug. 8, 1863, Oneida County, N.Y. (writing about visit to Yorktown, Va.), AFIC Records, box 1, folder 33, HO; Corporal Sykes Testimony, AFIC Records, file 2, reel 200, frame 169, NARA; C. B. Wilder Testimony, AFIC Records, file 2, reel 200, frame 148, NARA; Jared Fuller letters to wife Sarah, Fuller Papers, SHSI.; Lucy Chase to folks at home, March 4, 1863, Craney Island, Va., in Swint, *Dear Ones at Home,* 59. The quotation from Russell is from Russell to Assistant Secretary of War John Tucker, Jan. 11, 1863, Boston, AFIC Records, box 3, folder 92, HO. The incident on the Newport News wharf is also referred to in FSSP, ser. 1, 2:137, editor's note mid-page.

49. C. B. Wilder Testimony, AFIC Records, file 2, reel 200, frames 142, 146, NARA.
50. Lucy Chase to "Our folks at Home," Jan. 15, 1863, Craney Island, Va., in Swint, *Dear Ones at Home,* 25.
51. Lucy Chase Testimony, AFIC Records, file 2, reel 200, frames 153–55, NARA.
52. On burning the *Merrimack,* the wood shortage generally, and the constant cold, see Lucy Chase Testimony, AFIC Records, file 2, reel 200, frames 152 and 155, NARA and letter home, Jan. 20, 1863, in Swint, *Dear Ones at Home,* 26–27; for the *Merrimack*'s foundering off Craney, see *OR,* ser. 1, 7:335–36. On the sawmill six miles from Hampton, see Honorable F. W. Bird Testimony, AFIC Records, file 2, reel 200, frame 173, NARA.
53. Palmer Litts to S. S. Jocelyn, Dec. 1, 1862, Craney Island, Va., AMA, H1-4606.
54. On finding the sacking, see Lucy Chase Testimony, AFIC Records, file 2, reel 200, frame 156, NARA. On immediately starting up sewing operations, see Lucy Chase to home folks, Jan. 26, 1863, entry in letter begun Jan. 20, 1863, in Swint, *Dear Folks at Home,* 29.
55. About grain sacks: Lucy Chase Testimony, AFIC Records, file 2, reel 200, frame 156, NARA.
56. Lucy Chase to home folks, Jan. 26, 1863, entry in letter begun Jan. 20, 1863, in Swint, *Dear Folks at Home,* 29; Lucy Chase Testimony, AFIC Records, file 2, reel 200, frames 158–59, NARA. The "A.B.C. card" was probably a chart with the alphabet on one side and short words on the other, which the volunteer Palmer Litts had asked the American Missionary Association to send to Craney when he made his investigatory visit in Dec. 1862. See Litts to Jocelyn, Dec. 1, 1862.
57. Lucy Chase Testimony, AFIC Records, file 2, reel 200, frame 152, NARA.
58. On government farms, see Testimony of F. W. Bird (an independent inspector who twice went to investigate in and around Craney and Suffolk, Va.), AFIC Records, file 2, reel 200, frames 170–73, NARA.
59. Fuller to wife Sarah, May 19, 1862.
60. On the layout of Uniontown, see William O. King to S. S. Jocelyn, April 11, 1863, AMA H1-4717. Sykes Testimony, frame 169. For Portsmouth and Norfolk, see Testimony of Dr. Brown (superintendent of contrabands at Norfolk), AFIC Records, file 2, reel 200, frames 162–63, NARA.
61. H. C. Sanford to American Missionary Association, March 26, 1863, Suffolk, Va., AMA H1-4700; King to Jocelyn, April 11, 1863.
62. On work, see Fuller to Sarah, May 19, 1862; Sykes Testimony, frame 169; Dr. Brown Testimony, frames 162–63, NARA.
63. In Aug. 1863, a frustrated LeBaron Russell was still trying to track down the payrolls for hospital workers in Norfolk and Newport News hospitals, which he had forwarded to Washington, D.C., months earlier. Russell to Howe, Aug. 12 [1863], MacKaye Papers.
64. Sykes Testimony, frame 169.
65. For Wild's Raid, see Edward Augustus Wild Report, Dec. 28, 1863, Edward Augustus Wild Papers, folder 2, Southern Historical Collection, University of North Carolina, Chapel Hill; Richard Reid, "Raising the African Brigade: Early Black Recruitment in Civil War North Carolina," *North Carolina Historical Review* 70 (1993): 266–301; Barton A. Myers, "A More Rigorous Style of Warfare: Wild's Raid, Guerrilla Violence, and Negotiated Neutrality in North-

eastern North Carolina," in *North Carolinians in the Era of the Civil War and Reconstruction*, ed. Paul D. Escott (Chapel Hill: University of North Carolina Press, 2008), 37–68.

66. Myers, "More Rigorous Style of Warfare," and Wayne K. Durrill, *War of Another Kind: A Southern Community in the Great Rebellion* (New York: Oxford University Press, 1990).

67. Corporal John A. Williams (Tenth Virginia Heavy Artillery) to sister, April 22, 1863, near Richmond, John A. Williams Letters, Virginia Historical Society; Dr. Brown to G. T. Chapman, May 25, 1863, Portsmouth, Va., MacKaye Papers; correspondence between Major Generals John Peck, E. D. Keyes, Joseph Hooker, and Henry W. Halleck, April 13, 1863, in *OR*, ser. 1, vol. 25, pt. 2, pp. 206–9. For an account of Suffolk, see Steven A. Cormier, *The Siege of Suffolk: The Forgotten Campaign* (Lynchburg, Va.: H. E. Howard, 1989).

68. See, for example, the report of Colonel Benjamin F. Onderdonk (First New York Mounted Rifles), Aug. 20, 1863, Portsmouth, Va., in *OR*, ser. 1, vol. 29, pt. 1, pp. 70–71.

69. Captain Henry Chambers (Forty-Ninth North Carolina) Diary, March 9, 1864, Suffolk, Va., Henry Chambers Papers, NCDAH; *OR*, ser. 1, 33:3; George S. Burkhardt, *Confederate Rage, Yankee Wrath: No Quarter in the Civil War* (Carbondale: Southern Illinois University Press, 2007), 99–100.

70. Click, *Time Full of Trial*, 10–11. Plymouth was not actually the largest recipient of those liberated by Wild's Raid. Many more went to Roanoke Island, North Carolina, as noted by the Roanoke Island missionary Elizabeth James in a letter to George Whipple, Dec. 19, 1863, Roanoke Island, N.C., AMA 99726. See also Elizabeth James's Feb. 1864 account sent to *American Missionary* and printed April 7, 1864. Most of the approximately twenty-five hundred actually went north to Virginia, which is why Plymouth's increase was not higher. See Myers, "More Rigorous Style of Warfare."

71. Affidavit of Sergeant Samuel Johnson (Second U.S. Colored Cavalry) July 11, 1864, in FSSP, ser. 2, *The Black Military Experience*, 588–89; Durrill, *War of Another Kind*, 204–8.

72. Colonel George Wortham (Fiftieth North Carolina) explained the policy very clearly to one James Lamberton, an owner who made inquiries, in a letter sent from Plymouth on June 28, 1864, Thomas Merritt Pittman Papers, Civil War Correspondence, 1861–1865, NCDAH. He was referring to a Confederate act of Congress, chap. 62, sec. 1, passed Oct. 13, 1862, which stated that slaves recaptured by Confederate forces were "to be sent to nearest depot without unnecessary delay with a register of place & date of arrest but slaves may be at once delivered to owner if claim satisfactorily proved." Section 4 of that same law provided for captured slaves to be put to forced "employment at depot until removed." See W. N. H. Smith, *Abstract of the Law*, in Pittman Papers.

73. The apple brandy promise came from Elisha Cromwell to Captain and Assistant Commissary Lucien D. Starke (Seventeenth North Carolina) May 4, 1864, Tarboro, N.C., Pittman Papers, NCDAH.

74. Perkins to Wortham, June 20, 1864, Edenton, N.C., Pittman Papers (PC 123.16), NCDAH. See also Loftin Hargrave to Wortham, June 2, 1864, Hertford County, N.C., in which Hargrave asked Wortham to "examine your list of captured Negroes, and inform me whether there are any belonging to: C. M. Laverty, Dr. J. T. P. C. Cohoon," of Elizabeth City, "Richard G. Cowper, or Samuel

Moore" of Hertford County, or "Miss Emily Walker," residence unlisted. Pittman Papers. The Pittman Papers are full of similar missives to Wortham and his subordinate officers.

75. Pvt. J. A. Bracy (Fortieth North Carolina) to father, May 4, 1864, Fort Holmes, N.C., Lyman Wilson Sheppard Collection, folder 4, NCDAH.

76. W. N. H. Smith to Wortham, Aug. 2, 1864, Hertford County, N.C., and J. Edmunson (post adjutant) to Major Thomas Sparrow, Aug. 29, 1864, Plymouth, N.C., Pittman Papers, NCDAH.

77. William H. Taylor to Wortham, May 14, 1864, Colerain, Bertie Co., N.C., Pittman Papers, NCDAH.

78. Elisha Cromwell to Captain and Assistant Commissary Lucien D. Starke, May 4, 1864, Tarboro, N.C., Pittman Papers, NCDAH.

79. Pierce, "Contrabands at Fortress Monroe," 640; Richard A. Sauers, *"A Succession of Honorable Victories": The Burnside Expedition in North Carolina* (Dayton, Ohio: Morningside House, 1996), 17–24; Cecelski, *Fire of Freedom*, 51.

80. *OR*, ser. 1, 4:614.

81. For the original Hotel De Afrique, see *Frank Leslie's Illustrated Magazine*, Nov. 1861. For an illustration showing that the hotel had grown and moved by Feb. 1862, see *Harper's Weekly*, Feb. 15, 1862.

82. Burnside to Stanton, March 21, 1862, in *OR*, ser. 1, 9:199–200; Click, *Time Full of Trial*, 9–14.

83. Corporal Samuel Storrow (Forty-Fourth Massachusetts) to parents, Nov. 19, 1862, Newbern, N.C., Samuel Storrow Papers, MHS.

84. Vincent Colyer's Report to the AFIC, May 1863, AFIC Records, file 4, reel 200, frame 445, NARA.

85. Gaston Becton Affidavit, Pension File of Gaston Becton (Thirty-Sixth U.S. Colored Infantry) RG 15, NARA.

86. Kirwan, *Soldiering in North Carolina*, 51–53. Kirwan goes on to say that Nero was an early recruit into Wild's Brigade, suggesting that he might have been Nero Kornegay, who appears in the 1890 Census Schedule of Soldiers and Sailors in the War of the Rebellion as a veteran of the Second North Carolina Colored Infantry; "Kornegay" was a variant of "Carnegie" distinctive to black families in the swath of North Carolina from Duplin County to Lenoir County. There are Kornegays among pension applicants and affiants from those counties (for example, in Gaston Becton's application) and among Freedman's Savings Bank depositors in eastern North Carolina. "United States Freedman's Bank Records, 1865–1874," index and images, FamilySearch, https://familysearch.org/.

87. Colyer's Report, 1863, AFIC Records, file 4, reel 200, frame 430, NARA; Horace James Report to AFIC, Nov. 13, 1863, New Bern, N.C., AFIC Records, box 2, folder 55, HO; Click, *Time Full of Trial*, 10–11. Horace James, Statistics Prepared from the Census of Blacks, in April 1863, and sent with Report to AFIC, 1863, AFIC Records Box 2 HO. 2. According to that census, of 8,302 in New Bern, 4,468 were men, and 4,607 (both men and women) were between the ages of thirteen and fifty. The total under eighteen was 3,024 with slightly more (1,529) males than females, and the total of men and women over age fifty was 671 with men predominating slightly in the fifty-to-eighty age group, and women predominating in the ninety-to-one-hundred and over-one-hundred age groups.

88. Private Edward Bartlett (Forty-Fourth Massachusetts) to sister Martha, Dec. 6,

1862, New Bern, N.C., Edward J. Bartlett Correspondence, MHS; Pension File of Becton; James, *Annual Report*, 41.

89. James Rumley Diary, numerous entries including March 25, 1862, and May 1862 passim, Levi Woodbury Pigott Collection, NCDAH; Sergeant Charles Tubbs (Twenty-Seventh Massachusetts) to wife, July 20, 1862, New Bern, N.C., Charles Henry Tubbs Papers, NCDAH; James Report to AFIC, 1863, 11, AFIC Records, HO; Colyer's Report to the AFIC, 1863, AFIC Records, file 4, reel 200, frames 430–31, 447, and 454–55, NARA; Colyer, *Brief Report of the Services Rendered by the Freed People; Register of Colored Nurses Under Contract [Department of the East] July 16, 1863, to June 14, 1864,* 9–12, RG 94, entry 591, box 1, vol. 1, NARA.

90. Kirwan, *Soldiering in North Carolina,* 51–53; Stanly to Stanton, June 12, 1862, in *OR,* 9:400–401; Colyer's Report to the AFIC, 1863, AFIC Records , file 4, frames 457–58, NARA; James Report to AFIC, 1863, 15, AFIC Records, HO; Judkin Browning, *Shifting Loyalties: The Union Occupation of Eastern North Carolina* (Chapel Hill: University of North Carolina Press, 2011), 76–80, 101.

91. See David Cecelski, *The Waterman's Song: Slavery and Freedom in Maritime North Carolina* (Chapel Hill: University of North Carolina Press, 2001).

92. F. B. Mitchell to Chesson, June 27, 1862, Scotland Neck, N.C., and J. McLean to Chesson, March 1862, John B. Chesson Papers, NCDAH. The McLean letter does not include an exact date, but McLean could hear the "fighting at Newbern," which took place March 14, 1862, as he wrote.

93. To take one example, the fifteen men, women, and children who made it from Sneads Ferry, Onslow County, to Beaufort in a tiny open boat on Aug. 23, 1863 (Rumley Diary, Aug. 23, 1863), were just one small part of the reason for the attempted ban. Salt makers wrote to Major General William Whiting in protest the following month; see James Manney(?) (resident) et al. to Whiting, Sept. 24, 1863, Masonboro Sound. Whiting replied, "The parties named may use their boats under supervision of Col. Washington." Pittman Papers, NCDAH.

94. Gould, *Diary of a Contraband.* Gould's diary aboard the *Cambridge* and the *Niagara* appears on pp. 103–303. His published account of his escape first appeared in the *Anglo-African* on June 11, 1864, under the pen name "Oley" and is reprinted in *Diary of a Contraband,* 73–75.

95. While Union forces controlled the coastal waters of North Carolina with relative security, the amount of actual land they held was slim and always precarious. The precariousness of that hold is a theme in Horace James's *Annual Report.* The diary of James Rumley, a Confederate civilian stuck in Beaufort for the war, persistently records attacks and rumors of attacks on Beaufort, New Bern, and surrounding locales. Finally, the *Official Records* are full of orders and after-action reports that testify to Union forces' shaky hold and constant need for defensive activity in eastern North Carolina.

96. Rumley Diary, Feb. 8, 1865, Beaufort, N.C., NCDAH.

97. Colyer's Report to the AFIC, AFIC Records, file 4, reel 200, frames 435–40, NARA. It is just possible that the man was Gaston Becton's father, who was alternately known as Bill Smith or Bill Carnegie (or Kornegay), because Becton's father (before his father's sale away) and mother lived on plantations in the exact same locations described by Colyer's spy, until the war when his father returned. Becton never named his father but clearly viewed him as a man of daring and initiative. Also, the one child that Colyer's spy mentioned by name was

called Thomas Becton. Gaston Becton's similar slight build (measuring only five feet two inches at the time of his enlistment in 1863 and later obtaining a full height of five feet eight) is suggestive, if certainly not conclusive. Also preventing conclusive identification is the detail that Gaston Becton came into Union lines by himself a bit earlier than Colyer reports the older man returning with his wife and children.

98. Mann, *History of the Forty-Fifth Regiment Massachusetts Volunteer Militia,* 301–2; "News from North Carolina: Progress of the Negro Enlistments," *New York Herald,* June 1, 1863, 5; File of Gaston Becton; Reid, "Raising the African Brigade"; Myers, "More Rigorous Style of Warfare." For the banner from the women of New Bern, see James, *Annual Report,* 23. Becton was almost certainly not eighteen, because he grew roughly six more inches from the time of enlistment until he reached full height.

99. According to Horace James, about forty white families, totaling roughly two hundred individuals, remained on the island. See James Report to AFIC, 1863, 18, AFIC Records, HO.

100. Elizabeth James, "From Miss E. James," *American Missionary* 8 (June 1864): 140–41.

101. James, *Annual Report,* 21.

102. Horace James, Letter to the Public, June 27, 1863, New York City, reprinted in Click, *Time Full of Trial,* app. C, 211–12. James also explicated that same purpose in nearly identical language in the *Annual Report,* 21–22.

103. James Report to AFIC, 1863, 18, AFIC Records, folder 55, HO.

104. For the notion of autonomy as an alternative to liberal individualism, see Tutino, *Capitalism and Community, Patriarchy and Revolution.*

105. James, prefatory notice, in *Annual Report,* 2.

106. Ibid., 24–25, 43; James Report to AFIC, 1863, AFIC Records, box 3, folder 55 HO; James, "A Fragment of the Plan for Colonizing Roanoke Island, NC, with the Families of Colored Soldiers, and Invalid Negroes," RG 105, ser. 2821, NARA. This map is probably the map James refers to in his Nov. 1863 Report and promises to send later under separate cover. Elizabeth James to George Whipple, Dec. 19, 1863, Roanoke Island, N.C., AMA; Lucy Chase to Sarah Chase, Jan. 12, 1865, Roanoke Island, N.C., in Swint, *Dear Ones at Home,* 136–41.

107. James, *Annual Report,* 24; Lucy Chase to Sarah Chase, Jan. 12, 1865, in Swint, *Dear Ones at Home,* 136–41.

108. By Command of Major General Peck, General Orders No. 12, Headquarters District of North Carolina, New Berne, N.C., Sept. 10, 1863, reprinted in James, *Annual Report,* 24. Two paragraphs later on that same page of his *Report,* James reiterated that freedpeople were "to be absolute owners of the soil." He also emphasized the ownership point in his Nov. 1863 Report to the AFIC Records, box 3, HO.

109. James, *Annual Report,* 40–43; Lucy Chase to Sarah Chase, Jan. 12, 1865, 138–39.

110. James Report to AFIC, 1863, 8–9, AFIC Records, box 3, HO ; E. A. Williams, "Industrial School, Roanoke Island," *National Freedman,* Dec. 15, 1865, 347–48; Sarah Freeman, "Industrial School, Roanoke Island," *National Freedman,* Aug. 15, 1865, 215–16.

111. James Report to AFIC, 1863, 2, AFIC Records, box 3, HO.

112. Elizabeth James to George Whipple, Dec. 25, 1863, portion of a letter begun Dec. 19, 1863, AMA.

113. On stovepipes, which soldiers were especially likely to filch from schoolrooms, see Lucy Chase to Sarah Chase, Jan. 12, 1865, in Swint, *Dear Ones at Home*, 139.

114. "Letter from Mrs. S. P. Freeman," *Freedmen's Advocate,* Oct. 1864, 34, and "A Letter to Be Read and Circulated, in Public and Private Meeting, in Aid of the Freedmen," *Freedmen's Advocate,* Nov. 1864, 38.

115. James Report to AFIC, 1863, AFIC Records box 3, HO.

116. James, *Annual Report*, 16, 18, 22; Horace James Report to AFIC, 1863, AFIC Records, box 3, HO.

117. James Report to AFIC, 1863, 11, AFIC Records, box 3, HO.

118. Freedmen of Roanoke Island, N.C., to Mr. President, March 9, 1865, and Roanoke Island to Secretary of War, March 9, 1865, Letters Received, ser. 15, Washington Headquarters, RG 105, NARA, also reprinted in FSSP, ser. 1, 2:231–35.

119. James to Colonel J. S. Fullerton, July 10, 1865, New Bern, N.C., Letters Received, ser. 15, Washington Headquarters, RG 105, NARA, also reprinted in FSSP, ser. 1, 2:231–35.

120. Elizabeth James to George Whipple, Dec. 19, 1863, Roanoke Island, N.C., AMA; James, *Annual Report*, 15; *Register of Colored Nurses Under Contract [Department of the East], July 16, 1863, to June 14, 1864,* 9–12, NARA.

121. Rumley Diary, Jan. n.d., 1864, Beaufort, N.C., NCDAH.

122. James, *Annual Report,* 15–16.

123. Ibid., "Appendix, Jan.–June 1865," 57–58.

124. Rumley Diary, April 14, 1865, Beaufort, N.C., NCDAH.

125. On Samuel Arms, see Whitney Gould, "Black Settlers Leave Mixed Memories," *Milwaukee Journal Sentinel,* Jan. 7, 1997; Jack Holzhueter Papers: Black Settlers in Early Wisconsin Collection, box 1, folder 2, SHSW; and U.S. Census 1910, Forest District Vernon County, Wisconsin, Enumeration District 136, sheet 6B, family 122, NARA, microfilm publication T624.

126. War Journal, Benjamin Franklin Heuston Papers, box 1, folder 3, Special Collections and Area Research Center, Murphy Library, University of Wisconsin–La Crosse.

127. Will Sherman, WPA Narratives, 3:292–96.

128. Colonel Charles D. Kerr (126th Illinois Cavalry) quoted in Anne Sarah Rubin, *Through the Heart of Dixie: Sherman's March and American Memory* (Chapel Hill: University of North Carolina Press, 2014), 89–90.

129. B. K. Lee Testimony, AFIC Records, file 3, reel 299, frames 229–30, NARA.

130. Robert Smalls Testimony, AFIC Records, file 3, reel 200, frames 278–79, NARA; "Robert Smalls, Captain of the Gun-Boat 'Planter,'" *Harper's Weekly,* June 14, 1862, 372–73; Admiral Samuel Du Pont to Gideon Welles, May 14, 1862, in FSSP, ser. 1, 1:122; War Journal, Heuston Papers, box 1, folder 3, University of Wisconsin-La Crosse; General Rufus Saxton to William Eaton, March 11, 1865, Beaufort, S.C., N. Ritter to Eaton, May 25, 1865, Beaufort, S.C., and A. J. Ketchum to Eaton, June 14, 1865, Savannah, William F. Eaton Letters, Maine Historical Society.

131. Franklin Sanborn, "Harriet Tubman," *Commonwealth,* July 10, 1863, in *Harriet Tubman and the Fight for Freedom: A Brief History with Documents,* ed. Lois E. Horton (Boston: Bedford/St. Martin's, 2013), 132–33.

132. On numbers, see Report of Edward L. Pierce to Secretary Chase, Feb. 3, 1862, in *The Rebellion Record: Supplement I,* ed. Frank Moore (New York: G. P. Putnam's Sons, 1864), 303; AFIC, *Preliminary Report* (1863); Rufus Saxton Testi-

mony, AFIC Records, file 3, reel 200, frame 180, NARA; Lee Testimony, AFIC Records, file 3, reel 200, frame 226, NARA; Edward Philbrick, Feb. 19, 1862, in Pearson, *Letters from Port Royal,* 1.

133. In 1865, Edward Philbrick's clerk contrasted the "shivery, hungry, so lean and bony and sickly" condition of the former slaves who followed Sherman's army from "the interior of Georgia" to the Department of the South with the comparatively wholesome condition of "persons left in their own homes, and with their own clothing and property, besides their share of the plunder from their masters' houses" in 1861 when Confederates fled the Sea Islands and Union occupation began. See "W.C.G.," Jan. 23, 1865, Savannah, in Pearson, *Letters from Port Royal,* 307–8.

134. On African Americans' preference for growing food over cotton, see Pierce, Report to Chase, Feb. 3, 1862, 317; Laura Towne Diary, April 18, 1862, Coffin Plantation on St. Helena Island, and Laura Towne to family, April 24, 1862, Pope's Plantation, St. Helena's Island, in Holland, *Letters and Diary of Laura M. Towne,* 9, 16–18. On food abundance and monotony in 1861 and 1862, see Edward Philbrick to wife, March 14, 1862, Coffin's Point, S.C., in Pearson, *Letters from Port Royal,* 13, and Testimony of Frederick A. Eustis (who especially complained about too much acreage devoted to corn and potatoes), AFIC Records, file 3, reel 200, frame 333, NARA. Distribution complications did make for isolated occasional food shortages, as Commodore Samuel DuPont noted in a Feb. 25, 1862, letter to Henry Winter Davis, cited in Willie Lee Rose, *Rehearsal for Reconstruction: The Port Royal Experiment* (1964; Athens: University of Georgia Press, 1999), 20.

135. Lee Testimony, AFIC Records, file 3, reel 200, frame 226, NARA; Laura Towne Testimony, AFIC Records, file 3, reel 200, frame 252, NARA; New England Freedmen's Aid Society Records, MS N-101 Massachusetts Historical Society.

136. Sherman to Nobles, Dec. 3, 1861, Port Royal, S.C., in *OR,* ser. 1, vol. 6, chap. 15, pp. 200–201.

137. Rose, *Rehearsal for Reconstruction,* 67–69.

138. Saxton Testimony, AFIC Records, file 3, reel 200, esp. frame 183, NARA; Pierce, report to Chase, Feb. 3, 1862, 301–14; the 2.5 million pounds of cotton figure comes from Pierce, 304.

139. Pierce, Second Report to Secretary Chase, June 2, 1862, in Moore, *Rebellion Record: Supplement I,* 317.

140. General Thomas W. Sherman, General Orders No. 9, Requesting Help with Freedmen, Feb. 6, 1862, in *OR,* ser. 1, vol. 6, chap. 15, pp. 223–24.

141. For initial expectations, see, for example, the Reverend Mansfield French to American Missionary Association, Jan. 4, 1862, Washington, D.C., AMA; Hughes, *Letters and Recollections of John Murray Forbes,* chap. 12. The clash between various constituencies and their differing hopes and expectations is a main theme of Willie Lee Rose's classic work, *Rehearsal for Reconstruction.* Participants at the time also recognized the clash; see, for example, Forbes to Senator Charles Sumner, April 1862, Beaufort, S.C., in Hughes , *Letters and Recollections of John Murray Forbes,* 300–302. That Forbes was wrong in his assumptions of slavery's inefficiency is made clear by Baptist, *The Half Has Never Been Told.*

142. The Gideonite Elizabeth Botume includes the full text of the oath, to which others also referred, in Botume, *First Days Amongst the Contrabands,* 30.

143. Rose, *Rehearsal for Reconstruction*, chap. 2; New England Freedmen's Aid Society Records; Pearson, *Letters from Port Royal;* Solomon Bradley Testimony, AFIC Records, file 3, reel 200, frames 274–77, NARA.
144. Saxton Testimony, AFIC Records, File 3, reel 200, frames 193–96, 200–207, NARA; Tax Commissioner A. D. Smith Testimony, AFIC Records, file 3, reel 200, frames, 213–24, 225, NARA; Rose, *Rehearsal for Reconstruction*, chap. 10.
145. Charles P. Ware, July 30, 1862, and Aug. 14, 1862, Beaufort, S.C., in Pearson, *Letters from Port Royal*, 75, 83.
146. A. J. Ketchum of the Quartermaster Department explained paying by task to AFIC commissioners: A. J. Ketchum Testimony, AFIC Records, file 3, reel 200, frames 315–19, NARA. Variation existed as to how big a "task" was. Harry McMillan, the freedman quoted just below, defined a "task" as half an acre. The variations might have had to do with soil fertility, because the number of rows a quarter acre of rich soil could support might have approximated the number of rows half an acre of more marginal soil could support. On the variability of task size in South Carolina agriculture, see Saville, *Work of Reconstruction*, 53, n60.
147. Harry McMillan Testimony, AFIC Records, file 3, reel 200, frames 311–12, NARA.
148. Clara Barton Diary, May 23, 1863, Clara Barton Papers, reel 1, LOC. On Barton and Gage, see Stephen B. Oates, *A Woman of Valor: Clara Barton and the Civil War* (New York: Free Press, 1994), pt. 3, and Ishbel Ross, *Angel of the Battlefield: The Life of Clara Barton* (New York: Harper, 1956), chap. 5.
149. Rose, *Rehearsal for Reconstruction*, 294–96.
150. "The Constitution of the Educational Commission" (later renamed the New England Freedmen's Aid Commission, then the Freedmen's Aid Society) adopted at the Feb. 7, 1862, meeting, Boston, New England Freedmen's Aid Society Records, MS N-101, box 1, folder 1, MHS.
151. See Mansfield French to George Whipple, March 8 and 18, 1862, Hilton Head, S.C., AMA; New England Freedmen's Aid Society Records; W.C.G. (clerk to Edward Philbrick), May 30, 1862, Pine Grove plantation, St. Helena, S.C., in Pearson, *Letters from Port Royal*, 60; Rose, *Rehearsal for Reconstruction*.
152. Harriet Ware, April 29, 1862, St. Helena Island, S.C., in Pearson, *Letters from Port Royal*, 24–25.
153. Botume, *First Days Amongst the Contrabands*, 41–49, 62, 66. Freedpeople referred to refugees who came to Beaufort either singly or as a result of Union raids as "Combees"; see, for example, ibid., 93.
154. Taylor, *Reminiscences of My Life in Camp*, 34, 37–38, 52.
155. Harriet Ware, June 9, 1862, St. Helena, S.C., in Pearson, *Letters from Port Royal*, 65–66.
156. Map Showing the Distribution of the Slave Population of the Southern States of the United States Compiled from the Census of 1860, Geography and Map Division, LOC; Peter Wood, *Black Majority: Negroes in Colonial South Carolina from 1670 Through the Stono Rebellion* (New York: W. W. Norton Reissue, 1996); FSSP, ser. 1, 1:103–4.
157. See Russell Duncan, *Freedom's Shore: Tunis Campbell and the Georgia Freedmen* (Athens: University of Georgia Press, 1986).
158. Charles Wood, "Manuscript History Concerning the Pension Claim of Harriet Tubman," Records of the House of Representatives, 1789–2011, Accompanying Papers of the 55th Congress, RG 233, NARA. See also Kate Clifford Larson,

Bound for the Promised Land: Harriet Tubman, Portrait of an American Hero (New York: Ballantine Books, 2004), chap. 10.

159. The recklessness that irritated the mature women had a basis in early brain development: recent neuropsychological research confirms that development in men's brains' prefrontal cortex, the region associated with restraint, judgment, and impulse control, lags well beyond women's all through adolescence and early adulthood, not evening out until the late twenties or early thirties. For a concise overview of recent research aimed at general readers, see Sandra Aamodt and Sam Wang, *Welcome to Your Child's Brain: How the Mind Grows from Birth to University* (New York: Oneworld, 2011).

160. Harriet Ware, May 13, 1862, St. Helena, S.C., in Pearson, *Letters from Port Royal*, 43.

161. Harriet Ware, May 22, 1862, St. Helena, S.C., in ibid., 52. In general, white Northern men were less apt than women to recognize black expertise, but even Harriet's brother Charles admitted, "They have not been working cotton for nothing for so many years," and he could even concede workers' point when they insisted, "We won't be driven by nobody . . . either by white man or black man." Charles P. Ware, Nov. 16, 1862, Beaufort, S.C., in Pearson, *Letters from Port Royal*, 111–12.

162. Laura Towne, April 27, 1862, St. Helena, in Holland, *Letters and Diary of Laura M. Towne*, 18–19; Harriet Ware, April 29, 1862, St. Helena, in Pearson, *Letters from Port Royal*, 24–25; New England Freedmen's Aid Society Records, MS N-101, MHS. Thavolia Glymph writes of the "politics of dress" among white and black women after emancipation, underscoring that the importance of what she wore to a woman who had spent her life enslaved and in possession of a single (and unchosen) garment a year was far from trivial, although Glymph's emphasis differs a bit from that here, in that in her analysis the significance of buying ready-made clothes (not dry goods to make them) to the freedwoman Virginia Newman and the former slave Mollie was the materiality of a specific article of clothing rather than the autonomy of making or choosing it. See Glymph, *Out of the House of Bondage*, 10, 204–9.

163. Towne Testimony, AFIC Records, file 3, reel 200, frame 253, NARA. On this point, Towne at least showed willingness to stand by her belief by remaining in South Carolina for over two decades.

164. Lee Testimony, AFIC Records, file 3, reel 200, frames 231–32, NARA.

165. All from testimony to AFIC, AFIC Records, file 3, reel 200, NARA. Saxton, frames 186–87; Higginson, frame 336; Hooper, frames 402–3; Ketchum, frames 320–22.

166. Henry Judd Testimony, AFIC Records, file 3, reel 200, frames 265–77, NARA.

167. Smalls Testimony, AFIC Records, file 3, reel 200, frames 281–83, NARA.

168. Saxton Testimony, AFIC Records, file 3, reel 200, frame 184, NARA.

169. Towne Testimony, frame 244; Smalls Testimony, frame 284, both AFIC Records, file 3, reel 200, NARA.

170. Taylor, *Reminiscences of My Life in Camp*, 45.

171. Barton to Brown and Duer (editors of the *American Baptist*), March 13, 1864, Washington, D.C. (but writing about Hilton Head), Clara Barton Papers, reel 63, LOC; Ross, *Angel of the Battlefield*, chaps. 10 and 11; David H. Burton, *Clara Barton: In the Service of Humanity* (Westport, Conn.: Greenwood Press, 1995), chap. 5; American Red Cross, www.redcross.org/about-us/history.

172. Barton Diary, April 7, 1863, Barton Papers, reel 1.

173. "How the Freedmen Live," *St. Augustine (Fla.) Commercial Advertiser,* Aug. 21, 1863.

174. Susie Butler, Aug. 1862, St. Simons Island, Ga., in Taylor, *Reminiscences of My Life in Camp,* 40–41. In later years, Susie Butler King Taylor remembered, "Several of the men disappeared . . . in this way."

175. Harriet Ware, May 13, 1862, St. Helena, S.C., in Pearson, *Letters from Port Royal,* 43.

176. Towne Diary, May 12, 1862, St. Helena, S.C., in Holland, *Letters and Diary of Laura M. Towne,* 41.

177. On nonpayment, see Rufus Saxton to Secretary of War Stanton, Oct. 29, 1862, Beaufort, S.C., in FSSP, ser. 2, 53. On slow enlistment, see Edward Philbrick, Jan. 2, 1863, and Harriet Ware, Feb. 8, 1863, St. Helena, S.C., in Pearson, *Letters from Port Royal,* 136, 153.

178. Saxton to Stanton, Aug. 16, 1862, in *OR,* ser. 1, 14: 364–66; Laura Towne, July 14, 1862, St. Helena, S.C., in Holland, *Letters and Diary of Laura M. Towne,* 73–76; S. W. Gordon to Flag Officer DuPont, March 30, 1862, in FSSP, ser. 1, 1:118–20; Philbrick, Jan. 2, 1863, and Harriet Ware, Jan. 31, 1863, St. Helena, S.C., in Pearson, *Letters from Port Royal,* 136, 150; Rose, *Rehearsal for Reconstruction,* 180–83.

179. Special Field Orders, No. 15, Headquarters Military Division of the Mississippi, Jan. 16, 1865, Orders and Circulars, ser. 44, Adjutant General's Office, RG 94, NARA.

180. "A Great Scheme for the Georgia Negroes," *New Orleans Tribune,* Jan. 31, 1864, 2.

181. Articles of furniture and other property were specific items cited by a three-man committee who would later protest to both the Freedmen's Bureau and the president when the lands on which they established homesteads were returned to former Confederate landowners (see chapter 5). Henry Bram et al. to Major General O. O. Howard [Oct. 28?, 1865]; and Henry Bram et al. to the President of these United States, Oct. 28, 1865; B-53 1865 and P-27 1865, Letters Received (ser. 15), Washington Headquarters, RG 105, NARA.

182. William Eaton (captain and Freedmen's Bureau agent) to Saxton, Jan. 1, March 11, April 12, and May 25, 1865, Savannah, Eaton Letters, Maine Historical Society; Saxton to Eaton, March 11, 1865, Beaufort, S.C., Eaton Letters; Douglas R. Egerton, *Wars of Reconstruction: The Brief, Violent History of America's Most Progressive Era* (New York: Bloomsbury Press, 2014), 93–97. The library was on St. Simons.

183. Campbell to Eaton, Oct. 12, 1865, St. Catherine Island, Ga., Eaton Letters, Maine Historical Society.

TWO · CONSTANT TURBULENCE

1. Photograph: Former slaves of Jefferson Davis at Baton Rouge, ca. 1863, owned by Louisiana State Museum, http://www.louisianadigitallibrary.org/cdm/sin gleitem/collection/AAW/id/107/rec/2.

2. For more on this point, see chapter 3 below.

3. Ulysses S. Grant, General Orders No. 14, Feb. 26, 1862, Fort Donelson, Tenn., in Simon, *Papers of Ulysses S. Grant,* 4:290–91, digital edition at http://digital .library.msstate.edu/cdm/compoundobject/collection/USG_volume/id/17403

/rec/4. On slaves owned by Woods, Lewis, and Company, see Susan Hawkins, "The African American Experience at Forts Henry, Heiman, and Donelson, 1862–1867," *Tennessee Historical Quarterly* 61 (Winter 2002): 224. For more on Forts Henry and Donelson, see John Cimprich, *Slavery's End in Tennessee, 1861–1865* (Tuscaloosa: University of Alabama Press, 1985).

4. Corporal Mitchell Andrew Thompson (Eighty-Third Illinois) to wife Eliza, April 10, 1863, Fort Donelson, Tenn., Mitchell Andrew Thompson Letters, Civil War Collection, reel 17, box F24, folder 6, TSLA.

5. Thompson to wife Eliza, June 8 and 26, 1864, Fort Donelson, Tenn., Thompson Letters, Civil War Collection, reel 17, box F24, folder 6, TSLA. The June 26 letter was the last that Thompson wrote before being killed by Confederate guerrillas, demonstrating the ever presence of danger at Fort Donelson.

6. "Ground Plot of Ethiopian Hospitals, Nashville, Tennessee," "Ground Plot of Contraband Camp, Nashville, Tennessee," "Quarters for Railroad Employees," "Government Bakery on College Street," "Commercial Structure on College St. Between Broad & Spring—Hospital No. 16 (Colored)," all in James Allen Hoobler Collection, box 4, TSLA.

7. *OR*, ser. 1, vol. 27, pt. 2, p. 268.

8. Morton to Captain R. D. Massey (adjutant of U.S. Colored Troops), Dec. 4, 1863, Nashville, filed with AFIC Records, file 7, reel 201, frames 89–91, NARA; George Stearns Testimony, AFIC Records, file 7, reel 201, frames 69–70, NARA; Buell to Morton, Aug. 20 and 29, 1862, in *OR*, ser. 1, vol. 26, pt. 2, p. 408; Hood and Bostwick, "Letter to the Secretary of War," in Bostwick and Hood, *Report upon the Condition and Treatment of Colored Refugees*. For an overview of black labor at Fort Negley, see Bobby Lovett, "Nashville's Fort Negley: A Symbol of Blacks' Involvement with the Union Army," *Tennessee Historical Society Quarterly* 41, no. 1 (1982).

9. Stearns to Robert Dale Owen, Nov. 24, 1863, Nashville, AFIC Records, file 7, reel 201, frames 85–88, NARA. The letter was not part of the AFIC's file 7 testimony originally, but Owen filed it with that testimony. The point of Stearns's letter was to demonstrate to the AFIC that tactics other than those used by Morton not only were possible but would yield better results.

10. Roll of Negroes Impressed for Service on the North-Western Railroad, Oct. 1863, TSLA.

11. See William Mark Eames Papers, TSLA (letter of July 2, 1862, about the berries), and Abigail Dutton Papers, TSLA.

12. The Northwestern Freedmen's Aid Commission reported sending teachers to Nashville in the minutes of its very first annual meeting. NWFAC, *Minutes of the First Annual Meeting*, NL. Benjamin Franklin Heuston of the Twenty-Second Wisconsin commented frequently on schools in Nashville; see Heuston Papers, box 1.

13. Corporal Benjamin Franklin Heuston Diary, Dec. 25, 1863, Heuston Papers, box 1, folder 6.

14. See Dutton to Dear Ones at Home, Nov. 4 and 7, 1864, Nashville, Dutton Papers, for implementation of the Special Diet Kitchen. In Feb. 1865, Dutton stayed with Superintendent Barnard's young children so that he and his wife could travel to Chattanooga, Huntsville, and Decatur to encourage the adoption of Special Diet Kitchens there. See Dutton to father, Feb. 21, 1865 Dutton Papers, TSLA. By that time, Dutton herself had been reassigned to oversee the

Orphan's Home at Nashville, run by the Freedmen's Aid Society (see letter of Feb. 5, 1865).

15. General John Phelps, Proclamation to the Loyal Citizens of the South-West, Dec. 4, 1861, in FSSP, ser. 1, 1:199–201.

16. Several works discuss the war in New Orleans, including Chester G. Hearn, *The Capture of New Orleans, 1862* (Baton Rouge: Louisiana State University Press, 2005); Chester G. Hearn, *When the Devil Came Down to Dixie: Ben Butler in New Orleans* (Baton Rouge: Louisiana State University Press, 2000); Peyton McCrary, *Abraham Lincoln and Reconstruction: The Louisiana Experiment* (Princeton, N.J.: Princeton University Press, 1978); Rodrigue, *Reconstruction in the Cane Fields;* and Adam Rothman, *Beyond Freedom's Reach: A Kidnapping in the Twilight of Slavery* (Cambridge, Mass.: Harvard University Press, 2015). On Paine and Williams, see Paine, *Wisconsin Yankee in Confederate Bayou Country.*

17. The quartermaster and other army records are full of freedpeople working for the army. For one specific personal account of constructing Forts Jackson and St. Philip and working on the artillery guns, see Major John W. DeForest to My Dear Friend Lillie, Aug. 7, 1862, Camp Parapet, Carrollton, La., Lillie Devereaux Blake Papers, box 6, folder 9, MOHS.

18. Cecelski, *Fire of Freedom,* 51–57; Paine, *Wisconsin Yankee in Confederate Bayou Country;* Reports of Scout Horace Bell, Oct. 1864, reported in office of Chief Signal Officer, New Orleans, Correspondence, Reports, Appointments, and Other Records Relating to Individual Scouts, Guides, Spies, and Detectives, 1861–1867, RG 110, entry 36, box 1, NARA.

19. For a starting point on the Louisiana Native Guards, see James G. Hollandsworth, *The Louisiana Native Guards: The Black Military Experience During the Civil War* (Baton Rouge: Louisiana State University Press, 1998).

20. DeForest to "My Dear Friend," Oct. 8, 1862, New Orleans, Blake Papers, box 9, folder 6, MOHS.

21. NWFAC, *Second Annual Report,* 14, NL.

22. Major General William F. Smith, Judge Advocate Nicolas Bowen, and Jas. T. Brady, Esqr., Smith-Brady Commission on Corrupt Practices in the South, *Final Report,* Sept. 23, 1864, RG 94, entry 737, NARA.

23. Private George Flanders (Fifth Kansas Cavalry) to brother, July 22, 1862, Helena, Ark., George E. Flanders Letters, Kansas State Historical Society.

24. Officer in Fourth Iowa Cavalry to Samuel J. Kirkwood (governor of Iowa), Aug. 31, 1862, Helena, Ark., Samuel J. Kirkwood Papers, box 1, folder 18, SHSI; George Flanders to brother, July 22, 1862.

25. George Flanders to brother, Helena, Ark., Flanders Letters, Kansas State Historical Society; Corporal Samuel Kirkpatrick (Eleventh Wisconsin) to parents and siblings, Aug. 7, 1862, Old Town, Ark., Samuel Kirkpatrick Letters, SHSW. Flanders approved of the freedom certificates; Kirkpatrick did not. For Curtis's careful protestations about "enticement," see, for example, Luther T. Collier et al. to Curtis, Dec. 8, 1862, Chillicothe, Mo.; and Lieutenant Colonel A. Jacobson to Major H. Z. Curtis (assistant adjutant general, Dept. of Missouri), Feb. 23, 1863, Rolla, Mo., with endorsements on back from S. R. Curtis, Department of Missouri, RG 393, box 9, pt. 1, entry 2593, NARA.

26. George Flanders to brother, July 22, 1862, George E. Flanders, Kansas State Historical Society.

27. Lieutenant and Acting Assistant Quartermaster B. O. Carr to General Curtis,

July 18, 1862, Helena, Ark., in FSSP, ser. 1, 3:659–60; Private Friedrich Leder-garber (Twelfth Missouri) to uncle, Sept. 2, 1862, Helena, Ark., Engelmann-Kircher Papers, box 4½, ISHL.

28. William A. Pile Testimony, AFIC Records, file 7, reel 201, frame 139, NARA; Captain W. R. Hodges, "The Western Sanitary Commission and What It Did for the Sick and Wounded of the Union Armies from 1861 to 1865, with Mention of the Services of Companion James E. Yeatman, Therewith" (read before the Commandery of the State of Missouri Military Order of the Loyal Legion of the United States, Feb. 3, 1906), St. Louis Sanitation Collection, folder 1, MOHS.

29. Major General B. M. Prentiss to Major General J. M. Schofield, June 16, 1863, Helena, Ark., Department of Missouri, RG 393, box 9, pt. 1, entry 2593, NARA; Brockett and Vaughan, *Woman's Work in the Civil War*, 701; Maria R. Mann to the Reverend Ropes, April 13, 1863, Helena, Ark., Mary Peabody Tyler Mann Papers, LOC.

30. Brigadier General James R. Slack (Forty-Seventh Indiana) to wife, Sept. 11, 1862, Helena, Ark., James R. Slack Papers, box 1, folder 12, INSL.

31. See, for example, FSSP, ser. 1, vol. 3, 3:674–76. The superintendent of freedmen schools and Sanitary Commission agent William Allen commented on how variable white Union troops could be in their moods and attitudes, particularly in bad weather. In the rainy fall of 1864, he attributed Missouri soldiers' bad treatment of freedpeople to bad weather. "They are heartily tired of dallying here in this disagreeable hole," Allen noted. See William Allen to wife, Oct. 6, 1864, Helena, Ark., William F. Allen Family Papers, box 2, folder 1, SHSW. By the end of that same month, Allen claimed treatment had notably improved.

32. Coffin, *Reminiscences*, 640–46; Sperry, *History of the 33d Iowa Volunteer Regiment*, 264 n14; Gregory J. W. Urwin, "'We Cannot Treat Negroes . . . as Prisoners of War': Racial Atrocities and Reprisals in Civil War Arkansas," *Civil War History* 42 (Sept. 1996): 193–210.

33. Solomon Lambert, Arkansas Narratives, vol. 2, pt. 4, pp. 231–32, WPA Narratives; Roster of the 2nd LA Battery USCT Light Artillery at American Civil War Research Database, accessed via asp6n32.alexanderstreet.com.proxy.library .georgetown.edu/cwdb and also available at http://www.civilwardata.com; Dyer, *Compendium of the War of the Rebellion*, vol. 3. Other regiments also participated in the guarding of Helena, for example, the Fifty-Fourth, Sixty-Third, Sixty-Fourth, and Sixty-Ninth U.S. Colored Troops, mentioned by Allen in his Oct. 6, 1864, letter to his wife, Allen Family Papers, box 2, folder 1, SHSW.

34. John Eaton to Reverend C. B. Boynton, Sept. 11, 1863, Headquarters at Vicksburg, Miss. (reporting on Helena and Memphis), RG 105, M1914, NARA; Pile Testimony, AFIC Records, File 7, reel 201, frame 141, NARA.

35. Northwestern Freedmen's Aid Commission, *Minutes of the First Annual Meeting*, 11, NL; Ladies' Contraband Relief Society Testimony, St. Louis, AFIC Records, file 7, reel 201, frame 178, NARA; David Todd to brother, Pine Bluff, Ark., April 16, 1864, David Todd and Charlotte Farnsworth Letters, Illinois History and Lincoln Collection, University of Illinois.

36. Allen to wife, Sept. 27, 1864, Helena, Ark., Allen Family Papers, box 2, folder 1, SHSW.

37. Allen to wife, Oct. 31, 1864, Helena, Ark., Allen Family Papers, box 2, folder 1, SHSW.

38. Allen to wife, Oct. 14–16 and 31, 1864, Helena, Ark., Allen Family Papers, box 2, folder 1, SHSW.; Moore, "Reminiscences," 292.
39. Pile Testimony, AFIC Records, File 7, reel 201, frame 145, NARA.
40. Eaton, *Lincoln, Grant, and the Freedmen,* 2–3.
41. For one example of livestock and implements brought to camp and appropriated by the Union army, see James Alexander to John Eaton included in Eaton's 1863 Report to Jocelyn of the AMA, AFIC Records, file 6, reel 200, frame 574, NARA.
42. Grant, *Personal Memoirs of U. S. Grant,* 1:353. For an example of Grant's lack of strong leanings on slavery, see, for example, a letter to his father in which he admits, "I have no hobby of my own with regard to the negro, either to effect his freedom or to continue his bondage," but says that above all he would "execute" any measure passed by Congress or advocated by the president. As far as he was concerned, "one enemy at a time is enough, and when he is subdued it will be time enough to settle personal differences." Ulysses S. Grant to Jesse Grant, Aug. 3, 1862, in Simon, *Papers of Ulysses S. Grant,* 5:264, available online at http://digital.library.msstate.edu/cdm/ref/collection/USG_volume/id/17896.
43. See Transportation Orders Issued 1862, RG 393, pt. 2, entry 1102, NARA.
44. Pierson Cade: June 9–11, 1861; John, Bill, and Ann: June 17, 1861, Camp Defiance Report of Guard Mounted for June 1861, RG 393, pt. 2, entry 1100, 1097, NARA.
45. Naval officers of the Red Rover, for example, delivered nine "contrabands" discovered working on "rebel fortifications" while garbed in full Confederate uniform in May 1862. Miscellaneous Records, 1861–1866, RG 393, pt. 2, entry 1105, NARA.
46. Correspondence between A. G. Baxter (chief quartermaster for the District of Cairo) and Stanton, Jan. 1863, Consolidated Correspondence file, "Cairo, Illinois," RG 92, NARA. Simon, *Papers of Ulysses S. Grant,* 6:317, long annotation, available online at http://digital.library.msstate.edu/cdm/ref/collection/USG_volume/id/14868. Part of the reason for the shortage was that wages (at that point, to the predominantly white labor force) were both delayed and short—only 40 percent of what had been offered at time of hiring—and so workers were refusing to work and sometimes leaving Cairo entirely.
47. Consolidated Correspondence file, "Cairo, Illinois" RG 92, ; Special Orders No. 34, Aug. 29, 1862, RG 393, pt. 2, entries 1084, 1094, NARA; Brigadier General James M. Tuttle to Stanton, Sept. 18, 1862, Cairo, Ill., and Stanton to Tuttle, Sept. 18, 1862, in *OR,* ser. 3, 2:569, 663.
48. Engelmann to sister Josephine, Aug. 9, 1862, Bolivar, Tenn., Engelmann-Kircher Papers, box 3.
49. *General Laws of the State of Illinois, Passed by the Eighteenth General Assembly, Convened January 3, 1853,* 57–60.
50. Corporal Mitchell Thompson to brother William, Sept. 2, 1862, Cairo, Ill., Thompson Letters, Civil War Collection, reel 17, box F24, folder 6.
51. *Chicago Tribune,* Sept. 23, 1862.
52. *Salem Advocate,* Oct. 2, 1862.
53. Davis to Lincoln, Oct. 14, 1862, Abraham Lincoln Papers, LOC.
54. Michael Johnson, "Out of Egypt: The Migration of Former Slaves to the Midwest During the 1860s in Comparative Perspective," in *Crossing Boundaries: Comparative History of Black People in Diaspora,* ed. Darlene Clark Hine and Jacqueline McLeod (Bloomington: Indiana University Press, 1999), 232. For a

book-length treatment of freedpeople's wartime migration into the Midwest, see Leslie A. Schwalm, *Emancipation's Diaspora: Race and Reconstruction in the Upper Midwest* (Chapel Hill: University of North Carolina Press, 2009).

55. See Rogers, *War Pictures*, chaps. 6, 7, and 10, http://babel.hathitrust.org/cgi /pt?id=loc.ark:/13960/t7np2gw6m;view=1up;seq=18; *Fond du Lac Weekly Commonwealth*, Sept. 24 and Oct. 22, 1862.

56. *Fond du Lac Weekly Commonwealth* and *Weekly Patriot* throughout Sept. and Oct. 1862. The "tombstone" line comes from *Weekly Patriot*, Oct. 25, 1862, 5.

57. Robert Cook, *Baptism of Fire: The Republican Party in Iowa, 1838–1878* (Ames: Iowa State University Press, 1994), esp. 142–45.

58. See, for example, Private Thomas Stuart Birch (Second Iowa) Diary, vol. 4, June 11, 1862, near Corinth, Miss., Thomas Stuart Birch Papers, Special Collections, Woodruff Library, Emory University, for one example of a berry-picking episode, and Coffin, *Reminiscences*, 632–35.

59. Colonel J. S. Wilcox (Fifty-Second Illinois) to *Bureau County Republican*, July 15, 1862, near Corinth, Miss., *Bureau County Republican*, Aug. 7, 1862, 2, ISHL; Private Stephan Werly, (Twenty-First Missouri) Diary, Aug. 10, 1862, near Corinth, Miss., WHMC-Columbia.

60. General Ulysses S. Grant, Special Orders No. 15, Nov. 11, 1862, La Grange, Tenn., in Eaton, *Grant, Lincoln, and the Freedmen*, 5. Prior to Eaton's appointment, Grant appointed superintendents for single locations, such as Grenville M. Dodge at Grand Junction in Aug. 1862, RG 393, pt. 2, entry 6159, NARA. Even though the terms of the Emancipation Proclamation issued two months earlier rendered the term "contraband" obsolete throughout much of the occupied South by denominating former slaves as freedpeople once the Final Proclamation went into effect on Jan. 1, 1863, personnel in charge of the camps continued to be known as superintendents of contrabands. As Chaplain James Alexander, the superintendent of contrabands at Corinth, noted in 1863, "contraband" was "the term by which the Freedmen are better known in the South-West than other." Alexander to Samuel G. Howe, Sept. 1, 1863, AFIC Records, box 1, folder 1, HO.

61. Coffin, *Reminiscences*, 626.

62. Both Cam Walker in "Corinth" and Timothy B. Smith in *Corinth 1862: Siege, Battle, Occupation* (Lawrence: University Press of Kansas, 2012) identify Corinth as a "model" that was "superior to most other camps," despite its many imperfections. Writing from Corinth in Aug. 1863, the Reverend A. D. Olds stated, "It is believed that at this present time our camp is in the most healthy & prosperous state of any in the South West." See Olds to AFIC commissioners, Aug. 20, 1863, Corinth, Miss., AFIC Records, box 2, folder 73, HO. Levi Coffin also singled Corinth out as preferable to most, despite its shortcomings. See Coffin, *Reminiscences*, 636–37, 646–47. The *American Missionary* (publication of the AMA) called Corinth "the most thoroughly systematized, cleanest, and most healthy camp I have ever seen." See *American Missionary* 17, no. 5 (1863): 141.

63. Sometimes the number dipped as low as 2,000 and at other times topped 6,000, but most of the time it hovered between 3,600 and 3,900. See Walker, "Corinth," and Smith, *Corinth 1862* (which also provides the 1,200 prewar population on p. xviii). AMA records often cite roughly 2,500. The Reverend Abner Olds in an Aug. 20, 1863, letter to the AFIC and Levi Coffin in his *Reminiscences* both claimed 6,000 freedpeople to be under the jurisdiction of the Union army "in

the district of Corinth," including surrounding areas. Two places where actual counts appear are a table compiled by John Eaton for AFIC Records, file 6, reel 200, frame 571, NARA, in which he records a total of 3,657 (658 men, 1,440 women, and 1,559 children), and a letter from Olds to the AFIC commissioners in which he states a "total of 3879 persons" in the actual camp at Corinth (AFIC Records, box 2, folder 73, HO).

64. Alexander to Howe, Sept. 1, 1863. AFIC Records, box 1, HO.

65. Ibid.

66. Captain L. F. Booth to AFIC, Sept. 14, 1863, Corinth, Miss., AFIC Records, box 1, folder 15, HO; Olds to AFIC, 1863, Miss., AFIC Records, box 7, HO. See also Coffin, *Reminiscences,* and Walker, "Corinth."

67. Alexander to Howe, Sept. 1, 1863; AFIC Records, box 1, HO; Alexander's response to query 2 of Eaton's Questionnaire, AFIC Records, file 6, reel 200, frame 573, NARA; John Eaton Report to AFIC, April 29, 1863, AFIC Records, file 6, reel 200, NARA. For improved cabins by 1863 and the daily sweeping ritual, see Olds to AFIC, 1863, AFIC Records, HO.

68. Responses of superintendents to Eaton's Questionnaire, AFIC Records, file 6, reel 200, NARA; Brent, *Occupied Corinth,* 13–14, ISHL.

69. On architecture at Corinth, see Brent, *Occupied Corinth,* 31–33 and figs. 6 and 7.

70. Alexander to Eaton included in Eaton's 1863 Report to Jocelyn of the AMA, AFIC Records, file 6, reel 200, frame 572, NARA.

71. For hunger in the cotton South, see Johnson, *River of Dark Dreams,* 178–80, 185–89, 463 n7, which meticulously calculates a two-thousand-calorie-per-day deficit between a slave's average daily food intake and labor output.

72. Alexander to Eaton included in Eaton's 1863 Report; Eaton, *Grant, Lincoln, and the Freedmen;* Coffin, *Reminiscences.* For ration amounts, start date, and lack of hominy and soap, see Alexander's responses to Eaton's questionnaire, included in Eaton's 1863 Report, AFIC Records, file 6, reel 200, frame 573, NARA.

73. Corinth's vegetable gardens seem to be almost famous: mention of them appears *everywhere.* See, for example, John Eaton to Jocelyn of the AMA, May 18, 1863, Memphis, RG 105, M1914, reel 1, frames 226–28, NARA. For seed and farm implements, see NWFAC, *Annual Reports* (Chicago, 1864 and 1865). For acreage, see Coffin, *Reminiscences,* 637; Olds to AFIC, Aug. 1863, AFIC Records, HO; Booth, Sept. 14, 1863, AFIC Records, HO. For free transportation, see Coffin, *Reminiscences,* and John Eaton to Assistant Quarter Master in Charge of Transportation Captain Lyman, April 23, 1863, Memphis, RG 105, M1914, NARA.

74. John Alexander to Eaton included in Eaton's 1863 Report, AFIC Records, file 6, reel 200, frames 571 and 576, NARA.

75. Sergeant William Donaldson (First Missouri Light Artillery) to father, Aug. 16, 1863, Corinth, Miss., William R. Donaldson Papers, Civil War Correspondence, folder 1, MOHS.

76. On Bridge Creek, see Brent, *Occupied Corinth,* 15.

77. Of the nearly limitless sources testifying to black labor for the army at Corinth, see Olds to AFIC, Aug. 20, 1863, Corinth, Miss., AFIC Records, box 2, folder 73, HO; Alexander to Howe, AFIC Records, HO; Alexander to Eaton included in Eaton's 1863 Report, AFIC Records, file 6, reel 200, frame 571, NARA; Birch Diary, June 11, 1862, near Corinth, Miss.; Wilcox to *Bureau County Republican,* July 15, 1862, *Bureau County Republican,* Aug. 7, 1862, 2. On farming: Levi Cof-

fin reported 1,000 acres under cultivation at Corinth with 175 acres dedicated to vegetable gardens growing for army use and the rest to cotton (*Reminiscences,* 637), while the Reverend Abner Olds a few months later reported 50 acres in vegetable garden for freedpeople's own use and 250 acres planted in cotton, from which he anticipated "good wages" and "a handsome surplus for the Government." Olds to AFIC, 1863, AFIC Records, HO. The same sources, plus Booth to AFIC, Sept., 14, 1863, AFIC Records, HO, also mention schools, including details like number of structures, books, and students, as well as churches, including details of sermons and services.

78. On weddings generally, see Eaton, *Grant, Lincoln, and the Freedmen;* Coffin, *Reminiscences;* Alexander to Howe, Sept. 1, 1863, AFIC Records, HO; and Booth to AFIC, Sept. 14, 1863. AFIC Records, HO. For the forty weddings in late Nov. 1862, see Corporal Austin Andrews (Twelfth Illinois Infantry) to his sister, Dec. 2, 1862, Corinth, Miss., Andrews Family Papers, folder 1, ISHL.

79. On the recruitment of the First Alabama Infantry of African Descent at Corinth, see Smith, *Corinth 1862,* and Walker, "Corinth," as well as Sergeant William R. Donaldson to father, May 24 and 31, 1863, Corinth, Miss., Donaldson Papers, folder 1, MOHS; Alexander to Howe, Sept. 1, 1863 (in response to Howe to Alexander letter of Aug. 26, 1863), Corinth, Miss., AFIC Records, HO; James Spikes (or Spight), Arkansas Narratives, vol. 11, pt. 6, WPA Narratives; "Roster and History of the 55th United States Colored Troops," in Dyer, *Compendium of the War of the Rebellion,* vol. 3, available via American Civil War Research Database, www.civilwardata.com.

80. Private John Garriott (Eighteenth Missouri) to sister, June 12, 1863, near Corinth, Miss., John Garriott Letters, folder 3, WHMC-Columbia.

81. Robert Cartmell Diary, Jackson, Tenn., July 10 and Dec. 20, 1863, TSLA. Coffin's *Reminiscences* also notes dangers posed by raids in and around Corinth.

82. See *OR,* ser. 1, 32 (pt. 2): 70, 76, 84, 124–25, 134–35, 157–58, 167–68, 180–81, 190–91, 200–1, 213, 630, and Special Orders 146, Jan. 24, 1864, Special Post Fund Orders Issued, RG 393, entry 296, NARA.

83. For a summary of the dates of departure to Memphis for these camps, see John Cimprich, *Slavery's End in Tennessee, 1861–1865* (Tuscaloosa: University of Alabama Press, 1985), 49–52.

84. Julia Dodge to her father, April 19, 1863, quoted in Brent, *Occupied Corinth,* 619. Coffin also remarked on the war-torn appearance in his *Reminiscences,* 619.

85. Camp Superintendent Responses to Interrogatories About Shelter, AFIC Records, file 6, reel 200, frames 572–73, NARA. For the blankets and brush at La Grange, see Coffin, *Reminiscences,* 632. On emergency measures taken because of the Hatchie River flood, see John Eaton to General J. D. Webster (superintendent of Memphis railroad), May 1863, RG 105, M1914, NARA.

86. Sergeant Cyrus Boyd (Fifteenth Iowa) Diary, vol. 1, Aug. 10, 1862, Bolivar, Tenn., Cyrus F. Boyd Collection, Special Collections, Kansas City Public Library, Mo.; AFIC Records, file 6, reel 200, frame 572, NARA.

87. AFIC Records, file 6, reel 200, NARA, has a series of interrogatories about health conditions; frame 576 makes particular reference to the smallpox hospital at La Grange. Hospitals for the district were authorized by Special Field Order No. 9 signed by Assistant Adjutant General John A. Rawlings upon the order of Major General U. S. Grant on Nov. 27, 1862, at La Grange, Tenn., RG 105, M1914, reel 1, NARA.

88. Coffin, *Reminiscences*, 633–35. From Dec. 1862 through June 1863, Robert Cartmell regularly grumbled over reports of his former slaves moving in and out of Bolivar and the camp at Jackson, which was located about three-quarters of a mile from his property on the Jackson-to-Huntingdon Road. Cartmell Diary, TSLA. Requisitions, Jackson, Tenn., May 6, 7, 10, 11, 12, 16, 18, 20, 21, 25, 26 and June 1, 2, 1863, RG 393, pt. 4, entry 599, NARA.

89. Cartmell Diary, June 7, 1863, near Jackson, Tenn., TSLA.

90. Grant to Lincoln, June 11, 1863, near Vicksburg, Miss., quoted in Eaton, *Lincoln, Grant, and the Freedmen*, 65.

91. AFIC Records, file 6, reel 200, frames 574, 577, NARA.

92. On McClernand, see Christopher C. Meyers, *Union General John A. McClernand and the Politics of Command* (Jefferson, N.C.: McFarland, 2010).

93. For reports of freedpeople's various activities in camps in the region, see Boyd Diary, July 31, Aug. 10 and 26, 1862, Bolivar, Tenn., Kansas City Public Library; Engelmann to sister Josephine, Aug. 2 and 9, 1862, Bolivar, Tenn., Engelmann-Kircher Papers, box 3, ISHL; Sergeant James Jessee (Eighth Illinois) Diary, Nov. 17, 1862, La Grange, Tenn., Kansas Collection, Spencer Research Library, University of Kansas; Surgeon Thomas Hawley (111th Illinois) to parents, Jan. 17, 1863, La Grange, Tenn., Thomas S. Hawley Papers, MOHS; AFIC Records, file 6, reel 200, NARA; RG 393, pt. 4, entry 599, NARA; Coffin, *Reminiscences;* and Eaton, *Lincoln, Grant, and the Freedmen*.

94. James C. Vanderbilt (Twenty-Third Indiana) to mother, Aug. 1, 1862, Bolivar, Tenn., James Cornell Vanderbilt Papers, INSL.

95. AFIC Records, file 6, reel 200, frame 576, NARA.

96. Hawley to parents, Jan. 17, 1863.

97. See, for example, Coffin, *Reminiscences*, 630–31.

98. See Sperry, *History of the 33d Iowa Infantry Volunteer Regiment*, 17.

99. Prentiss to Curtis, June 16, 1863, Helena, Ark., Department of Missouri, box 9, RG 393, pt. 1, entry 2593, NARA. For suffering (among both soldiers and freedpeople) due to deteriorating sanitary conditions related to the river, see Prentiss to Curtis, Feb. 28, 1863, Helena, Ark., Department of Missouri, box 9, RG 393, pt. 1, entry 2593, NARA; Moore, "Reminiscences," 292.

100. Prentiss to Curtis, June 16, 1863.

101. Fifteen hundred one day in Feb.: Prentiss to Curtis, Feb. 28, 1863. Judge Advocate Lucien Eaton later reported that they made it to St. Louis; see Lucien Eaton to Major General John Schofield, May 30, 1863, St. Louis, Department of Missouri, box 9, RG 393, pt. 1, entry 2593, NARA. Members of the Ladies' Contraband Relief Society also reported the arrival of refugees from Helena's flooding. See Ladies' Contraband Relief Society Testimony, AFIC Records, file 7, reel 201, frame 179, NARA.

102. Descriptive List of Enlisted Men on the U.S.S. *Ouachita*, MOHS. African American men could enlist directly in the navy from the outset of war, so they were serving in the Mississippi River squadron even before black enlistment into the army was authorized.

103. Charles A. Davis to wife, Nov. 1864, Cairo, Ill., George Davis Family Papers, WHMC-St. Louis; Adam Isaac Kane, "The Western River Steamboat: Structure and Machinery, 1811 to 1860" (master's thesis, Texas A&M University, 2001), http://anthropology.tamu.edu/papers/Kane-MA2001.pdf; *Arrival and Departures Port of Cairo*, District, Division, and Post of Cairo, Ill., 1862–1865

Miscellaneous Records, RG 393, pt. 2, entry 1106, NARA; "Cairo, Evansville Packet Co." file, RG 92, NARA. For the remains of soldiers from wealthy families transported in metal caskets, see Faust, *This Republic of Suffering.*

104. For renewal of the specifically government-financed transportation of freedpeople from camps in the South to the Midwest, see S. A. Duke to Curtis, March 9, 1863, St. Louis, Department of Missouri, box 9, RG 393, pt. 1, entry 2593, NARA. For the surge in March and April 1863, see *Arrival and Departures Port of Cairo.*

105. Curtis to Prentiss, Feb. 28, 1863, in *OR*, ser. 1, vol. 22, pt. 2, p. 147. For the divided state of St. Louis opinion, see Louis S. Gerteis, *Civil War St. Louis* (Lawrence: University Press of Kansas, 2001). Judge Advocate Lucien Eaton also noted that "the severity—the barbarism—of our state laws" made it far too easy for black people in St. Louis to be re-enslaved. See Lucien Eaton to Schofield, May 30, 1863.

106. Lucien Eaton to Schofield, May 30, 1863; Contraband Relief Society Circular Letter, Feb. 1863, Civil War Collection folder B132, MOHS; Ladies' Contraband Relief Society Testimony, Dec. 2, 1863, AFIC Records, file 7, reel 201, frames 161–83, NARA; Joe M. Richardson, "The American Missionary Association and Black Education in Civil War Missouri," *Missouri Historical Review* 69 (July 1971): 433–48; John L. Richardson to Rev. S. S. Jocelyn, April 10, 1863, St. Louis, AMA.

107. For a detailed accounting of the construction of barracks in St. Louis, see Alex Phillips (superintendent of mechanics) to Assistant Quartermaster E. Wuerzel, July 9, 1864, St. Louis, Department of Missouri, box 16, RG 393, pt. 1, entry 2593, NARA.

108. See Wuerzel to Chief Quartermaster Colonel William Myers, Sept. 27, 1864, St. Louis, Department of Missouri, box 16, RG 393, pt. 1, entry 2593, NARA.

109. Rogers, *War Pictures,* 214–15.

110. Edward Noyes, "The Contraband Camp at Cairo, Illinois," *Selected Proceedings of the Sixth Northern Great Plains History Conference,* ed. Lysle E. Meyer (1972), 212; Rogers, *War Pictures,* chap. 10; Responses to John Eaton's Questionnaire Sent to Superintendents Throughout the Mississippi Valley Spring 1863, AFIC Records, file 6, reel 200, frames 571–84, 616, NARA.

111. "The African Methodist Episcopal Church of Cairo," Illinois Writers Project "Negro in Illinois" Collection, box 17, folder 3, Vivian G. Harsh Research Collection, Woodson Regional Branch, Chicago Public Library.

112. See, for example, Rogers, *War Pictures,* 214; Rogers's responses to Eaton's 1863 Questionnaire, AFIC Records, file 6, reel 200, frame 577, NARA; George T. Allen (medical inspector, U.S.A.) to Mayor S. S. Taylor of Cairo, Jan. 24, 1864, Cairo, Ill., Edward Wade Papers, box 1, MOHS.

113. Ann grew up and went to school as a full member of the Bicknell family in Fort Atkinson, Wisconsin. Years later, Ann met John Ellis, a Louisiana-born man who also ended up in Wisconsin after securing his own freedom by making his way to the camp of the Twenty-Ninth Wisconsin during the war. They married and opened a candy shop in Fort Atkinson. Ann's sister, Millie, however, slips from the record, leaving no more trace than whispers of poor treatment by a Wisconsin family who hired and then overworked her. Ellis Family Materials at Fort Atkinson Hoard Museum, Holzhueter Papers: Black Settlers in Early Wisconsin Collection, box 2, folder 8, SHSW.

114. Columbus is about two dozen miles downriver from Cairo. For numerous references to there-and-back-in-a-day journeys between Cairo and Columbus, see *Arrival and Departures Port of Cairo.*

115. On enslaved labor building Confederate fortifications at Columbus, see Brigadier General James Slack to wife Ann, July 13, 1862, Memphis, Slack Papers, box 1, folder 3, INSL.

116. "Description of Government Buildings at Columbus, Kentucky, in charge of Capt. H. W. Persing, A.Q.M.," Consolidated Correspondence file, "Columbus, KY," RG 92, NARA.

117. Assistant Adjutant General J. Lovell to Columbus Provost Marshal, Oct. 3, 1862, and Lovell to Assistant Quartermaster O'Brien, Nov. 14, 1862, Columbus, Ky., Letters Sent Oct. 1862–July 1864 [from Columbus, Ky.], RG 393, pt. 2, entry 986, NARA. Regular pay receipts appear in Provost Marshal Accounts for Columbus, Ky., RG 393, pt. 2, entry 1105, vol. 3, NARA.

118. On repeated action along rail lines between Columbus and Jackson, see Cartmell Diary. On the Dec. 24 rumored attack and account of moving all stores from warehouses onto boats, see Cox to Colonel T. F. Haines, Dec. 24 and 26, 1862, Columbus, Ky., Consolidated Correspondence file, "Columbus, KY," RG 92, NARA. One wharf boat was so overloaded that Cox had to send for an additional steamer in the Mississippi River Squadron, the *Ravenna,* to be sent immediately on Christmas Day to transfer some stores onto, to prevent sinking. By Dec. 26, Cox reported that the rumored attack "along the line from Jackson to this place" appeared to be beaten back.

119. Orders received to deliver Frederick R. Huston to Washington, D.C., under guard, Dec. 3, 1863, and orders received to ready prisoners and witnesses in case of Yocum and Huston for transportation to Washington for trial, Dec. 6 and 8, 1863, Letters Sent Oct. 1862–July 1864 [from Columbus, Ky.] and Nov. 1864–Aug. 1865 [from Cairo], RG 393, pt. 2, entry 986, NARA.

120. Report of Brigadier General Smith on the nonappearance of McComb and Gant (or Grant) before a military commission in July and Aug. 1863, Oct. 24, 1863, Columbus, Ky.; Smith to Cairo Post Commander Reid, Oct. 17, 1863, Letters Sent Oct. 1862–July 1864 [from Columbus, Ky.], RG 393, pt. 2, entry 986, NARA; Correspondence between Brigadier General John Buford and Colonel W. F. Shaw (Fourteenth Iowa), Cairo, Ill., Letters Sent March 1863–April 1866, RG 393, pt. 2, entry 1085, NARA; David L. Phillips to Lincoln, Oct. 23, 1863, Lincoln Papers, LOC.

121. Lucien Eaton to John Schofield, May 30, 1863.

122. Senator Benjamin Gratz Brown Testimony, AFIC Records, file 7, reel 201, frame 152, NARA. *The Daily Missouri Democrat* ran a series of articles about the auctioning in March 1863. For more on kidnapping and selling by police in St. Louis, see Schwalm, *Emancipation's Diaspora,* 53–54. For additional examples of kidnapping and sale on both the Missouri and the Illinois sides of the Mississippi River, see Records Relating to Confiscated and Contraband Property, Department of Missouri, RG 393, pt. 1, entry 2797, NARA.

123. John Eaton to Robert N. Carroll (corresponding secretary of the Contraband Relief Society of Cincinnati), spring 1863, Corinth, Miss., RG 105, M1914, reel 1, frames 14–15, NARA.

124. Eaton to Alexander, March 1863, Memphis, RG 105, M1914, reel 1, frame 17, NARA.

125. Eaton to Carroll, spring 1863, RG 105, M1914, reel 1, NARA.
126. Special Orders No. 40, HQ Sixteenth Army Corps with additional orders to Binmore, enclosed with Eaton to Assistant Quartermaster Lyman, March 31, 1863, Memphis, RG 105, M1914, frames 15–17, NARA; Transportation Records in Miscellaneous Records, District, Division, and Post of Cairo, Ill., 1862–1865, RG 393, pt. 2, entry 1106, NARA.
127. NWFAC, *Second Annual Report*, 11, 18.
128. "Report of Public Buildings, Barracks etc. Belonging to the Quartermasters Department at Cairo Illinois Under the Charge of Captain M. Manigan A.Q.M.," May 27, 1865, Consolidated Correspondence file, "Cairo, Illinois." RG 92, NARA.
129. Post Commander J. E. Cornelius to B. F. Smith, Aug. 9, 1865, Cairo, Ill., Letters Sent March 1863–April 1866, RG 393, pt. 2, entry 1085, NARA; Commander L. C. Skinner, Oct. 2, 1865, Cairo, Ill., Letters Sent March 1863–April 1866, RG 393, pt. 2, entry 1085, NARA. For records of whites in jail for antiblack violence, see Register of Prisoners in Military Prison, Camp Cairo, Cairo, Ill., Misc. Records 1861–1866, RG 393, pt. 2, entry 1105, vol. 2, NARA.
130. Haviland, *Woman's Life-Work*, 246–47.
131. Asboth to Hurlbut, April 8, 1863, and Asboth to Major Henry Brinmore, April 8, 1863, Letters Sent Oct. 1862–July 1864 [from Columbus, Ky.], RG 393, pt. 2, entry 986, NARA.
132. Haviland, *Woman's Life-Work*, 250–51.
133. Ibid., 252–55.
134. The "Freedmen's Wood Yards" lasted for the duration of the war, and even beyond. See Brigadier General M. L. Smith, General Orders No. 27, Feb. 25, 1865, and Special Orders No. 55, March 9, 1865, Headquarters for District of Vicksburg, RG 105, M1914, reel 1, NARA; Lieutenant and Assistant Quarter Master D. M. Dick to Colonel H. M. Whittlesley, Nov. 15, 1865, Vicksburg, Miss., Consolidated Correspondence file, "Islands in Mississippi River," RG 92, NARA.
135. William Allen to wife, Sept. 26, 1864, Memphis, Allen Family Papers, box 2, folder 1.
136. Asboth, May 6, 1863, Columbus, Ky., Letters Sent Oct. 1862–July 1864, RG 393, pt. 2, entry 986, NARA.
137. Allen to wife, Sept. 26, 1864.
138. John Eaton to Provost Marshal Smith of the Memphis District, May 22, 1863, Memphis, RG 105, M1914, reel 1, frame 29, NARA.
139. Allen to wife, Sept. 26, 1864.
140. Haviland, *Woman's Life-Work*, 266–67.
141. Eaton, *Lincoln, Grant, and the Freedmen*, 35; Haviland, *Woman's Life-Work*, 267; Stearns Testimony, AFIC Records, file 7, reel 201, frames 71–72, NARA.
142. John Eaton to Senator Henry Wilson, [no day] 1863, Memphis, RG 105, M1914, reel 1, NARA; Lieutenant Colonel A. L. Mitchell to Major W. H. Morgan, July 28, 1864, District of West Tennessee, in FSSP, ser. 2, 1:720 n; Special Orders No. 10, para. 8, Memphis, Dec. 17, 1864, RG 105, M1914, reel 1, NARA. When William Allen visited President's Island on Sept. 26, 1864, he noted that Union army troops were "transferring [all black noncombatants] as fast as they can get ready for them, over to President's Island," and that on that particular day many soldiers of the Sixty-First U.S. Colored Troops were visiting their families there.

See Allen to wife, Sept. 26, 1864. See also Cimprich, *Slavery's End in Tennessee,* 50, 73–74.

143. Haviland, *Woman's Life-Work,* 264–65.

144. Answers to Interrogatories, AFIC Records, file 6, reel 200, frames 571–76, NARA; Cimprich, *Slavery's End in Tennessee,* 58. For an account of black Union soldiers' health, see Margaret Humphreys, *Intensely Human: The Health of the Black Soldier in the American Civil War* (Baltimore: Johns Hopkins University Press, 2008). For a treatment of health crises that allows nothing to dim its bold claims, see Jim Downs, *Sick from Freedom.*

145. Asboth to Hurlbut, May 16, 1863, Letter of introduction for the Reverend H. W. Goff of the Freedman's Aid Commission of Cincinnati (who wanted to ascertain conditions in the Memphis camps), Letters Sent Oct. 1862–July 1864 [from Columbus, KY], RG 393, pt. 2, entry 986, NARA; Coffin, *Reminiscences,* 630–31; Haviland, *Woman's Life-Work,* 264–65.

146. Allen to wife, Sept. 26, 1864.

147. William D. Butler (U.S. Christian Commission) to William G. Eliot, Sept. 1, 1863, St. Louis, William D. Butler Papers, MOHS.

148. Matilda Bass, Arkansas Narratives, vol. 2, pt. 1, p. 126, WPA Narratives.

149. Butler to Eliot, Sept. 1, 1863.

150. Ibid.; General James Wadsworth Testimony, AFIC Records, file 5, reel 200, frame 547, NARA. In successive months, thousands of freedpeople were transferred out of camps and onto leased plantations (as discussed later in this chapter), yet even with that relocation, by Sept. 1864, there were 4,585 freedpeople in camps just within Vicksburg alone, compared with about 3,000 there in the summer of 1863. See Tri-monthly Report of Freedmen and Employees in Freedmen Department to Draw Rations, and of Animals to Draw Forage, Sept. 29, 1864, RG 105, M1914, reel 1, frame 296, NARA.

151. John Eaton to Reverend C. B. Boynton (secretary of Western Freedmen's Aid Commission in Cincinnati), Sept. 11, 1863, RG 105, M1914, reel 1, frame 35, NARA.

152. William D. Butler (agent of the Western Sanitary Commission) to James Yeatman, July 16, 1863, near Vicksburg, Miss., William D. Butler Papers, MOHS.

153. Eaton to Boynton, Sept. 11, 1863.

154. Butler to Yeatman, July 16, 1863.

155. Ibid.; Eaton to Boynton, Sept. 11, 1863; "Condition of the Negroes Who Came into Vicksburg with Sherman's Army, as Described by Mr. N. M. Mann, Agent of the Western Sanitary Commission," March 7, 1864, Vicksburg, Miss., St. Louis Sanitation Collection, folder 1, MOHS.

156. "Condition of the Negroes Who Came into Vicksburg with Sherman's Army, as Described by Mr. N. M. Mann."

157. James E. Yeatman et al. to Lincoln, "Letter to the President of the United States," Rooms of the Western Sanitary Commission, St. Louis, Nov. 6, 1863, William Greenleaf Eliot Papers, box 2, folder 21, MOHS.

158. "My African Grandfather," compiled from the Reverend Daniel Flickinger's wartime diaries by his granddaughter, by Florence Wolff, IHS.

159. Ibid.; John Eaton to Levi Coffin (Western Freedmen's Aid Commission), Nov. 10, 1863, Vicksburg, Miss., RG 105, M1914, reel 1, frames 46–47, NARA.

160. Flickinger in "My African Grandfather."

161. John B. Clark (secretary of the United Presbyterian Church in the U.S.A. Board

of Missions for Freedmen) to Howe and AFIC, Aug. 20, 1863, Allegheny City, Pa., AFIC Records, box 3, folder 109, HO.

162. John Eaton to H. B. Spellman, Oct. 2, 1863, RG 105, M1914, reel 1, frame 40, NARA.

163. John Eaton to Martin Camp and the Contraband Committee of Summit County, Ohio, Nov. 2, 1863, Vicksburg, Miss., RG 105, M1914, reel 1, frames 45–46, NARA.

164. David O. McCord to John Eaton, Final Report of Medical Director and Inspector for the Freedmen's Department, filed July 1865, RG 105, M1914, reel 1, frames 359–95, NARA.

165. Pile Testimony, AFIC Records, file 7, reel 201, frame 360, NARA.

166. Ladies' Contraband Relief Society Testimony, AFIC Records, file 7, reel 201, frame 178, NARA.

167. Adjutant General Lorenzo Thomas, Special Orders No. 114, Dec. 1, 1863, Vicksburg, Miss.; McCord's Report, 1, RG 105, M1914, reel 1, frame 359, NARA; David O. McCord, Special Orders No. 38, Jan. 27, 1864, Vicksburg, Miss., RG 105, M1914, reel 1, frame 62, NARA.

168. McCord's Report, 23, RG 105, M1914, reel 1, frame 382, NARA.

169. Ladies' Contraband Relief Society Testimony, AFIC Records, file 7, reel 201, frame 178, NARA; NWFAC, *Second Annual Report.*

170. Albert Johnson and "Citizens of Cincinnati" to Office of the Provost Marshal of Freedmen, Feb. 3, 1865, Records of the Mississippi Freedmen's Department ("Pre-Bureau Records"), RG 105, M1914, reel 5, frame 8, NARA; S. S. Livermore on behalf of J. V. Farwell to Office of the Provost Marshal, March 16, 1865, Vicksburg, Miss., RG 105, M1914, reel 5, frame 13, NARA. That application was refused by Lieutenant Stuart Eldridge, because comparable stores were already in place. Special Orders regulated trade at the stores in order to guard against cheating former slaves. See Special Orders No. 83 Ex. IV from District of Vicksburg HQ, April 10, 1865, the protest of the merchants Ellet and Huggins against it, April 13, 1865, and Provost Marshal Lieutenant Eldridge's scathing reprimand of Ellet and Huggins, May 15, 1865, Vicksburg, Miss., RG 105, M1914, reel 5, frames 20–21, NARA.

171. NWFAC, *Second Annual Report;* McCord's Report, 2, RG 105, M1914, reel 1, frame 360, NARA. Chaplain J. A. Hawley, Superintendent of Colored Schools for District of Vicksburg, Special Orders No. 79, Oct. 8, 1864, Memphis, and Rev. L. H. Cobb, Special Orders No. 81, Oct. 13, 1864, Memphis, RG 105, M1914, reel 1, frame 140, NARA.

172. McCord's Report, 23–24, RG 105, M1914, reel 1, frames 382–83, NARA; Tri-monthly Report, Colored Orphan Asylum, Vicksburg, Miss., June 27, 1865, RG 105, M1914, reel 1, frames 647–50, NARA.

173. Surgeon T. J. Wright to Provost Marshal M. Brobst, July 29, 1864, Freedmen's General Hospital, Vicksburg, Miss., and Brobst to Wright, same day, with Endorsement of the Superintendent of Freedmen, RG 105, M1914, reel 1, frames 116–17, NARA.

174. Bass, Arkansas Narratives, vol. 2, pt. 1, p. 126.

175. McCord's Report, 1–2, RG 105, M1914 reel 1, frames 359–60, NARA.

176. Ibid., 7, 24–25, frames 366, 383–84.

177. McCord's Report, 1–6, frames 359–65, details the conflict. For mortality and morbidity numbers, see Tri-monthly Report of Freedmen and Employees in

Freedmen Department to Draw Rations, and of Animal to Draw Forage, Sept. 9, 29; Oct. 19, 30; Nov. 9, 19, 29; Dec. 9, 19, 30, 1864, RG 105, M1914, reel 1, frames 294, 296, 300, 302, 304, 306, 310, 312, 314, 316, NARA.

178. The pecuniary motivation is obvious, because selling cotton remained so prodigally lucrative. For one assertion of the belief that moving freedpeople out of crowded camps, which he called "depots," and situating them on rural plantations, where he believed they would breathe cleaner air and engage in the kind of work to which they were accustomed and therefore enjoy better health, see Wadsworth Testimony, AFIC Records, file 5, reel 200, frames 512–13, NARA.

179. Dubois, *Avengers of the New World;* Fick, *Making Haiti.*

180. General John Hawkins to Honorable Gerritt Smith, Oct. 21, 1863, Goodrich's Landing, La., AFIC Records, file 5, reel 200, frames 90–91, NARA.

181. Provost Marshal James S. Matthews, "List of the Planters, Leasees [*sic*], Employers, and Numbers of Acres of Land Tilled and Untilled in the Second District of North Mississippi," June 1864, RG 105, M1914, reel 5, frames 90–91, NARA; McCord, Special Orders No. 38, Jan. 27, 1864; Hawkins to Smith, Oct. 21, 1863, AFIC Records, file 5, reel 200, frames 90–91, NARA.

182. Hawkins to Smith, Oct. 21, 1863, AFIC Records, file 5, reel 200, frames 557–58, NARA.

183. Nelson Allen to Colonel Samuel Thomas, Aug. 30, 1864, Goodrich's Landing, La., RG 105, M1914, reel 5, frame 130, NARA.

184. James S. Matthews to Colonel Samuel Thomas, May 9, 1864, Goodrich's Landing, La., RG 105, M1914, reel 5, frames 46–47, NARA; Chaplain H. S. Fisk to Thomas, Nov. 28, 1864, Reporting on plantations in District of Vicksburg, RG 105, M1915, reel 5, frames 144–47, NARA.

185. For threats right at Goodrich's Landing, see James Matthews to Colonel Samuel Thomas, July 7, 1864, Goodrich's Landing, La., RG 105, M1914, reel 5, frames 99–104, NARA. On the raids throughout the region, including Milliken's Bend and Terrapin Neck, see Lieutenant D. McCall to Thomas, May 9 and 22, 1864, RG 105, M1914, reel 5, frames 51–53, NARA. On removal of the Sixty-Sixth U.S. Colored Troops, see Lieutenant C. F. Keller, Sixty-Sixth U.S. Colored Troops to Thomas, June 3, 1864, Goodrich's Landing, La., RG 105, M1914, reel 5, frame 74, NARA. On the 1st Regiment Plantation Guards, see Special Orders No. 22, para. 5, issued by the Headquarters of the Department of Mississippi, Memphis, Dec. 27, 1864, RG 105, M1914, reel 1, frames 174–75, NARA. The First Plantation Guards were to be paid partially from a tax levied on plantation lessees.

186. Hawkins to Smith, Oct. 21, 1863, AFIC Records, file 5, reel 200, frame 558, NARA.

187. Matthews to Thomas, May 9, 1864; Wadsworth Testimony, AFIC Records, file 5, reel 200, frames 517–18, NARA; Fisk to Thomas, Nov. 28, 1864. On Haiti, see Dubois, *Avengers of the New World,* and Fick, *Making Haiti.*

188. Wadsworth Testimony, AFIC Records, file 5, reel 200, frames 542–43, NARA. Sancho's story recalls the concept of slave "neighborhoods" as discussed by Anthony Kaye in *Joining Places: Slave Neighborhoods in the Old South* (Chapel Hill: University of North Carolina Press, 2007). The names of Sancho's followers are not recorded, so it is not possible to tell if they all hailed from the same prewar plantation or not, but lists of workers on many leased plantations do not exactly match the lists of slaves owned by the plantation's prewar

owner. They often feature many names from that plantation but not all, while also featuring the names of some people who had been slaves at adjoining or nearby plantations. Shared surnames suggest that kinship and family groups often tried to hire on together, though the names alone cannot establish that probability beyond doubt. Groups of freedpeople sharing the last name Dickerson and coming from Greenville, Mississippi, for example, tended to appear on lists of hired laborers at DeSoto Landing, Mississippi, and Goodrich's Landing, Louisiana. See James Matthews to Samuel Thomas, June 1864, Goodrich's Landing, La., RG 105, M1914, reel 5, frames 90–91, NARA; Lieutenant Ben Cheney, Record of Hands Hired from Camp Around DeSoto Landing, March 1865, RG 105, M1914, reel 1, frame 598, NARA. Two Dickersons also enlisted in the U.S. Colored Troops together near Vicksburg; see *Monthly Report of Enlisted Men Detailed in the Freedmen Department, Oct. 31st, 1864,* RG 105, M1914, reel 1, frames 801–2, NARA.

189. Wadsworth Testimony, frame 532.
190. On the colony at Davis Bend, see Janet Sharp Hermann, *The Pursuit of a Dream* (New York: Oxford University Press, 1981).
191. Fisk to Thomas, Nov. 28, 1864.
192. Hawkins to Smith, Oct. 21, 1863, AFIC Records, file 5, reel 200, frames 90–91, NARA.
193. See orders arresting Captain A. L. Thayer, Special Orders No. 7 signed by Adjutant General Lorenzo Thomas, Jan. 24, 1865, and letter from Thomas to John Eaton of that same date, RG 105, M1914, reel 1, frames 191–92, NARA.
194. Moore, "Reminiscences," 291.
195. Ibid.
196. See the Deposition of Mr. Andrew A. Ripka, prospective lessee from New York, investigating conditions near Natchez, Miss., AFIC Records, file 11, reel 201, frames 632–33, NARA; Brigadier General M. L. Smith, Special Orders No. 22, Extract 2, March 4, 1865, Vicksburg, Miss., RG 105, M1914, reel 1, frame 217, NARA.
197. Assistant Provost Marshal O. A. A. Gardner to Major General Curtis, Feb. 16, 1863, Mexico, Mo., Department of Missouri, box 9, RG 393, pt. 1, entry 2593, NARA.
198. W. R. Penick to General Benjamin Loan, telegram, March 28, 1863; Loan to General Samuel Curtis, March 29, 1863, Jefferson City, Mo., in *OR,* ser. 1, vol. 22, pt. 2, p. 183; Report of Major General Samuel R. Curtis, U.S. Army Headquarters, St. Louis, April 3, 1863, in *OR,* ser. 1, vol. 22, pt. 1, pp. 245–46; Curtis to Halleck, telegram, April 7, 1863, St. Louis, in *OR,* ser. 1, vol. 22, pt. 2, p. 203; *New York Times,* March 30, 1863.
199. Brigadier General Thomas Ewing to Lieutenant Colonel C. W. Marsh (assistant adjutant general of the Department of Missouri), Aug. 3, 1863, St. Louis, Department of Missouri, box 9, RG 393, pt. 1, entry 2593, NARA.
200. Deposition of Leonard Babcock, May 10, 1863, Provost Marshal Office, Ray County, Mo., Records Relating to Confiscated and Contraband Property, Department of the Missouri, RG 393, pt. 1, entry 2797, NARA.
201. See letters of Captain Reeves Leonard for early 1863, esp. Jan. 4, 1863, in Abiel Leonard Family Papers, folder 461, WHMC-Columbia; Guitar to Major Reeves Leonard, Aug. 5, 1863, HQ for District of N. MO, Macon City, Mo., Leonard Family Papers, folder 465; M. English to Leonard, Aug. 17, 1863, Glasgow, Mo.,

Leonard Family Papers, folder 465; Colonel J. B. Douglass to Guitar, including the depositions of William G. Carter, James Wilson, Lewis Hendrick, James H. Beasley, and Joseph Harking, Aug. 22, 1863, Audrain Co., Mo., Odon Guitar Collection, folder 7, WHMC-Columbia. Guitar found himself constantly at loggerheads with Company C of the Ninth Missouri Militia under his command, whose members refused to return slaves. He had even more trouble with troops from outside the state, such as the Twenty-Eighth Iowa Infantry. Major J. R. Murphy of the Twenty-Eighth Iowa Infantry managed to get himself imprisoned and then expelled from Missouri by General Guitar for defying orders to return slaves. See J. R. Murphy Testimony, AFIC Records, file 7, reel 201, frames 122–23, NARA. Guitar eventually resigned in 1864.

202. Higgins affidavit, in FSSP, ser. 1, 2:680–90. For more on expulsion, see Richard D. Sears, *Camp Nelson, Kentucky: A Civil War History* (Lexington: University Press of Kentucky, 2002).

203. Major D. C. Fitch and Captain M. A. Jewett Testimony, AFIC Records, file 7, reel 201, frames 32–34, NARA.

INTERLUDE · REFUGE WITHOUT WATER

1. Fuller to wife Sarah, Nov. 28, 1861, Fort Monroe, Va., Fuller Papers, SHSI.

2. Pierce, "Contrabands at Fortress Monroe," 626.

3. A robust school of historiographical thought takes this uncomplicatedly critical view, which in an earlier era of historical writing when the history of emancipation was hard to distinguish from hagiography served very necessary corrective purposes. As an example of an early corrective that was crucial at the time it was written and helped give rise to much important scholarship since, see Robert Engs's judgment of the Union army's "unwillingness to care for the freedmen or to do the job with any degree of good will," leading to a "disastrous" policy at Fort Monroe, from which the entire Union army and government "did not learn" and therefore went on to doom "every ensuing encounter" to unremitting "failure." Robert Engs, *Freedom's First Generation: Black Hampton, Virginia, 1861–1890* (Philadelphia: University of Pennsylvania Press, 1979), 42–43. Thanks to Engs's work and all we have learned since, it is now possible to consider contraband camps, emancipation, and the Union army with more precision than simple "good/bad" dichotomies permit.

4. Office of the United Nations High Commissioner for Refugees, *Protecting the Most Vulnerable;* UNHCR Web site, http://www.unhcr.org/cgi-bin/texis/vtx /home; Alan Taylor, "The World's Largest Refugee Camp Turns 20," *Atlantic,* April 14, 2011.

5. The notion of noncombatants displaced by war as refugees deserving of assistance in any institutional sense dates back no further than the civilians of Belgium in World War I. The massive numbers of displaced people dislodged by the cataclysm of World War II certainly heightened worldwide sensitivity to the need for systematic relief for war refugees, but official, coordinated relief operations materialized even later than that. According to the UNHCR, the official refugee agency of the UN, the very first "major emergency" for which the UNHCR "became operational" was in response to the Hungarian uprising of 1956, more than nine decades after the close of the U.S. Civil War. See *Protecting the World's Most Vulnerable* and "A Repository of the Past."

6. See http://www.sitesofconscience.org.

7. See http://www.sitesofconscience.org/resources/.

8. Samuel Moyn, *The Last Utopia: Human Rights in History* (Cambridge, Mass.: Harvard University Press, 2010), 1–2, chaps. 1 and 4.

9. Webber to the Brown family in Kansas, April 24, 1862, Tipton, Mo., John S. Brown Family Papers, reel 2, Kansas State Historical Society.

10. Richard Baxter, "Human Rights in War," *Bulletin of the American Academy of Arts and Sciences* 31, no. 2 (Nov. 1977): 4–13; Richard Shelly Hartigan, *Military Rules, Regulations, and the Code of War: Francis Lieber and the Certification of Conflict* (New Brunswick, N.J.: Transaction, 2011); Arthur Nussbaum, *A Concise History of the Law of Nations* (New York: Macmillan, 1947).

11. Dunant, *Un souvenir de Solférino,* https://archive.org/stream/unsouvenirdesolo1 dunagoog#page/n9/mode/2up. This version was a later edition of the original, published in 1863. It was quickly translated into most European languages, including English, and has since been translated into many more. Modern edition online copies are available in French and English from the International Committee of the Red Cross Web site, https://www.icrc.org/fre/assets/files /publications/icrc-001-0361.pdf.

12. Baxter, "Human Rights in War"; Nussbaum, *Concise History of the Law of Nations.*

13. For more on the Lieber Code, see chapter 3.

14. Lieber to Sumner, July 26, 1864, New York, Francis Lieber Papers to Charles Sumner, microfilmed from Harvard College Library, MSS Mfilm 00001 reel 1, HL.

15. Barton herself specifically noted the impression that Andersonville made on her. See Barton to Henry Wilson, Oct. 27, 1865, New York, Barton Papers, reel 63. Digital version available at http://www.loc.gov/resource/mss11973.063_0161 _0194/#seq-20. See also Ross, *Angel of the Battlefield,* chaps. 10 and 11; Burton, *Clara Barton,* chap. 5; American Red Cross, www.redcross.org/about-us/history.

16. Barton to Brown and Duer, March 13, 1864, Barton Papers, LOC.

17. Barton to "My most esteemd & dear friend," July 5, 1864, Point of Rocks, Va., Barton Papers, reel 63, LOC.

18. UNHCR, *Protecting the Most Vulnerable.*

THREE · PRECARIOUS ROUTES TO FREEDOM

1. Heuston Diary, Oct. 16 and 23, 1862, Georgetown, Ky., box 1, folder 3, and letters to wife, Oct. 23, 1862, Georgetown, Ky., and Nov. 16–17 and 18, 1862, Nicholasville, Ky., box 1, folder 5, Heuston Papers University of Wisconsin-La Crosse; William M. Fliss, "Wisconsin's 'Abolition Regiment': The Twenty-Second Volunteer Infantry in Kentucky, 1862–1863," *Wisconsin History* (Winter 2002–2003): 2–17; Quiner, *Military History of Wisconsin.*

2. Jan Furman, ed., *Slavery in the Clover Bottoms: John McCline's Narrative of His Life During Slavery and the Civil War* (Knoxville: University of Tennessee Press, 1998), 43–44.

3. William Sewell Jr., "A Theory of Structure: Duality, Agency, and Transformation," *American Journal of Sociology* 98, no. 1 (1992): 19. Historians, anthropologists, and sociologists all talk about "social structures" in this way. The scholar probably most associated with crystallizing the concept is Richard N. Adams. See his *Energy and Structure: A Theory of Social Power* (Austin: University of

Texas Press, 1975). See also Elizabeth S. Clemens, "Toward a Historicized Sociology: Theorizing Events, Processes, and Emergence," *American Review of Sociology* 33 (April 2007): esp. 528; William Sewell Jr., *Logics of History: Social Theory and Social Transformation* (Chicago: University of Chicago Press, 2005); John Tutino, *Making a New World: Founding Capitalism in the Bajío and Spanish North America* (Durham: Duke University Press, 2011), esp. 44–53.

4. In theory, a black person would be accepted as free rather than slave once he or she proved free status, but that was a singularly hard feat to achieve in Southern courts where state laws prohibited black people from testifying against white people, and even in federal court once the Fugitive Slave Law eliminated alleged slaves' access to a court to demonstrate free status. For more on the presumption of slave status, see Thomas Morris, *Free Men All: The Personal Liberty Laws of the North, 1780–1861* (Baltimore: Johns Hopkins University Press, 1974). In *Freedom National* and *The Scorpion's Sting*, James Oakes vigorously outlines the logic of the opposite assumption: that any person in the United States was at first presumed to be free rather than enslaved because freedom was the national default, and slavery a peculiarity that existed only by force of state or local law. As evidence, Oakes cites the disapproval that Republicans expressed in 1860 and 1861 of things like Texas annexation, the failure of the Wilmot Proviso, the Fugitive Slave Law, and the Kansas-Nebraska Act (*Scorpion's Sting*, 26), all of which is true and all of which demonstrates that Oakes is exactly right to portray the Republican Party as committed to the "freedom national" doctrine. But before 1861, the Republican Party had no power to act on its ideas, and the way the federal government *did* act was in direct opposition to those ideas, as is shown by the long list of federal actions of which Republicans disapproved. It is absolutely the case that Republicans did not *like* the presumption of slavery structure. It is not the case that their dislike dislodged it or neutralized its power before the Civil War.

5. See John K. Mahon, *History of the Militia and the National Guard* (New York: Macmillan, 1983). One recent consideration of the problem of civil and military relations can be found in John Casey, "Marked by War: Demobilization, Disability, and the Trope of the Citizen-Soldier in *Miss Ravenel's Conversion*," *Civil War History* 60, no. 2 (June 2014): 123–51.

6. Kantrowitz, *More Than Freedom;* Smith, *Civic Ideals.*

7. Oakes, *Scorpion's Sting*, 146–52. The Seminole example is a little complicated. American slaves owned by Southern masters had fled to the Seminoles before and during the wars. When U.S. forces defeated the Seminoles, Seminoles were transported out of Florida to west of the Mississippi. Some military officers at that time sent slaves who had fled white American masters west along with the rest of the Seminoles, rather than hunt down each one's previous owner for individual return; in that sense, fugitives escaped from their masters in time of war by being deported rather than returned. Even in the Seminole Wars, though, at least one of the officers in question, the U.S. major general Thomas Jesup, reverted to re-enslavement at the express direction of Secretary of War Lewis Cass. The various levels of complication make the Seminole Wars a very interesting case, though not a clear and unambiguous precedent for any one course of action.

8. On "The Star-Spangled Banner," and especially on the circumstances surround-

ing the composition of the third verse, which exalts, "No refuge could save the hireling and slave / From the terror of flight or the gloom of the grave," see Andrew Cockburn, "Washington Is Burning: Two Centuries of Racial Tribulation in the Nation's Capital," *Harper's Magazine,* Sept. 2014, 44–48.

9. Michael D. Doubler, *Civilian in Peace, Soldier in War: The Army National Guard, 1636–2000* (Lawrence: University Press of Kansas, 2003), 99–100; Mahon, *History of the Militia and the National Guard,* esp. 85, 96.

10. Sewell, "Theory of Structure," 19, and *Logics of History,* 228. For an extended discussion of slavery as a state of war, see Beckert, *Empire of Cotton.*

11. Slemmer to Lieutenant Colonel L. Thomas (assistant adjutant general, U.S. Army), March 18, 1861, Fort Pickens, Fla., in *OR,* ser. 2, vol. 1, pt. 1:750.

12. Butler to Hicks, April 23, 1861, Annapolis, Md., in *OR,* ser. 2, vol. 1, pt. 1:750.

13. George McClellan, May 26, 1861, in Stephen W. Sears, *Civil War Papers of George B. McClellan,* 26. Also available in *OR,* ser. 2, vol., I, pt.1: 753.

14. *Cong. Globe,* 37th Cong., 1st sess., 77. On Illinois as "an important exception, but the only one, to the idea that people in the North incorporated into law the presumption that all men are born free," see Morris, *Free Men All,* xii.

15. *Cong. Globe,* 37th Cong., 1st sess., 186.

16. Sylvia Frey, *Water from the Rock: Black Resistance in a Revolutionary Age* (Princeton, N.J.: Princeton University Press, 1992), 113; Woody Holton, "Rebel Against Rebel: Enslaved Virginians and the Coming of the American Revolution," *Virginia Magazine of History and Biography* 105, no. 2 (1997): 157–92; John Fabian Witt, *Lincoln's Code: The Laws of War in American History* (New York: Free Press, 2012), 29.

17. See Jasanoff, Liberty's Exiles; Martin, *Narrative of Some of the Adventures, Dangers, and Suffering of a Revolutionary Soldier,* 173–75.

18. Oakes, *Scorpion's Sting,* 108–30.

19. Witt, *Lincoln's Code,* 66–77. On the aftermath of 1812, see Rothman, *Slave Country.*

20. John Quincy Adams Diary, 31, Jan. 1, 1819–March 20, 1821, Adams Family Papers, MHS.

21. Adams Dispatches to U.S. Minister to Russia, Middleton, and letter to Benjamin Rush, July 1820, reprinted in "Views of John Quincy Adams," *Washington Intelligencer,* Sept. 2, 1862, pasted into Francis Lieber, 1862 "Notebook on Slavery," Lieber Papers, box 23, HL. Adams in this instance provides a good example of national policy trumping the ideas of individuals who believed in the freedom national principle, for his actions in this instance went against his own inclinations. By the time of the Civil War, Republicans like Charles Sumner focused on the inclinations, not the actions, to assert a long pedigree for military emancipation. In a Senate speech delivered on June 27, 1862, Sumner argued that Adams's advocacy of slaveholders' rights in the wake of the War of 1812 caused Adams "bitterness of heart" and went on to quote an 1842 House of Representatives speech in which Adams explained, "It was utterly against my judgment and wishes; but I was obliged to submit" to the dictates of his boss, the slaveholding president, James Monroe. Sumner's general argument is plausible regarding Adams's own personal sentiments, as Adams's 1820 diary shows, but the evidence Sumner uses shows that the case for wartime liberation was much murkier than he was letting on: the Adams speech quoted had noth-

ing to do with the liberation of slaves in the War of 1812 but rather referred to a dispute with the British over the right to search naval vessels. Sumner's dilemma was almost certainly that he felt confident of Adams's personal inclinations, and rightly so, but could not find public statement of them, precisely because at the time Adams was obligated to take the standard administration view, which denied the legitimacy of military emancipation. See Sumner, "War Powers of Congress," 5, and *Cong. Globe,* 27th Cong., 2nd sess., 1841–1842, 2:424. I thank Patrick Rael for drawing my attention to Sumner's 1862 speech.

22. See, for example, *New York Tribune* and *New York World,* Aug.–Sept. 1862; *Washington Intelligencer,* Sept. 2, 1862.

23. See, for example, Dix to S. R. Richardson, Oct. 12, 1861, and Colonel Augustus Morse, Oct. 14, 1861, in *OR,* ser. 2, 1:772–74.

24. Shadd Cary to *Liberator,* Nov. 29, 1861, accessed via American Periodicals Series Online, 191.

25. *Cong. Globe,* 37th Cong., 1st sess., 32.

26. G.L.M. (Sixth Wisconsin Infantry) to *Journal and Courier* (Wis.), July 13, 1861, Camp Randall, Wis., E. B. Quiner Correspondence of Wisconsin Volunteers, reel 1, 1:235–36, SHSW.

27. The military historian James Johnson Turner provides a very helpful frame of reference for the existing norms of warfare in the mid-nineteenth century. While popular cliché has it that before the Civil War, warfare was comparatively bloodless and consisted of armies who lined up in elaborate formations and displayed their force rather than actually deploying it, while noncombatants were scrupulously left alone, Johnson shows that such an image is patently false. "Limited warfare" fought according to agreed-upon rules did predominate in the European wars of the eighteenth century, but after the French Revolution, and certainly by the Napoleonic Wars, according to Johnson, wars were about "nations" and not just territory, which meant that everyone, including civilians, counted as fair game. Warfare by the mid-nineteenth century, then, was no-holds-barred: it was typically *not* limited, nor had it yet generated any kind of norm for the protection of the life or property of noncombatants. Johnson acknowledges that "a tradition of military regulations governing the conduct of armies to the early modern period" existed in theory but carefully and convincingly shows that it was not applied in practice, nor did any "customary-law standards of restraint rigorously [applied] as formal orders" exist until midway through the U.S. Civil War with General Orders No. 100. For the most concise iteration of these basic points, see James Turner Johnson, "Lieber and the Theory of War," in *Francis Lieber and the Culture of the Mind,* ed. Charles R. Mack and Henry H. Lesesne (Columbia: University of South Carolina Press, 2005), 61–68.

28. Kent, *Commentaries on American Law,* 4 vols., http://www.constitution.org /jk/jk_000.htm; Francis Lieber, *Manual of Political Ethics,* https://archive.org /details/manualofpolitico1lieb; Halleck, *International Law.* On the status of Kent's *Commentaries on American Law* as the "best-selling law book of the nineteenth century," see Witt, *Lincoln's Code,* 71. Arthur Nussbaum's classic *Concise History of the Law of Nations* confirms the absence of any formal precedents for dealing with noncombatants of any kind until the 1860s. What changed then, according to Nussbaum, was Henry Dunant, the International Committee of the Red Cross (1863), and the First Geneva Convention (1864). Richard Baxter's seminal article, "Human Rights in War," makes quick mention of Dunant,

the Red Cross, and Geneva as a brief warm-up before the bulk of the article, which clearly treats the whole notion of noncombatants' wartime existence, let alone rights and proper procedures concerning them, as twentieth-century phenomena.

29. Butler, *Private and Official Correspondence*, 1:105–7. For a discussion of the practice of hiring out, see Jonathan Martin, *Divided Mastery: Slave Hiring in the American South* (Cambridge, Mass.: Harvard University Press, 2004).

30. Butler, *Private and Official Correspondence*, 1:105–7. For the original handwritten copy, see Benjamin F. Butler, May 24, 1861, Benjamin F. Butler Papers.

31. "What Shall We Do with the Slaves?," *New York Times*, Dec. 14, 1861.

32. Butler, *Private and Official Correspondence*, 1:112–14. Edward L. Pierce, a private in the Third Massachusetts Infantry who was detailed to oversee fugitive slaves housed at Fort Monroe, similarly pointed to international law, the "law of nations," and "Common Law" to justify the seizure "as lawful prize" of "contraband goods, which are directly auxiliary to military operations." See Pierce, "Contrabands at Fortress Monroe," 626–40.

33. Butler, *Private and Official Correspondence*, 1:114.

> Head Quarters Department of Virginia, May 28, 1861
> *Col.* Phelps
> ALL able-bodied negroes within your lines will be taken and set to work in the trenches and on the works. Rations will be served to them and their families. An accurate record of the time when they came, and of their services, as well as of the rations supplied to them, will be kept. Their names, descriptions, and the names of their owners will also be correctly kept for further use.
> *By order of* B. F. BUTLER, *Maj. Genl. Comdg*

34. Ibid., 1:113. In "Contrabands at Fortress Monroe," Pierce agreed that the fugitive slaves presented "a new question, and a grave one, on which the Government had as yet developed no policy."

35. Cameron to Butler, May 30, 1861, in FSSP, ser. 1, 1:72.

36. On Republican antislavery strategy right from the beginning of the war, and Cameron's enthusiasm for that strategy, see Oakes, *Freedom National.*

37. *U.S. Statutes at Large, Treaties, and Proclamations of the United States of America* (Boston, 1863), 12:319.

38. Cameron to Butler, Aug. 8, 1861, in *OR*, ser. 2, 1:761–62. Copies of the same letter went out to Union commanding officers throughout the field of war. I wish to thank James Oakes for drawing my attention to these instructions.

39. Loring to Butler, Aug. 6, 1861, Salem, Mass., in Butler, *Private and Official Correspondence*, 1:192. For a concise treatment of fears of a standing government dating back even earlier than the founding of the republic, see James Kirby Martin and Mark Edward Lender, *A Respectable Army: The Military Origins of the Republic, 1763–1789* (Chichester, UK: John Wiley & Sons, 2015).

40. Lieber to A. D. Bache, Dec. 14, 1861, Lieber Papers, box 23, HL.

41. Lieber to Charles Sumner, June 1, 1861, New York City, Lieber Papers, box 42, HL.

42. Lieber to Sumner, Nov. 29, 1861, New York, Lieber Papers, box 42, HL. For more on these concerns, see Mancini, "Francis Lieber, Slavery, and the 'Genesis' of the Laws of War," and Dennis K. Boman, *Lincoln and Citizens' Rights in Civil*

War Missouri: Balancing Freedom and Security (Baton Rouge: Louisiana State University Press, 2011).

43. Secretary of War Simon Cameron, Aug. 8, 1861, in *OR*, ser. 2, 1:761–62.

44. Cameron to Butler, May 30, 1861.

45. *U.S. Statutes at Large, Treaties, and Proclamations*, 12:319. For Stevens, see *Cong. Globe*, 37th Cong., 1st sess., 415.

46. Cameron, Aug. 8, 1861, in *OR*, ser. 2, 1:761–62.

47. Brown to Assistant Adjutant General Lieutenant Colonel E. D. Townsend, June 22, 1861, Fort Pickens, Fla., in *OR*, ser. 2, 1:756.

48. Circular of General George McClellan, Dec. 16, 1861, Headquarters of the Army of the Potomac, Washington, D.C., in *OR*, ser. 1, 5:52. McClellan hired Allan Pinkerton, who operated under the pseudonym of E. J. Allen, to collect intelligence from escaped slaves and other fugitives to the Union army.

49. Commander O. S. Glisson to Flag Officer Silas H. Stringham, July 15, 1861; Stringham to Gideon Welles, July 18, 1861; Welles to Stringham, July 22, 1861, all in FSSP, ser. 1, 1:75–76. For the weather on July 14–15, see Robert K. Krick, *Civil War Weather in Virginia* (Tuscaloosa: University of Alabama Press, 2007), 30. For the phase of the moon, see NASA moon tables at http://eclipse.gsfc.nasa.gov/phase/phases1801.html.

50. "Doings in South Carolina," *Liberator*, Nov. 29, 1861.

51. Nussbaum, *Concise History of the Law of Nations*. The notion of freedom as the natural state of humans was generally known as the freedom principle in Europe centuries before importation into the United States via England and the *Somersett* case of 1772, discussed by Blackburn in *American Crucible*, 125–34, and Seymour Drescher in *Abolition: A History of Slavery and Antislavery* (New York: Cambridge University Press, 2009). For discussion of the freedom principle and the law of nations in mainstream Republican thinking during the Civil War, see Oakes, *Freedom National*, esp. ix–xiii, 8–14, 22–34, 43–51, 106–44.

52. Lieber to Sumner, Dec. 19, 1861, New York, Lieber Papers, box 42, HL.

53. *Cong. Globe*, 37th Cong., 1st sess., 216–17. See Oakes, *Freedom National*, 137–39.

54. James Buchanan, Reply to a Memorial of Citizens of Connecticut on Kansas, Washington City, Aug. 15, 1857, in Moore, *Works of James Buchanan*, 10:120. For the sway of the "slavery national" point of view over the federal government before the Civil War, see Fehrenbacher, *Slaveholding Republic*.

55. W.D.W. (Seventh Wisconsin) to hometown newspaper, Dec. 16, 1861, Arlington Heights, Va., Quiner Correspondence of Wisconsin Volunteers, reel 1, 2:5–6, SHSW. For just one of many examples of intra-army conflict over policy regarding slave refugees, see Colonel John Edwards (Eighteenth Iowa) to Major General Samuel Curtis, Jan. 19, 1863, Springfield, Mo., Records of the Department of Missouri, box 9, RG 393, pt. 1, entry 2593, NARA.

56. *OR*, ser. 1, 3:466–67; Basler, *Collected Works of Abraham Lincoln*, 3:506–7, 517–18.

57. Francis Lieber to S. A. Allibone, Oct. 5, 1861, Lieber Papers, box 22, and Lieber to Sumner, Nov. 28, 1861, Lieber Papers, box 42, HL.

58. Captain William Dunham (Thirty-Sixth Ohio) to wife, Oct. 28, 1861, and to father-in-law, Nov. 15, 1861, Summersville, Va., William Dunham Letters, Civil War Military Collection, U.S. Army Military History Institute.

59. Halleck, *International Law*, esp. chap. 18, sec. 24, p. 443.

60. *OR*, ser. 2, 1:778.

61. Halleck to Asboth, Dec. 26, 1861, St. Louis, in *OR*, ser. 2, 1:796.

62. Halleck to Colonel William Carlin (Commanding Ironton), Jan. 9, 1862, St. Louis, in *OR*, ser. 2, 1:799.

63. Grant to Colonel J. Cook, Dec. 25, 1861, Cairo, Ill., Letters Sent Aug. 1861–Oct. 1862, RG 393, pt. 2, entry 2730, NARA.

64. E. C. Hubbard (Thirteenth Illinois) to sister Laura, Dec. 31, 1861, Rolla, Mo., E. C. Hubbard Letters, Special Collections, University of Arkansas. A soldier in the Eighth Wisconsin Infantry stationed in Sulphur Springs, Missouri, similarly admitted to defying General Orders No. 3 in any way possible without getting in trouble for open violation of orders. See S. C. Mc to *Gazette* (Wis.), Dec. 13, 1861, Sulphur Springs, Mo., Quiner Papers Correspondence of Wisconsin Volunteers, reel 1, 2:29, SHSW.

65. Sgt. John Boucher (Tenth Missouri Infantry) to wife, Nov. 31, 1861, Camp Holmes, Mo., Boucher Family Papers, Civil War Miscellaneous Collection, 2nd ser., U.S. Army Military History Institute.

66. *Cong. Globe,* 37th Cong., 2d sess., 1143; *U.S. Statutes at Large, Treaties, and Proclamations,* 12:354.

67. Corporal Rufus Kinsley (Eighth Vermont) Diary, pt. 1, June 22, 1862, near Lafourche, La., Vermont Historical Society.

68. Paine, June 5–12, 1862, Paine to Williams, June 5 and 10, 1862, and subsequent Paine diary entries recorded in his Memoir, June–Aug. 1862, in Paine, *Wisconsin Yankee in Confederate Bayou Country,* 77–85, 87–88, 90, 102–3, 113.

69. Cartmell Diary, March 29, 1863, Madison County, Tenn., TSLA.

70. See Oakes, *Freedom National,* chaps. 1 and 8.

71. The District of Columbia Emancipation Act, April 16, 1862, http://www .archives.gov/exhibits/featured_documents/dc_emancipation_act/.

72. Petition of Ann E. Beall (former owner of Barbary and Robert), May 2, 1862, RG 217.6.5, M520, reel 2, NARA, and available online at http://civilwardc.org /texts/petitions/cww.00006.html; Allan Johnston, *Surviving Freedom: The Black Community of Washington, D.C., 1860–1880* (New York: Garland, 1993); Masur, *Example for All the Land.*

73. *New York World,* Feb. 25, 1865; *Boston Herald,* June 4, 1863. For eyewitness accounts of conditions among the new arrivals, see the Testimony of William Slade, Mrs. Daniel Breed, and Mr. George E. H. Day, AFIC Records, file 1, reel 200, frames 120–31, NARA.

74. Hunter's Proclamation (General Orders No. 11, Headquarters of the Department of the South, Hilton Head, S.C., May 9, 1862) and Lincoln's Proclamation countermanding it both appear in *OR*, ser. 2, 1:818–19.

75. Lieber to Bates, June 8, 1862, New York, plus enclosures, Lieber Papers, box 23, HL.

76. *U.S. Statutes at Large, Treaties, and Proclamations,* 12:589–92.

77. Emancipation Deeds of Lucinda, Alice, and Winnie Walker, Oct. 26, 1863, St. Louis, Walker Family Papers, MOHS.

78. Lieber to Sumner, Sept. 6, 1862, Lieber Papers, box 42, HL; Freidel, *Francis Lieber,* 323, 331; Lieber, *Law and Usages of War* (Notebook No. 7), Feb. 4, 1862, cited in Witt, *Lincoln's Code,* 227–28; Francis Lieber, "A Memoir on the Military Use of Coloured Persons, Free or Slave, That Come to Our Armies for Support or Protection, Written at the Request of Hon. Edwin M. Stanton, Secretary of War," Lieber Papers, box 27, HL.

79. Lieber, "Memoir on the Military Use of Coloured Persons."

80. For a recent survey of the long-running debate on the Emancipation Proclamation, see Louis P. Masur, *Lincoln's Hundred Days: The Emancipation Proclamation and the War for the Union* (Cambridge, Mass.: Harvard University Press, 2012). For a collection of recent work on the proclamation, see Blair and Younger, *Lincoln's Proclamation*.

81. *Chicago Times*, Oct. 14, 1862, Illinois Writers Project "Negro in Illinois" Collection, box 10, folder 41, Harsh Research Collection Chicago Public Library; Cartmell Diary, Nov. 2, 1862. Cartmell also notes the influence of the proclamation in spurring slaves to run in diary entries of Dec. 1 and 13, 1862, TSLA.

82. Charles Tubbs (Twenty-Seventh Massachusetts) to wife, Dec. 28, 1862, New Bern, N.C., Tubbs Papers. Tubbs himself was ambivalent at best about the incoming numbers, but other soldiers reacted with more fellow feeling, which they conveyed to New Englanders back home informally and also formally, such as through Superintendent of Contrabands James Means's communication to the New England Freedmen's Aid Society "asking relief for destitute negroes" in and near New Bern in the wake of the Emancipation Proclamation; see New England Freedmen's Aid Society Records, MS N-101, box 1, folder 1, MHS.

83. On uncertainty about the final proclamation, see Masur, *Lincoln's Hundred Days*, esp. chaps. 5–9. Union soldiers and freedpeople in contraband camps felt and echoed the uncertainty. See, for example, Benjamin Heuston to wife, Nov. 15, 1862, Nicholasville, Ky. (near Kentucky's Camp Nelson contraband camp), Heuston Papers, box 1, folder 5, University of Wisconsin-La Crosse.

84. For Union soldiers' reactions to the Emancipation Proclamation, see Manning, *What This Cruel War Was Over*, 83–102. On the one-and-a-half-inch copies of the proclamation printed by John Murray Forbes and distributed by Union soldiers, see Masur, *Lincoln's Hundred Days*, 233.

85. Cartmell Diary, Feb. 28, 1863, Madison County, Tenn., TSLA.

86. Wilder Testimony, AFIC Records file 2, reel 200, frame 148, NARA.

87. For records of slaves thronging Union steamers in the early months of 1863, see *Arrival and Departures Port of Cairo*, March 13, 1863, NARA.

88. Eaton to AFIC, AFIC Records, file 6, reel 200, frame 622, NARA.

89. Ayers and Nesbit, "Seeing Emancipation," 17.

90. On Dilla Best, Margaret (no last name), and men and boys from Huntsville and Murfreesboro at work on Fort Negley, see correspondence of Eames (Twenty-First Ohio) to wife, April–Aug. 1862, Murfreesboro and Nashville, Tenn., especially letters of July 31 and Aug. 13, 1862, Eames Papers MOHS. For more on Fort Negley, see General D. C. Buell to Captain James Morton, Aug. 6, 1862, Huntsville, Ala., in *OR*, vol. 16, pt. 2, p. 268 (and subsequent correspondence, p. 269); Stearns Testimony, frames 69–70; *Nashville Daily Times and True Union*, June 21, 1864.

91. *Alexandria Gazette*, Dec. 1, 1862. On high mortality rates, see all the AFIC files, chapters 1 and 2 above, and Downs, *Sick from Freedom*.

92. Greer Davis to son Lowndes Henry Davis, Feb. 24, 1863, Jackson, Mo., and Lowndes Davis to wife Mary, March 24 and April 6, 1863, Jackson, Mo., Lowndes Henry Davis Papers, MOHS; Greer Davis to Major General Samuel Curtis, Feb. 24, 1863, Jackson, Mo., Department of the Missouri, box 9, RG 393, pt. 1, entry 2593, NARA. At least one of the men, John, formerly owned by the Davises, made it even farther than Cape Girardeau, all the way to Chicago.

93. For an enlisted man's account of the Twenty-Second Wisconsin's adventures in

Kentucky, including Colonel Utley's travails, see Heuston Diary, Oct. and Nov. 1862, and the following letters: Heuston to wife, Oct., 23, 1862, Georgetown, Ky.; Heuston to wife, Nov. 16 and 18, 1862, Nicholasville, Ky., Heuston Papers, box 1, folders 3 and 5. University of Wisconsin-La Crosse. Other accounts of the Twenty-Second can be found in Coffin, *Reminiscences,* and Quiner, *Military History of Wisconsin.* William M. Fliss discusses the adventures of the Twenty-Second in an article titled "Wisconsin's 'Abolition Regiment.'"

94. Nat Leonard to Abiel Leonard, Oct. 6, 1862, Ravenswood, Mo., Leonard Family Papers, WHMC. Letters among Leonard families all fall, in fact, bemoaned the loss of slaves.

95. Eames to wife, July 20, 1862, Murfreesboro, Tenn., Eames Papers, box 1, folder 3, TSLA.

96. Morris, *Free Men All,* 4. On the aftermath of the Revolution, see Jasanoff, *Liberty's Exiles.* On the North's gradual emancipation alongside the South's strengthening of slavery, see Joanne Pope Melish, *Disowning Slavery: Gradual Emancipation and "Race" in New England, 1780–1860* (Ithaca, N.Y.: Cornell University Press, 2000), and Zilversmit, *First Emancipation.*

97. Rothman, *Slave Country.*

98. Dubois, *Colony of Citizens.*

99. Blanchard, *Under the Flags of Freedom,* esp. chaps. 7 and 8; Leitman, "Black Ragamuffins"; and conversation with the historian of Brazil Bryan McCann about his work in progress on the Ragamuffin Revolt.

100. Dubois, *Avengers of the New World;* Fick, *Making Haiti.*

101. "What Shall We Do with the Slaves?," *New York Times,* Dec. 14, 1861.

102. *U. S. Statutes at Large, Treaties, and Proclamations,* 12:589–92.

103. Provost Marshal General Bernard G. Farrar to Rombauer, April 2, 1862, St. Louis, in *OR,* ser. 2, 1:814.

104. Bostwick and Hood, *Report upon the Condition and Treatment of Colored Refugees,* 10.

105. John Eaton Report, AFIC Records, file 6, reel 200, frame 622, NARA.

FOUR · UNEASY ALLIANCES

1. Collier et al. to Curtis, Dec. 8, 1862, Chillicothe, Mo.; and Jacobson to Major H. Z. Curtis (assistant adjutant general, Department of Missouri), Feb. 23, 1863, Rolla, Mo., with endorsements from Major General Samuel R. Curtis, Department of Missouri, box 9, RG 393, pt. 1, entry 2593, NARA.

2. See Don H. Doyle, *The Cause of All Nations: An International History of the American Civil War* (New York: Basic Books, 2014).

3. Edward E. Hale, "The Man Without a Country," *Atlantic Monthly,* Dec. 1863, 665–80.

4. Daryle Williams, "Rethinking the Christie Affair: Free Africans, Citizenship, and Nation During the Anglo-Brazilian Conflict, 1861–1865" (unpublished paper, Dec. 15, 2012; cited with permission), 22–24, and subsequent e-mail correspondence with the author, Dec. 2012 and March 2013.

5. I first began to think seriously about the destabilizing threat posed by statelessness and how such a perceived threat might have influenced Northerners' views of slaves freed by war when I heard Linda K. Kerber's presidential address, "The Stateless as the Citizen's Other: A View from the United States," at the 121st

Annual Meeting of the American Historical Association held in Atlanta, 2007, and reprinted on the History and Archives page of the American Historical Association Web site, http://www.historians.org/about-aha-and-membership /aha-history-and-archives/presidential-addresses/linda-k-kerber. See also Kerber, "Toward a History of Statelessness in America," *American Quarterly* 57, no. 3 (2005): 727–49.

6. *Bryan v. Walton* (1853), quoted in William M. Wiecek, "Emancipation and Civic Status: The American Experience, 1865–1915," in Tsesis, *Promises of Liberty,* 81.

7. *Dred Scott v. Sandford,* 60 U.S. 393 (1857), http://laws.findlaw.com/us/60/393 .html.

8. Olds to AFIC commissioners, Aug. 20, 1863, AFIC Records, box 2, HO.

9. Lieber to Charles Sumner, March 25, 1864, New York, Lieber Papers, box 44, HL.

10. Laura E. Richards, *Samuel Gridley Howe, by His Daughter* (New York: D. Appleton-Century, 1935). The range of Howe's interests and reforming activities was vast. He is best known for his work with the blind and for his antislavery activities.

11. John Hodges to Howe, April 29, 1863, MacKaye Papers, LOC.

12. William Christie, "Our Relations with Brazil," *Macmillan's Magazine,* Oct. 1863, 488–97.

13. See Prentiss to Major General Samuel Curtis, Feb. 28, 1863, Helena, Ark.; Hanford (agent of the Pacific Railroad) to L. M. Hissock (general superintendent of the Pacific Railroad), May 3, 1863, Jefferson City, Mo.; and Major Lucien Eaton to Major General Schofield, April 13, May 9 and 30, 1863, all in Department of Missouri, box 9, RG 393, pt. 1, entry 2593, NARA. See also Lucien Eaton Papers, MOHS.

14. Eaton to Schofield, May 30, 1863. Records reveal that Hanford was disciplined for refusing transport to the group, but they do not reveal when or if the group ever managed to take the train out of Jefferson City.

15. Strawbridge to Brigade Surgeon Holston (medical director, District of West Tennessee), Sept. 11, 1862, General Hospital, Jackson, Tenn., and Strawbridge to McClernand, Aug. 15, 1862, General Hospital, Jackson, Tenn., RG 393, pt. 2, entry 2732, NARA.

16. For more on McClernand, see Michael Todd Landis, *Northern Men with Southern Principles: The Democratic Party and the Sectional Crisis* (Ithaca, N.Y.: Cornell University Press, 2014).

17. Brigadier General Thomas Williams, General Orders No. 46, June 5, 1862, Baton Rouge, La.; Paine to Williams, June 5, 1862, Baton Rouge, La.; Lieutenant and Assistant Adjutant Quartermaster Henry Elliott to Paine, June 7 and 10, 1862, Baton Rouge, La.; Paine to Elliott, June 10, 1862, Baton Rouge, La.; Williams to Paine, June 11, 1862, Baton Rouge, La.; Paine to General Benjamin Butler, June 14, 1862, Baton Rouge, La., in Paine, *Wisconsin Yankee in Confederate Bayou Country,* 77–85. Senator Timothy Howe, *Cong. Globe,* 37th Cong., 2nd sess., 3341–42.

18. Jessee Diary, vol. 1, Aug. 16, 1862, Jackson, Tenn., University of Kansas.

19. Ibid., Oct. 27, 1862.

20. Colyer Report to AFIC, 1863, AFIC Records, file 4, reel 200, frames 430–31, NARA; Rumley Diary, March 25, 1863, Beaufort, N.C., NCDAH.

21. Rumley Diary, March 25, 1863, Beaufort, N.C.

22. Nichols Testimony, AFIC Records, file 1, reel 200, NARA. Numbers of women:

frame 107; value of their labor: frame 112; confrontation with Virginia slave owner: frames 118–19.

23. John Eaton, AFIC Records, file 6, reel 200, frames 570-588, NARA. For "Interrogatory 9th" about women's and men's labor, see frame 577.

24. AFIC Records, file 6, reel 200, NARA. Tables: frame 571. Quotations: frames 592–600.

25. Colyer, *Brief Report of the Services Rendered by the Freed People*.

26. Prentiss to Schofield, June 16, 1863, Helena, Ark., Department of Missouri, box 9, RG 393, pt. 1, entry 2593, NARA.

27. AFIC, *Preliminary Report*, June 20, 1863, sec. 1, para. 1, AFIC Records, reel 199, NARA.

28. AFIC Questionnaire, short and long forms, 1863, AFIC Records, box 1, folder 25, HO. The query about value to the community was question 13. Towns from Massachusetts, Connecticut, Vermont, Rhode Island, Pennsylvania, New York, Ohio, and Kansas responded. See boxes 1–4, HO.

29. "The War in Tennessee," *New York Times*, Sept. 10, 1863.

30. AFIC Records, file 6, reel 200, NARA. Quotations: frames 592–600.

31. Emberton, "Only Murder Makes Men," 380.

32. Quoted in Robert B. Edgerton, *Hidden Heroism: Black Soldiers in America's Wars* (Boulder, Colo.: Westview Press, 2001), 39.

33. Nussbaum, *Concise History of the Law of Nations*; Blackburn, *American Crucible*, 125–34; and Drescher, *Abolition;* Oakes, *Freedom National;* Eaton, *Lincoln, Grant, and the Freedmen;* Lieber Papers, HL.

34. Butler to Cameron, July 30, 1861, Private and Official Correspondence, 187.

35. Elizabeth James to Whipple, Dec. 19, 1863; James, *Annual Report*, 15; *Register of Colored Nurses Under Contract [Department of the East] July 16, 1863, to June 14, 1864*. For Martha and Albert Pool, see pp. 9–10. To trace the Pools and their son, Benjamin, see Deposit Records for Alfred Pool and Martha Pool, citing Bank New Bern, Craven, N.C., FSB microfilm 928586.

36. The ban was first enacted in 1802. See *Public Statutes at Large of the United States of America from the Organization of the Government in 1789 to March 3, 1845*, 2:191. In 1828, Congress went even further to not even allow black workers (free or slave) to lift a mail sack out of a carriage without specified white supervision. See Leon F. Litwack, "The Federal Government and the Free Negro, 1790–1860," *Journal of Negro History* 43, no. 4 (Oct. 1958): 270. The postal service Web site notes that the 1828 ban was lightened by Congress in 1862. See Jenny Lynch, "African-American Postal Workers in the 19th Century," U.S. Postal Service, http://www.usps.com/postalhistory/_pdf/AfricanAmericanWorkers19thc.pdf.

37. See, for example, Amy Dru Stanley, *From Bondage to Contract: Wage Labor, Marriage, and the Market in the Age of Slave Emancipation* (New York: Cambridge University Press), 1998. Quotations from pp. x and 2.

38. William Graham Sumner, *What Social Classes Owe to Each Other* (New York: Harper and Brothers, 1883), 25.

39. Perry Miller, *Errand into the Wilderness* (Cambridge, Mass.: Harvard University Press, 1956); Edmund Morgan, *Puritan Political Ideas* (Indianapolis: Bobbs-Merrill, 1965); Stanley, *From Bondage to Contract*, esp. 6–8.

40. For one example of the application of social contract theory to the United States in the Civil War, see Drew Gilpin Faust, *Mothers of Invention* (Chapel Hill: University of North Carolina Press, 2004).

41. Much influential scholarship has argued that nineteenth-century African Americans, and black women in particular, rejected predominant white notions of freedom, including the primacy of contract, because they did not accept the tenets of liberal individualism. See, for example, Elsa Barkley Brown, "Negotiating and Transforming the Public Sphere: African American Political Life in the Transition from Slavery to Freedom," *Public Culture* 7 (Winter 1994): 107–46, and Jacqueline Jones, *Labor of Love, Labor of Sorrow: Black Women, Work, and the Family from Slavery to the Present* (New York: Basic Books, 1985). While I am not confident that all former slaves defined anything, let alone freedom, in exactly the same way, I agree that many freedpeople navigated by lights other than liberal individualism, but here I argue that those lights led them not so much to reject the notion of contract as to understand it in terms other than the free-market ones that came to predominate after the war.

42. For example, see Lieber to Sumner, March 11, 1864, making reference to correspondence with McKaye, Howe, and Owen of the "Freedmen Commission" as well as to the Loyal Publication Society, Lieber Papers, box 44.

43. Lieber, *Amendments of the Constitution, Submitted to the Consideration of the American People;* Lieber to Sumner, March 5, 1864, New York, Lieber Papers, box 44.

44. Lieber to Sumner, March 10, 1864, Lieber Papers, box 44.

45. Lieber to Sumner, March 20 and 25, 1864, Lieber Papers, box 44.

46. *Opinion of Attorney General Bates on Citizenship* (Washington, D.C.: Government Printing Office, 1863), http://quod.lib.umich.edu/m/moa/aew6575.0001 .001/1?view=image&size=100.

47. Ibid., 1, 3, 9, 14, 7, 4.

48. Fife to Dr. S. G. Howe, May 28, 1863, Va., MacKaye Papers.

49. John Eaton, AFIC Records, file 6, reel 200, frame 624, NARA.

50. Banks (Department of the Gulf) to James McKaye, March 28, 1864, Alexandria, La., included in McKaye's supplemental report, "The Emancipated Slave Face to Face with His Old Master, Valley of the Lower Mississippi," AFIC Records, reel 199, frame 388–89, NARA. McKaye criticizes Banks's excessive sympathy toward planters several times in his report.

51. See, for example, Matthews, "List of the Planters, Leasees, Employers, and Number of Acres of Land Tilled and Untilled in the Second District of North Mississippi," RG 105, M1914, reel 5, frames 90–91, NARA.

52. On the Third South Carolina protests and Walker's court-martial, see FSSP, ser. 2, 1:391–394.

53. Hugh Davis, *"We Will Be Satisfied with Nothing Less": The African American Struggle for Equal Rights in the North During Reconstruction* (Ithaca, N.Y.: Cornell University Press, 2011), esp. chap. 1.

54. AFIC, *Final Report*, 99, AFIC Records, reel 199, NARA.

55. Lieutenant Stuart Eldridge (Sixty-Fourth U.S. Colored Infantry) and provost marshal of freedmen, to Colonel George M. Zeigler (Fifty-Second U.S. Colored Infantry), June 12, 1865, Vicksburg, Miss.; Zeigler to Eldridge, June 12, 1865, and Eldridge's endorsement of June 12, 1865, RG 105, M1914, reel 5, frames 23–24, NARA.

56. McKaye, "Emancipated Slave Face to Face with His Old Master," AFIC Records, reel 199, frames 363–68, NARA.

57. George Hanks, Testimony, AFIC Records, file 11, reel 201, frame 615, NARA.

58. "Additional Particulars: Interesting Details of the Expedition," *New York Times*, March 7, 1864, 1.

59. Provost Marshal General of Freedmen and Colonel of Sixty-Fourth U.S. Colored Infantry Samuel Thomas, Jan. 31, 1865, Vicksburg, Miss., RG 105, M1914, reel 5, frames 6–7, NARA.

60. See Cartmell Diary, Aug. 19, 1862, outside Jackson, Tenn. See also Rumley Diary; Alice Williamson Diary, DU, http://scriptorium.lib.duke.edu/williamson/p01 /williamson-p01.html.

61. Andrew to sister, Dec. 2, 1862, Corinth, Miss., Andrews Family Papers, folder 1, TSLA.; Hinshaw to cousin Benjamin Beeler, July 15, 1865, Marshall, Tex., William Hinshaw Letters, ISHL; Rice to My Children, Sept. 3, 1864, Benton Barracks, Mo., enclosed in F. W. Diggs to General Rosecrans, Sept. 10, 1864, in FSSP, ser. 2, 689–90; Lavinia Bell Testimony, AFIC Records, file 7, reel 201, frames 105–7, NARA. See also Stanley, "Instead of Waiting for the Thirteenth Amendment."

62. Message of the President of the United States, Communicating, in Compliance with a Resolution of the Senate of the 5th Instant; A Report from the Secretary of States, upon the Subject of the Supposed Kidnapping of Colored Persons in the Southern States for the Purpose of Selling Them as Slaves in Cuba, 39th Cong., 1st Sess. (18660, S. Ex. Doc. 30, ser. 1238, p. 18-19), in Rothman, *Beyond Freedom's Reach*, 193-197.

63. AFIC Records, reels 199–201, NARA. Quotation from *Final Report*, chap. 3, p. 109.

64. *Chicago Times*, Oct. 5, 1864, Illinois Writers Project "Negro in Illinois" Collection, box 14, folder 21, Chicago Public Library.

65. Testimony in virtually every one of the AFIC files makes this point. See AFIC Records, reels 199–201, NARA.

66. Correspondence between Chaplain J. A. Hawley and Provost Marshal of Freedmen Stuart Eldridge, April 1865, Vicksburg, Miss., RG 105, M1914, reel 5, frames 13–14, NARA. There is a *huge* existing literature on freedpeople's education generally and as an aspect of citizenship; rehearsing it here would be redundant, especially when the topic is already so well covered in James D. Anderson, *The Education of Blacks in the South, 1860–1935* (Chapel Hill: University of North Carolina Press, 1988); Ronald Butchart, *Schooling the Freed People: Teaching, Learning, and the Struggle for Black Freedom, 1861–1876* (Chapel Hill: University of North Carolina Press, 2010); Jacqueline Jones, *Soldiers of Light and Love: Northern Teachers and Georgia Blacks, 1865–1873* (Athens: University of Georgia Press, 1992); Rose, *Rehearsal for Reconstruction*.

67. William Sherman, Florida Narratives, 3:286, WPA Narratives; Thomas Smallwood Testimony, AFIC Records, files 10 and 10:2, reel 201, frame 314, NARA. In these files, several freeborn black migrants to Canada, as well as Canadian-born black men, emphasize the importance of access to courts.

68. See Dylan Penningroth, *The Claims of Kinfolk: African American Property and Community in the Nineteenth-Century South* (Chapel Hill: University of North Carolina Press, 2003).

69. William Bolles Testimony, AFIC Records, file 2, reel 200, frame 140, NARA. Testimony in file 1 (Washington, D.C.), file 2 (Department of the South), file 4

(North Carolina), file 7 (Kentucky, Tennessee, and Missouri), and files 10 and 10.2 (Canada) repeatedly emphasizes access to courts.

70. Penningroth, *Claims of Kinfolk*, 112.

71. "Testimony of a Colored Man (Name Unknown)," AFIC Records, file 7, reel 201, frame 98, NARA.

72. Albert Butler Testimony, AFIC Records, file 10, reel 201, frame 313, NARA.

73. Martin Hauser to Morton, April 21, 1863, Newbern, Ind., Governor Oliver P. Morton Papers, reel 5, Indiana State Archives.

74. Record of Soldiers and Citizens Arrested by Provost Guard to Be Disposed of by C.M.P., Records of the Provost Marshal, Department of Alabama (Decatur, Huntsville), July 1864–Aug. 1865, RG 393, pt. 4, entry 1411, NARA.

75. R. S. Donaldson (Fifty-Fourth U.S. Colored Infantry) by order of Post Adjutant S. D. Barnes, General Orders No. 5, April 13, 1865, Davis Bend, RG 105, M1914, reel 1, frames 242–43, NARA.

76. Report of Arrests Made March 1862–1864, Cairo, Ill., RG 393, pt. 2, entry 1105, vol. 2, NARA.

77. Palmer Letts and C. P. Day to AFIC commissioners, Aug. 8, 1863, Oneida County, N.Y. (about Yorktown, Va.), AFIC Records, box 1, folder 33 HO.

78. Fraser and Gordon, "Genealogy of Dependency," 315. Northern newspapers also echoed the dependent/independent debate in their columns. In 1862 and 1863, former slaves from the Mississippi valley resettled in Wisconsin, prompting state Democrats to use that migration, far more than the Emancipation Proclamation, as a divisive political issue. Republican newspapers responded by portraying former slaves as a population "noted for industry, upright conduct, morality and business," as the *Lancaster Herald* put it on Feb. 19, 1863. Pleasant Ridge file, Holzhueter Papers: Black Settlers in Early Wisconsin Collection, box 3, folder 1, SHSW.

79. Corporal Jackson Cherry, Company I, Thirty-Fifth U.S. Colored Troops, to editor, *South Carolina Leader* (Charleston), Dec. 16, 1865, 2.

80. David Todd to brother John Todd, April 16, 1864, Pine Bluff, Ark., Farnsworth Letters, University of Illinois; AFIC, *Final Report,* esp. chap. 3 (quotation from p. 100), AFIC Records, reel 199, NARA.

81. John Dix Testimony, AFIC Records, file 2, reel 200, frame 136, NARA; Dr. Brown Testimony, AFIC Records, file 2, frame 164, NARA.

82. Butler to Lincoln, Nov. 28, 1862, quoted in *Preliminary Report of the American Freedmen's Inquiry Commission,* 4, AFIC Records, reel 199, NARA.

83. Colyer to AFIC, AFIC Records, file 4, reel 200, frames 447–48, NARA.

84. Eaton to Wilson, Feb. 1863, Memphis, RG 105, M1914, reel 1, NARA.

85. Eaton to Robert Carroll (secretary of the Contrabands' Relief Commission), Feb. 9, 1863, Memphis, RG 105, M1914, reel 1, NARA.

86. Colyer's Report to the AFIC, 1863, AFIC Records, reel 200, frames 447–51, NARA.

87. Elsa Barkley Brown argues that "collective autonomy," as opposed to personal independence, was what slaves most desired. See "Negotiating and Transforming the Public Sphere," esp. 124–27.

88. Northwestern Freedmen's Aid Commission, *Minutes of the First Annual Meeting,* 5.

89. James, *Annual Report of the Superintendent of Negro Affairs in North Carolina,* 4.

INTERLUDE · INTO THE WILDERNESS

1. Adam Goodheart, *1861: The Civil War Awakening* (New York: Knopf, 2011), 382. There were no longer slaves in and around Fort Monroe, but not because of the Emancipation Proclamation, which had not applied to Elizabeth City County. Rather, the combined effects of War Department orders of Aug. 1861, a March 1862 federal law prohibiting the army from returning fugitive slaves, and the Second Confiscation Act of July 1862 all meant that enslaved men, women, and children who got themselves to Union lines in and around Fort Monroe were no longer their former owners' property.

2. Surgeon General V. K. Barnes to William H. Seward, July 22, 1865, War Department Pass No. 663 Signed by L. H. Pelonge, Assistant Adjutant General, William Seward to General David Hunter, July 25, 1865, Wood, "Manuscript History Concerning the Pension Claim of Harriet Tubman," all in HR 55 A-D1, Papers Accompanying the Claim of Harriet Tubman, RG 233 (Records of the House of Representatives), NARA; General Affidavit of Harriet Tubman Davis, 1898, RG 233, NARA, http://www.archives.gov/legislative/features/claim-of-harriet-tubman/.

3. Affidavits of Gaston Becton, Pension File of Gaston Becton (one of Becton's affidavits mentions his growth spurt); "36th U.S. Colored Troops Infantry Regiment (Union)," in Dyer, *Compendium of the War of the Rebellion*, vol. 3; James K. Bryant, *The 36th Infantry United States Colored Troops in the Civil War: A History and Roster* (Jefferson, N.C.: McFarland, 2012).

4. Private Charles Beman (Fifth Massachusetts Cavalry) to father, April 5, 1865, Richmond, reprinted in the *Anglo-African*, April 22, 1865, 1; Lieutenant Edward Bartlett (Fifth Massachusetts Cavalry) to sister, April 3, 1865, Bartlett Correspondence; Sergeant Major Griffin (Twenty-Ninth Connecticut) to editor, April 12, 1865, *Anglo-African*, April 29, 1865, 1; Ella Roper, April 20, 1865, Roanoke Island, N.C., "From Miss Ella Roper," *American Missionary* 9 (July 1865): 157.

5. Charles L. Perdue Jr., Thomas E. Barden, and Robert K. Phillips, *Weevils in the Wheat: Interviews with Virginia Ex-slaves* (Charlottesville: University Press of Virginia, 1976), 39. For discussion of reaction to Appomattox, see Elizabeth R. Varon, *Appomattox: Victory, Defeat, and Freedom at the End of the Civil War* (New York: Oxford University Press, 2014). Gregory P. Downs's *After Appomattox: Military Occupation and the Ends of the War* (Cambridge, Mass.: Harvard University Press, 2015), which came out too late to be considered in this study, emphasizes continuity of war for years after Appomattox. That view is not incompatible with the recognition of Appomattox and the spring of 1865 as turning points, for even though violence continued and the army was still needed, as Downs shows, two significant changes took place with immediate and real effects on people's lives: the Confederacy ceased to exist and the conflict went from high intensity to low intensity. Low intensity does not mean "gentle" or "nice" violence; it means different violence. Mark Grimsley has usefully described the low-intensity post-1865 conflict as an insurgency. See "Wars for the American South: The First and Second Reconstructions Considered as Insurgencies," *Civil War History* 58, no. 1 (March 2012): 6–36.

6. Sperry, *History of the 33d Iowa Infantry Volunteer Regiment*, 163.

7. Corey, "Reminiscences."
8. See Records of the Mississippi Freedmen's Department ("Pre-Bureau Records") for April 1865, RG 105, M1914, reel 5, NARA.
9. Richard Etheredge, William Benson, and other men of the Thirty-Sixth U.S. Colored Infantry to General Oliver Otis Howard, May 1865, City Point, Va., in FSSP, ser. 2, 1:729–30, which dates the petition either May or June, but it had to have been May if it came from City Point, because the Thirty-Sixth left City Point for Fort Monroe on May 24 and began shipping out for Texas by the end of the month. By June, the regiment was in Brazos Santiago, Texas.
10. Roper, "From Miss Ella Roper," 158. For discussion of a wide range of responses to Lincoln's death, see Martha Hodes, *Mourning Lincoln* (New Haven, Conn.: Yale University Press, 2015).
11. David Todd to brother John Todd, May 6, 1865, Pine Bluff, Ark., Farnsworth Letters University of Illinois.
12. Taylor, *Reminiscences of My Life in Camp*, 125.
13. See Fehrenbacher, *Slaveholding Republic*. On Albert and Martha Pool, pp. 216–218, 349 n. 35.
14. James, *Annual Report of the Superintendent of Negro Affairs in North Carolina*, 59.
15. Judge A. D. Smith (chairman of the board of U.S. Direct Tax Commissioners for state of South Carolina) Testimony, AFIC Records, file 3, reel 200, frame 210, NARA.
16. T. J. Wright to Lieutenant D. M. Dick, May 20, 1865; Dick to Colonel Samuel Thomas, May 20, 1865, Vicksburg, Miss., RG 105, M1914, reel 5, frame 21, NARA. Thomas's endorsement instructs the assistant quartermaster "to make the repairs on the Hospital, as asked for."

FIVE · IMPERFECT PLOWSHARES

1. Daughty to Eaton, Jan. 29, 1866, Brunswick, Ga., Eaton Letters, Maine Historical Society. This particular letter written in Jan. capped off the previous months' tussles over Frashior and the boat.
2. Eaton to Rufus Saxton, April 12, 1865, Savannah and St. Simon's Island, Ga.; Captain A. P. Ketchum to Eaton, Aug. 21, 1865; Willard Saxton to Eaton, Sept. 14, 1865, Beaufort, S.C.; Campbell to Eaton, Oct. 12, 1865, St. Catherine's, Ga.; Ketchum to Eaton, Jan. 6, 1866, Charleston, S.C.; Eaton Letters. Quotation from Saxton to Eaton, Sept. 14, 1865, all in Eaton Letters.
3. Gregory Downs and Scott Nesbit echo the point about the army's presence as a crucial condition for the enforcement of freedpeople's rights in the Reconstruction South. See Gregory P. Downs and Scott Nesbit, *Mapping Occupation: Force, Freedom, and the Army in Reconstruction*, accessed June 2015, http://mappingoccupation.org, published March 2015.
4. "Horrible Treatment of a Negro Woman," *Liberator*, Nov. 10, 1865, 180.
5. "Proceedings of the Louisiana Conference of the African Methodist Episcopal Zion Church, New Orleans, May 17, 1865," in *Proceedings of the Black National and State Conventions, 1865–1900*, ed. Philip S. Foner and George E. Walker (Philadelphia: Temple University Press, 1986), 2–28.
6. "Address from the Colored Citizens of Norfolk to the People of the United States. Also an Account of the Agitation Among the Colored People of Virginia

for Equal Rights, June 1865," in ibid., 80–103; "State Convention of the Colored Men of Tennessee, Nashville, Aug. 7, 1865," in ibid., 112–27.

7. "State Convention of the Colored People of North Carolina, Sept. 29, 1865, Raleigh, N.C.," in ibid., 177–81.

8. "Proceedings of the Convention of the Colored Citizens of the State of Arkansas, Nov. 30–Dec. 2, 1865, Little Rock, Ark.," in ibid., 187–95.

9. "Proceedings of the First Annual Meeting of the National Equal Rights League, Held in Cleveland, Ohio, October 19, 20, and 21, 1865," in ibid., 40–68.

10. See Kantrowitz, *More Than Freedom,* and Taylor, "'To Make the Union What It Ought to Be,'" chap. 7.

11. Hazen Parsons's ca. 1874 account, quoted in *Mukwonago Chief,* Nov. 14, 1984, Holzhueter Papers: Black Settlers in Early Wisconsin Collection, box 1, folder 1, SHSW. Cowen died suddenly after a brief illness on Jan. 17, 1873.

12. Hager helped resettle freedpeople in Cincinnati, Springfield, Urbana, Mechanicsburg, Landau, and Xenia. RG 105, M999, reel 10, frames 351–55, NARA, and Sears, *Camp Nelson, Kentucky,* 312–24.

13. See *National Freedman,* 1865–1866; *Worcester Daily Spy,* 1865–1860; Janette Greenwood, "Southern Black Migration and Community Building in the Era of the Civil War," in *Faces of Community: Immigrant Massachusetts, 1860–2000,* ed. Reed Ueda and Conrad Wright (Boston: Massachusetts Historical Society, 2003); Janette Greenwood, *First Fruits of Freedom: The Migration of Former Slaves and Their Search for Equality in Worcester, Massachusetts, 1862–1900* (Chapel Hill: University of North Carolina Press, 2009), especially p. 197, notes 2, 12, and 13.

14. See Heather Andrea Williams, *Help Me to Find My People: The African American Search for Family Lost in Slavery* (Chapel Hill: University of North Carolina Press, 2012).

15. Holmes, "Reminiscences."

16. Liberty pole celebration in Darlington, Sept. 22, 1865, recounted in the journal of Provost Judge John Mead Gould Diary, Sept. 22, 1865, *Civil War Journals of John Mead Gould,* 500–501, Maine Historical Society.

17. On Andrew Johnson and Reconstruction, see Michael W. Fitzgerald, *Splendid Failure: Postwar Reconstruction in the American South* (Chicago: Ivan R. Dee, 2007), chap. 2; Eric L. McKitrick, *Andrew Johnson and Reconstruction* (New York: Oxford University Press, 1988); Michael Perman, *Reunion Without Compromise: The South and Reconstruction, 1865–1868* (New York: Cambridge University Press, 1973); Hans L. Trefousse, *Andrew Johnson: A Biography* (New York: Norton, 1997). For a recent apologia on Johnson's presidency as seen exclusively from Johnson's point of view, see Paul H. Bergeron, *Andrew Johnson's Civil War and Reconstruction* (Knoxville: University of Tennessee Press, 2011).

18. Johnson to Governor Oliver P. Morton and Indiana delegation, April 21, 1865, in *The Papers of Andrew Johnson,* ed. LeRoy P. Graf and Ralph W. Haskins (Knoxville: University of Tennessee Press, 1967–1986), 7:612–13, and *The Papers of Andrew Johnson,* vols. 7 and 8, ed. Paul Bergeron (Knoxville: University of Tennessee Press, 1990).

19. See Brooks D. Simpson, LeRoy P. Graf, and John Muldowny, eds., *Advice After Appomattox: Letters to Andrew Johnson, 1865–1866* (Knoxville: University of Tennessee Press, 1987).

20. Andrew Johnson, June 9, 1864, Nashville, in Edward McPherson, *The Political History of the United States of America During the Period of Reconstruction* (Washington, D.C.: Solomons & Chapman, 1875), 56.

21. Andrew Johnson, Proclamations of Amnesty and Reconstruction, May 29, 1865, in *A Compilation of the Messages and Papers of the Presidents*, ed. James D. Richardson (Washington, D.C.: Government Printing Office, 1896–1899), 6:312–13.

22. Donald Nieman, "Andrew Johnson, the Freedmen's Bureau, and the Problem of Equal Rights, 1865–1866," *Journal of Southern History* 44, no. 3 (Aug. 1978): 399–420.

23. Chase to Johnson, May 4, 1865, Beaufort, N.C., in Simpson, Graf, and Muldowny, *Advice After Appomattox*, 17. See also Whitelaw Reid, *After the War: A Tour of the Southern States, 1865–1866* (London: S. Low, Son & Marston, 1866).

24. Carl Schurz to Margarethe Schurz, July 26 and 30, 1865, and Schurz's letters to Johnson, July–Sept. 1865, in Simpson, Graf, and Muldowny, *Advice After Appomattox*, 69, 78–150.

25. J. W. Shaffer Testimony, Jan. 22, 1866, in *Report of the Joint Committee on Reconstruction at the First Session Thirty-Ninth Congress* (Washington, D.C.: Government Printing Office, 1866), pt. 4, p. 55.

26. William Driver Diary, n.d. but early 1870s about the immediate postwar, Nashville, William Driver Papers, TSLA.

27. D. E. Haynes Testimony, Jan. 30, 1865, in *Report of the Joint Committee on Reconstruction*, 60–61; Joseph E. Roy Testimony, in ibid., 63.

28. The woman set out with a band of fellow freedpeople, some of whom escaped into the woods, witnessed these events, and then reported them when they finally did make it to U.S. troops. See Roy Testimony, Jan. 30, 1865, 63. For more on violence after the war, see Dan Carter, *When the War Was Over: The Failure of Self-Reconstruction in the South* (Baton Rouge: Louisiana State University Press, 1985); Douglas R. Egerton, *The Wars of Reconstruction: The Brief, Violent History of America's Most Progressive Era* (New York: Bloomsbury Press, 2014); Hannah Rosen, *Terror in the Heart of Freedom: Citizenship, Sexual Violence, and the Meaning of Race in the Postemancipation South* (Chapel Hill: University of North Carolina Press, 2009); Kidada E. Williams, *They Left Great Marks on Me: African American Testimonies of Racial Violence from Emancipation to World War I* (New York: New York University Press, 2012), chap. 1.

29. Swayne to Alabama judges, Sept. 9, 1865, RG 105, M809, reel 1, NARA.

30. Private J. A. Bracy (Fortieth North Carolina) to father, June 13, 1863, Fort Caswell, N.C., Sheppard Collection, folder 3, NCDAH.

31. McKaye, "Emancipated Slave Face to Face with His Old Master," AFIC Records, reel 199, frame 366, NARA.

32. *Cong. Globe*, 38th Cong., 1st sess., 19, 1314.

33. Repeal of Fugitive Slave Law, June 28, 1864, 13 *Stat. at Large* (38th Cong.), 410.

34. *Cong. Globe*, 38th Cong., 1st sess., 2995.

35. "Abolition of Slavery: Adoption of the Amendment to the Constitution by Congress," *New York Herald*, Feb. 1, 1865, 1.

36. See, for example, "Rejoicings over the Passage of the Constitutional Amendment," *Boston Herald*, Feb. 3, 1865, 2; Captain Peter Eltinge (156th New York) to father, Feb. 6, 1865, Savannah, Eltinge-Lord Family Papers, box 4, folder 3, DU.

37. On the passage and ratification of the Thirteenth Amendment, see Michael Vorenberg, *Final Freedom: The Civil War, the Abolition of Slavery, and the Thir-*

teenth Amendment (New York: Cambridge University Press, 2001), and Oakes, *Freedom National,* chap. 12.

38. The Reverend O. G. Wheeler to AFIC, Sept. 24, 1863, South Hero, Vt., AFIC Records, box 4, HO.

39. Lieber to Sumner, March 10, 1864, Francis Lieber Papers, box 42. HL.

40. Gould Diary, July–Oct. 1865, in *Civil War Journals of John Mead Gould,* Maine Historical Society.

41. Captain and Provost Marshal W. R. Kennedy to Lieutenant A. L. Cavender (commander of Post Brownsboro, Ala.), Aug. 5, 1865, Huntsville, Ala., Letters Sent by the Provost Marshal, Department of Alabama (Decatur, Huntsville), July 1864–Aug. 1865, RG 393, pt. 4, entry 1411, NARA. "The Old Slaveholding Spirit," *Liberator,* Dec. 29, 1865, 208.

42. See Rothman, *Beyond Freedom's Reach.*

43. General John M. Palmer to President Andrew Johnson, July 29, 1865, Louisville, Ky., Department of Kentucky, RG 393, pt. 1, entry 2164, NARA. Palmer estimated the numbers of black Kentuckians affected as follows: 230,000 were enslaved at the start of the war, of whom approximately 64,568 remained enslaved at the end of the war, the balance having been freed by enlistment, the act of Congress freeing soldiers' families, the First or Second Confiscation Act, and/or War Department orders forbidding Union soldiers to help recapture fugitive slaves.

44. Mary Wilson affidavit, June 17, 1865, in FSSP, ser. 1, 1:623–24.

45. Secretary of State William Seward's official proclamation of the ratification (which he issued Dec. 18) can be found in *Statutes at Large* (Boston, 1866), 774–75.

46. On slavery and emancipation in Delaware, see Patience Essah, *A House Divided: Slavery and Emancipation in Delaware, 1638–1865* (Charlottesville: University Press of Virginia, 1996), and William H. Williams, *Slavery and Freedom in Delaware, 1639–1865* (Wilmington, Del.: Scholarly Resources, 1996).

47. John M. Palmer, Circular No. 6, Louisville, Ky., in FSSP, ser. 1, 1:658–59.

48. Fehrenbacher, *Slaveholding Republic;* Jasanoff, *Liberty's Exiles;* Pybus, *Epic Journeys of Freedom;* "Liberty and Union, Now and Forever, One and Inseparable: Views of John Quincy Adams," *New York World,* Sept. 2, 1862, reprinted in *Washington Intelligencer;* Francis Lieber, "Notebook on Slavery," Sept. 1862, Lieber Papers, box 23, HL.; Cockburn, "Washington Is Burning"; Rothman, *Slave Country.*

49. *Right Way,* Dec. 23 and 30, 1865, Maine Historical Society.

50. Both Stephen Kantrowitz (*More Than Freedom*) and Michael Vorenberg (*Final Freedom,* 79, 82–86) note little interest in the ratification of the Thirteenth Amendment among black activists. Taylor's "'To Make the Union What It Ought to Be'" similarly posits that African American community leaders in the North skipped over the Thirteenth Amendment to focus on tangible benefits like landownership, hallmarks of full citizenship like legal equality, and black suffrage.

51. Wiecek, "Emancipation and Civic Status," 82. In this passage, Wiecek is describing what he sees as a Southern view of the relationship between emancipation and citizenship, which contrasted with a more variegated Northern view that ranged widely in different times and places, until the *Dred Scott* decision of 1857 nationalized the Southern view. Wiecek then skips over the Civil War itself to

assert that after the war there was a more unified Northern view of emancipation conveying formal rights, which would eventually lose out once again to a more stripped-down Southern version of the rights that inhered in freedom. A closer look at the war years and the latter half of 1865 reveals that far from having come to clear agreement on this question, Northerners were still trying to figure it out during and immediately after the war.

52. Senator Garrett Davis, April 5, 1865, *Cong. Globe*, 38th Cong., 1st sess., 1424.

53. Alabama legislature, Dec. 2, 1865, in McPherson, *Political History*, 21.

54. John Mercer Langston (National Equal Rights League), "Special Notice," Aug. 14, 1864, Philadelphia, in *Christian Recorder*, Aug. 19, 1865.

55. James Lynch, "The Word 'African' in Our Denominational Title," *Christian Recorder*, May 6, 1865. For fuller discussion of the absence of citizenship from the Thirteenth Amendment, see Vorenberg, "Citizenship and the Thirteenth Amendment," 58–77.

56. Bettie S. Pritchett to Carr Waller Pritchett, Jan. 1864 and Oct. 1864 through Feb. 1865, Fayette, Mo., Pritchett Family Papers, folders 3 and 4, WHMC. Quotation from letter of Jan. 13, 1864.

57. Bettie S. Pritchett to Carr Waller Pritchett, Feb. 5, 1865, Fayette, Mo., Pritchett Family Papers, folder 4.

58. McPherson, "Legislation Respecting Freedmen," in *Political History*; *Laws of the State of Mississippi, Passed at a Regular Session of the Mississippi Legislature, Held in Jackson, October, November, and December, 1865* (Jackson, Miss.: J. J. Shannon & Co., State Printers, 1866), 82–93, 165–67.

59. Phillip A. Bell, editorial, *Elevator*, July 28, 1865.

60. Major George Grubbs (Forty-Second U.S. Colored Troops) July 7, 1865, Chattanooga, George W. Grubbs Letters, INSL. The African American delegation to Johnson on Feb. 6, 1866, also explicitly emphasized, "We are citizens." See "A Delegation of Colored Men at the Executive Mansion, Interview with President Johnson, Feb. 7, 1866," in Walker and Foner, *Proceedings of the Black National and State Conventions*, 214.

61. Rumley Diary, July 4, 1865, Beaufort, N.C.

62. Fields Cook et al., "Address of Delegates to the President: Statement of Wrongs and Oppression," composed at "a meeting of colored people," June 8, 1865, Richmond, printed in *New York Daily Tribune*, June 17, 1865, 1.

63. Gregory P. Downs argues that the postwar level of antiblack violence in North Carolina made freedpeople's need for federal protection so overwhelming that they were willing to forgo the language of rights and citizenship, go along with paternalistic white notions, and resort to throwing themselves on Union officials' mercy in something that looked like a patron-client relationship predicated more on dependence and inequality than on assertions of partnership and rights. See Downs, *Declarations of Dependence*, esp. chap. 3. Without question, a black family in immediate danger would argue in whatever terms were most likely to keep children safely through the night, but overall, claims on Union protection were less begging for mercy and more calling on the Union to keep up its side of the war-forged bargain, as freedpeople's persistent reminders of black contributions to the Union war effort emphasized. Downs also argues that North Carolina whites as well as blacks adopted a politics of inequality rather than equality, so his argument is not one about specifically black acceptance of deference but rather a powerful questioning of modern-day assumptions of the timelessness

of rights arguments. Precisely because such arguments are not timeless, freed-people's insistence on the United States and former slaves living up to mutual obligations stands out as important.

64. Wildon and Shipherd, *Second Annual Report of the Board of Directors of the North-western Freedmen's Aid Commission*, 6, 9, and back cover, NL.

65. William Darrah Kelley, "The Equality of All Men Before the Law Claimed and Defended," June 22, 1865, Concert Hall, Philadelphia. The speech was reprinted as a pamphlet of the same name by the Social, Civil, and Statistical Association of Colored People of Pennsylvania (Philadelphia: Merribew & Printers, 1865), and in the *New Orleans Tribune*, July 11, 1865, 3.

66. *Iowa State Register* (Des Moines), Jan. 24, 1865, 2.

67. *Alexandria Gazette*, April 12, 1865.

68. Palmer to Pullen, Aug. 22, 1865, Headquarters, Department of Kentucky, Lou-isville, Ky., Prisoners, &c in the District of Western KY 1865, RG 393, pt. 2, entry 1012, NARA.

69. Kirkpatrick to Mr. Kingsbury, Oct. 13, 1865, Davidson, N.C., NCDAH.

70. Newspaper clipping unsigned but almost certainly written by Lucy Chase, June 25, 1865, Norfolk, Va., in Swint, *Dear Ones at Home*, 165–69.

71. For discussion of the unintended and inadequately foreseen violent consequences of too-hasty demobilization, see Downs, *Declarations of Dependence*, 76–79. For a visual representation of where troops left and where they remained, see Downs and Nesbit, Mapping Occupation. Troop totals for Dec. 1865 come from adding up all the Dec. 1865 figures in the Troop Table and Raw Data documents on that Web site (see Gregory P. Downs, Mapping Occupation Troop Locations Dataset, 2015), which yields the sum of 123,176.

72. The earliest branch locations included New York City, Washington, D.C., New Orleans, Huntsville, Louisville, Memphis, Nashville, Wilmington, N.C., Rich-mond, Norfolk, and Beaufort. On the Freedman's Savings Bank, see House Ex. Doc. No. 70, 39th Cong., 1st sess.; Walter Lynwood Fleming, "The Freedmen's Savings Bank," *Yale Review*, May and Aug. 1906, 40–146; and "United States, Freedman's Bank Records, 1865–1874," FamilySearch, http://familysearch.org.

73. Application 211, Record for Sam Fobs, Tallahassee, Leon, Florida, FSB. The family information included in deposit records provides very useful evidence for reconstructing community and family relationships; one essay that has done so in important and innovative ways is Susan E. O'Donovan, "Mapping Freedom's Terrain: The Political and Productive Landscapes of Wilmington, North Caro-lina," in *After Slavery: Race, Labor, and Citizenship in the Reconstruction South*, ed. Bruce E. Baker and Brian Kelly (Gainesville: University Press of Florida, 2013), 176–98.

74. Fleming, "Freedmen's Savings Bank," 49.

75. Taylor, *Reminiscences of My Life in Camp*, 172.

76. Fleming, "Freedmen's Savings Bank"; Carl Osthaus, *Freedmen, Philanthropy, and Fraud: A History of the Freedman's Savings Bank* (Champaign: University of Illinois Press, 1976).

77. Accounts of the creation and history of the Freedmen's Bureau abound. Some good places to start include Bureau of Freedmen and Refugees, "Report to Accompany House Bill No. 598," March 18, 1868, 40th Cong., 2nd sess., Report 30; Paul A. Cimbala, "The Freedmen's Bureau, the Freedmen, and Sherman's Grant in Reconstruction Georgia, 1865–1867," *Journal of Southern History* 55, no.

4 (Nov. 1989): 597–632; Paul Cimbala and Randall Miller, eds., *The Freedmen's Bureau and Reconstruction: Reconsiderations* (New York: Fordham University Press, 1999); LaWanda Cox, "The Promise of Land for the Freedmen," *Mississippi Valley Historical Review* 45 (1958): 413–40; Egerton, *Wars of Reconstruction*, chap. 3; Mary Farmer-Kaiser, *Freedwomen and the Freedmen's Bureau: Race, Gender, and Public Policy in the Age of Emancipation* (New York: Fordham University Press, 2010); Eric Foner, *Reconstruction: America's Unfinished Revolution, 1863–1877* (New York: Oxford University Press, 1988). For the AFIC recommendation that Congress establish a "freedmen's bureau" as a temporary government agency to oversee the transition to freedom, see *Final Report of the American Freedmen's Inquiry Commission to the Secretary of War* (1864), 109.

78. Barton to Henry Wilson, March 9, 1865, Barton Papers, reel 63; Saxton to William Eaton, Aug. 15, 1865, Beaufort, S.C., Eaton Letters, Maine Historical Society.

79. Samuel Riddick, North Carolina Narratives, vol. 9, pt. 2, p. 210, WPA Narratives.

80. This description of the joint work of the bureau and voluntary organizations comes from a piece in the *Des Moines Register* announcing the consolidation of several Freedmen's Commissions into the American Freedmen's Aid Commission, an agent of which was visiting Des Moines soliciting aid to supplement the efforts of the bureau, which was "taxed beyond its means to furnish relief." See "Freedmen's Commission," *Des Moines Register*, Jan. 19, 1866.

81. Clinton B. Fisk Testimony to Joint Committee on Reconstruction, Jan. 30, 1866, in *Report of the Joint Committee on Reconstruction*, pt. 1, "Tennessee," 111–14.

82. Maggie Westmoland, Arkansas Narratives, vol. 2, pt. 7, pp. 100, 102–3, WPA Narratives.

83. Louisa Jacobs, *Freedmen's Record*, March 1866, 55.

84. Barry A. Crouch, "'To Enslave the Rising Generation': The Freedmen's Bureau and the Texas Black Code," in Cimbala and Miller, *Freedmen's Bureau and Reconstruction*, 267–78.

85. Several other steamers, including the *Cosmopolitan* and the *Canonicus*, also took part in these supplying missions, which feature regularly in the correspondence of the bureau agent William Eaton. See, for example, Eaton to Saxton, April 12, 1865; Nathan Ritter to Eaton, May 25 and Aug. 19, 1865; and Captain James Low to Eaton, April 21, 1866, Eaton Letters, Maine Historical Society.

86. See, for example, Mary Ames's observations of former slaves going "once a month for rations," in her account of her experiences as a teacher employed by the Freedmen's Bureau at Edisto Island, South Carolina, in May 1865. Ames, *New England Woman's Diary in Dixie*, 17.

87. William French to Brigadier General Clinton B. Fisk, Aug. 8, 1865, Fayetteville, Tenn., in FSSP, ser. 1, 2:470–72. French was a white Unionist to whom the freedpeople dictated the letter expressing their concerns.

88. Fisk made few friends among local whites for taking such action. See, for example, the letter of Mrs. S. H. Hayes of Nashville complaining that her property had been used as Wilson Hospital for Union soldiers during the war, then commandeered by Fisk "for the use of the Bureau of Refugees, Freedmen, etc." and was now, much to her disgust, "occupied by Refugees, etc. by order from Genl. Fisk." See Mrs. S. H. Hayes to Major General George Thomas, Jan. n.d. 1866, Nashville, Lawrence Family Papers, box 1, folder 12, TSLA.

89. Lieutenant William Bristoll (U.S. Arsenal) to the Reverend Wm. DeLoss Love (secretary of the American Missionary Association for the Northwest), Jan. 6, 1866, Baton Rouge, La., William DeLoss Love Papers, box 1, folder 3, SHSW.

90. Vicksburg Colored Schools Report, May 26, 1865, Records of the Mississippi Freedmen's Department, RG 105, M1914, reel 1, frame 776, NARA. Geography was also the favorite subject of Sarah Jane Foster's pupils in Martinsburg, West Virginia. See Reilly, *Sarah Jane Foster, Teacher of the Freedmen*, esp. 55–57.

91. Bristoll to Love, Jan. 6, 1866. Louisa Jacobs also noted that most of the teachers in Savannah freedmen's schools "are colored . . . natives of this place," *Freedmen's Record*, March 1866, 56.

92. Richard Paul Fuke, "Land, Lumber, and Learning: The Freedmen's Bureau, Education, and the Black Community in Post-emancipation Maryland," in Cimbala and Miller, *Freedmen's Bureau and Reconstruction*, 296.

93. Randall Miller, "The Freedmen's Bureau and Reconstruction: An Overview," in Cimbala and Miller, *Freedmen's Bureau and Reconstruction*, xxvii–xviii. The bureau also constructed schools, in cooperation with benevolent associations, in areas not in the former Confederacy, such as border states, the District of Columbia, and West Virginia. For example, the Freewill Baptist Home Mission Society and the Freedmen's Bureau established the Shenandoah Mission in four different West Virginia locations in 1865. See Freewill Baptist Home Mission Society, *Thirty-Second Annual Report* (Dover, N.H., 1866), 82–89, quoted in Reilly, *Sarah Jane Foster, Teacher of the Freedmen*, 134n1.

94. Nieman, "Andrew Johnson, the Freedmen's Bureau, and the Problem of Equal Rights," 400.

95. See, for example, Rosen, *Terror in the Heart of Freedom*, and Williams, *They Left Great Marks on Me*.

96. See Rothman, *Beyond Freedom's Reach*.

97. Gould Diary, Darlington, S.C., July 1865–March 1866, in *Civil War Journals of John Mead Gould*, Maine Historical Society; quotation from Aug. 8, 1865. See also the Provost Court records of Vicksburg, Miss., April 1865 (and following months), RG 105, M1914, reel 5, NARA.

98. *New Orleans Tribune*, July 20, 1865.

99. "Review of the Work of the Freemen's [*sic*] Bureau," *New Era*, Jan. 20, 1870.

100. Memorial of the Colored Men of the Second Congressional District of Georgia, Setting Forth Their Grievances, and Asking Protection, Dec. 4, 1868, Albany, Ga., in Lee Formwalt, "Petitioning Congress for Protection: A Black View of Reconstruction at the Local Level," *Georgia Historical Quarterly* 73, No. 2 (Summer 1989): 309–10. For more on Andrew Johnson's actions as increasingly sympathetic to slaveholders and deleterious to the bureau in the later months of 1865, see Paul A. Cimbala, "Reconstruction's Allies: The Relationship of the Freedmen's Bureau and the Georgia Freedmen," in Cimbala and Miller, *Freedmen's Bureau and Reconstruction*, esp. 318–21; Nieman, "Andrew Johnson, the Freedmen's Bureau, and the Problem of Equal Rights"; "Prologue," in Simpson, Graf, and Muldowny, *Advice After Appomattox*.

101. Reverend Squire Dowd, North Carolina Narratives, vol. 11, pt. 1, p. 266, WPA Narratives.

102. Randy Finley, "The Personnel of the Freedmen's Bureau in Arkansas," in Cimbala and Miller, *Freedmen's Bureau and Reconstruction*, 100–101.

103. An Act to Establish a Bureau for the Relief of the Freedmen and Refugees,

U.S. Statutes at Large, Treaties, and Proclamations of the United States of America (Boston, 1866), 13:507–9; Paul A. Cimbala, *Under the Guardianship of the Nation: The Freedmen's Bureau and the Reconstruction of Georgia, 1865–1870* (Athens: University of Georgia Press, 1997); Rose, *Rehearsal for Reconstruction.*

104. For a book-length treatment of Davis Bend, see Janet Sharp Hermann, *The Pursuit of a Dream* (New York: Oxford University Press, 1981). There were a few other examples of the Freedmen's Bureau overseeing the direct transfer of land to freedpeople in the Mississippi valley—for example, in the summer of 1865, hundreds of black families successfully applied to Assistant Commissioner Thomas W. Conway directly for land in Louisiana—but direct possession of land was by and large more common in the East than in the West. See Circular No. 10, Aug. 28, 1865, "Letter from the Secretary of War, in Answer to a Resolution of the House of March 9, Transmitting a Report, by the Commissioner of the Freedmen's Bureau, of All Orders Issued by Him or Any Assistant Commissioner," *House Executive Document,* 39th Cong., 1st sess., no. 70, p. 19. John Rodrigue notes the "hundreds of applications representing thousands of freedmen" flooding bureau headquarters in the summer of 1865 in "The Freedmen's Bureau and Wage Labor in the Louisiana Sugar Region," *Journal of Southern History* 67, no. 1 (Feb. 2001): 201.

105. Black landownership after emancipation is also one of the ways in which the contrast between emancipation in Haiti and the United States is most pronounced.

106. Nathaniel Banks, General Orders No. 23, Headquarters, Department of the Gulf, Feb. 3, 1864, in FSSP, ser. 1, 3:512–17; Rodrigue, *Reconstruction in the Cane Fields.*

107. Fisk Testimony to Joint Committee on Reconstruction, 112.

108. Complaint of the planter R. C. Martin Jr. in John C. Rodrigue, "The Freedmen's Bureau and Wage Labor in the Louisiana Sugar Region," in Cimbala and Miller, *Freedmen's Bureau and Reconstruction,* 198. For more on the bureau as labor advocate for former slaves in the postwar Louisiana sugar industry, see Rodrigue, *Reconstruction in the Cane Fields.*

109. S. Barnes, General Orders No. 16, Sept. 15, 1865, Records of the Virginia Field Office, RG 105, M1048, NARA.

110. Erin McClam, "Many Americans Blame 'Government Welfare' for Persistent Poverty, Poll Finds," June 6, 2013, inplainsight.nbcnews.com.

111. For elaboration on this theme, see Farmer-Kaiser, *Freedwomen and the Freedmen's Bureau.* For an example of callousness in service to a quick shutdown, see the case of Camp Nelson, Kentucky, which Clinton Fisk was eager to effect within the year initially allotted to the Freedmen's Bureau, especially because Kentucky had never been a Confederate state, which made any bureau presence in it legally tenuous. Richard D. Sears details the breakup of Camp Nelson in *Camp Nelson, Kentucky,* chaps. 6 and 7.

112. According to *The Cotton Plant: Its History, Botany, Chemistry, Culture, Enemies, and Uses* (Washington, D.C.: Government Printing Office, 1896), 262–63, in the nineteenth century cotton was planted on the South Carolina coast the final week of March, would sprout in roughly two weeks, and would bud forty-one days after sprouting, or in May.

113. Ames, *New England Woman's Diary in Dixie.*

114. Ibid., 90.

115. Ibid., 88–89.

116. Ibid., 23.

117. Ibid., 25–26.

118. Ibid., 92–95.

119. Meade to Secretary of War Edwin Stanton, Sept. 20, 1865, Philadelphia, in Simpson, Graf, and Muldowny, *Advice After Appomattox,* app. 1; Botume, *First Days Amongst the Contrabands,* 197–98; Nieman, "Andrew Johnson, the Freedmen's Bureau, and the Problem of Equal Rights"; Brooks Simpson, "Ulysses S. Grant and the Freedmen's Bureau," in Cimbala and Miller, *Freedmen's Bureau and Reconstruction,* 8–9.

120. Botume, *First Days Amongst the Contrabands,* 195–96. William S. McFeely, *Yankee Stepfather: General O. O. Howard and the Freedmen* (New Haven, Conn.: Yale University Press, 1968), 130–48. See also John Cox and LaWanda Cox, "General O. O. Howard and the 'Misrepresented Bureau,'" *Journal of Southern History* 19, no. 4 (Nov. 1953): 427–56.

121. Ames, *New England Woman's Diary,* 97–98.

122. Henry Bram et al. to Major General O. O. Howard [Oct. 28?, 1865], B-53 1865, Letters Received (ser. 15), Washington Headquarters, RG 105, NARA. This petition has become famous and is also available on many Web sites that make teaching resources available.

123. Bram et al. to Howard, Oct. 1865, and Henry Bram et al. to the President of these United States, Oct. 25, 1865, Edisto Island, S.C., P-27 1865, Letters Received (ser. 15), Washington Headquarters, RG 105, NARA. The letter written to Andrew Johnson at the same time is also available in Ames, *New England Woman's Diary,* 101–2.

124. Bram et al. to Howard, Oct. 1865.

125. Schurz, *Report on the Condition of the South,* https://archive.org/stream /senateexecutivedoounit#page/n77/mode/2up. Besides continuation of a firm federal presence, Schurz advocated black suffrage.

126. "Letter of General Grant Concerning Affairs at the South," Dec. 18, 1865, Sen. Exec. Doc. No. 2, 39th Cong., 1st sess. (Washington, D.C., 1866), 107, https:// archive.org/stream/senateexecutivedoounit#page/n77/mode/2up; Truman to Johnson, Oct. 13, 1865, Mobile, Ala., in Simpson, Graf, and Muldowny, *Advice After Appomattox,* 186.

127. Howard to Senator Henry Wilson, Nov. 25, 1865, quoted in Nieman, "Andrew Johnson, the Freedmen's Bureau, and the Problem of Equal Rights," 415.

128. Report of General Oliver O. Howard, *House Executive Documents,* 39th Cong., 1st sess., No. 11, Serial 1255 (Washington, D.C.: Government Printing Office, 1865), 32–33.

129. Schuyler Colfax, Speech in Response to a Serenade, Nov. 18, 1865, Washington, D.C., in Willard H. Smith, "Schuyler Colfax and Reconstruction Policy," *Indiana Magazine of History* 39, no. 4 (1943): 325–26.

CONCLUSION

1. Kate Wiltrout, "Army Hands Over Historic Fort Monroe in Hampton," *Virginia-Pilot,* Sept. 16, 2011.

2. "Fort Monroe Stands Down After 188 Years of Army Service," *Daily Press,* Sept. 15, 2011.

3. Fort Monroe National Monument Foundation Document Part 1, Planning Vision Statement, and Public Comment Analysis Report, http://parkplanning .nps.gov/documentsList.cfm?parkID=533&projectID=41444.; Contraband Historical Society, Vision and Mission Statement, http://contrabandhistoricalso ciety.org/vision-mission.shtml.

4. Nieman, "From Slaves to Citizens"; Stanley, *From Bondage to Contract,* esp. 55.

5. For the full text of the Fourteenth Amendment, see http://constitutioncenter .org/constitution/the-amendments/amendment-14-citizenship-rights. Section 1 declared all persons born or naturalized in the United States to be citizens with equal rights to life, liberty, and property and entitled to equal protection of the laws. Section 2 based congressional representation on the number of legal voters rather than pure population; its purpose was to encourage states to enfranchise African American men or else have their representation in Congress reduced, but it did not yet take the step of placing the federal government in charge of voting. Section 3 prevented high-ranking Confederate leaders who had once taken but then violated oaths of allegiance to the United States from holding high public office in the United States without a two-thirds vote of Congress (a provision that did not stop Confederate leaders as high up as the vice president from serving in Congress before Reconstruction was over). Section 4 repudiated the Confederate debt. Section 5 gave Congress the power to pass laws to enforce the amendment.

6. For a concise account of the drafting, adoption, and ratification of the Fourteenth Amendment, see Nelson, *Fourteenth Amendment,* esp. chap. 3. Nelson throughout the book judiciously balances the concern for principles of equality and the commitment to federalism that sometimes ran at cross-purposes with each other, but which both mattered to Republican framers of the amendment. Additional useful overviews of the Fourteenth Amendment include Robert J. Kaczorowski, "Revolutionary Constitutionalism in the Era of the Civil War and Reconstruction," *New York University Law Review* 61 (1986), http://ir.lawnet .fordham.edu/faculty_scholarship/466/; Earl M. Maltz, *Civil Rights, the Constitution, and Congress, 1863–1869* (Lawrence: University Press of Kansas, 1990); Earl M. Maltz, "The Fourteenth Amendment as Political Compromise—Section One in the Joint Committee on Reconstruction," *Ohio State Law Journal* 45 (1984): 933–80; Bernard Schwartz, ed., *The Fourteenth Amendment: Centennial Volume* (New York: New York University Press, 1970); Wiecek, "Emancipation and Civic Status." On ratification, see Joseph B. James, *The Ratification of the Fourteenth Amendment* (Macon, Ga.: Mercer University Press, 1984).

7. Wiecek, "Emancipation and Civic Status," 88.

8. I am neither a legal scholar nor a Fourteenth Amendment specialist, and make no pretense of wading into the debate about the Fourteenth Amendment and rights generally, or the incorporation of the Bill of Rights specifically, but for those interested in that debate, good starting points include Raoul Berger, *The Fourteenth Amendment and the Bill of Rights* (Norman: University of Oklahoma Press, 1989); Charles Fairman and Stanley Morrison, eds., *The Fourteenth Amendment and the Bill of Rights: The Incorporation Theory* (New York: DaCapo Press, 1970); Hermita Herta Heyer, *The History and Meaning of the Fourteenth Amendment: Judicial Erosion of the Constitution Through the Misuse of the Fourteenth Amendment* (New York: Vantage Press, 1977).

9. For an analysis of the Fourteenth Amendment that emphasizes its narrowness and interprets it as restricting and limiting rather than expanding the Thirteenth Amendment specifically, and wartime gains generally, see Vorenberg, "Citizenship and the Thirteenth Amendment."

10. The Southern Claims Commission Papers: Question Sheet Used in Depositions, Valley of the Shadow, accessed April 2011, http://valley.lib.virginia.edu /VoS/claims/SCC_questions.html.

11. Good starting points for Republicans' ultimately unsuccessful strategies to encourage black suffrage with the Fourteenth Amendment, and Southern response, include Eric Foner, *A Short History of Reconstruction* (New York: Harper & Row, 1990), chaps. 5 and 6, and Nelson, *Fourteenth Amendment*, chap. 3.

12. List of Local Affiliates of the Pennsylvania State Equal Rights League, 1865; Business Committee Report, Aug. 9, 1865, *Proceedings of the Annual Meeting of the Pennsylvania State Equal Rights League, Held in Harrisburg,* Aug. 9 and 10, 1865; Pennsylvania State Equal Rights League Memorial to Congress, Feb. 20, 1866; *Proceedings of the Annual Meeting of the Pennsylvania State Equal Rights League 1866* (and all successive years); William Nesbit and Jacob C. White correspondence (about the Fourteenth Amendment) in 1868; all in the Papers and Proceedings of the Pennsylvania State Equal Rights League, Leon Gardiner Collection of American Negro Historical Society Records, reel 1, Historical Society of Pennsylvania. The emphasis on black men's military service and voting also grows stronger in the 1866 and later proceedings in Foner and Walker, *Proceedings of the Black National and State Conventions.* Much of the secondary literature on black citizenship and suffrage in Reconstruction reflects this emphasis on former soldiers and voting rights. See, for example, Berry, *Military Necessity and Civil Rights Policy;* Samito, *Becoming American Under Fire;* and Taylor, "'To Make the Union What It Ought to Be.'"

13. Saidiya Hartman makes similar points about violence in the power relationships between white and black people in *Scenes of Subjection: Terror, Slavery, and Self-Making in Nineteenth-Century America* (New York: Oxford University Press, 1997).

14. See especially Gregory P. Downs's beautiful essay, "Anarchy at the Circumference: Statelessness and the Reconstruction of Authority in Emancipation North Carolina," in Baker and Kelly, *After Slavery,* 98–121.

15. I am very grateful to the Fort Monroe Authority and the Casemate Museum for the many materials they so generously provided me concerning water at Fort Monroe, including Drawing of Fort Monroe Cistern (probably 1819), the original drawing of which is located in RG 77, drawer 57, sheet 107, NARA, College Park and Artesian Well at Fortress Monroe, 1866, RG77, drawer 58, sheet 169, NRA, College Park, and with a copy at the Casemate Museum at Fort Monroe. Additional drawings from 1843, 1884, and 1894 and a ca. 1900 photograph in the possession of the Casemate Museum show seventeen individual cisterns within the inner fort. An 1834 letter (also in the possession of the Casemate Museum at Fort Monroe) from Lieutenant Robert E. Lee, then an engineer at Fort Monroe, describes water collected by the cisterns "attached to the permanent quarters" as "suitable for all purposes except drinking."

Bibliography of Primary Sources

Secondary sources may be found in the notes.

ARCHIVAL SOURCES

Alexandria (Va.) Archaeology Museum
Artemel, Janice G., Elizabeth A. Crowell, and Jeff Parker. *The Alexandria Slave Pen: The Archaeology of Urban Captivity.* 1987.
Kraus, Lisa, John Bedell, and Charles Lee Decker. *Joseph Bruin and the Slave Trade.* Prepared for Columbia Equity Trust, Inc., 2007.
Isaac and Amy Kirby Post Family Papers, transcribed from Rush Rhees Library, University of Rochester

American Antiquarian Society
Freedmen's Record

Amistad Research Center at Tulane University
American Missionary Association Archives, 1839–1882, accessed via *Slavery and Antislavery: A Transnational Archive,* pt. 4: Age of Emancipation, www.gale.com /DigitalCollections

Chicago Public Library, Woodson Regional Branch
Vivian P. Harsh Research Collection, Illinois Writers Project: "Negro in Illinois" Collection, boxes 1–51

Duke University
Eltinge-Lord Family Papers
Constant Hanks Papers
Alice Williamson Diary, http://scriptorium.lib.duke.edu/williamson

Emory University
Thomas Stuart Birch Papers

Historical Society of Pennsylvania
James Buchanan Papers
Pennsylvania State Equal Rights League Records

Houghton Library, Harvard University
U.S. American Freedmen's Inquiry Commission Records

Huntington Library
Francis Lieber Papers

Illinois History and Lincoln Collection, University of Illinois
David Todd and Charlotte Farnsworth Letters

Illinois State Historical Library
Andrews Family Papers
Brent, Joseph E. *Occupied Corinth: The Contraband Camp and the First Alabama Regiment of African Descent, 1862–1864.* Prepared for the City of Corinth, Miss., and the Siege and Battle of Corinth Commission, Feb. 1995.
Engelmann-Kircher Papers
William Hinshaw Letters

Indiana Historical Society
Carrington, H. B. *Address in Aid of the Erection of a New Church Edifice for the Methodist Episcopal (Colored) Society,* Indianapolis, 1869.
Martha Mace Lattimore Papers
Frances Patterson Papers
Elijah Roberts Collection
Audrey C. Werle Papers
Wolff, Florence. "My African Grandfather: A Compilation of the Diaries of Daniel Flickinger."

Indiana State Archives
Clark County Register of Negroes and Mulattoes
Governor Oliver P. Morton Papers
Vigo County Register of Negroes and Mulattoes

Indiana State Library
George W. Grubbs Letters
Salmon Hall Letter
Oliver P. Morton Papers
James R. Slack Papers
Kate Starks Letters
James Cornell Vanderbilt Papers
Anna W. Wright Papers

Kansas City Public Library Special Collections
Cyrus F. Boyd Collection

Kansas Collection, Spencer Research Library, University of Kansas
James W. Jessee Diaries

Kansas State Historical Society
John S. Brown Family Papers
George E. Flanders Letters

Library of Congress
Clara Barton Papers
Benjamin F. Butler Papers
Abraham Lincoln Papers
James Morrison MacKaye Papers
Maria Tyler Mann Papers

Maine Historical Society
Civil War Journals of John Mead Gould, 1861–1866, edited by William B. Jordan.
"Conditions on Malaga Island," 1911
"Discovering Malaga Island" Program and Research Materials
William F. Eaton Letters
The Right Way (published by the Impartial Suffrage League of Boston)
John Varney Research Materials

Massachusetts Historical Society
Adams Family Papers
African Civilization Society. "An Appeal in Behalf of the Education of the Freedmen
    and Their Children," 1864.
Edward J. Bartlett Correspondence
"Come Back You Black Rascal," Two Patriotic Covers C-BL-77 and C-BL-78
Educational Commission (Boston). *Extracts from Letters Received by the Educational
    Commission of Boston, from Teachers Employed at Port Royal and Its Vicinity,* 1862.
Ellis, Britton & Eaton's Novelty Works (Springfield, Vt.). "Employment for Eman-
    cipated Negroes."
Knox, Thomas P. *Startling Revelations from the Department of South Carolina,* 1864
New England Freedmen's Aid Society Records, 1862–1876
Edward Lillie Pierce Journals
Pierce, Edward L. *The Negroes at Port Royal: Report of E. L. Pierce, Government Agent,
    to the Hon. Salmon P. Chase,* 1862
Soldiers' Memorial Society Miscellany
Soldiers' Memorial Society Records
Samuel Storrow Papers
White slave girl [photograph], ca. 1861–1865, photograph 2.129

Missouri Historical Society, St. Louis
Lillie Devereaux Blake Papers
William D. Butler Papers
Contraband Relief Society Circular Letter
Lowndes Henry Davis Papers
William R. Donaldson Papers
William Greenleaf Eliot Papers
Thomas S. Hawley Papers
Kennett Family Papers
Ladies' Union Aid Society Minute Books, 1865–1868

Kenneth McKenzie Papers
Moody Family Papers
St. Louis Sanitation Collection
Slaves and Slavery Collection: The Story of Peter Boyd's Life
U.S.S. *Ouachita* Descriptive List
Edward Wade Papers
Walker Family Papers

National Archives and Records Administration, Washington, D.C. (NARA Downtown)

General Affidavit of Harriet Tubman Davis, 1898, RG 233
Manuscript History Concerning the Pension Claim of Harriet Tubman, Written by Charles Wood, Records of the House of Representatives, 1789–2011, Accompanying Papers of the 55th Cong., RG 233
Records of the Adjutant General's Office, RG 94
Records of the American Freedmen's Inquiry Commission, RG 94 Letters Received by the Office of the Adjutant General (Main Series), 1861–1870, 1863-328-0, Microfilm Collection 619, reels 199–201
Records of the Department of Veterans Affairs, RG 15
Records of the Provost Marshal General's Bureau (Civil War), RG 110
Records of U.S. Army Continental Commands, 1821–1920, RG 393
Register of Colored Nurses Under Contract [Department of the East], Record Group 94, entry 591

Newberry Library, Chicago

Northwestern Freedmen's Aid Commission. *Minutes of the First Annual Meeting . . . Held in the Second Presbyterian Church in Chicago, on Thursday Evening, April 14th, and on Friday Morning, April 15th, 1864. With an Appendix, Containing a List of Annual and Life Electors, and Other Data.* Chicago: James Barnet, Printer, 1864.
———. *The Second Annual Report of the Board of Directors of the Northwestern Freedmen's Aid Commission: Presented at the Second Anniversary Meeting, Held in Bryan Hall, Chicago, Ill., on Thursday Evening, April 13th, 1865. With Accompanying Documents and Data.* Chicago: James Barnet, Printer, 1865.
Putnam, Lewis H. *The Review of the Revolutionary Elements of the Rebellion, and of the Aspect of Reconstruction, with a Plan to Restore Harmony Between the Two Races in the Southern States, by a Colored Man.* Brooklyn, 1868.
Southern Refugee Relief Association. *Organization at a Public Meeting Held at the Grand Pacific Hotel in Chicago, on Monday, February 9th, 1880.* Chicago, 1880.

North Carolina Division of Archives and History

Henry Chambers Papers
John B. Chesson Papers
Civil War Collection, Miscellaneous Papers
J. L. Kirkpatrick Letter
Levi Woodbury Pigott Collection
Thomas Merritt Pittman Papers, Civil War Correspondence, 1861–1865
Lyman Wilson Sheppard Collection
Charles Henry Tubbs Papers
Whedbee Freedmen Papers

Southern Historical Collection, University of North Carolina, Chapel Hill
Edward Augustus Wild Report, Dec. 28, 1863, Edward Augustus Wild Papers, folder 2,
  http://www2.lib.unc.edu/mss/inv/w/Wild,Edward_Augustus.html#folder_2#1

Special Collections, Murphy Library, University of Wisconsin–La Crosse
Benjamin Franklin Heuston Papers

State Historical Society of Iowa, Des Moines
Joseph A. Dugdale Correspondence
Jared and Sarah Fuller Papers
Hartsock, James R. "Remarks in Favor of the Adoption of the Resolution Offered by
  Mr. Ed. Russell of Davenport to Strike the World 'White' from the Constitution
  of the State of Iowa," 1868.
Iowa Women's Suffrage Records
Samuel J. Kirkwood Papers
Russell, Charles Edward. *A Pioneer Editor in Early Iowa: A Sketch of the Life of Edward
  Russell by His Son, Charles Edward Russell*. Washington, D.C.: Ransdell, 1941.
Annie Turner Wittenmyer Papers
Works Progress Administration Federal Writers Project: "The Negro in Iowa"
  Research Materials

Tennessee State Library and Archives
Robert Cartmell Diary
William Driver Papers
Abigail Dutton Papers
William Mark Eames Papers
James Allen Hoobler Collection
Lawrence Family Papers
Roll of Negroes Impressed for Service on the North-Western Railroad
Mitchell Andrew Thompson Letters, Civil War Collection

University of Arkansas Special Collections
E. C. Hubbard Letters

Valley of the Shadow Project
Southern Claims Commission Papers

Vermont Historical Society
Rufus Kinsley Papers

Virginia Historical Society
John A. Williams Letters

Western Historical Manuscripts Collection, University of Missouri
George Davis Family Papers
John Garriott Letters
Samuel C. Gold Papers
Odon Guitar Collection
Ladies' Union Aid Society Reports

Abiel Leonard Family Papers
Missouri Collection
Pritchett Family Papers
Stephan Werly Diary

Wisconsin Historical Society (formerly known as State Historical Society of Wisconsin)
William F. Allen Family Papers
Annual Reports of the General Assembly's Committee on Freedmen, of the Presbyterian Church in the United States of America, 1867–1885.
John O. Holzhueter Papers: Black Settlers in Early Wisconsin Collection M2001-011
John O. Holzhueter Research Files
Samuel Kirkpatrick Letters
William DeLoss Love Papers
Symanthia Gillespie Marshall Papers
E. B. Quiner Papers: Correspondence of Wisconsin Volunteers, 1861–1865

NEWSPAPERS AND PERIODICALS

Alexandria (Va.) Gazette
American Missionary
Anglo-African
Baptist Home Mission Monthly
Boston Herald
Bureau County (Ill.) Republican
Chicago Tribune
Christian Recorder
Commercial Advertiser
Commonwealth
Daily Missouri Democrat
Elevator
Fond du Lac Weekly Commonwealth
Frank Leslie's Illustrated Magazine
Frederick Examiner
Freedman's Advocate
Freedmen's Record
Harper's Weekly
Iowa State Register (Des Moines)
Liberator
Nashville Daily Times and True Union
National Freedman
New Bern (N.C.) Daily Journal
New Era
New Orleans Tribune
New York Herald
New York Times
New York Tribune
New York World
Salem (Ill.) Advocate

South Carolina Leader
Washington Intelligencer
Weekly Patriot (Madison, Wisconsin)
Worcester Daily Spy

ELECTRONICALLY AVAILABLE COLLECTIONS

American Civil War Research Database, http://www.civilwardata.com/
Black Abolitionist Papers, 1830–1865, http://www.proquest.com/products-services/blk_abol_pap.html
Born in Slavery: Slave Narratives from the Federal Writers' Project, 1936–1938, http://memory.loc.gov/ammem/snhtml/snhome.html
The District of Columbia Emancipation Act, April 16, 1862, http://www.archives.gov/exhibits/featured_documents/dc_emancipation_act/
Mapping Occupation: Force, Freedom, and the Army in Reconstruction, http://www.mappingoccupation.org/
Slavery and Anti-slavery: A Transnational Archive, www.gale.com/DigitalCollections
U.S. Freedman's Bank Records, 1865–1874, Freedman's Savings and Trust Company, National Archives and Records Administration, Washington, D.C., http://familysearch.org
U.S. Statutes at Large, Treaties, and Proclamations of the United States of America, http://memory.loc.gov

PUBLISHED GOVERNMENT AND MILITARY PRIMARY SOURCES

Bates, Edward. *Opinion of Attorney General Bates on Citizenship.* Washington, D.C.: Government Printing Office, 1863.
Bostwick, S. W., and Thomas Hood. *Report upon the Condition and Treatment of Colored Refugees in Kentucky, Tennessee, and Alabama, 1864.* Senate Reports, 38th Cong., 2nd sess., Ex. Doc. No. 28. Washington, D.C.: Government Printing Office, 1864.
Bureau of Refugees, Freedmen, and Abandoned Lands. "Report to Accompany House Bill No. 598," March 18, 1868, 40th Cong., 2nd sess., Report 30. 1868.
Congressional Globe. Washington: Blair & Rives, 1834–1873, http://memory.loc.gov/ammem/amlaw/lwcg.html.
The Cotton Plant: Its History, Botany, Chemistry, Culture, Enemies, and Uses. Washington, D.C.: Government Printing Office, 1896.
Dred Scott v. Sandford. 60 U.S. 393 March 6, 1857, http://laws.findlaw.com/us/60/393.html.
Dyer, Frederick A. *A Compendium of the War of the Rebellion.* 3 vols. Des Moines: Dyer, 1908.
General Laws of the State of Illinois, Passed by the Eighteenth General Assembly, Convened January 3, 1853. Springfield, Ill.: Lanphier and Walker, Printers, 1853.
Grant, U. S. "Letter of General Grant Concerning Affairs at the South," Dec. 18, 1865. Sen. Exec. Doc. No. 2, 39th Cong., 1st sess. Washington, D.C.: Government Printing Office, 1866.
House Executive Doc. No. 70, 39th Cong., 1st sess. 1866.
Howard, Oliver O. *Report.* House Executive Documents, 39th Cong., 1st sess., No. 11, Serial 1255. Washington, D.C.: Government Printing Office, 1865.

Instructions for the Government of Armies of the United States in the Field, Prepared by Francis Lieber, LL.D., Originally Issued as General Orders No. 100, Adjutant General's Office, 1863. Washington, D.C.: Government Printing Office, 1898.

Laws of the State of Mississippi, Passed at a Regular Session of the Mississippi Legislature, Held in Jackson, October, November, and December, 1865. Jackson, Miss.: J. J. Shannon & Co., State Printers, 1866.

Moore, Frank, ed. *The Rebellion Record.* New York: G. P. Putnam's Sons, 1861–1865.

Public Statutes at Large of the United States of America from the Organization of the Government in 1789 to March 3, 1845. Vol. 2. Boston: Charles C. Little and James Brown, 1850.

Report of the Joint Committee on Reconstruction at the First Session Thirty-Ninth Congress. Washington, D.C.: Government Printing Office, 1866.

Schurz, Carl. *Report on the Condition of the South,* Nov. 1865, Senate Exec. Doc. No. 2, 39th Cong., 1st sess. Washington, D.C.: Government Printing Office, 1866.

The War of the Rebellion: A Compilation of the Official Records of the Union and Confederate Armies. Washington, D.C.: Government Printing Office, 1888–1922.

OTHER PUBLISHED PRIMARY SOURCES

Ames, Mary. *A New England Woman's Diary in Dixie in 1865.* Norwood, Mass.: Plimpton Press, 1906.

Anderson, John Q., ed. *Brokenburn: The Journal of Kate Stone, 1861–1868.* Baton Rouge: Louisiana State University Press, 1995.

Basler, Roy P., ed. *The Collected Works of Abraham Lincoln.* New Brunswick, N.J.: Rutgers University Press, 1953.

Blight, David. *A Slave No More: Two Men Who Escaped to Freedom, Including Their Own Narratives of Emancipation.* New York: Mariner Books, 2009.

Botume, Elizabeth. *First Days Among the Contrabands.* Boston: Lee and Shepard, 1893.

Brockett, Linus Pierpont, and Mary C. Vaughan. *Woman's Work in the Civil War: A Record of Heroism, Patriotism, and Patience.* Philadelphia: Zeigler, McCurdy, 1867.

Butler, Benjamin. *Butler's Book: Autobiography and Personal Reminiscences of Major-General Benjamin F. Butler.* Boston: A. M. Thayer, 1892.

———. *Private and Official Correspondence of Gen. Benjamin F. Butler During the Period of the Civil War.* Norwood, Mass.: privately issued by Jessie Ames Marshall, 1917.

Christie, William D. "Our Relations with Brazil." *Macmillan's Magazine,* Oct. 1863, 488–97.

Coffin, Levi. *Reminiscences of Levi Coffin: The Reputed President of the Underground Railroad.* 1876. New York: Augustus M. Kelley Reprints of Economic Classics, 1968.

Colyer, Vincent. *Brief Report of the Services Rendered by the Freed People to the United States Army in North Carolina, in the Spring of 1862.* New York: Vincent Colyer, 1864.

Corey, Charles H. "Reminiscences." *Baptist Home Mission Monthly* 10 (1888): 284–85.

Derby, William P. *Bearing Arms in the Twenty-Seventh Massachusetts Regiment of Volunteer Infantry During the Civil War, 1861–1865.* Boston: Wright & Potter, 1883.

Dunant, J. Henry. *Un souvenir de Solférino.* Geneva: Jules-Guillaume Fick, 1863.

Eaton, John. *Lincoln, Grant, and the Freedmen: Reminiscences of the Civil War with Special Reference to the Work for the Contrabands and Freedmen of the Mississippi Valley.* New York: Longmans, Green, 1907.

Foner, Philip S., and George E. Walker, eds. *Proceedings of the Black National and State Conventions, 1865–1900.* Philadelphia: Temple University Press, 1986.

French, Mrs. A. M. *Slavery in South Carolina and the Ex-slaves; or, The Port Royal Mission.* New York: Winchell M. French, 1862.

Furman, Jan, ed. *Slavery in the Clover Bottoms: John McCline's Narrative of His Life During Slavery and the Civil War.* Knoxville: University of Tennessee Press, 1998.

Gould, William B., IV, ed. *Diary of a Contraband: The Civil War Passage of a Black Sailor.* Stanford, Calif.: Stanford University Press, 2001.

Graf, LeRoy P., and Ralph W. Haskins, eds. *The Papers of Andrew Johnson.* Knoxville: University of Tennessee Press, 1967–1986.

Grant, Ulysses S. *Personal Memoirs of U. S. Grant.* New York: Century, 1895.

Hale, Edward E. "The Man Without a Country." *Atlantic Monthly,* Dec. 1863, 665–80.

Halleck, Henry Wager. *International Law; or, Rules Regulating the Intercourse of States in Peace and War.* San Francisco: H. H. Bancroft, 1861.

Haviland, Laura. *A Woman's Life-Work: Labors and Experiences.* Cincinnati: Walden & Stowe, 1882.

Holland, Rupert Sargent, ed. *Letters and Diary of Laura M. Towne: Written from the Sea Islands of South Carolina, 1862–1864.* Cambridge, Mass.: Riverside Press, 1912.

Holmes, J. H. "Reminiscences." *Baptist Home Mission Monthly* 10 (1888): 286–87.

Hughes, Sarah Forbes, ed. *Letters and Recollections of John Murray Forbes.* Vol. 1. Boston: Houghton Mifflin, 1899.

James, Horace. *Annual Report of the Superintendent of Negro Affairs in North Carolina, 1864, with an Appendix Containing the History and Management of the Freedmen in This Department to June 1st, 1865.* Boston: W. F. Brown, 1865.

Kelley, William Darrah. "The Equality of All Men Before the Law Claimed and Defended." Philadelphia: Merribew & Printers, 1865.

Kent, James. *Commentaries on American Law in Four Volumes.* New York: O. Halsted, 1826.

Kirwan, Thomas. *Soldiering in North Carolina.* Boston: Thomas Kirwan, 1864.

Lieber, Francis. *Amendments of the Constitution, Submitted to the Consideration of the American People.* New York: Loyal Publication Society, 1865.

———. *Manual of Political Ethics Designed Chiefly for the Use of Colleges and Students at Law.* 2 vols. Boston: Little, Brown, 1838–1839. 2nd ed., Philadelphia: J. B. Lippincott, 1875.

Livermore, George. *An Historical Research Respecting the Opinions of the Founders of the Republic on Negroes as Slaves, as Citizens, and as Soldiers.* Boston: New England Loyal Publication Society, 1863.

Lockwood, Lewis C. *Mary S. Peake, the Colored Teacher at Fortress Monroe.* Boston: American Tract Society, 1862.

Mann, Albert W. *History of the Forty-Fifth Regiment Massachusetts Volunteer Militia.* Jamaica Plain, Mass.: Brookside Print, 1908.

Martin, Joseph Plumb. *A Narrative of Some of the Adventures, Dangers, and Suffering of a Revolutionary Soldier; Interspersed with Anecdotes of Incidents That Occurred Within His Own Observation.* Hallowell, Me.: Glazier, Masters, 1830.

McPherson, Edward. *The Political History of the United States of America During the Period of Reconstruction.* Washington, D.C.: Solomons & Chapman, 1875.

Moore, Joanna P. *"In Christ's Stead": Autobiographical Sketches.* Chicago: Women's Baptist Home Mission Society, 1902.

———. "Reminiscences." *Baptist Home Mission Monthly* 10 (1888): 289–92.

Moore, John Bassett, ed. *The Works of James Buchanan: Comprising His Speeches, State Papers, and Private Correspondence.* Vol. 10. New York: Antiquarian Press, 1960.

Paine, Halbert Eleazer. *A Wisconsin Yankee in Confederate Bayou Country: The Civil War Reminiscences of a Union General.* Edited by Samuel C. Hyde Jr. Baton Rouge: Louisiana State University Press, 2009.

Pearson, Elizabeth Ware, ed. *Letters from Port Royal: Written at the Time of the Civil War.* Boston: W. B. Clarke, 1906.

Perdue, Charles L., Jr., Thomas E. Barden, and Robert K. Phillips, eds. *Weevils in the Wheat: Interviews with Virginia Ex-slaves.* Charlottesville: University Press of Virginia, 1976.

Pierce, Edward L. "The Contrabands at Fortress Monroe." *Atlantic Monthly,* Nov. 1861, 626–40.

Quiner, E. B. *Military History of Wisconsin: A Record of the Civil and Military Patriotism of the State, in the War for the Union.* Chicago: Clarke, 1866.

Reid, Whitelaw. *After the War: A Tour of the Southern States, 1865–1866.* London: S. Low, Son, & Marston, 1866.

Reilly, Wayne E., ed. *Sarah Jane Foster, Teacher of the Freedmen: A Diary and Letters.* Charlottesville: University Press of Virginia, 1990.

Richardson, James D., ed. *A Compilation of the Messages and Papers of the Presidents.* Washington, D.C.: Government Printing Office, 1896–1899.

Rogers, James B. *War Pictures: Experiences and Observations of a Chaplain in the U.S. Army, in the War of the Southern Rebellion.* Chicago: Church & Goodman, 1863.

Sears, Richard D. *Camp Nelson, Kentucky: A Civil War History.* Lexington: University Press of Kentucky, 2002.

Sears, Stephen W., ed. *The Civil War Papers of George B. McClellan.* New York: DaCapo Press, 1992.

Simon, John Y., ed. *The Papers of Ulysses S. Grant.* Carbondale: Southern Illinois University Press, 1967–2012. Digital edition at http://digital.library.msstate.edu.

Simpson, Brooks D., LeRoy P. Graf, and John Muldowny, eds. *Advice After Appomattox: Letters to Andrew Johnson, 1865–1866.* Knoxville: University of Tennessee Press, 1987.

Sperry, A. F. *History of the 33d Iowa Volunteer Regiment, 1863–1866.* Edited by Gregory J. W. Urwin and Cathy Kunzinger Urwin. Fayetteville: University of Arkansas Press, 1999.

Sumner, Charles. "War Powers of Congress: Speech of the Honorable Charles Sumner of Massachusetts on the House Bill for the Confiscation of Property and the Liberation of Slaves Belonging to Rebels." Washington, D.C.: Scammell, 1862.

Swint, Henry L., ed. *Dear Ones at Home: Letters from Contraband Camps.* Nashville: Vanderbilt University Press, 1966.

Taylor, Susie King. *Reminiscences of My Life in Camp with the 33rd U.S. Colored Troops, Late 1st South Carolina Volunteers.* Edited by Patricia W. Romero, with a new introduction by Willie Lee Rose. New York: Markus Wiener, 1988. Originally published in 1902.

Willcox, Orlando B. *Forgotten Valor: The Memoirs, Journals, and Civil War Letters of Orlando B. Willcox.* Edited by Robert Garth Scott. Kent, Ohio: Kent State University Press, 1999.

Yellin, Jean Fagin, ed. *The Harriet Jacobs Family Papers.* Chapel Hill: University of North Carolina Press, 2008.

MISCELLANEOUS

International Coalition of Sites of Conscience. http://www.sitesofconscience.org.

National Trust for Historic Preservation. "Preserving and Interpreting Historic Places Associated with Civil War–Era Freedom Seekers." 2011.

Shephard, Steven J. "Excavations at the Contrabands and Freedmen Cemetery and the Concept of the Proper Coffin in the Mid-19th Century," Oct. 27, 2010, Lyceum, Alexandria, Va.

United Nations High Commission for Refugees. http://www.unhcr.org/pages/49da o66c6.html.

Index

Page numbers in *italics* refer to illustrations and maps.

Illustration Credits

p. 44   *Gwine to de Field, Hopkinson's Plantation, Edisto Island, S.C.*, Henry P. Moore, 1862. William Gladstone Collection of African American Photographs, Library of Congress, Washington, D.C. Courtesy of the Library of Congress.

p. 96   *Former Slaves of Jefferson Davis*, ca. 1863. Louisiana State Museum, Baton Rouge, Louisiana. Courtesy of the Louisiana State Museum.

A NOTE ABOUT THE AUTHOR

Chandra Manning graduated summa cum laude from Mount Holyoke College, received the M.Phil. from the National University of Ireland, Galway, and took her Ph.D. at Harvard University. She has taught history at Pacific Lutheran University in Tacoma, Washington, and at Georgetown University in Washington, D.C. Currently, she serves as special adviser to the dean of the Radcliffe Institute for Advanced Study at Harvard University. She lives in Braintree, Massachusetts, with her husband and children.

A NOTE ON THE TYPE

This book was set in a modern adaptation of a type designed by the first William Caslon (1692–1766). The Caslon face, an artistic, easily read type, has enjoyed more than two centuries of popularity in the English-speaking world. This version with its even balance and honest letterforms was designed by Carol Twombly for the Adobe Corporation and released in 1990.

Composed by North Market Street Graphics,
Lancaster, Pennsylvania

Printed and bound by Berryville Graphics,
Berryville, Virginia

Designed by Cassandra J. Pappas